THE VALUATION OF PRIVATELY-HELD BUSINESSES

State-of-the-Art Techniques for Buyers, Sellers, and Their Advisors

Updated to include the Tax Reform Act.

By *IRVING L. BLACKMAN*

PROBUS PUBLISHING COMPANY
CHICAGO, ILLINOIS

Library of Congress Cataloging in Publication Data
Blackman, Irving L.
   The valuation of privately-held businesses.

   Includes index.
   1. Close corporations—Valuation.   I. Title.
HG4028.V3B48   1986   657′.73   86-20498

ISBN 0-917253-27-2

Printed in the United States of America

 2 3 4 5 6 7 8 9 0

Contents

Preface

If there is an area in the field of taxation where uncertainty is the hallmark, it is the area of valuation of an interest in a closely held business.

Valuation causes frustration to accountants, who are used to adding and subtracting precise numbers and coming up with results that produce sheets that are in balance. It also frustrates lawyers, who are used to finding cases in point that, when taken in series, produce a brief that neatly proves their client's case. Probably the most frustrated of all is the closely held business owner; uncertainty reigns supreme, and often the financial life of a business and a family hangs in the balance.

Every company to be valued has its own set of facts and circumstances, and each valuation is unique, different from every other valuation. Two companies in the same business with almost identical numbers can have significantly different values because of just one fact difference. No set of general rules or volumes of books can bring out the importance of unique facts.

The valuation process is an art, not a science, but just as art has its discipline, so too does valuation. The discipline lies mainly in approaches and techniques, rather than in some magic formula or an all-too-easy reference to market prices of so-called comparable businesses that are publicly traded. The inquiry is not only on how to select the right approach, but also on how to attain the desired results for the business owners, their families, and sometimes, their heirs.

As you read this book, bear in mind that a valuation is *always*:

1. as of a particular *point in time*—
   A difference of only a few months in the valuation date can introduce (or eliminate) a fact of crucial significance. Events affecting the perceived value of the business, such as the loss or gain of a

major client, can occur overnight. Fluctuating interest rates affecting the cost of capital can enhance or detract from a business' worth if its capital needs are great.

2.   for a particular *purpose—The value of a business may vary significantly depending upon the purpose of the valuation. If the valuation is for estate tax purposes, the taxpayer's goal is to come up with a low value. If the valuation is for loan security purposes, the taxpayer's goal is to come up with a high value. Accordingly, different valuation methods often are used to come up with different valuation amounts to fit the specific purpose of the taxpayer even though the same business is being valued. But one thing is certain: significant variations between the "different valuation amounts" means an incorrect method or valuation theory was used.*

Any valuation must begin with this question: What is the purpose of the valuation? Is it for a purchase? sale? Or is the valuation for tax purposes? A buyer's or a seller's estimation of value naturally will be prejudiced. A similar prejudice is present for tax purposes. Why? Because in that instance all mistakes are paid to an imaginary buyer—the IRS.

This book demonstrates these fundamentals:

1.   how to value a specific business for a specific purpose
2.   how to control valuation results without the IRS dictating adverse tax consequences
3.   how to plan a valuation to accomplish lifetime planning as well as estate planning

The following definition of valuation should be kept in mind throughout the book: *A valuation is a determination of the value of the business on a certain date for a specific purpose.*

However, regardless of the specific purpose, there is also an ultimate purpose to any valuation, which is also the ultimate purpose of this book: to serve the ends of the closely held business owner.

Foreword

If you attain financial success, chances are the Internal Revenue Service will wind up with more of your dollars than you or your family will. Our forebearers fought a war to stop double taxation. Yet, success forces you *to pay taxes on taxes*. You pay tax when you make it; your estate pays tax when you transfer it to your heirs. New and changing tax laws—supercharged by inflation–continue to shave your share: the IRS gets more; you get less. Yes! And it gets worse with every change of overly complex tax laws that increase the tax on success.

In almost every field, the average American is capable of probing, pushing, thinking, and being creative, but not so in the tax field. As taxpayers, most Americans become paralyzed. The ability to save taxes under this nation's scheme of things is more an art than a science. Both Congress and the Internal Revenue Service are aligned toward the same end. It is the job of Congress to enact new tax provisions and at the same time close existing loopholes. The Internal Revenue Service has the unpopular but necessary task of overseeing every aspect of the tax law, carrying out the congressional intent. The match-up is one-sided: the Average American against the System (of laws, regulations, rulings, and cases engineered and maintained by Congress and the IRS).

Over the years, a void has developed between Taxpayers (who need to understand and solve tax problems) and Tax Advisors (who must bring their knowledge to bear on their clients' tax needs).

This book fills the void in the area of valuing a privately held business.

This book has been long overdue. As far as I know it is the first book of its kind in two respects:

First, it puts in one place sample valuations, IRS rulings, and court cases.

Second, it tells it like it is. It discusses and explains the theory of valuation and the various methods, but it also shows how, for real businesses, in real life, between real buyers and sellers, the price at which a business will change hands is determined. This method brings the appraiser as close to the true value of the business as possible. Only a real sale between a real buyer and a real seller could produce a more accurate price (valuation).

It is hoped that this book will be relished by every American Taxpayer who has accumulated enough wealth to possibly feel the sting of the Estate Tax Collector. It is also hoped that tax advisors will find this work not only a how-to book but also a valuable research tool.

Irving L. Blackman, C.P.A., J.D.
Partner, Blackman Kallick Bartelstein
Certified Public Accountants,
Chicago Illinois

PART 1
Fundamentals of Valuation

CHAPTER 1
Valuation, Future Expectation, and Uncertainty

HOW BUSINESSES CHANGE HANDS IN REAL LIFE

When a business is sold in real life, two people—a real seller and a real buyer—negotiate and hammer out a real price. If the two parties can't agree on value, the seller will simply walk away and look for another buyer.

The value of a business stems from

1. the value of its operating and nonoperating assets, and
2. the return on investment those assets can generate.

Ultimately, if the business's operations continually generate a large negative cash flow or net loss, an owner must liquidate. He cannot sell it as a going concern that might require a determination of value; the best he/she could do is a sale at liquidation value. However, the anticipated monetary benefits that a business can generate through its operations as a going concern are what determines the value of the business in the buyer's mind. A business is only one of many places buyers can invest their money, and is an alternative they won't pursue if they can find a higher return on investment elsewhere.

The principle that underlies the valuation of a closely held business is the same principle that underlies the valuation of any investment. *Businesses are valuable not because of what they have done but because of what they are capable of doing.* It is the future expectation of the rate of return that a business can generate that determines its value.

VALUATION IN GENERAL

The valuation of an investment is based upon investors' calculation and expectation of approximately what return on investment they will garner at some point in the future. This is true whether the investment is a commodities futures contract bought in the morning and sold that afternoon, a long-term bond held for decades, or an operating business. This principle—future expectations of return on investment—is the foundation of valuation. Buyers determine the value of a commodity—how much they want to pay for it today—based on the rate of return on investment they think the commodity will make for them over a future period of time.

The next few paragraphs and examples are simplistic. Yet they are extremely important as a base on which this book builds in later chapters.

The *rate of return* of an investment is the percentage earned on the amount of money invested. The higher the percentage, the higher the rate of return. The higher the rate of return on an investment in a commodity, the more valuable it is, and the higher the price an investor is willing to pay for it. The lower the rate of return, the lower the price an investor will pay. For the moment, assume the investment has no risk.

Example

Two ten-year bonds each have a face value of $1,000. The average rate of interest, or market rate, paid by such bonds is 10 percent. However, the one bond pays 5 percent interest, while the other pays 15 percent. An investor would be willing to pay more than $1,000 for the bond yielding 15 percent, and less than $1,000 for the bond yielding 5 percent. The amount of money over the face value of the 15 percent bond that the investor would pay is called bond *premium*. The amount below face value that an investor would pay for the 5 percent bond is called bond *discount*. In this case, to at least equal the 10 percent market rate, the 15 percent bond would sell for a premium of $1,561.58, and the 5 percent bond at a discount of $691.26.

The price of a closely held business is determined in much the same manner. It is the future earning power of the business that determines its worth to a buyer and sets the price he/she is willing to pay. Again, only for the moment, assume no risk and that the earning power of the business is the only factor being considered.

Example

Suppose a business has a book value of $1 million, and over the past five years has returned 20 percent on the owner's investment. A buyer would be willing to pay a premium over that book value because he/she highly values the sustained, proven earning power of the business. Suppose instead, however, that an identical business with the same book value has returned only 2 percent over a five-year period. A seller would have to be willing to discount the value of the business in order to price it the right way to lure the cash for the sale out of a willing buyer's pockets.

The purpose of this book is to illustrate how a buyer or a seller, a taxpayer or the IRS, or a borrower or a lender, arrives at the right premium or discount when valuing a business. If one keeps the basic principle of valuation firmly in mind—future expectation of return on investment—the process becomes one of fine-tuning the price of the business using as many factors as desired or necessary to fit the specific purpose of the valuation.

Anyone endeavoring upon a valuation should also heed these two aphoristic clichés: "One person's sorrow is another's pain," and "Nothing is etched in stone." Why?

1. Any valuation usually has two adversaries valuing a business for diametrically opposite purposes. A fact that one party puts great stock in may seem inconsequential to another.
2. Valuations are also ephemeral. Locked into a certain point in time, and wedded to a specific purpose, the myopic vision of their makers, with the passage of time, usually makes valuations as useless as yesterday's newspapers.

The combination of these two factors makes valuation more of an art than a precise science.

THE IMPACT OF TAX REFORM ON VALUATION

The Tax Reform Act of 1986 did many things. For valuation purposes, it did one important thing—lower tax rates significantly.

How do lower tax rates (assuming risk—along with all other facts—remains constant) affect the value of a business? Since taxes levied on income will be lower, after-tax profits will be higher. Result: a higher return on investment. And it is a basic principal of valuation: The higher the return on investment, the more valuable the underlying asset—in this case, the entire business—producing that return.

The higher-value theory holds in only two possible circumstances: (1) if the business is a successful moneymaker, the premium (see the two preceding examples) should be higher. (2) On the other hand, a business that is losing money should trade hands at a slightly smaller discount (again, see examples).

For many reasons: VIVA LOWER TAX RATES!

UNCERTAINTY IN VALUATION

Welcome to the world of uncertainty. It is uncertainty that makes any valuation at best an unreliable indicator of future worth. The following are some of the uncertainties that professional appraisers face in most valuation situations:

- They are uncertain about when, if ever, the owner will sell the business.
- They are uncertain about how long the owner will live.
- They are uncertain if business will get better or worse, be it a specific business, industry, or the economy in general.
- They are uncertain about the rate of inflation.
- They are uncertain about what estate tax bracket the owner will be in when he/she dies.

The uncertainties are as infinite and indeterminable as life itself. With death comes certainty: at that point, the moment of truth for valuation purposes arrives. All that then remains to be done is to apply the appropriate estate tax bracket to the final valuation.

All business owners, whether they like it or not, must someday face the fact that they will have to value their business for tax purposes. They can do it voluntarily during life, or the IRS will do it for them in an involuntary situation, after they die. The only "out" is to sell the business in a real transaction while they are alive.

For some business owners, selling doesn't make sense. In particular, if the business owner wants to transfer the business to the next generation or if he/she wants to keep on working until retirement or death, selling is not generally a reasonable option. Chapter 2 illustrates reasons for closely held business owners to undertake periodic valuations, even if they want to keep their businesses. The uncertainty that surrounds future expectations demands that the closely held business owner be prepared to meet any and all contingencies.

CHAPTER 2
Why Valuation Is a Must: Specific Purposes for Valuing the Closely Held Business

THE CLOSELY HELD CORPORATION: A DEFINITION

This book concerns itself with the closely held business. Although a closely held business can be any one of many entities (such as partnership, sole proprietorship, joint venture, and so on), this book focuses its attention on the *closely held corporation*. The same valuation principles applicable to closely held corporations, *mutatis mutandi,* can be applied to unincorporated closely held businesses such as sole proprietorships, partnerships, or joint ventures. An IRS valuation ruling (Rev. Rul. 65–192, 1965–2 C.B. 259, 260) specifically states that its valuation principles are applicable to closely held businesses of whatever legal form.

The IRS defines a closely held corporation as follows:

> a corporation whose market quotations are either unavailable or of such scarcity that they do not reflect the fair market value.
> (Rev. Rul. 59–60, 1959–1 C.B. 237)

> a corporation . . . the shareholders of which are owned by a relatively limited number of stockholders. Often the entire stock issue is held by one family. The result of this situation is that little, if any, trading in the shares takes place. There is, therefore, no established market for the stock, and such sales as occur at irregular intervals seldom reflect all the elements of a representative transaction as defined by the term ''fair market value.''
> (Rev. Rul. 59–60, 1959–1 C.B. 237)

As the following list and explanations illustrate, failure to incorporate may severely limit financial and tax-planning opportunities of the business owner. The idea is clear: in most cases, a business owner who hasn't incorporated should.

WHY PERIODIC VALUATIONS ARE A MUST

Without reliable knowledge of the value of the business, an owner cannot

A. Plan effectively to minimize *estate taxes* by
  1. Having shares redeemed by the corporation (a *redemption* is when a corporation buys its own stock from one or more of its shareholders) at the least tax cost (see Chapter 14)
  2. Planning a *recapitalization* to freeze the value of the business for estate purposes (see Chapter 11)

3. Selling shares to an *ESOP* (Employee Stock Ownership Plan) as a tax-wise means of transferring the business to a third party (see Chapter 13)
4. Negotiating proper *buy-and-sell stock agreements* (see Chapter 10)
5. Developing a *gift program* of business property (see Chapter 15)

B. Negotiate realistically for possible *sale* or *merger*
C. *Spin-off* part of the business for cash-flow, regulatory, or operational purposes
D. Reach an equitable property settlement in a *divorce* that properly divides the closely held business between husband and wife
E. Obtain *financing* using the closely held business as collateral
F. Buy out dissident minority shareholders
G. Restructure the capital makeup of the company in a tax-free *reorganization*
H. Make tax-deductible *charitable contributions* of the closely held corporation's stock

In each of the various valuation purposes listed, the relationship of the parties, the objectives to be accomplished, and a host of other factors might cause the fair market value to fluctuate. Much depends on the eye of the beholder. Honest, competent people have different ideas of the fair market value of the same business.

The theoretical goal in any valuation is precision. Yet, the true goal is to value the business within a range. The narrower the range, the better.

MINIMIZING ESTATE TAXES

The Fiction of the Estate Tax

Of all the reasons for valuing a closely held business, defeating the estate tax is probably the most important. Valuing a business for purchase or sale is straightforward: a real seller and a real buyer hammer out the price and terms. When you try to value that same business for tax purposes, the entire perspective changes.

This is the estate tax valuation challenge: a *real business* must be valued. It will be sold by an *imaginary seller* (who may be alive or dead, and if dead, represented by heirs or an executor) to an *imaginary buyer*. This fiction is employed to arrive at a *"real price"* to be used for tax purposes—a price that was determined in an *imaginary deal* made by *imaginary people*.

How Estate Tax Can Destroy a Closely Held Business

What follows illustrates what can happen to a closely held business that is not armed with the correct valuation.

Take for example a real business worth more than $500,000, and still growing in value. This book is must reading for the business owner who might own all or a portion of such a business when he dies. Why? Because when he dies, the IRS becomes his partner.

It's an old cliché, but here it has meaning: there are only two sure things in life—death and taxes. The IRS has found a way to combine the two into the estate tax that can rob business owners, their families, and business associates of everything the business owners worked hard for during their lives.

How much the IRS can posthumously tax the deceased owner depends on two factors: *how much* the person is worth when he/she dies, and *when* the person dies.

The Economic Recovery Tax Act of 1981 (ERTA) changes the rules of the game, lowering tax rates and raising the amount exempt from tax. ERTA increases the uni-credit that is being phased in over a six-year period. The following schedule shows the period, amount of credit, amount of the estate exempted from tax, and the maximum and lowest rates (updated to include the rate deferral under the Tax Reform Act of 1984).

Year	Amount of Uni-credit	Amount of Estate Exempt from Tax	Maximum Rate	Lowest Rate
1982	$ 62,800	$225,000	65%	32%
1983	79,300	275,000	60	34
1984	96,300	325,000	55	34
1985	121,800	400,000	55	34
1986	155,800	500,000	55	37
1987	192,800	600,000	55	37
1988 and	192,800	600,000	50	37

Under ERTA, the closely held business owner gets a big break: The "Amount of Uni-credit" protects the "Amount of Estate Exempt from Tax." For example, death in 1986 means the first $500,000 of an estate escapes tax. Then the IRS starts to get its share.

Here's an example. If you are the owner of a small, closely held business, fill in your own numbers to get an idea of what fate could await you.

Example

Right now the owner of the closely held business is alive and the business is worth $500,000. The future prospects of the business are good enough that the business probably will be worth more by the time the owner dies. All things being equal, inflation and business growth are likely to kick the value into seven figures. How much will the tax be? Assume the owner has other property worth $600,000 on the day he/she dies (after 1987) and that his/her spouse is also dead. The schedule shows the federal estate tax bite:

If the business is worth	The estate tax will be
$ 500,000	NONE
1,000,000	$153,000
1,500,000	363,000
2,000,000	588,000
2,500,000	833,000 (plus 50% of the excess over $2.5 million)

These figures illustrate the potential size of the valuation problem in the estate tax context. The obvious question is "Where will the money come from to pay the tax?" Unfortunately, the money is often just not there.

Because the potential tax stakes are so high, placing a value on an owner's interest (usually stock) in a closely held business (usually a corporation) often leads to serious conflict with the Internal Revenue Service. The IRS is the closely held business owner's adversary. Valuation is sort of a game—a game without clearly defined rules. The score is kept in dollars—*the closely held business owner's dollars*. Unlike the publicly traded stock, whose value is published in the daily newspapers, the value of closely held stock must be individually determined. All too often such determinations run as follows:

by the IRS	much higher than the value reported by the taxpayer, arrived at by comparing the business to comparable businesses whose stock is publicly traded
by the taxpayer	much lower than the value claimed by the IRS agents
by the courts	somewhere in between, arrived at by weighing various factors that concern the business

The schedule following the preceding example gives an idea of the size of the tax payments that may hinge on the outcome of a dispute with the IRS. Professional fees for the fight are high. Result? Business liquidations (at sacrifice prices) sometimes become necessary to pay estate taxes, because a deceased owner failed to foresee the high value that the IRS could successfully claim for his/her closely held stock.

The most common reason for this unfortunate occurrence is inadequate planning concerning a valuation of the company's stock. For the most independent business people, their business will be the biggest asset in their estate. If the IRS wins a valuation battle, the business loses. Everything the closely held business owner worked a lifetime to build might have to be dismantled overnight to pay taxes.

THE NEW LAW AND CAPITAL GAINS

Tax reform has increased the complexity of the tax maze. Worse yet, false rumors, based on some tax truth, abound—try this tax truth: under the new law, starting in 1987, long-term capital gains are taxed at the same rate as other ordinary income. Now, the false tax rumor: Long-term gains don't matter.

Let's analyze the rumor. Understanding the new law correctly is a must. First, let's look at the definition of a long-term capital gain, which remains unchanged by the new law. Such gains still arise when you sell property held for more than six months.

Next, let's take a look at the two most common scenarios—a net long-term capital gain (gains) and a net long-term capital loss (losses). For 1987, the highest personal tax rate is 38.5 percent. But get this—gains are capped at 28 percent, a 10.5 percent saving. Starting in 1988, net gains will in fact be taxed the same as ordinary income. But remember, capital gains (long-term or short-term) can be used to offset net capital losses.

What about net losses? Sorry, but you can only deduct $3,000 of losses (including short-term losses) in any one year. The balance of the losses can be carried forward to the next year (1988, 1989, etc.) until used up.

What is most important is this fact: *Capital* gains still matter after tax reform. For that reason, transactions that would have resulted in a capital gain under the old law continue to result in capital gains under the new law. The balance of the material in this book, therefore, identifies capital-gain-resulting transactions as such.

How to Beat the Estate Tax: Planning Tools

The estate tax is a transfer tax. It is levied on the closely held business owners' property that is transferred to their heirs and to those they wish to receive it when they die. Transferring a closely held business at the least tax cost could be the subject of another book altogether, yet it and valuation of the business are inextricably intertwined.

There are three common types of tax-disaster problems in the business-transfer area; they result from the following things:

1. the transfer not being done because the founder doesn't know how to solve the particular transfer problem, which compounds as the potential tax cost continues to mount
2. procrastination
3. the transfer being made, but being made unwisely from a tax standpoint, and the owner, business, or family being clobbered taxwise

Never fear. The government-transfer-tax-machine can be beat.

A variety of tax-saving transfer-of-ownership techniques have been used by "sophisticated business people" for generations. Their use has been limited to those fortunate few who have been able to translate their objectives and applicable tax law into a workable transfer plan. The sooner the plan is put into effect, the greater the tax savings.

In most cases, planning the transfer of a closely held corporation means freezing the owner's estate. A good transfer plan is part of an overall estate plan that attempts to get the asset-freezing process into place as soon as possible. If you can cut wealth off before it accumulates, serious tax problems can be avoided.

Asset freezing is really a generic term for describing the various methods that have been designed to limit the estate tax value of a closely held business:

1. transferring future growth,
2. providing the owner a flow of income during life, and
3. keeping control of the business in the owner for as long as he/she lives.

These methods involve both transfer and valuation. An asset freeze simply seeks to achieve all (or almost all) of the owner's specific objectives. The freeze is usually the most important part of a transfer plan. Following is a list of popular tools employed in asset freezing.

Redemption. A redemption occurs when a shareholder sells stock back to the corporation. The corporation is said to "redeem" the stock. The proceeds from the sale are treated as dividends to the shareholder, unless

1. the number of shares redeemed is disproportionate to the number of shares held by the shareholder,
2. the redemption terminates the shareholder's entire interest in the corporation,
3. the redemption is not substantially equivalent to a dividend, or
4. the redemption is made to a noncorporate shareholder in partial liquidation.

If the redemption falls into any of these four categories, it is treated as a sale or exchange. Then any property or cash received by the shareholder that results in a profit is taxed as a capital gain.

Here is a typical redemption scenario: The owners' children own a small number of shares, which they purchased from their parents, or received as a gift. The parents sell the balance of their shares to the corporation. The selling of all the parents' shares qualifies under the second exception just mentioned. It is a complete termination of their interest in the corporation.

This method accomplishes the freeze—the children own 100 percent of the future growth. However, there are some drawbacks: the parents must still pay tax on the profit, and the corporation cannot deduct the payments. Not only are the parents out of control, but the tax rules prohibit them from working for the corporation for ten years. If they do, the capital gain may turn into ordinary income—a tax disaster.

Example

In *L.V.Seda* (82 TC 484), a husband and wife who were the sole shareholders in a family corporation had all their stock in the company redeemed, and at the same time, resigned all of their positions as directors and officers of the company. Their son became the sole shareholder. Unfortunately, at the request of the son, the father continued to work for the company as a salaried advisor at $1,000 a month salary.

That continued advisory capacity was enough to constitute an "interest in the corporation" that turned the father's capital gain into ordinary income.

What this case illustrates is that redemptions, although effective tools for freezing the owner's interests in a corporation by removing it, carry with them disadvantages for the closely held business owner who desires to continue working in the business or who wants to nurture the next generation of owners. The owner has to choose: capital gain (not much of an advantage after tax reform) and no control, or ordinary income and a majority shareholder position. This and other tax pitfalls of redemption are discussed in detail in Chapter 14.

Recapitalization. Often, the best way to freeze the value of the corporation so any appreciation will not be included in the owner's estate is by a recapitalization.

Here's how a recapitalization works:

1. The owner of the closely held corporation exchanges his/her voting common stock for preferred stock in the corporation.
2. The younger generation [the owner's children], and anyone else the owner wishes to transfer the business to, receives common stock. (The owner also could first receive the common stock and then gift it to the same parties.)
3. The value of the corporation is locked-in, frozen, in the preferred stock, and any future appreciation will be reflected in the common stock, which will be excluded from the owner's estate.
4. The owner maintains control of the corporation during his/her life by giving the preferred stock voting control.

Result: The owner is able to retain control of the corporation for life without exposing the future growth of the corporation to the estate tax. All this is accomplished tax-free with no current income tax. In addition, the owner is assured of income after retirement, through dividends (which can continue to a spouse in the event of the owner's death).

Recent IRS rulings on recapitalizations, claiming that preferred stock is overvalued (unless it meets specific requirements), have attacked the value assigned to the preferred stock. This gives rise to a larger-than-anticipated gift of common stock to the owner's successors, because if the preferred stock is worth less, the common stock must be worth more.

We have come full circle. Recapitalization is a means of freezing the closely held business owner's estate so as to gain a low valuation for that portion of the estate comprised of the business. However, the IRS has now made valuation of the preferred stock a gift tax issue. If they can't get the taxpayers in their graves with the estate tax on preferred stock, they'll try to get them while alive with the gift tax on the common stock.

This means that a recapitalization involves valuation of three components: the closely held business as a whole, the preferred stock, and the common stock. The total value of the preferred and common stock must equal the value of the company as a whole. The larger the value of the common stock (and lower the value of the preferred stock), the larger the gift tax problem when the recapitalization is consummated. The larger the value of the preferred stock (and lower the value of the common stock), the larger the potential estate tax problem upon the owner's death.

The gift tax problem is the more serious and imminent of the two. The estate tax often can be defeated with various estate planning techniques. Some of the techniques can be put into effect immediately, but others, such as an effective gift program, must be implemented over a period of time. However, the gift tax problem on the common stock is something that must be defeated at the time of the recapitalization.

The valuation assigned to the two classes of stock depend on the features they possess, such as voting rights, dividends, liquidation preference, and so on. These and other recapitalization issues are discussed in detail with planning solutions in Chapter 11.

Employee Stock Ownership Plans (ESOPs).   If the owner cannot or does not want to transfer the corporation to family members, an ESOP might be the answer. ESOPs can be used to facilitate the transfer of a closely held corporation to nonfamily buyers or the company's employees by creating a market for its shares. Best of all, it lets the owner take cash out of the corporation at capital gains rates or defer the gain by reinvesting the ESOP distribution in domestic common stocks.

An ESOP is a *qualified defined contribution plan*, which is similar to a typical profit-sharing plan but is designed to invest primarily in the employer's stock or securities. Technically, an ESOP can be either a stock bonus plan or a combination stock bonus and money purchase pension plan.

Here's an overview of a common method of operating an ESOP.

1. An Employee Stock Ownership Trust (ESOT) is established by the employer.
2. The ESOT invests in the employer's stock or securities. The ESOT can acquire the employer's stock from
    a. the stockholder of the employer corporation,
    b. the employer corporation, or
    c. both
3. It can get the cash for the purchase either
    a. by a direct deductible contribution from the employer, or
    b. by borrowing the money from a bank.
4. Subsequent contributions to the ESOT, which are used to pay off principal and interest on funds borrowed to purchase employer stock, are deductible by the employer corporation as made.

The ESOT, with all the rights and benefits of a shareholder, holds the stock for the benefit of participating employees. The stock is distributed to the participants when they are eligible to receive it—upon retirement, disability, or death. Usually, the ESOT or the corporation repurchases the distributed stock from the employees. This flow of stock "to, from, and back" to the trust or corporation, combined with very favorable tax breaks applicable to ESOPs, makes the ESOP an interesting planning tool.

These and other aspects of ESOPs, including valuation of closely held stock sold to an ESOP, are discussed in detail in Chapter 13.

Buy-Sell Agreements.   A typical buy–sell agreement is

1. a contract between shareholders of a closely held corporation (or between the shareholders and the corporation itself), in which the parties agree
2. that any shareholder transferring corporation stock—because of death, disability, gift, bankruptcy, or any other reason—must sell or transfer the shares
3. to the other shareholders (or the corporation) at a specified price and on specified terms.

If the agreement is structured properly, the agreed price will be honored by the courts as the correct valuation of the deceased's closely held stock for estate tax purposes. The courts have held that for estate tax purposes the IRS is bound to honor the price specified in the buy–sell agreement, if the following conditions are met:

1. The price of the shares fixed in the buy–sell agreement have been arrived at according to some reasonable valuation method.
2. The agreement has a *bona fide* business purpose and is not, in the IRS' words, "a device to pass the decedent's shares to the natural objects of his/her bounty for less than adequate and full consideration"; in other words, the agreement is not a testamentary device used to defeat the estate tax. This issue is raised by the IRS when the parties to the agreement are related.
3. The estate of the deceased is legally bound to sell the shares to the parties specified in the agreement after the shareholder's death.
4. The parties to the agreement cannot dispose of their stock in their lifetime unless the other parties have a right of first refusal.

If careful drafting does not satisfy the above requirements, the IRS is free to use its own valuation method to arrive at what is usually a higher value for the stock (Reg. 20.2031-2(h); *Estate of O.B. Littick*, 31 TC 181).

Here is an example of how the IRS attacks a buy–sell agreement. Recently, it agreed to the result of the 17-year-old *Littick* case, but disagreed with its reasoning. In *Littick*, three brothers, one of whom had terminal cancer, were sole shareholders of a family corporation. They executed a buy–sell agreement that provided a selling price for the stock of $200,000, even though the agreement stipulated it had a fair market value (FMV) of more than $250,000. The terminally ill brother died shortly thereafter.

The IRS claimed the agreement was a testamentary device, demanding the decedent's stock be included in his estate at FMV. The court upheld the business purpose of the agreement, which was to keep control of the business in the family, and honored the set price. Why? Even though one brother was terminally ill, it was possible that the healthy brothers could die before him.

After brooding for 17 years over its defeat, the IRS is attempting to do with the gift tax what is couldn't do using the estate tax. It now says that the terminally ill brother's shortened life expectancy made his promise to sell worth more than the promise of his brothers. Therefore, there was an immediate gift. Nonsense!

(The factors just mentioned, as well as other IRS methods of attacking the valuation price in buy–sell agreements, are discussed in detail in Chapter 10.)

Gifts of Closely Held Stock to Family Members. A program of gifting closely held stock can transfer stock worth up to $10,000 ($20,000 if the donor's spouse consents to the gift) annually to each donee (family members, and so on) without paying gift tax. Such gifts save estate taxes in two ways: the value of the stock will not be subject to the estate tax when the donor dies, and any appreciation in the stock after the gift is made also escapes estate tax.

That portion of an annual gift over $10,000 ($20,000 if married) will be included in the donor's estate.

Another consideration for recapitalization purposes is that if a gift results from the creation of common stock in recapitalization, the statute of limitations under which the IRS has time to challenge the valuation of the common stock does not begin to run unless a gift tax return is filed and a gift tax paid. Therefore, enough value may be needed to consume the unified credit and pay the tax in order to start the statute running. The use of a gift program that passes IRS muster is discussed in Chapter 15.

SALE, PURCHASE, OR MERGER

Sale or Purchase

The sale or purchase of a closely held business calls for the application of the appraisal techniques described in detail in this book as well as the utilization of a competent, professional appraiser. Those techniques are the meat of this book.

Merger

Most states allow corporations to merge. A not uncommon scenario involves the merger of a closely held corporation into a publicly held corporation, or the merger of two closely held corporations. The shareholders of the former corporation usually exchange their shares for shares of the surviving corporation. Valuation of these shares is important for tax purposes and for protecting and satisfying minority shareholder rights.

State law usually provides that shareholders of the corporation that would cease to exist after the merger have a right to a court hearing to determine whether the price offered for their stock by the surviving corporation is adequate. That hearing usually turns into a battle of valuation experts, not unlike psychiatrists testifying as to sanity of a defendant in a criminal trial; the difference is that the value of the closely held corporation's stock, not a defendant's state of mind, is the bone of contention.

SPIN-OFF OF THE CLOSELY HELD BUSINESS

Most closely held corporations don't have subsidiaries, but those that do may find it necessary to spin-off (sell) the subsidiary for reasons such as these:

1. compliance with government agency regulations (SEC, IRS, FTC, and so on)
2. infusion of working capital into the parent closely held business
3. resolving disputes between shareholders regarding the operations and objective of the business

Usually, shareholders of the parent company receive the subsidiary's stock for a set price. The transaction can be tax free if it is for a legitimate business purpose of the parent company. Whether tax free or not, valuation is necessary to justify the selling price and may be necessary to determine the basis of the stock of the new corporation.

DIVORCE PROPERTY SETTLEMENT

Divorce, in and of itself, can be an unpleasant experience. If one or both of the divorcing spouses are owners of a closely held business, reaching a property settlement can be extremely difficult.

Suppose, for example, that one spouse knows that the other has depreciated the business' assets heavily at an accelerated rate or has depressed income by use of excessive entertainment expense deductions. That spouse will be reluctant, and rightly so, to accept any valuation that does not make appropriate adjustment for these factors.

The property settlement usually ends up with one spouse transferring stock in the corporation to the other. Valuation of the stock is the cornerstone to reaching a settlement. The parties relying upon the valuation are in conflict, often bitter. This can make valuation very difficult.

The Transfer Tax Problem for Pre-July 19, 1984 Transfers

The transfer tax problem that plagued closely held business owners going through a divorce before enactment of the Tax Reform Act of 1984 (TRA) is a real mess.

Example

Mr. Entrepreneur owns 100 percent of the stock of a substantial business. His tax basis is $200,000. Mr. Entrepreneur transfers 25 percent of the stock, with a value of $550,000, to Ms. Entrepreneur as part of a property settlement pursuant to a divorce decree entered into on July 18, 1984. Mr. Entrepreneur suffers a taxable gain (technically, a capital gain) of $500,000 ($550,000 less $50,000—25 percent × $200,000—of basis).

Not only does Mr. Entrepreneur get hung for a current tax on the transfer, but Ms. Entrepreneur shares in the future growth of the business. Often this result can be avoided by recapitalizing the business and transferring preferred (nongrowth) stock, instead of common stock, to the spouse.

The Transfer Problem Shifts for Post-July 18, 1984 Transfers

TRA provides that no gain or loss is recognized to either spouse on the transfer of property between them incidental to divorce. The transferee spouse takes a carryover basis in the transferred property. The transfer problem is shifted from the shoulders of the spouse transferring the property to the shoulders of the spouse receiving it.

Example

Consider the same facts as the previous example, except that Mr. Entrepreneur transfers the stock to Ms. Entrepreneur pursuant to a divorce decree entered into after July 18, 1984. Mr. Entrepreneur recognizes no gain or loss. He is able to take appreciated property and use its fair market value to fulfill his divorce obligations with no adverse tax consequences. Ms. Entrepreneur, however, steps into Mr. Entrepreneur's shoes as owner of the transferred property, and is stuck with his low basis. If she sells the stock she will be the one who suffers a taxable capital gain of $500,000.

Frequently, the net result is that the dispute over valuation ends up in court, with both parties spending money on attorneys' and accountants' fees that they should be dividing between themselves instead. Periodic valuations made before the divorce can narrow the range of disputed value between the parties and make a settlement easier to reach.

Careful planning is essential. A valuation that satisfies both parties makes sharing the transfer tax burden easier in settlement negotiations.

OBTAINING FINANCING

A lender is more apt to furnish capital funds to a business if that business can demonstrate that it possesses valuable assets and that it also generates substantial revenue and profit from those assets. Valuations that show these factors over and above what is shown on the business' financial statements can make obtaining financing easier.

BUY-OUT OF DISSIDENT MINORITY SHAREHOLDERS

Most states have laws that protect the interests of minority shareholders. Often, articles of incorporation provide for contingent buy-outs of minority interests. Valuations of such minority interests that fairly reflect value minimize costly court battles that can drain a business's finances and often cast a cloud of uncertainty over its future.

Valuation of minority interests usually must be discounted for lack of marketability. Such discounting is discussed in Chapter 9.

REORGANIZATION OF A TROUBLED BUSINESS

Often, a closely held corporation finds itself cash-poor and unable to meet current obligations, yet projects a profitable future. A restructuring of capital may make a business more attractive for financing short-term as well as long-term obligations, and so reassure creditors that the business will pay its liabilities.

First the business is valued on a debt-free or reduced debt basis; then the reorganization creates a capital structure that allows the business to survive so the creditors have a better chance of receiving all or part of the amount due to them. This approach can be voluntary or made by a bankruptcy court.

CHARITABLE CONTRIBUTIONS

If a closely held corporation or its shareholders make charitable contributions of the corporation's stock, the donor is entitled to a deduction. Under current law, the deduction is limited to 10 percent of a corporation's taxable income for such contributions, while shareholders are allowed to deduct up to 50 percent of their incomes. Contributions that exceed these limitations can be carried forward to future tax years, according to specific rules. The exact amount allowable as a deduction depends on the value of the shares contributed. Not surprisingly, the IRS has taken a keen interest in the valuation of such contributed shares.

CHAPTER 3
The Legal Approach to Valuation

FAIR MARKET VALUE

The concept of *fair market value* is mostly a legal device used by the courts and the IRS to settle valuation disputes in estate and gift tax matters. It has little use between a real seller and real buyer who are hammering out the sale price of a real business. The price arrived at in such situations is what the seller will accept and the buyer is willing to pay. That price can vary depending on the buyer and the seller. The process of valuation—using discounts and premiums—described in Chapter 1 is what really happens in the sale and purchase of a business.

However, valuations are made for many purposes other than buying and selling a business, as demonstrated in Chapter 2. The courts and the IRS frequently get involved in valuations, and what they consider to be fair market value in those situations is of paramount importance.

IRS Definition of Fair Market Value

In every valuation matter before the IRS, the meaning of "fair market value" is at center stage and is used to decide the issue. For purposes of estate tax (Regulations 20.2031–1(b)) and gift tax (Regulations 25.2512–1), fair market value is defined this way:

> The price at which the property would change hands between a willing buyer and a willing seller when the former is not under any compulsion to buy and the latter is not under any compulsion to sell, both parties having reasonable knowledge of relevant facts.

This definition is universally accepted in federal taxation. Regulation 1–1001(a) states, "fair market value is a question of fact, but only in rare and extraordinary cases will property be considered to have no fair market value." As Chapter 4 illustrates, fair market value, value, or the price of a closely held business is a determination based on particular facts and circumstances.

Judicial Definition of Fair Market Value

The term "fair market value" has been defined by the courts as the price which property will bring when it is offered for sale by one who is willing but is not obligated to sell it, and is bought by one who is willing or desires to purchase but is not compelled to do so" (*H.H.Marshman*, 279 F.2d 27.).

Uncertainty of Fair Market Value

As a practical matter, it is impossible to pinpoint the exact price two parties would arrive at in an actual transaction. This is particularly true when a major block of stock is involved, because the price agreed upon is normally determined through a bargaining process. In addition to the underlying economics of the company and its industry, the bargaining skill and the individual circumstances of the two parties also affect the actual price. These highly subjective considerations make a valuation study by an independent analyst imprecise, at best.

The key question is this: Who has the advantage when the uncontested fact is that fair market value is a matter of uncertainty, floating on a wavy sea of opinion—the IRS or the taxpayers? I maintain the advantage is clearly on the taxpayers' side—provided they know what they are doing.

Many sections of the Internal Revenue Code refer to fair market value (it is mentioned 173 times), but neither these sections nor the applicable regulations give any precise definition. Most practitioners assume that the definition for estate and gift tax purposes is universally applicable. So far this assumption has proved correct.

Fair Market Value as It Really Is

In 1928 the court (in *James Couzens*, 11 B.T.A. 1040) really said it like it is:

> It has been said that value is a price at which a willing seller and a willing buyer would agree to trade if they both were aware of the facts. . . . Recognizing all the facts in existence, and from them attempting reasonably to predict those to come, being neither unduly skeptical nor unduly optimistic, we sought to determine what an intelligent and reasonable seller and an intelligent and reasonable buyer would in their fairly mercenary interest have been most likely to agree upon as a price for the property in question.

In the real world, when valuing the stocks of closely held corporations for federal tax purposes, instead of a mythical willing seller and a mythical willing buyer, we have as traditional adversaries a real taxpayer (or the taxpayer's heirs or donees) and the "unreal" IRS. The many litigated cases and the more numerous compromise settlements clearly show each adversary considers the other anything but willing and reasonable.

VALUATION AS THE IRS SEES IT

How the Valuation Tax Game Is Played

In every valuation of a business for tax purposes, the IRS is looking over the taxpayer's shoulder, scouting out the taxpayer as a potential opponent. The way to win the valuation game is to know in advance what the IRS is looking for and how it plays the valuation game.

There are three sources the IRS looks to for guidance in order to best the taxpayer at the game:

1. the Internal Revenue Code,
2. IRS regulations, and
3. rulings.

The referees overseeing the conflict between the IRS and taxpayers are the courts: Tax Court (which also has a small claims division), U.S. District Courts, U.S. Appellate Courts, and the U.S. Supreme Court.

According to information published yearly in the IRS *Statistics of Information Bulletin*, past practice has shown that the higher in the court system a taxpayer goes, the smaller the taxpayer's chance of winning the game.

A Small Business Administration study (SBA Market Research Summary No. 124, April 1963) summarizes the results of cases involving estate tax valuations of closely owned businesses as follows:

1. The IRS usually employs whatever approach to "fair market value" that results in the highest value and, as a result, yields the highest tax liability. The study cautions that the cases may not be wholly representative, since it is the extreme cases that most likely end up in court.
2. There was a strong tendency for the IRS to adopt a rigid formula approach to valuation that considered the enterprise in a vacuum.

Market condition studies were rarely undertaken unless the IRS was forced to defend its position in court.

3. Taxpayers usually contended for unrealistically low valuation, as might be expected. However, some cases were lost by default because taxpayers were inadequately prepared to justify their own valuation figures.

4. The courts afforded taxpayers protection by making the IRS justify its valuations with thorough expert testimony and documentation.

5. The final valuation amount reached by the courts in their decisions tended to compromise between the higher figure of the IRS and the lower figure of the taxpayer. This tendency is an incentive for both the IRS and the taxpayer to present an extreme initial valvation.

6. Often, the decision in a case turned not on the merits of the accuracy of contending valuations and their methods but on legalistic procedural and evidentiary rules that prevented the court from considering facts that would result in a fully formed decision.

When reading the following sections of this chapter, which contain statutory and regulatory provisions concerning valuation, take notice of the concept of comparing similar businesses engaged in similar industries as useful guides at arriving at the value of a closely held business. These "comparable" companies, or comparables, can be closely held or publicly traded. You can see the ease of using a publicly traded comparable by turning to the page of *The Wall Street Journal* that contains the market price of the stock selected.

As will be posited in Chapter 6 the use of comparables, although appropriate in some instances, can be deceptively easy for the IRS but is usually disastrous for the closely held business owner.

Estate Tax Code Section

Section 2031(b) of the Code, covering valuation for estate tax purposes of unlisted securities, provides the following:

> In the case of stock and securities of a corporation the value of which, by reason of their not being listed on an exchange and by reason of the absence of sales thereof, cannot be determined with reference to bid and

asked prices or with reference to sales prices, the value thereof shall be determined by taking into consideration, in addition to all other factors, *the value of stock or securities of corporations engaged in the same or a similar line of business which are listed on an exchange.* [Author's Italics.]

Estate Tax Regulations

The estate tax regulations (Reg. 20.2031.2–(f)) provide in part

Where selling prices or bid and asked prices are unavailable. If . . . actual sales prices and bona fide bid and asked prices are lacking, then the fair market value is to be determined by taking the following factors into consideration:

(1) In the case of corporate or other bonds, the soundness of the security, the interest yield, the date of maturity, and other relevant factors; and

(2) In the case of shares of stock, the company's net worth, prospective earnings power and dividend-paying capacity, and other relevant factors.

Some of the "other relevant factors" referred to in subparagraphs (1) and (2) of this paragraph are: the good will of the business; the economic outlook in the particular industry and its management; the degree of control of the business represented by the block of stock to be valued; and *the values of securities of corporations engaged in the same or similar lines of business which are listed on a stock exchange.* However, the weight to be accorded such comparisons or any other evidentiary factors considered in the determination of a value depends upon the facts of each case. Complete financial and other data upon which the valuation is based should be submitted with the return, including copies of reports of any examinations of the company made by accountants, engineers, or any technical experts as of or near the applicable valuation date.

The Genesis of Valuation, ARM 34: The Rigid Formula Approach

The IRS first tried to set valuation criteria by issuing Appeals and Review Memorandum (ARM) 34 in 1920. The theory of the ARM 34 was that a business is expected to earn a normal profit on its tangible assets and that any actual profit greater than normal profit must be attributed to intangible assets. ARM 34 thus distinguished between tangible and intangible assets and attributed a set value to each.

This was done by use of a rigid formula. The IRS considered normal profit to be an 8 to 10 percent return on the net book value of tangible assets, a 15 to 20 percent return on intangibles.

Example

> If a business with $2 million in tangible assets earned $250,000 a year and its normal profit (according to the IRS) was $160,000 (8 percent of $2 million), then $90,000 ($250,000 minus $160,000) was its profit on intangible assets. The $90,000 profit on intangible assets was capitalized at 15 percent (100 percent divided by 15 percent = 6.666), this produced $600,000(6.666 × $90,000), the value of the intangible assets. The $600,000 in intangible assets was then added to the $2 million in tangible assets to produce a total value of $2.6 million.

The Arm 34 method is disarmingly simple. Using it, valuation is made without considering any peculiar facts or circumstances concerning the business.

Because of this lack of knowledge about the individual business, the computation of valuation is in fact made in a vacuum. This caused ARM 34 to be hotly contested by taxpayers. Among other faults, ARM 34 did not account for discrepancies in book value and fair market value of operational assets; it did not distinguish between capital-intensive and labor-intensive businesses; it arbitrarily assigned the same rate of return to all businesses, regardless of industry and regardless of nature (such as disparities between retail, wholesale, and manufacturing concerns).

Because of these shortcomings, ARM 34 finally was limited in its use (Rev. Rul. 65–192, 1965–2 C.B. 259).

The Most Important IRS Ruling

Recognizing that simplistic formulas do not work, in 1959 the IRS issued Revenue Ruling 59–60, 1959–1 C.B. 237 (see Appendix B for the full text). This is now the most significant legal guideline in valuations. At least, it is the place to start in determining the value of a business.

Revenue Ruling 59–60's Approach to Valuation. Revenue Ruling 59–60's basic approach is set forth as follows:

.01.   A determination of fair market value, being a question of fact, will depend upon the circumstances in each case. No formula can be devised that will be generally applicable to the multitude of different valuation issues arising in estate and gift tax cases. Often, an appraiser will find wide differences of opinion as to the fair market value of a particular stock. In resolving such differences, he should maintain a reasonable attitude in recognition of the fact that valuation is not an exact science. A sound valuation will be based upon all the relevant facts, but the elements of common sense, informed judgment, and reasonableness must enter into the process of weighing those facts and determining their aggregate significance.

.02.   The fair market value of specific shares of stock will vary as general economic conditions change from "normal" to "boom" or "depression," that is, according to the degree of optimism or pessimism with which the investing public regards the future at the required date of appraisal. Uncertainty as to the stability or the continuity of future income from a property decreases its value by increasing the risk of loss of earnings and value in the future. The value of shares of stock of a company with very uncertain future prospects is highly speculative. The appraiser must exercise his judgment as to the degree of risk attached to the business of the corporation which issued the stock, but that judgment just be related to all of the other factors affecting value.

.03.   Valuation of securities is, in essence, a prophesy as to the future and must be based on facts available at the required date of appraisal. As a generalization, the prices of stocks which are traded in volume in a free and active market by informed persons best reflect the consensus of the investing public as to what the future holds for the corporations and industries represented. When a stock is closely held, is traded infrequently, or is traded in an erratic market, some other measure of value must be used. *In many instances, the next best measure may be found in the prices at which the stocks of companies engaged in the same or similar line of business are selling in a free and open market.* [author's italics.]

The Many Factors of Valuation.   The last few pages illustrate the IRS'
emphasis on the fact that to value a closely held corporation it is necessary
to consider the value of stock or securities of corporations engaged in the
same or a similar line of business, which are listed on an exchange, *in
addition to considering all other factors*. To consider "all other factors" is
an endless task. One of the most important aids in determining what those
"other factors" are is Revenue Ruling 59–60.

   Revenue Ruling 59–60 lists eight factors to consider in valuing a
closely held business:

1.   the nature of the business and the history of the enterprise from
     its inception
2.   the economic outlook in general, and the condition and outlook of
     the specific industry in particular
3.   the book value of the stock and the financial condition of the
     business
4.   the earnings capacity of the company
5.   the dividend-paying capacity
6.   whether the enterprise has goodwill or other intangible value
7.   sales of the stock and the size of the block to be valued
8.   the market price of stocks of corporations engaged in the same or
     similar line of business having their stock actively traded in a free
     and open market, either on an exchange or over-the-counter

Revenue Ruling 59-69 emphasizes that the eight factors do not necessarily
have equal weight and that determination of value is a matter of *judgment*
and *common sense* to be arrived at after *consideration of all factors*.

Expanded Application of Revenue Ruling 59–60.   Revenue Ruling 59–60
by its express terms limits the factors it creates to valuations for estate and
gift tax purposes. However, Revenue Ruling 65–192, 1965–2 C.B. 259
states

   .01   The general approach, methods, and factors outlined in Reve-
         nue Ruling 59–60 are equally applicable to valuations of corpo-
         rate stocks for income and other tax purposes as well as for
         estate and gift tax purposes. *They apply also to problems in-
         volving the determination of the fair market value of business
         interests of any type, including partnerships, proprietorships,
         and so on.* and of intangible assets for all tax pur-
         poses. [Author's italics.]

Although this book deals solely with the incorporated closely held business, as far as the IRS is concerned the same principles involved in valuing a closely held corporation are equally applicable to unincorporated businesses of whatever form.

Some Comments on the Factors.

Nature and History of the Business.   The nature of the business is usually the starting point of a valuation. The characteristics of the enterprise and the specific industry within which it operates and competes must be established.

A detailed study of the history of the corporation is needed to enable the appraiser to form an opinion of the degree or risk involved in the enterprise. This factor covers a broad area involving degrees of stability, growth, and diversity of operations, plus analyses and information that will reflect the general nature of the business: its risks, its hazards, and its ability to withstand adverse economic swings.

Nonrecurring items should be discounted, since value has a close relation to future expectancy.

The Economic Outlook in General and the Condition of the Business.   Determination of fair market value must include consideration of the outlook of the economy in general as well as the particular industry.

Usually, this determination begins with an examination of financial data and comparison of earnings. In addition, several questions should be asked: Would the public be an eager investor in the company? Is it a one-person company? Will future management be able to take over in the event of the death or retirement of a key person? Will the loss of key personnel be offset by insurance? Will the market for the company's products grow, decline, or remain stable? Will the general economy sustain the company's future?

Often the figures of the company itself tell a complete economic story. Consider the earnings of three different companies, all with the same total earnings in the past five years:

	Down, Inc.	Yo-Yo, Inc.	Up, Inc.
1981	$ 30,000	$ 20,000	$ 15,000
1982	24,000	24,000	17,000
1983	20,000	18,000	20,000
1984	16,000	22,000	23,000
1985	10,000	16,000	25,000
TOTALS	$100,000	$100,000	$100,000

Obviously the appraiser must consider the earnings pattern in any valuation. One way of computing the ultimate value while still placing primary emphasis on later years is to utilize a weighted average. The most common method of making the computation for Down, Inc. is as follows:

1981	$30,000 ×	1 =	$ 30,000
1982	24,000 ×	2 =	48,000
1983	20,000 ×	3 =	60,000
1984	16,000 ×	4 =	64,000
1985	10,000 ×	5 =	50,000
TOTALS		15	$252,000

$252,000 ÷ 15 = $16,800 (weighted average earnings)

The exact weighting to be used is flexible. For example, the appraiser might have used a weighting of 1,1,2,3,3 or 1,1,2,3,4 or any number of other combinations.

Sometimes a weighted average does not give the best results. Remember, it is only one of the many methods that can be used to emphasize recent events.

Competition is always a key issue. At the valuation date, the company's current and past performance compared to its competitors should be determined. The competitive trend, the impact on profits, and the ability to overcome the competition must be examined.

The Gallo Case: The IRS Strikes Out

A good example of what a court will look at concerning the nature and history of a business, the outlook of the specific industry in particular, and the effect that consideration has on the final valuation decision is provided in *Estate of Mark M. Gallo* (TCM 1985–363).

In that case, the Tax Court was called upon to value the shares of stock of a holding company closely held by Ernest and Julio Gallo and their families, whose principal asset was all the stock of the well-known Gallo Winery. The shares were part of the estate of a grandson of Julio Gallo, and comprised less than 1 percent of all the issued and outstanding stock of the holding company. The year of the valuation was 1978.

The court reviewed both the state of the U.S. wine industry, including its relation to the worldwide industry, and Gallo's position in that industry in 1978. It summarized that position as follows:

> In sum, although Gallo remained the largest wine producer in the United States, with a market almost double that of the second largest producer, its performance in the years immediately preceding the valuation date and its prospects for the future were not bright as its record prior to 1972. Gallo experienced a substantial decline in its total market share and weakness in its traditional areas of strength. In light of its image as a quantity producer of inexpensive wines, Gallo appeared ill-equipped to take advantage of emerging trends in the industry.

The court went on to reject the valuation of the IRS' expert appraiser because, among other things, he ignored the historical trend within the wine industry.

> The emerging consumer preference for higher price wines with perceived higher quality was apparent as of the valuation date, as was Gallo's actual past and expected future inability to exploit this trend. . . . Because of these and other factors mentioned in our findings, Gallo's earnings exhibited a sharp downward trend after 1972. By virtually any measure of investment merit, Gallo was significantly less attractive on the valuation date than in 1972.

The *Gallo* case was not decided upon this factor alone. But it does illustrate that a valuation that ignores the nature and the history of the business and the industry it operates within, reaches its conclusions in a factual vacuum, and does so at its peril.

Book Value (Net Value) and Financial Condition.   Often, the computation of book value is an essential starting point for determining fair market value of stock of a closely held corporation. Generally, book value is acquisition cost (less accumulated depreciation) minus liabilities. It is also referred to as owner's equity. The courts have held that book value, although one of many factors of valuation, is not related to other factors such as earning power, fair market value, or even liquidation value. In *Nellie I. Brown*, (25 TCM 498–1966), the Tax Court stressed this fact in rejecting an IRS' expert witness appraisal that relied solely on book value.

What the courts have used book value for can be illustrated in *Albert L. Luce, Jr.*, (ClmsCt, 84–1 USTC 13,549). Book value is floor value. The courts are reluctant to let any valuation fall below book value. In *Luce*, controlling shareholders of a closely held manufacturing company gave stock to their children and to trusts for the benefit of their children. For gift tax purposes, the shareholders gave the stock a value below book value. In the ensuing court case, the shareholders' expert witness attempted to justify the lower-than-book value by using the capitalization of earnings method and a minority discount.

The court rejected that approach and held book value to be at least one of the proper indicators of worth for the business for the following reasons:

> If a company's net worth consists of substantial write-ups of intangible value acquired in mergers and corporate acquisitions, if it has paid inflated prices for its assets, or if its machinery and equipment are obsolete, and it has been consistently unable to obtain a fair return on investment, then the fair market value of the company may be understandably less than book value. But the undisputed evidence here is that as of the valuation date Blue Bird's [the closely held company at issue] ownership had been in the same family since it was organized, its net worth was not inflated by any substantial tangible value, and its plant and equipment were in good condition and enabled it to be a dominant company in its industry. Moreover, Mr. Shelton's [the expert witness] own computations showed that the company's returns on its tangible net worth ranged between 16.1 and 28.4 percent, with an average of 19.2 percent, over the preceding 5 years, returns far in excess of those earned in the closest comparable industries Mr. Shelton could find. A seller could hardly have been expected to be willing to accept 25 percent less for the company than the cost of duplicating the net depreciated tangible assets alone, without regard to its value as a going concern with goodwill, qualified personnel, an established national distributor's organization and high earning capacity; and a hypothetical buyer could hardly have expected that he could obtain it for that price. In such circumstances, it is reasonable to conclude that book value is at least a floor under fair market value, which an appraiser may not properly ignore.

Book value alone, however, is a poor indicator of value. The court in *Luce,* and other courts, only requires that book value not be discarded and that a highly profitable going concern dare not attempt to dip below it. The values of assets and liabilities on a corporation's books do not necessarily reflect fair market values. For example, the value of plant and equipment, which is carried on the books at cost less depreciation, may be inaccurate because an accelerated method of depreciation was employed or because inflation and other market factors make the assets much more valuable than the book figures.

Remember, balance sheets are almost always stated at cost. For example, land carried on the books at cost for a number of years probably has a fair market value due to appreciation—in real value, inflation, or both. For valuation purposes, the balance sheet should be adjusted to reflect the higher value of the land, providing a more realistic worth of the company.

The importance of book value as a measure of fair market value also depends upon the nature of the enterprise. It is considered by the courts as a poor measure for operating companies where earnings and dividend-paying capacity are the most relevant criterion:

> Book value is a factor to be considered, still it is not a reliable measure of fair market value. I am certain the investor is inclined to give earning power and dividend prospects much more weight in appraising the worth of any security. What the buyer is acquiring are the profits and dividends which the business will provide in the future (*Bader* v. *U.S.*, 172 F.Supp. 833 (D.C.Ill. 1959)). A prospective buyer would give some consideration to the book value of $145 a share. He would realize, however, that the company was a going concern, and that, even if it was assumed that the book value could be realized upon the liquidation of the corporation, there was not indication that it was to be liquidated.(*Mathilde B. Hooper, Admnx.*, 41 B.T.A. 114 at 119, acq. and nonacq. 1942–1 C.B. 9, 24).

However, the IRS takes book value as a good indicator of the value of investment and real estate holding companies where the underlying value of the assets closely approximates the worth of the corporation. It states that "computing the book value per share of stock, assets of the investment type should be revalued on the basis of their market price and the book value adjusted accordingly" (Rev. Rul. 59–60, 1959–1 C.B. 237).

Assets not essential to the operation of the business should be identified by an examination of current and past balance sheets. Management should be consulted to identify nonoperating assets that cannot be segregated by looking at the financial statements. These assets may add to or detract from the stock's value, depending on their separate value and earning power. Nonoperating assets must be revalued at current market prices for publicly traded securities or fair market value for other nonoperating assets. The value of the nonoperating assets should be added to the value determined for the operating assets. In effect, two valuations must be made: one for the nonoperating assets and another for the operating assets. The sum of these two values yields the fair market value of the whole.

A valuation analysis should include comparative annual balance sheets and profit and loss statements for at least five years before the valuation date.

Earnings Capacity. Potential future income of the closely held corporation is a prime factor affecting its value. According to Revenue Ruling

59–60, *earnings should be the most important valuation factor when appraising an operating company.*

For an operating company, earnings are usually the most important factor in valuation (*Kline* v. *Commissioner*, 13 F2d 742–1942), but the use of historical earnings may be misleading and must be adjusted for trends and nonrecurring items.

For an investment company, the fair market value of underlying assets is usually more important than earnings (*William Hamm, Jr.*, 325 F2d 934–1964).

As stated by Judge Learned Hand in an early valuation case:

> Everyone knows that the value of the shares in a commercial or manufacturing company chiefly depends on what it will earn.
> (*Borg* v. *International Silver*, 11 F.2d 147, 152, CA–2, 1925).

In other words, as stated in Chapter 1, it is essential to keep in mind the central theme of this book: A willing buyer will pay a willing seller a price for a closely held business determined by a valuation based upon the expected future earnings power or capacity of that business.

Revenue Ruling 59–60 states: "Prior earnings records usually are the most reliable guide as to future expectancy." You should examine detailed income statements, preferably for five or more years.

Previous years' earnings are not simply averaged. In most cases, they are weighted with the most recent earnings years under consideration being given the highest importance. This applies whether the trend is an increasing or a decreasing one. "If, for instance, a record of progressively increasing or decreasing net income is found, then greater weight may be accorded the most recent years' profits in estimating earning" (Rev. Rul. 59–60, 1959–1 C.B. 237).

Once the weighted figure is reached, it should be capitalized at an appropriate rate to reach a final valuation (see Chapter 7).

An excellent example of the weighting process necessitated by an earnings trend took place in *Central Trust Co.* v. *U.S.*, 305 F.2d 393 (for the full text, see Appendix C). There the court took a favorable earnings trend and gave earnings from the five most recent fiscal years a weighting of 5,4,3,2,1, respectively, with 5 for the most recent year.

Analysis of gross income by product line, major deductions from operations, net income, and taxes, will enable you to form opinions regarding future profitability and value of the business. Additional information regarding nonrecurring expenses, officer's salaries, depreciation methods, substantial rental expense, and historical trends with regard to sales, costs, and new income would be discovered through this analysis. Nonrecurring items may require adjustments to reflect normal or fair earnings, and distortions—caused by erroneous or inconsistent practices—must be "normalized." Generally, past earnings experience is indicative of future expected earnings, but reliance on past history, without regard to present trends in both the company and the industry, is not likely to produce a realistic valuation.

The IRS in its *IRS Valuation Guide for Income, Estate, and Gift Taxes: IRS Appeals Officer Valuation Training Guide* has this to say about earnings capacity:

> The earnings of the business have been held by many valuation authorities to be the essence of fair market value. Certainly, investors have a primary concern with the earning power inherent in the securities they are buying or selling.
>
> One of the most frequently used indicators of earning power of a business is the income statement. We have to analyze the income statement to understand the operating results of the company. Usually income statements for a five-year period are obtained for comparison purposes.
>
> Trends in net sales, operating expenses, various classes of expenses or income and net profit should be noted because this will indicate the company's progress in the period preceding the valuation date.

Any valuation based on earnings capacity must be based on the actual historical earnings of the company to be valued. It must not be based on what the company should be earning if not for extraordinary conditions. For example, in *E.J.Fehrs*, (556 F.2d 1019), a gift tax case, the IRS attempted to have the stock of a closely held company engaged in the heavy road and industrial equipment business valued without regard to a poor earnings record. The IRS, instead, wanted to substitute the historical earnings record for the industry, which was higher than the business being valued. This would have resulted in a higher valuation and consequently, higher gift tax. The court stopped the government in its tracks, citing the following problem with this approach:

> the fact that the expert entirely avoided the use of Rental's [the company at issue] own earnings as a basis for the application of the earnings multiplier in favor of a reconstructed earnings base derived wholly from the profitability levels of companies other than Rental. This, as the court sees it, is an approach that proceeds not by comparison but by substitution and, in the last analysis, represents the valuation of a non-existent company.

To be sure, prospective earnings are important in the determination of share price. However, a valuation that completely disregards the recognized importance of actual earnings as a factor in the assessment of future expectations must rest on something more than the naked speculation that a dramatic change in corporate fortunes would follow from a change in corporate management.

Dividend-Paying Capacity. This is seldom a significant factor since the stockholders in control of a closely held business usually pay little or no dividends. The capacity to pay dividends rather than the actual dividend payout history is what counts.

> Primary consideration should be given to the dividend-paying capacity of the company rather than to the dividends paid in the past. Recognition must be given to the necessity of retaining a reasonable portion of profits in a company to meet competition. Dividend-paying capacity is a factor that must be considered in an appraisal, but dividends paid in the past may not have any relation to dividend-paying capacity. Specifically, the dividends paid by a closely held family company may be measured by the income needs of the stockholders or by their desire to avoid taxes on dividend receipts, instead of by ability of the company to pay dividends. Where an actual or effective controlling interest in a corporation is to be valued, the dividend factor is not a material element, since the payment of such dividends is discretionary with the controlling stockholders. The individual or group in control can substitute salaries and bonuses for dividends, thus reducing net income and understating the dividend-paying capacity of the company. Dividends are less reliable criteria of fair market value than other applicable factors.
> (Rev. Rul. 59–60, 1959–1 C.B. 237).

Once that dividend-paying capacity is determined, it is capitalized in a manner similar to that for earnings. However, remember that dividend-paying capacity capitalization rates will be lower than those for earnings simply because dividends come from earnings, and corporations rarely pay out all their earnings as dividends.

Although not as important as earnings, failure to take dividend-paying capacity into account can be and has been reason for the courts to disregard a valuation (*Louis* v. *U.S.*, 369 F.2d 263, CA–7, 1966).

Goodwill and Other Intangibles. Goodwill stems from various factors, the most significant of which is favored or "excess" earnings capacity. According to Revenue Ruling 59–60:

> In the final analysis, goodwill is based upon earning capacity. The presence of goodwill and its value, therefore, rests upon the excess of net

earnings over and above a fair return on the net tangible assets. While the element of goodwill may be based primarily on earnings, such factors as the prestige and renown of the business, the ownership of a trade or brand name, and a record of successful operations over a prolonged period in a particular locality, also may furnish support for the inclusion of intangible value . . .

In other words, the presence and value of goodwill depends on the measure of any unusually high earnings and rate of return the company enjoys. It may also be the result of a patent, an unusually acceptable product, an outstanding distribution or sales system, a location that attracts customers, and so on. While it usually is not accorded a separate value, goodwill is part of the earnings capacity and indicates a more valuable company.

Goodwill is not a factor in the valuation of an investment company.

Normally, the analysis of a business considering the other factors outlined in this book encompasses both the valuation of goodwill and other intangibles.

In many cases, the intangible value of a business, including goodwill, cannot be determined without reference to the tangible assets of the business. Such a case, Revenue Ruling 68–609, 1968–2 C.B. 327 (see Appendix B), provides that the formula approach of ARM 34, as restated, should be used. This revenue ruling is must reading. It provides authority for a valuation approach that in practice has proven to be the best method of making the valuation when no other method is capable of getting the job done right. Note, however, that despite its prevalent use, the IRS believes it should be used only as a last resort. (See Chapter 8 for a more detailed discussion of goodwill valuation.)

Sales of Stock and the Size of the Block to be Valued.   Prior sales of stock are said to be the best evidence of value if the sales were close in time to the valuation date and under comparable circumstances (*Louis* v. *U.S.*, 369 F.2d 263). There is no exact period of time at which a valuation becomes outdated. The main factor in determining the weight a representative sale should be given depends primarily on the change, if any, in the financial condition of the business since the date of the representative sale.

There are other factors besides proximity in time that are looked at. Here is what Revenue Ruling 59–60 has to say:

Sales of stock of a closely held corporation should be carefully investigated to determine whether they represent transactions at arm's length. Forced or distress sales do not ordinarily reflect fair market value, and isolated sales in small amounts do not necessarily control as the measure of value. This is especially true in the valuation of the controlling interest in a corporation. Since, in the case of the closely held stocks, no prevailing market prices are available, there is no basis for making an adjustment for blockage. Those stocks should be valued after a consideration of all the evidence affecting the fair market value. The size of the block of stock is a relevant factor to be considered. Although a minority interest in an unlisted corporation's stock is more difficult to sell than a similar block of listed stock, control of a corporation, either actual or in effect, representing an added element of value, may justify a higher value for a specific block of stock.

The closer the size of the representative sale is to the block of stock to be valued, the more likely the representative sale value will be accepted as controlling. In *Estate of Vandenhoek* (4 T.C. 125, 1944), the Tax Court disregarded previous small lot sales of stock in valuing a much larger block.

Another factor given close scrutiny is whether the representative sale was reached at arm's length. Sales between family members especially are suspect, and are given little weight by most courts (*Estate of Anderson*, 31 T.C.M. 502, 1972).

However, in *Estate of Kaye* v. *Comm'r* (32 T.C.M. 1270, 1973), a sale of stock from a business associate of the decedent to the decedent's daughter two years after the decedent's death was held by the court to be representative of the value of the stock in the decedent's estate. This was because the estate presented three expert witnesses who defended the value while the IRS smugly rested upon its assertion of a higher value with no proof.

Here's a case where the court relied heavily on the sale of stock (*First National Bank of Fort Smith*, 85–2 USTC 13,627 DC–Ark.). A block of stock representing a 28 percent interest in a privately held corporation was the subject of this valuation dispute. Both sides used the traditional factors of valuation, yet the court gave great weight to the price paid for a block of stock representing only a 2 percent interest. The sale was made 16 months before the death of the decedent.

The court noted that the size of the blocks were different, but it felt the difference was not substantial. Even though the court did not use the sales price as the sole criterion, it held that the price was determined objectively, and that it could be used to measure other evidence of value.

Here is a checklist of factors that determine the weight given to a previous representative sale:

1. the proximity of the sale to the valuation date,
2. the amount of the disparity between the number of shares sold and the number of shares to be valued,
3. the motives surrounding the sale other than those aimed at arriving at a fair price, and
4. the amount of any intervening change in the economic or financial condition of the business and the environment from the sale date to the valuation date.

The buyer of a closely held business almost always wants 100 percent of the stock or none at all. Generally, even a controlling interest—if substantially less than all the stock—will sell at a discount below the price for 100 percent of the stock. A minority interest would be discounted even more (see Chapter 9).

Weighing the Factors: The Central Trust Case

The most instructive case to study to get an idea of how a court might use the factors of Revenue Ruling 59–60 in reaching its valuation decision can be found in *Central Trust Co.* v. *U.S.* (305 F.2d 393; Ct. Cls., 1962). The following summary is provided (see Appendix C for the full text) to illustrate that step-by-step process.

Facts. In 1954, a member of the board of directors of a closely held manufacturer of cans for food packaging gifted over 70,000 shares of stock in the company to various trusts for the benefit of his children. He died the next year. The executors of his estate first valued the shares at $10 per share and later amended that valuation to $7.50 for estate tax purposes. The IRS contended a value of $24 per share.

The court made the following findings of additional facts:

Nature of the business. Heekin (the company at issue) was a well-established can manufacturer. It had two main product lines: packer cans for shelved canned foods, and larger general line cans used for housewares, for picnic containers, and by institutions for bulk food storage. Annual sales were $17 million. Its main manufacturing facilities were housed in a multi-story plant. It also had four other, smaller facilities. The family members of the decedent were the controlling shareholders, with 79 members owning 71 percent of all outstanding stock.

Business relations. Heekin had six steady major customers accounting for over half its business. It was perfectly situated in the Ohio River Valley, which minimized transportation costs. At the time of the valuation, the canning industry, in general, was experiencing record demand.

Competitive Industry. Heekin was in an industry dominated by two mammoth corporations: American Can and Continental Can. They controlled over 75 percent of the canning market. Heekin accounted for less than 1 percent of the same market. Prices in the industry were set by the two giants, leaving Heekin at their mercy. As a result, Heekin secured and retained its customers by giving better personal service and a quality product.

Age of Equipment. The court highlighted the age and inefficiency of Heekin's plant and equipment as its main problem. It noted that Heekin had been unable to retool and keep up with the technological advancements in canning instituted by the two giant competitors because Heekin lacked the capital for a large-scale modernization program. As a result, Heekin's productivity was 300 cans per minute compared to 400–500 for the rest of the industry. However, this productivity disadvantage existed only in its packer can production. It was competitive with the two giants and the rest of the industry concerning manufacture of the larger general line cans.

Past Sales of Heekin Stock. Trading activity in Heekin stock was infrequent. Sales that did take place were struck at $7.50 per share and made to employees and friends of the Heekin family.

Estate's Expert Witness' Testimony. The Estate's first expert witness reached a valuation based on the following:

Past sales. Although made at the $7.50 per share value, the expert felt the past sales were too limited, and therefore consideration of the other factors listed in Revenue Ruling 59–60 was in order.

Book value. The company's balance sheet produced a book value of $33 per share. Because of the inefficiency and age of the company's plant and equipment, this was reduced by half to $16.60.

Earnings. Using income statements from the past three years, an average earnings per share of $1.77 was found, and was capitalized at a P/E ratio of 6 to 1, yielding a $10.62 per share value. However, recognizing the importance of earnings in valuation of an operating company, that figure was given double weight, resulting in a $21.24 per share value.

Dividend yield. Using a per annum dividend of 50 cents over the last three years, it was assumed that an investor would look for a 7 percent yield. This resulted in a $7.14 value per share.

Here is the result:

Book Value
    $33.20 × .50 × weighted average of 1 .... $16.60
Earnings
    $1.77 × 6 × weighted average of 2.......................... 21.24
Dividends
    $0.50 divided by .07 × weighted average of 1.................. 7.14
Past sales
    $7.50 × weighted average of 1 .... 7.50

Total all factors... $52.48
Divided by weighted average total of 5 .... 10.50
Less 25 percent lack of marketability............................. 2.62

Final per share value 7.88

The estate presented two other expert witnesses who used the same formula. Here is the most interesting result: They reached final valuation figures of $9.37 and $11.41 per share. Why the difference? Each made different assumptions. For example, the discount for lack of marketability (see Chapter 9) given by the three witnesses was 25, 5, and 20 percent, respectively. The weight given each of the four factors was different for each witness. Each used a slightly differing book value, and so on and so on. In other words, they differed on the quantitative aspects of the factors but were in approximate agreement as to their qualitative merits as belonging in the valuation process. Each expert juggled the numbers differently.

Court's Criticism of Estate's Witness' Testimony. The court had a field day, criticizing the valuation approach of the estate's witnesses on seven points:

1. The prior stock sales were too insignificant to warrant the weight given them.
2. Financial data used by the experts came from periods after the valuation date, and would have been unavailable to a prospective purchaser.

3. The third witness' data excluded financial data for the year before the valuation date.

4. Adjustments were not made in calculating the company's earnings for excessive income from government contracts as a result of the Korean War.

5. No allowances were made for detecting trends in historical earnings by giving greater weight to most recent earnings.

6. Despite the fact that earnings are the most important valuation factor to consider for a manufacturing company such as Heekin, two of the experts gave equal weight to earning power and dividend yield:

> Some investors may indeed depend upon dividends. In their own investment programs, they may therefore stress yield and even compare common stocks with bonds or other forms of investment to obtain the greatest yields. However, others, for various reasons, may care little about dividends and may invest in common stocks for the primary purpose of seeking capital appreciation. All investors, however, are primarily concerned with earnings, which are normally a prerequisite to dividends. In addition, the declaration of dividends is sometimes simply a matter of the policy of a particular company. It may bear no relation to dividend-paying capacity. Many investors actually prefer companies paying little or no dividends and which reinvest their earnings, for that may be the key to future growth and capital appreciation.

7. The experts took too great a discount for lack of marketability. The costs of creating a market for a block of the well-established company's shares should be closer to 12 percent (see Chapter 9).

Whether the court's criticisms are valid is not the point. What is important is to note the issues raised and the manner in which the court attacks them. The issues are such that reasonable people could differ over their solutions. These issues are common to most valuation cases, and an appraiser must be prepared to meet them head on. Needless to say, the court made it clear that it felt the valuation figures of the estate's witnesses were understated.

Ultimately, the court in *Central Trust* used the comparative approach, i.e., used comparable publicly traded companies, to reach an approximate value for the closely held manufacturing company. Since we have not discussed comparables in detail yet, the rest of the *Central Trust* case is reserved for Chapter 6 which discusses the proper use of comparables in detail.

VALUATION AS THE COURTS SEE IT: A SURVEY OF FACTORS DECIDING VALUATION CASES

The *Central Trust* case, which is the subject of an in-depth survey, is just one in the over 300 cases brought before various courts concerning valuations of closely held businesses. The particular facts in that case dictated what valuation approaches were appropriate to use.

However, aside from the assumption that particular facts dictate particular approaches, much can be learned from surveying the various factors that entered into many court decisions over a period from 1945–1984. The following is a list of 30 factors and the number of times in 327 closely

Valuation Factor	Number of Times Considered by Courts in Their Decisions
1. Historical earnings	139
2. Earning power	66
3. Capitalization of average earnings	24
4. Price/earnings ratio	30
5. Dividends paid or yield	68
6. Dividend-paying capacity	31
7. Book value	115
8. Tangible assets	85
9. Net working capital	21
10. Potential value	14
11. Replacement costs	4
12. Growth of net worth	17
13. Dividend arrearages	3
14. Nature of business	89
15. Position of industry	18
16. Character and quality of management	38
17. Sale of stock (or lack thereof)	165
18. Blockage	38
19. Restrictions	76
20. Marketability	69
21. Controlling interest	21
22. Minority interest	61
23. Comparative companies	37
24. Economic conditions	23
25. Stock market conditions	12
26. Goodwill	11
27. Cost of doing business	4
28. Expert testimony	130
29. Intent of liquidation	12
30. Lack of evidence	85

held business cases that each factor entered into the court's valuation decision. The raw numbers for the following table can be found in the excellent compendium on valuation cases: *Federal Tax Valuation Digest: Business Enterprises and Business Interests,* 1984 edition (John A. Bishop and Morton Mark Lee, Standard Research Consultants, Published By Warren, Gorham & Lamont, Boston).

As can be seen from the numbers, the eight factors listed in Revenue Ruling 59–60 predominate the courts' thinking.

If a factor was used in a case, it does not necessarily mean it was controlling. In many instances it was disregarded. What the survey shows, as does the *Central Trust* example, is what factors are considered, even if only for strawman purposes.

Like a golfer deciding which is the best club to use for an approach shot to the green, the factors are a smorgasbord from which valuation opponents and the courts can pick and choose in order to bolster their valuation decisions. As in the case of a golfer, it is not so much the club used as it is the skillful swing employed that makes a good shot. So too it is the skill of the appraiser, using the valuation factors to the best advantage, that counts.

CHAPTER 4
Blending in the Facts

FACT, NOT LAW, DETERMINES VALUE

Valuation experience dictates that each company to be valued has its own set of facts and circumstances, and each valuation is different from every other valuation. Two companies in similar lines of business with almost identical numbers can have quite different values because of one significant fact difference. No set of textbook rules can bring out the importance of unique facts.

Every valuation must commence with an examination of the balance sheet and operating statement; care must be taken to recognize that both are nothing but sets of numbers. It is important to distinguish between numbers and facts. Numbers represent historical earnings, margins, return on equity, book value, and so on. Numbers are precise and, if correct, are tough to argue—either for or against.

On the other hand, facts are the reason behind the numbers. Facts are not self-evident from a mere reading of the numbers. Facts have to be dug out, verified, assessed, and often discarded for lack of weight. Facts are found everywhere, and the search for them must go everywhere.

Numbers can have a fatal attraction in the valuation process because by their nature they are self-quantifying. Being wholly mathematical, numbers lend themselves all too easily by arithmetic process to translation into the valuation figure, which is also a number. Numbers are easy to work with, but to produce easy answers or quick answers is not to produce sound answers.

The objective of every valuation is to blend the numbers and the facts into a cohesive justification of a business's worth. In order to succeed, facts must be organized toward that end. The methods for doing so follow.

THE FACT-GATHERING PROCESS: A CHECKLIST

Balance Sheet

To arrive at "adjusted book value," examine the balance sheet in detail.

Inventory.   Question the quality of the inventory; a portion of it is almost always bad. Is it LIFO or FIFO? A LIFO inventory may have one value for going-concern purposes (requiring an adjustment to arrive at adjusted book value) and another value for liquidation purposes.

Receivables.   Review the aging and the quality of receivables. Failure to write off bad debts means equity and earnings are overstated.

Assets Not Essential to the Operations of the Business.   Assets (such as securities or real estate) that are not used in the operation of the business or will not be used in future expansion should be valued separately at fair market value. The value determined for these assets should be added as a separate item to the value of the operating portion of the business. Operating earnings also should be adjusted upward or downward because of profits or losses attributable to such nonessential assets.

Real Estate.   If any real estate used in the operations of the business has been on the books for a long period of time, the depreciated value probably is well under market value. Remember that the operating portion of the business may have little or no value, or be substantially reduced, because of the location of the real estate (if, for example, customers can get to the business only with great difficulty). At other times the real estate could be the whole ballgame (if, for example, a retail business owns a building in the highest traffic area in town; but what if the building is about to be taken by eminent domain?).

Tangible Personal Depreciable Property.   Should tangible personal depreciable property be adjusted to fair market value (usually called *appraisal value* at this initial stage)? If it is a nonoperating asset or an asset no longer to be used in operations, the answer is clearly "Yes!" But if the asset is used in operations, the answer usually must await further probing. Logically, increasing the value of the asset requires an upward adjustment of future depreciation. The increased appraisal value raises the ultimate fair market value, while the increased depreciation lowers future book profits and the ultimate value—one works against the other. Similar reasoning says that if a particular piece of equipment is worth more right now, future earnings will be reduced because of the increased cost of replacing that equipment when it wears out or becomes obsolete—more circular reasoning.

Quite often, even though tangible personal property is worth substantially more than book value, no adjustment is made for valuation purposes. The problem, if applicable, should be recognized in the appraisal report.

Age, Nature, and Efficiency of Assets. The age, nature, and efficiency of the company's assets will dictate its sales, earnings, and dividends capacity. Assets used efficiently, but with additional capacity, suggest the potential for growth without substantial spending: a positive valuation factor. If the assets are operating at, or close to, full capacity, further growth may dictate additional spending and financing: a negative factor.

Intangible Property. Intangible property should be either eliminated (because it has no intrinsic value) or adjusted to appraisal value as circumstances require.

Leasehold Improvements. On liquidation leasehold improvements are usually worth nothing; for a going concern, book value usually is used. However, if the improvements are valuable and can be removed, or if the increased value can be utilized over a long-term lease, this asset would be restated at fair market value.

Loans to Shareholders. Are loans to shareholders collectible or worthless? Do they bear interest, and if so at what rate?

Loans from Shareholders. Are loans from shareholders debt or equity? When in doubt, the appraiser should get written confirmation from the shareholder. Is accrued interest substantial? How would someone purchasing the assets and assuming the liabilities treat this apparent liability?

Operating Statement

When using any valuation approach involving earnings, the operating statement must be analyzed. Appropriate adjustments (increasing or decreasing profit as enumerated below) must be made for each year of operations being considered. (Remember that valuation is an attempt to predict the earning potential of an operating business.) To some degree, future earnings can be given a sharper focus by examining past earnings, as adjusted.

Salaries of Owners. If salaries are excessive, earnings are understated; the reverse is true if salaries are too low. But this part of the valuation process shouldn't stop with salaries. All of the owner's fringe benefits must be examined to determine whether they are excessive.

Depreciation. If accelerated depreciation methods are used, earnings may be understated, but the opposite will be true when acceleration runs out. Additional and immediate requirements for capital expenditures might have greater impact than past or anticipated future depreciation.

LIFO Reserve. Adjust to FIFO basis. When inventory is increased by the amount of the LIFO reserve, it must be done by only the after-tax amount on the balance sheet. Cost of sales and gross profit must also be adjusted for the before-tax difference for each year of operations considered, while net profits must be adjusted for the after-tax difference.

Extraordinary Items. Sale of land, equipment, or a division may generate a profit or loss, the effect of which should be eliminated, since this does not represent normal business operations.

Unusual Year. A year of abnormally high profit or loss should be excluded unless other circumstances indicate a recurring trend.

Nonoperating Assets. Exclude income and expense from portfolios, rental real estate, and so on, if it is not part of normal operations.

Earnings Trends. If earnings are erratic, average them; if rising or falling, you may want to weight the later years, but you should investigate the reasons for the changes. Consider the effect of such items as annual union wage increase on projected earnings.

Employee Benefit Contribution. If the company is to be sold to a buyer who has a benefit plan different from the seller's plan, adjust earnings up or down as required. Other employee benefits, of which there is an ever-growing list in the eyes of the IRS, must also be considered. The main goal of the benefit inquiry is to determine if the total benefit package is excessive, normal, or low.

Income Taxes. Adjustments to each income and expense item should be aggregated and an appropriate adjustment to income taxes must be made.

Intangibles. Some factors exercise either a positive or negative effect on the value of goodwill. They are these:
- Favorable location
- Reputation for service or special skills of the owner or employees

- Discount prices
- Majority of sales coming from only a few customers
- Failure of business to keep up with changing market conditions
- Occupancy of a location vital to success not assured by lease or ownership
- Dependence on personality or special skills of an individual who will not be available after the business is acquired (if the owner goes, so does the goodwill)

The first two items on the list are positive; the others are negative.

Other intangible assets, if they do exist, should be valued separately from the goodwill. They include these:

- Customer lists
- Covenant not to compete
- Licenses, to be transferred, restricted as to number by local ordinance
- Contracts that give a special advantage (for example, supply or price)
- Patents
- Trademarks

Other Points to Ponder

Loss of Key Personnel.   Is there backup management? Can key people be replaced? What would be the impact on business if one or more key people were lost? Will life insurance solve the problem until new people can be trained?

Present Plant.   Is the present plant condemned? Is it adequate for near-term, or will it have to be enlarged or replaced? Is the lease about to expire? How will the cost of these affect future earnings?

State of Industry.   If the state of the industry is static, what is the possibility of future growth for the company? What is the impact of present governmental regulations or the likelihood of new or changed regulations? Will necessary raw material be in short supply and put the company out of business? Or cause profits to skyrocket because the company has a source? Or could it be the other way around, with the market being flooded by an oversupply, killing profit margins?

Competitive Position.   If your company is one of many similar operations in the area, what is the outlook for growth, sales, and profits?

HINT: This checklist should be used every time a business is valued. Also use it when a valuation is updated. Add points to the list as required. However, using checklists does not automatically produce answers. For any given case, only one or two points on the checklist may be relevant— when a bell rings, research and evaluate the relevant point thoroughly.

EXAMPLES: HOW FACTS DETERMINE VALUE

Each of the following examples actually happened.

Example 1

A retail sporting goods store had in its most recent five-year period doubled its sales and earnings. These facts gave the initial impression that the company was doing better than average and should sell at a premium. This impression was erroneous. In each year the store space had expanded, yet sales per square foot were unchanged from year one to year five. The owner had to double his investment to double his sales and earnings. A buyer would have had to increase his investment beyond what he paid at the valuation date if he wished to increase his sales and earnings. This fact negated the impression that the historic five-year growth would continue automatically in the hands of the buyer. A premium was not warranted.

Example 2

A manufacturing concern had a steady five-year earnings record that justified a $1.5 million value. However, a potential buyer inspected the company's plant and found severe physical deterioration. The plant manager admitted that the building was condemned and that the company was actively searching for and planned to buy a new, more expensive plant elsewhere. The net cost for such a move was figured at $500,000. Despite the proven earnings record, what buyer would be willing to pay the $1.5 million knowing that another $500,000 outlay would be required to move the facility?

Example 3

A decedent held the stock of a corporation that owned a small parcel of land on which it operated a restaurant business. The decedent also held the beneficial interest in a land trust that owned a large parking lot adjacent to and leased by the restaurant. One person (a real estate appraiser) valued the parking lot at $70,000. Another person looked at the numbers for the restaurant and valued the restaurant at $400,000. By simple addition, the value of the two holdings equaled $470,000. Subsequently, it was pointed out that the restaurant was worth $400,000 only if the parking lot was available. If no parking lot had been available, the restaurant would be out of business and worth only salvage value. The IRS accepted the no-value-to-the-parking-lot approach and agreed to a $400,000 value for the two holdings.

Example 4

A decedent had been a member of a very small group that had for years owned and operated a successful company. When the lawyers, accountants, and advisors prepared to value the decedent's interest in the corporation, it was under the assumption that the decedent's 60 percent interest was represented by common stock.

Suddenly, someone remembered that the decedent did not own common stock but a voting trust certificate entitling the holder to receive 60 percent of the common stock upon expiration of the voting trust some eight years after date of death. A holder of a voting trust certificate has no voice in running the corporation; this power resides in the voting trustee. Despite the nominal representation of 60 percent control, the voting trust certificate holder has no more voice in management than the holder of a minority interest. This argument was made to the IRS and resulted in a 25 percent discount from the full value of 60 percent of the stock of the corporation.

The most important valuation factor in this example had nothing to do with the numbers but rather with the discovery of the precise nature of the interest in the company held by the decedent.

Example 5

A multiple-store retailer wanted to transfer the future growth of his business to his two sons. Both were active in the business. The business was being evaluated to support a recapitalization. For various reasons the 65 percent owner/founder wanted to have a larger value than what appeared from the usual facts. The other 35 percent was owned by the two sons.

Fortunately, the business rented a number of stores that had very favorable leases. Most of the leases had a number of years (from three to seven years) remaining. The rents were significantly lower than the current market rents.

When a lease has a remaining term at a rent below market, this difference has value (leasehold interest), which is a separately identifiable intangible asset and should not be included with goodwill. Usually, the value of a leasehold interest can be computed by capitalizing, at an appropriate rate for commercial real estate, the annual difference between market rent and actual rent over the remaining term of the lease.

EXAMPLE: Market Rent $20,000
             Less Actual Rent   14,000
             Annual Difference $ 6,000

The present value factor at 10 percent for four years (the remaining term of the lease) is 3.170. Therefore the value of the leasehold interest is $19,020 (3.170 × $6,000).

The value of the business was increased by almost $200,000 because of the value of the leases. Each lease was valued separately.

CHAPTER 5
The Eight Major Approaches to Valuation

It has been said that the number of different valuation approaches in existence at any point in time can be determined by multiplying all the appraisers in the world by the number of businesses to be valued.

Years of practice and experience have shown the following eight approaches as the most common valuation approaches:

1. comparative values of similar going concerns
2. reproduction or replacement value
3. present value of the cash flow
4. liquidation approach
5. book value
6. factor approach (often called a formula approach)
7. earnings approach
8. combinations and variations

Observation: At this point, it should be observed that basically there are only two approaches to valuation—the liquidation approach and the earnings approach. All other approaches are combinations.

Which is best? Which should be used and when? Actually there is no pat answer. Often an approach that is just right under one set of circumstances would give ridiculous results if the facts were changed slightly.

COMPARATIVE VALUES OF SIMILAR GOING CONCERNS

One widely used method of valuing closely held corporations entails an examination of comparable publicly held companies and the prices of actual transactions of such companies' securities on or near the valuation date.

The search for comparable companies might begin with *industry classification*. In theory, companies in the same industry share similar markets, and the potential for sales and earnings growth is usually dependent upon the characteristics of the growth rates of these markets. In addition, companies in the same industry are often affected by common operating (production and supply) characteristics. Upon reviewing all those public firms in the same industry classification, adjustments are made for *size*, *diversity, growth, stability, leverage, dividends*, and other factors.

This method is based on the observation that during any relatively short period of time the relative sales prices of the public common stocks within a given industry generally can be related to the stock of a closely held company. Somehow the relative investment characteristics of these larger, publicly traded corporations and the closely held corporations are supposed to be alike. As explained in Chapter 6 this is, more often than not, an incorrect supposition.

With rare exceptions, the comparative method does not make sense, for any but the very largest of closely held companies. It is difficult (and more often impossible) to find truly comparable companies; however, some large unlisted companies approach the comparability requirements of their listed counterparts (see Chapter 6).

REPRODUCTION OR REPLACEMENT VALUE

The production or replacement value approach is based on the amount of money it would take to replace or reproduce the facilities and systems of the business being valued, by going into the marketplace and obtaining replacement assets. This method is used for insurance purposes. Also, if the seller has unique property that is what the buyer really wants in terms of a physical plant that is operating, this method may be the first choice.

PRESENT VALUE OF THE CASH FLOW

The present value of the cash flow approach is concerned with the value of the cash flow of the business adjusted for the time value of money and the business and economic risks. The theory is that cash flow represents the recovery of the investment and the receipt of income produced by such investment. This method contains the following factors:

1. The expected growth rates in sales and earnings projected to a selected date on which the stock may be sold.
2. The time period between the valuation date and the sale date.
3. The dividend payout of the company (as it is or potentially could be).
4. An expected price-earning ratio or liquidation value at the end of the time frame. A perpetual dividend stream also could be used.
5. A rate of return investors might seek given their expectations of the four preceding factors, less a discount for the risk of not having such expectations realized.

Cash flow is assumed to be a more valid criterion of value than "book or accounting" profits. Only cash or cash equivalents can be used for reinvestment purposes.

This method (also called the *Discounted Cash Flow Approach* or *Investment Approach*) is often used for nontax purposes to arrive at a comparable price at which to establish an exchange ratio; or in certain other circumstances—for example, a merger.

Example

Suppose a rational investor decides the risk for the business she wants to buy merits a 15 percent return. She assumes an annual cash return of $10,000 a ycar for ten years and a liquidation value of $100,000.

The value today (right now), called the "present value," is $74.84. The following schedule shows how the investor would arrive at this value.

Year	Annual cash	+	Liquidation value	=	Total cash	×	Discount factor (15%)	Present value
1	$10,000				$ 10,000		.869	$ 8,690
2	$10,000				$ 10,000		.756	$ 7,560
3	$10,000				$ 10,000		.657	$ 6,570
4	$10,000				$ 10,000		.571	$ 5,710
5	$10,000				$ 10,000		.497	$ 4,970
6	$10,000				$ 10,000		.432	$ 4,320
7	$10,000				$ 10,000		.375	$ 3,750
8	$10,000				$ 10,000		.326	$ 3,260
9	$10,000				$ 10,000		.284	$ 2,840
10	$10,000		$100,000		$110,000		.247	$27,170
Total present value								$74,840

The mechanics of the preceding schedule are simple. If an investor had $8,690 on the first day of year one and it earned 15 percent for a full year ($1,310) she would have $10,000 at the end of the year ($8,690 plus $1,310), and so on.

LIQUIDATION APPROACH

Investment companies usually are valued on a liquidation basis. If an operating company has nonoperating assets, such assets should be segregated for valuation purposes. The operating assets and the income produced by such assets must be valued separately.

As a practical matter, every business is worth at least *liquidation value*. If the operating assets—particularly fixed assets—are left in place to be used in a continuing business, then the package has a minimum value at or near *reproduction or replacement* cost less depreciation. Replacement cost, unless the property is unique, means fair market value.

Liquidation value of a going business can be tricky: Costs, expenses, and losses must be estimated for selling the inventory, collecting receivables, terminating employees, selling assets as no longer needed, and a host of other winding-down activities.

BOOK VALUE

Among other names, the book value approach to valuation is called *net tangible asset value* or *adjusted book value*.

Tangible book value is obtained by reference to the business' most recent balance sheet. In essence, it is the net book value of the business: total assets minus total liabilities, with adjustments made for intangibles such as goodwill.

Adjusted book value is based on making the necessary adjustments to book value for such factors as economic depreciation of plant and equipment, appreciation of land and other real estate values, and understated or overstated inventories due to accounting method.

Typically, little or no judgment is required to value assets using this approach. If required, each asset on the balance sheet should be restated at fair market value. (See the Tangible Personal Depreciable Property item on the fact-gathering process checklist in Chapter 4 for an exception for depreciable personal property used in an operating business.)

Such a valuation can be accomplished mechanically by completing a schedule similar to the following:

Steps for Determination of Adjusted Book Value

1. Start with book value. $_____
2. Add(or subtract) the necessary figure to arrive at line 3.   _____
3. Appraisal or fair market value (the number for which all
   assets—like fixed assets and inventory—with any value could
   be sold if the company were to be liquidated).   _____

4. Subtract all intangibles on the books that have no value (that is, cannot be sold separately in liquidation), such as goodwill or a covenant not to compete. _____

5. Balance—adjusted book value. $_____

The adjusted book value approach is important because it is one of the elements used in the valuation approaches that follow.

Book value as the sole or predominant factor also makes sense in certain special situations:

1. a relatively new business
2. a business whose earnings have been unstable
3. a business whose sole owner is disabled or has died
4. a business for which an earnings approach to valuation is highly speculative—for example, where uncertainty due to things like supply shortages, strikes, government legislation, and product obsolescence makes the future unpredictable.

FACTOR APPROACH

According to the factor approach, three major factors are considered the most significant in determining value: earnings, dividend-paying capacity, and book value.

Earnings are normally the prime interest of the investor, but their weight, of course, must be tempered by consideration of the type of business being valued. Manufacturing companies and companies that sell a product or service usually give earnings heavier weight. On the other hand, gross revenue is the main factor in the valuation of a strictly service operation.

When an investment or holding company is valued, the greatest weight, up to 100 percent if appropriate, is given to the underlying net asset values. The payment of dividends does not permit much weight in the valuation of closely held stock.

The factor approach was used in two well-known cases, Bader (*Bader v. U.S.,* 172 F Supp. 833–1959) and Central Trust (*Central Trust Co., Exr v. U.S.,* 350 F2d 393–1962). Following is a comparison of the weight and values given to each factor in those two cases. Keep in mind that the weighting process is a subjective one: the full texts of each case (which can be found in Appendix C) should be read for the justifications behind the assumptions resulting in the actual weights assigned each factor.

	Capitalized value	Bader		Central Trust	
		Weight	Value	Weight	Value
1. Earnings:					
$50 × 12.5	$625	2	$1,250	.5	$312
2. Dividends:					
$25 × 24.0	600	1	600	.3	180
3. Book value:					
$800 × .6	480	1	480	.2	96
4. Total			$2,330		$588
5. Average			$ 582		$588
6. Discount:					
10.00 percent			58		
12.17 percent					72
7. Per share value			$ 524		$516

EARNINGS APPROACH

The earnings approach rarely is ignored in the valuation of an operating privately held business. However, the earnings approach can yield extremely different results depending on the purpose of the valuation and the nature of the entity to be valued. It is usually the investor's best method for calculating expected return on investment.

Judgment must be exercised at each of two significant levels when implementing the earnings approach.

At one level, the "true" earnings of the business must be determined. Adjustments must be made for such items as officers' salaries and expenses that would not be made (or if made, not in the same amount) by the usual self-serving owners of a privately held business. The number of operating years (three, four, or five) to be considered, eliminated (as not representative), or weighted (with greater weight given to the most recent years) must be selected.

At another level, after the "true earnings" have been determined, the appropriate multiple is applied, which will be higher for a low-risk business (seldom as much as ten) and lower for a high-risk business (often only one or two). The amount of the multiple is, of course, affected by the many facts, factors, and circumstances peculiar to the business.

Often an operating business is valued completely by earnings, ignoring the liquidation approach. This is true when a business is valued solely as a multiple of earnings. For example, under proper circumstances a business with average earnings over the preceding five years of $0.4 million after taxes might be valued at $2.0 million—a five times multiple of earnings.

COMBINATIONS AND VARIATIONS

This is the method by which most closely held businesses change hands between a willing buyer and a willing seller. It is also the method preferred by the courts and often employed by the IRS in practice. In most valuations of an operating business, a combination of several basic methods is employed to arrive at the final valuation. The variations used are at least equal to the number of businesses to be valued. A typical example would combine the adjusted book value and earnings approach. There is no single correct way.

Every valuation eventually has to face its alter ego. The valuation of the taxpayer must confront that of the IRS; the valuation of the seller that of the buyer. Each of the valuation approaches can be taken piecemeal, *a la carte* if you will, by a contending party to fit his or her purposes. The IRS is particularly adept at adopting whatever method generates the most tax dollars in a particular case.

Because of this fact, the courts have recognized that no one particular approach is controlling. Instead, they take the facts of each particular case, use the approach they deem appropriate to the facts, and make a judgment call in reaching a final valuation figure.

Ponder the lamentations of the Tax Court:

> Too often in valuation disputes the parties have convinced themselves of the unalterable correctness of their positions and have consequently failed successfully to conclude settlement negotiations—a process clearly more conducive to the proper disposition of disputes such as this. The result is an overzealous effort, during the course of the ensuing litigation, to infuse talismanic precision into an issue which should frankly be recognized as inherently imprecise and capable of resolution only by Solomon-like pronouncement.
> (*Messing* v. *Commissioner*, 48 T.C. 502)

Indeed, each of the parties should keep in mind that, in the final analysis, the Court may find the evidence of valuation by one of the parties suffi-

ciently more convincing than that of the other party, so that the final result will produce a significant financial defeat for one or the other, rather than a middle of-the-road compromise which we suspect each of the parties expects the Court to reach.
(*Buffalo Tool & Die Mfg. Co.* v. *Comm'r*, 74 T.C. 441, 1980)

In their effort to reach a compromise, the courts often resort to the combination approach.

CHAPTER 6
When to Use and When Not to Use Comparables

The use of the market price of stock of comparable publicly traded corporations as a measure of valuation of the stock of closely held corporations has become a prime valuation tool. It is resorted to much too frequently in unjustifiable situations; nevertheless, in certain situations the use of comparables is not only desirable but necessary.

THE BASICS OF HOW COMPARABLES ARE USED

Problems with Comparables

There are four basic problems with the use of comparables: difficulty finding comparables, fluctuating prices of publicly held stock, missed significance of adjusted book value, and lack of real buy-to-sell experience based on comparables.

Difficulty Finding Comparables.　The smaller the privately held business, the less likely that the appraiser will be able to find one or more comparable public companies. In fact, the appraiser has no duty to engage in a fruitless search when logic and experience dictate otherwise. On the other hand, when the nature and size of the company to be valued indicate the feasibility of using comparables, the appraiser has a duty to search for comparable public companies. If found, they should be used.

It is not always clear whether comparables can be found. An experienced and knowledgeable appraiser will not be stampeded into the use of comparables by such statements as "The IRS only accepts comparables," or even, "The IRS prefers comparables." What the business owner and other interested parties want and need is the right valuation. Forced use of comparables that are "close" but not really comparable can result in a correct valuation only by accident.

Often, when the comparables are not what the appraiser would like them to be, more than one method is used to make the valuation. Then, the results of the comparable method and other method are averaged (usually by weighting) to arrive at the final valuation. [Chapter 7 contains an example (Royal Oil, Inc.) of such a valuation.]

Fluctuating Prices of Publicly Held Stock.　Publicly held stocks often have wide fluctuations in price. The value of any particular stock or group of industry stocks can and does move up and down several times during a year. When such volatile stocks are used as comparables, what price from the wide, yearly range should be used? The value of the privately held stock, when aligned with such comparables, would have a value that would jump up and down along with the price of its volatile comparable. Is this realistic?

This fluctuating price problem runs directly counter to the principle that says a valuation is a determination of the value of a business on a specific date. However, the fluctuating price problem can largely be overcome by averaging or weighting prices of the publicly held stocks. [An excellent example of how this can be accomplished is contained in Chapter 7 (Royal Oil, Inc.).]

Missed Significance of Adjusted Book Value. Comparables use earnings as a basis of comparability. How valid is the use of comparables when the privately held business shows losses or low profits? Should comparables in similar dire financial straits be used? Of course not. Comparables just won't work in such a case. Adjusted book value less a discount for the lack of profit or liquidation value are two bases for valuing an unprofitable privately held business that make much more sense.

What about profitable privately held businesses that have large adjusted book values? Consider these four companies that are identical in all respects, including profits, except their names and adjusted book values:

Name	Adjusted book value	After-tax profits
Smallest	$500,000	$500,000
Small	$2,000,000	$500,000
Big	$8,000,000	$500,000
Biggest	$32,000,000	$500,000

The blind use of comparables would make the value of each of the four companies equal, based on their earnings. That is clearly an absurd result. Earnings, when large in comparison to book value, rule. However, it is the appraiser's job to make sure that the book value, as adjusted, does not get swallowed by a multiple of earnings controlled by the price-earnings ratio of comparables.

The problem of the overwhelming predominance of earnings in the comparable method can be overcome by using one of the combination methods of valuation discussed in Chapter 5.

Lack of Real Buy-Sell Experience. In the real world, buyers and sellers of a privately held company do not use comparables when they sit down to negotiate the price at which the business will be bought or sold. There are two exceptions to this rule: (1) when the buyer is a publicly traded company and (2) when the privately held business approaches its publicly traded comparable counterpart in sales, size, diversification, and other factors. "Willing buyers" and "willing sellers," as used in the legal definition of fair market value (see Chapter 3) simply do not use comparables (subject to the few exceptions) when fixing the price at which a privately held business will change hands.

In the final analysis, the appraiser must ask this question: What method will duplicate the price that would be hammered out by a real buyer and a real seller? That is the method that should be used.

THE IRS AND THE USE OF COMPARABLES

The main and most important proponent of the use of comparables has been and is the IRS. As noted previously, Revenue Ruling 59–60 and various provisions of tax law endorse the use of comparables. Here is what Revenue Ruling 59–60 says:

> Section 2031(b) of the Code states that, in valuing unlisted securities, the value of the stock or the securities of corporations engaged in the same or similar line of business which are listed on an exchange should be taken into consideration along with all other factors. An important consideration is that the corporations to be used for comparisons have capital stocks which are actively traded by the public. In accordance with Section 2031(b) of the Code, stocks listed on an exchange are listed first. If sufficient comparable companies whose stocks are listed on an exchange cannot be found, other comparable companies which have stocks actively traded on the over-the-counter market also may be used. The essential factor is that, whether the stocks are sold on an exchange or over-the-counter, there is evidence of an active, free public market for the stock as of the valuation date. In selecting the corporations for comparative purposes, care should be taken to use only comparable companies. Although the only restrictive requirement as to comparable corporations specified in the statute is that their lines of business be the same or similar, yet it is obvious that consideration must be given to other relevant factors in order that the most valid comparison possible will be obtained. For illustration, a corporation having one or more issues or preferred stock, bonds, or debentures in addition to its common stock

should not be considered to be directly comparable to one having only common stock outstanding. In like manner, a company with a declining business and decreasing markets is not comparable to one with a record of current progress and market expansion.

The IRS admits, then, that a comparable company must be just that—comparable. This reduces the use of the comparable approach to a search for a publicly traded corporation that closely resembles the closely held corporation to be valued. Needless to say, such a search is time-consuming and consequently very costly. Worse yet, in most cases the closely held company being valued does not have a true comparable counterpart. Close, unlike with horseshoes and hand grenades, counts for zero in comparable valuations.

What criterion should be used to measure similarity? How similar must a publicly traded corporation be to be valuable as a valuation guide? The answers to these questions are subjective, despite the objective nature of their goal. One is reminded of the Supreme Court justice who, when attempting to define pornography, stated, "You'll know it when you see it." The same could apply to the definition of a comparable. The use of comparables is not an exact science but only a method of approximation that can vary as much as the biases of individual appraisers and companies to compare and be compared to—which leads us back into the same discretionary and judgmental quandary that affects valuation in general.

Undaunted, proponents of comparables have attempted to set guidelines for determining comparability. These guidelines involve both financial and nonfinancial characteristics.

The irony of these guidelines is that instead of using facts and figures of the closely held corporation to be valued, the data of the publicly traded corporation, in effect, dictates the valuation process. This is because after the publicly traded corporation is deemed comparable, the only task that remains is to assign the price (by using the multiple of earnings) of the publicly traded corporation's stock to that of the closely held corporation's stock.

THE MOST IMPORTANT QUESTIONS

How does one go about finding a comparable publicly traded company? Consider the following. Suppose the closely held business to be sold does $10 million a year in sales in one county in a midwestern state and sells one product. The owner, who is also president and chief operating officer, has a back-up manager who is 60 years old. Before-tax profits, after subtracting the owner's compensation of $250,000, is $800,000. The owner spends three months of the year in Florida relaxing. Would a prospective buyer of such a company be well-served by determining an asking price by checking into the price-earnings ratio of comparable publicly traded companies?

Do buyers and sellers of closely held businesses use comparables? A survey of such buyers and sellers would reveal that closely held businesses are almost always bought and sold without a thought being given to the price at which any publicly traded company—comparable or otherwise—has or is selling for.

THE COURTS AND THE USE OF COMPARABLES

The use of comparables is widespread, however, in the imaginary world of the estate tax. Remember the imaginary buyer and seller and the determination of an imaginary price at which a business would be bought and sold?

The use of comparables has been forced on the courts by the IRS. The word "forced" is appropriate, because the courts have used almost every opportunity presented them to refrain from using the comparable method.

In *Tallichet* v. *Comm'r* (33 T.C.M. 1133, 1974), the Tax Court put forth the following factors to be considered in determining compatibility:

1. capital structure
2. credit status
3. depth of management
4. personnel experience
5. nature of the competition
6. maturity of the business

The *Tallichet* court went on to quote itself from another case, as if uncomfortable in its comparison task:

> In short, a publicly traded stock and a privately traded stock are not . . . the same animal distinguished only by the size, frequency, or color of its spots. The essential nature of the beast is different.
> (*Messing* v. *Comm'r*, 48 T.C. 502).

This schizophrenic ambivalence exhibited by the Tax Court regarding the use of comparables is confusing to say the least. It gives the comparable approach the credibility of a methodology that compares apples and oranges simply because they are fruit.

Needless to say, quite a few courts have rejected the IRS' use of comparables out of hand. In *Bader* v. *U.S.*, 172 F.Supp. 833 (DC–Ill., 1959), the court rejected the comparable method for the good reason that there were no publicly traded corporations in the same business (grain elevator operator). In *Worthen* v. *U.S.*, 192 F.Supp. 727 (DC–Mass., 1961), the court rejected the use of a comparable because it had sales four times that of the closely held business and because it was not engaged in wholesaling, as the closely held business was (trader in coarse paper products). Another court rejected the use of a comparable with different assets and in a different geographical location (*Estate of Tompkins* v. *Comm's*. 20 TCM 1763, 1961; real estate holding and development company).

All of these cases involved the IRS advocating a comparable company that produced a higher valuation of the closely held company and the court rejecting it. In an anamalous case, in *Estate of Gallo* (TCM 1985–363), the IRS argued against the use of comparables only because the closely held corporation to be valued was itself larger than any of the publicly traded corporations in the same business (wine making).

CENTRAL TRUST REVISITED: A LESSON IN THE USE OF COMPARABLES

The court in *Central Trust Company* v. *U.S.*, 305 F.2d 393 (Ct.Cl., 1962), used the economy of scale argument to hold that giant corporations such as Continental Can Company and American Can Company were sublimely different from the closely held corporation to be valued because of their mammoth manufacturing facilities and advanced automation. (See Chapter 3 for the facts of *Central Trust*.)

After knocking the wind out of the estate's expert witnesses' valuations, the court turned to the IRS' witness and did the same thing. However, while it rejected the government's bottom-line valuation figure, it accepted the comparable approach as the proper one. It just didn't like the companies chosen as comparable. It chose its own comparables instead. Here's a summary of that court's use of the comparable approach.

IRS' Expert Witness Testimony

The expert witness for the IRS presented a comprehensive survey of eight companies in the can and glass container industries. He developed percentage ratios for profits and dividends to net worth over a five-year period for the comparables and the period 1950–1954 for Heekin, the closely held company whose stock was at issue. He considered two of those eight companies to be comparable to Heekin, arriving at a price between $18.75 and $19.75 for a share of Heekin stock. After applying a marketability discount of 20 percent, he reached a valuation of between $16 and $15.25 per share.

That value, however, was approximately equal to book value. Therefore the IRS' expert felt it was too conservative. Using the price-earnings ratios and book values of 11 comparable companies, and the dividend yields of seven comparables, the IRS' expert reached a value of between $21.85 and $21.35 for each share of Heekin.

The Court's Critique of the IRS' Expert's Testimony

While the court lauded the thoroughness of the IRS' expert's valuation, it found fault with the two selected comparable companies. One was a bottle cap and bottling machinery manufacturer, and the other declared periodic stock dividends, which was ignored by the IRS' expert. The court remarked:

> Although no two companies are ever exactly alike, it being rare to have such almost ideal comparatives . . . so that absolute comparative perfection can seldom be achieved, nevertheless the comparative appraisal method is a sound and well-accepted technique. In employing it, however, every effort should be made to select as broad a base of comparative companies as is reasonably possible, as well as to give full consideration to every possible factor in order to make the comparison more meaningful . . . the selection of such companies as American Can and Continental Can as comparatives—companies held in esteem—will obviously give an unduly high result. It is simply not fair to compare Heekin with such companies and to adopt their market ratios for application to Heekin's stock. Furthermore, defendant's (IRS) use of the comparatives is confusing. The employment of different comparatives for different purposes is unorthodox. When the comparative appraisal method is employed the comparatives should be clearly identified and consistently used for all purposes.

The Court's Own Comparative Valuation Approach

The court picked its own comparatives, which while "by no means perfect comparables" were "at least reasonably satisfactory for the purpose in question.'' The court, in effect, made its own opinionated value judgment. Never mind why the companies were chosen. As stated before, all appraisers worth their salt could make cases for or against any given valuation assumption.

The court used earnings, book value, and dividend yield in its comparison of the closely held business to the five publicly traded ones. It accorded the most weight to the earnings factor, 50 percent; 30 percent to dividends yield; and 20 percent to book value.

As to the weight accorded book value, the court succinctly stated:

> Book value indicates how much of a company's net assets valued as a going concern stands behind each share of its stock and is therefore an important factor in valuing the shares. As defendant's expert pointed out, this is the factor that plays such a large part in giving a stock value during periods when earnings may vanish or be suspended. However, principally because book value is based upon valuing the assets as a going concern, which would not be realistic in the event of a liquidation of a corporation, a situation which a minority shareholder would be powerless to bring about in any event . . . this factor is, in the case of a manufacturing company with a consistent earnings and dividend record, normally not given greater weight than the other two factors.

The court then applied a marketability discount of 12.17 percent based on the costs of floating shares of the company for public trading. (As will be explained in Chapter 8, such a low discount is not common; the courts on the average have awarded discounts of 20 to 30 percent.)

As a final valuation figure, the court held that $15.50 a share was correct. Could any fault be found with the court's process and result? Of course it could. The important thing to note, however, as remarked in Chapter 3, is *how* it was reached.

The trend in these cases is not apparent. What is apparent is that a party opposed to the use of comparables need only build a case on the uniqueness of the closely held corporation in order to discredit the approach. Since all companies are unique, any competent advocate should be able to accomplish the objective: proper valuation of the particular business, with the full realization that the use of comparables will not yield the real strike price at which the business would be sold to a real buyer.

Do not, however, totally dismiss use of comparables as a means of valuation. If the comparable shoe fits, wear it! Use comparables where appropriate. The larger the closely held company, the more likely a comparable counterpart can be found in the marketplace. When one or more comparable companies can be found, not using these comparables as the only, or at least a significant, factor in the valuation opens the entire valuation to question. *Just as the use of comparables should not be forced, no other method should be forced if use of comparables is appropriate. The goal is always the same: the right valuation, by whatever method, rather than the use of any particular method.*

A good test is to use other methods being offered. If there is a wide discrepancy between two valuation amounts reached by two different methods, logic tells the appraiser that at least one of the methods must be discarded.

OTHER DRAWBACKS OF COMPARABLES

From a conceptual standpoint it is almost impossible to make valid comparisons of listed companies with privately held companies. Here's why:

- When the closely held company is small, the size differential alone makes comparison impossible.
- Closely held companies often pay large salaries and expense items that a public company would capitalize. Accounting treatment may also differ.
- Public companies have a depth of management that closely held companies often lack.
- Closely held companies usually are limited to one product, while a public company that makes the same product will usually have several other lines that may or may not be related.
- Public companies have access to credit lines unavailable to closely held companies.
- As an investor, a person might pay $100 per share for 500 shares of GM for one set of reasons; yet that same person might pay the same $500,000 (more or less) for 100 percent of the stock of a closely held manufacturing company as an investor/operator for a completely different set of reasons.

What impact do these drawbacks have on valuation in practice? Simply put, blind use of comparables often produces absurd results. The following example actually happened.

Example

A privately held company was in the retail business, and the valuation was based on 1974 data. Earnings for 1974 were 25 percent higher than those for 1973, and book value had increased substantially. Obviously, the company could not be worth less in 1974 than it was in 1973. The average price-earnings ratios, however, for two listed comparable companies fell from 20 in 1973 to 6.7 in 1974. If the numbers produced by the mechanistic use of comparables were used as the measure of value, the forced conclusion was that in 1974 the privately held company was worth only one-third of what it was worth in 1973. This result is absurd and illustrates the danger of using comparables.

PROPER USE OF COMPARABLES

The most appropriate situation for the use of comparables is when the closely held corporation is large enough that its economies of scale are on par with the publicly traded corporations it is compared to: the *size* of the closely held corporation makes its operations and financial condition similar to the comparables.

The task of finding the most appropriate comparable with which to value a particular closely held corporation is similar to that of a police detective who gradually, through thorough investigation, narrows the list of suspects in a crime. Like the police detective who compiles a list of suspects, the appraiser of a closely held business using the comparable approach must compile a list of publicly traded corporations. This is not an easy task and involves reasoned judgment and intuition.

The Search Begins

There are many sources from which to compile such a list. Since the starting point for the search is the industry in which the closely held corporation operates, an excellent place to begin the search is the *Standard Industrial Classification Manual* published by the U.S. Office of Management and Budget (OMB).It gives Standard Industrial Classifications (SIC) codes for each particular industry.

Once the industry of the business is established, the next step is to consult one of various financial directories—such as the Securities and Exchange Commission's (SEC's) *Directory of Companies Required to File Annual Reports* which lists companies with more than $1 million or more in assets and 500 or more shareholders.

Once a list of companies with the same financial statement character-istics as the closely held corporation is compiled from these directories, they should be contacted and their most recent financial reports for the past five years obtained. Then begins the real task.

Comparative Analysis

Needless to say, before any comparisons can be made, the financial data of the closely held corporation and the comparable must be organized in the same manner—digested and spit out in the same form so as to make similarities and differences identifiable. Otherwise the comparative analy-sis can be attacked for its sloppy methodology.

For example, several ratios could be used (see Appendix D), such as these:

1. *Liquidity ratios.* These measure the ability of the corporation to meet its current obligations.
2. *Leverage ratios.* These indicate the amount of the business' oper-ations and expenditures that are debt- rather than equity-fi-nanced.
3. *Activity ratio.* These measure the efficiency and productivity of the business in utilizing its available resources.
4. *Profitability ratio.* These measure the nitty-gritty of the busi-ness—does it make money by returns on its sales and invest-ments?

There are many other ratios that can measure other nuances of a business that may just prove the differences between comparability and disqualification.

The Process of Elimination. Once the data has been organized, objective criteria should be established. The data gathered has two purposes: (1) to help in the process of eliminating corporations that aren't comparable and (2) to provide guideposts in comparing the companies that are. Granted, the process, as described, is discretionary and could vary enormously depending upon who is governing it. However, the selection must still be made. It must be made with the thought in mind that no matter how thorough and logical the process of elimination and subsequent compari-son, someone will find fault with it.

MAKING THE COMPARISON

Once the comparable publicly traded companies have been selected, the following steps should be used in reaching a comparative value. The first three steps should be applied to each comparable company.

1. Determine the earnings per share (EPS) by using no more than five years (or a shorter period if this will be more comparable). Often only one year—the year closest to the valuation date—is used. If the information is available, earnings should be adjusted for extraordinary and nonrecurring items that would affect the income and accounting differences between the comparable and the closely held company.

2. Determine the average price per share (APS). This is usually done by using the price on the valuation date, taking an average of the high and low prices for the year, or using some averaging method to eliminate or reduce the impact of fluctuating stock prices.

3. Divide the APS by the EPS to arrive at the price-earnings ratio (P/E).

4. Determine an average P/E ratio for all the comparable companies being used. This is done by aggregating the P/E ratios of the selected companies and dividing by the total number of companies. The P/E of the individual public companies can be weighted to arrive at the average P/E ratio.

5. Apply the average P/E ratio to the average earnings per share (usually a five-year average) of the closely held company being valued.

[See Chapter 7 for an example of a valuation using comparables (Royal Oil, Inc.).]

An errant P/E should be excluded. For example, suppose the P/E for the four selected public companies ran between 4.5 and 11.3 for each of the five years selected. If there is one anomalous year of 26.8, it should be ignored.

There it is—the comparable approach. The comparable company (or companies) has been found and the market price of its stock assigned as the value of the closely held corporation's stock. Use it carefully, and remember: anyone who uses it indiscriminately may get burned.

CHAPTER 7
Valuation in Practice

This chapter pulls it all together. This is the chapter you want to mark up, underline, and return to as a starting point and reference. It fans out and refers to other chapters, as necessary, to organize all the elements needed to do a valuation in practice. What is most interesting is that, even in practice, the world of theory can never be left far behind.

This chapter brings into focus in one place the most important aspects of any valuation. In many respects, this chapter is like a checklist, although not every consideration for every valuation can be included.

In a nutshell, this is what the chapter covers:

- Avoiding a valuation altogether
- Making a valuation the easy, no-frills way
- Selecting the right method of valuation
- Reviewing the checklist of considerations
- Using valuations in practice

The first three of these are a sort of valuation pecking order. If the first solves the valuation problem, then the others are unnecessary. If the first can't do the job, move to the second. If the valuation can be completed there, the rest of the numbers can be ignored. Once you get to selecting a method for valuation—as is almost always necessary in practice—the valuation roller coaster ride begins. The considerations checklist and the actual practice examples, taken together, form a guide to the valuation of a privately held business.

AVOIDING VALUATION ALTOGETHER

What if the stock to be valued can be purchased for a price that has been fixed by an enforceable contract? Is another valuation, which would no doubt produce a value different from the fixed price, necessary? Of course not.

If a buy-sell agreement or other contractual arrangement exists, read it before beginning any valuation process. There are three possible results:

1. The price (value) is fixed in the contract without any doubt. Result: No valuation is necessary.
2. There is no question that the document does not set the value. Result: A valuation is necessary.
3. There is genuine doubt as to whether the document fixes the value. Result: A lawyer should be consulted to render an opinion

as to whether the document does or does not fix the value. If the doubt remains, all the parties involved must decide the next step: whether an appraisal should be made. If an appraisal is ordered, the appraiser must do at least the following:

- Obtain a letter from the principal stating that the valuation is to be made in spite of the possibility that it might not be necessary.
- Mention the problem, accompanied by an appropriate discussion, in the appraisal report.

(See Chapter 10 for a discussion of when a document might fix the value.)

MAKING A VALUATION THE EASY, NO-FRILLS WAY

Recent Sales of Stock

Sales of stock made by a willing seller to a willing buyer, which are close in time to the valuation date and made under similar circumstances, could fix the valuation number. (See Chapter 3 for a more detailed discussion.)

If such stock sales cannot be used in lieu of a complete valuation, then the sales would be a factor to be considered along with other factors in the valuation. Another possibility is to use the stock sales price or prices as one of the factors, along with other factors, and give the stock sales an appropriate numerical weight in determining the final valuation.

Industry Standard

The appraiser must determine if there is an established industry standard or some industry rule of thumb that is used to value the type of business under consideration. Sometimes the standards vary from one geographic area to another. Find out. Ask questions. These standards can take many forms: a percentage or multiple of gross sales or billings, so many cents or dollars for each unit sold (measured in terms of per gallon, barrel, pound, or other measure), a multiple of gross profit or net profit before taxes, and many other methods.

As in the case of a recent sale of stock, if the total valuation cannot be accomplished by using the established industry standard, it would be a factor to be considered or, possible, weighted along with other factors.

SELECTING THE RIGHT METHOD OF VALUATION

Review the eight basic methods of valuation described in Chapter 5. Select the method or methods to be employed.

Remember these two points:

1. If the comparable method is appropriate, use it. If it isn't, don't waste your time trying to put a square peg into a round hole.
2. The valuation must never produce a value less than liquidation value.

Since most valuations in practice use more than one method to accomplish the valuation, the examples used later in this chapter illustrate combination valuations. It is very rare indeed that an appraiser can resort to only one valuation method and not be subject to withering criticism.

REVIEWING THE CHECKLIST OF CONSIDERATIONS

The checklist is meant to be a memory jogger, not an exhaustive list of every possible consideration. Steps, procedures, and considerations that are obvious are intentionally omitted.

1. Scan the table of contents of this book noticing any subject or point that should be reviewed.
2. Review the eight factors listed in Revenue Ruling 59–60 (in Chapter 3).
3. Select the additional factors to be used from the list of 30 factors in the Valuation Factors table in Chapter 3.
4. Reread the material "The Fact-Gathering Process:—A Checklist Section" at the beginning of Chapter 4.
5. If one valuation method is not capable of producing proper valuation results, use more than one method and weight the methods.
6. After selecting the factors to be considered, determine the weight to be assigned, if any, to each factor. This is probably the most subjective part of the process—the one requiring the skill of a

winning trial lawyer to justify the assumptions behind the weighting.

7. After the prediscount value has been determined, select the discount, if any, that should be taken for any of the following (see Chapter 9 for more on discounting a valuation):

- Less than 100 percent of the stock of the privately held business being valued
- A general lack of marketability of the stock
- A minority interest

USING VALUATIONS IN PRACTICE

This section of the book could go on and on with hundreds of pages of examples of hundreds of valuations for hundreds of purposes using hundreds of methods. That being the case, and since such an overload of information tends to confuse rather than instruct, now seems a good time to divide the total appraisal report (valuation report) into its natural sections: the valuation numbers, support materials, and financial data.

The Valuation Numbers.   This chapter contains examples of how these numbers are set forth to accomplish the valuation.

Support Material.   This includes everything considered essential to support the valuation conclusion and give it validity—from the history of the company to the credentials of the appraiser. Examples of this support material are included in Appendix A.

Financial Data.   The report should include all essential financial data. At a minimum, the financial statements—balance sheet and profit-and-loss statement—for the years reviewed should be included. Various ratios (see Appendix D), statistics, or selected revenue or expense figures may be shown to highlight important data or indicate trends. (This book does not provide complete examples of financial statements, as they are readily available elsewhere. However, Appendix A contains examples of the type of raw financial data used in a valuation.)

Now let's examine some examples that put to work the methods discussed in this text.

A Basic Combination Approach That Works

This example employs a combination of two methods: adjusted book value and a multiple of earnings. Most privately held businesses are bought and sold using this method or some variation of the method. Essentially, this particular combination method asks two questions:

1. How much would be the total cost to a buyer to buy each of the assets now being used in the business? More simply put, how much must be invested in the operating assets of the business? (This question is answered by the adjusted book value method.)
2. How much can be earned on this investment? If the earnings produce more than a fair rate of return, a premium (goodwill) must be paid. On the other hand, if the business cannot produce a fair rate of return, it is worth less than the adjusted book value, and a discount must be allowed.

In actual negotiations, the buyer and seller discuss how each asset on the balance sheet should be valued for purposes of the potential sale. Then they hammer out the goodwill number or the discount. Often the goodwill will be recast in various ways for tax purposes: for example, assigning a specific dollar figure to a covenant not to compete, a patent, and other intangibles that might be written off over a fixed and determinable useful life. The tax consequences of buying and selling a business are not covered in this book; you should hire the best tax advisor you can to oversee the entire transaction from beginning to end.

The following six-step example is offered as *one of many* approaches that can give proper valuation results.

Sample Computation:

1. Determine the *average after-tax earnings* for the company for five years. $ 360,000

2. Determine the *average annual net tangible assets* (this is actually adjusted book value) in the business for the five-year period. $2,000,000

3. Apply a *fair rate of return* on the average net tangible assets computed in (2). Say 15 percent × $2,000,000. $ 300,000

4. Deduct (3) from (1): equals *excess earnings attributable to goodwill.* $ 60,000

5. Capitalize the excess earnings in (4) at a selected rate to yield the *value of goodwill* (or intangibles). Say 25 percent (or a multiple of 4 × $60,000). $ 240,000

6. Add net tangible assets of the company as of the valuation date to (5)
    a. Assuming net tangible assets (adjusted book value) at the valuation date $2,500,000
        PLUS
    b. Capitalized excess earnings from (5), and   240,000
    c. the fair market value is $2,740,000

Do businesses actually change hands by use of this simple computation? The mathematical result should not be the exclusive test. Every element of the business and every factor that affects it must be taken into consideration: the nature and history of the business, quality of management, future prospects, competition, general economic and industry outlook, all the rhetoric contained in this book, plus a liberal amount of the appraiser's gut feeling, which seems to improve with age and experience.

The seductive simplicity of the above example is that it looks objective, yet any experienced appraiser could point out the many things that make the approach extremely subjective. By changing any one of the several assumptions, the results can be altered significantly.

Keep in mind these notes on this approach:

1. This method can (and often does) produce a fair market value that is less than adjusted book value. Such a result is acceptable to a point. If the valuation figures dip below liquidation value (after deducting estimated liquidation expenses), then liquidation value must be used.

2. Whatever the fair market value as determined might be (no matter what valuation approach has been used), an appropriate discount must be taken.

Now comes the key question: Could $2,740,000 truly be the value of a real operating business as determined by the method shown? The answer is an emphatic *YES*. Although it can be argued skillfully that changing any one of the assumptions would change the fair market value mathematically arrived at, that does not invalidate the method itself. As a practical matter, the ability to change the numbers (for valid reasons) in any one of the steps allows the appraiser to fine-tune the appraisal.

Actually, this particular approach can be summarized as a combination of the two basic approaches to valuation:

1. *the liquidation approach*—Step 6a is the appraisal value of the assets minus the liabilities or adjusted book value—and
2. *the earnings approach*—Step 6b is, in effect, a separate valuation of the earnings of the business in excess of a reasonable rate of return required on the investment (adjusted book value).

The job of the appraiser is to combine the factors, methods, and procedures (for convenience these will be called "methodology") discussed in this book to allow the mathematical result to produce a "correct" fair market value.

The following is an analysis of how the appraiser might use the selected methodology in the sample computation to reach a correct valuation.

Step 1. Determine the *average after-tax earnings* for the business for five years. The earnings must be analyzed and adjustments made for non-recurring items, discretionary expenses, and so on. The task is to predict what profits will be in future years by eliminating those expenses and income items that are not likely to occur again and including anticipated future expenses and income.

What earnings should be used as average earnings if the after-tax profit of the business for the past five years has been as follows?

Year	Profit
1981	$120,000
1982	80,000
1983	50,000
1984	20,000
1985	480,000
TOTAL	$750,000

Would a simple average be appropriate? Should more weight be given to 1985 because it is the most recent year? The 1985 figure is an anomaly. Looking at the figures alone, it should be eliminated as an extraordinary year. So you would probe. Is 1985 the breakthrough year that will produce another Xerox? Or was this a one-time windfall to be disregarded?

Step 2. Determine the *average annual net tangible assets (adjusted book value)* used in the business for a five-year period. First, convert each item on the balance sheet to its adjusted book value. (For our purposes, adjusted book value means fair market value.)

There is not much room to manipulate the numbers, because the assets should, in fact, be stated at appraisal value. This average should be computed to reflect the amount actually invested in the business on the average over the past five years. Simply add the adjusted book values at the beginning of each of the five years and divide by five, as follows:

Year	Tangible assets at fair market value less all applicable liabilities
1	$1,560,000
2	1,720,000
3	2,040,000
4	2,180,000
5	2,500,000
Average net tangible assets	10,000,000 ÷ 5 = $2,000,000

Step 3. Determine a *fair rate of return*. What constitutes a fair rate of return is dependent upon the same factors that affect financial markets in general, such as inflation and the cost of money (interest rates). If U.S. Treasury bonds are yielding 10 percent, logic dictates the rate of return for an investment must be more than 10 percent. Also, if the cost of money is 11 percent, the business must earn more to repay borrowings. A good rule of thumb is to use a rate-of-return that is approximately one to three points over the prime rate of interest, with adjustments made for the industry rate of return, if known, and risk factors.

Comparisons should be made with investment returns for preferred stocks, tax-free municipal bonds, industrial bonds, and other appropriate investments.

Risk is the most volatile element of a fair rate of return. it must be quantified. Factors like competition, general economy, industrial outlook, and technological advancement all come under the heading of *risk*.

In the end, a fair rate of return is made up of two elements: (1) the right rate of return according to the present investment market, and (2) the degree of risk. Add the two together and the determination is complete. For example, a fair rate of return might be determined as follows:

Return On Investment	11%
Degree of Risk	4%
Total Fair Rate of Return	15%

Step 4. Determine the *excess earnings attributable to goodwill* by deducting the number arrived at in step 3 from the number arrived at in step 1. This can also be called the *intangible value of the business*.

Step 5. Capitalize excess earnings in step 4. The real challenge here is to select a capitalization rate (multiple of earnings). The same risk considerations come into play in this step as in step 3 where a fair rate of return was determined. Should the two rates be the same? Not necessarily so, but they usually are.

The multiple will be higher for a steady line of business, and lower for a business that is new, risky, or tends to have widely fluctuating profits. Any uncertainty concerning the business usually lowers the multiple.

Step 6. Determine the *fair market value of the business* by adding the net tangible assets as of the valuation date (*not* the five-year average of step 2) to the capitalized excess earnings amount from step 5. The sum of these two numbers should not be regarded as the exact value of the business but as a median figure within a value range. Suppose the figure is $2 million. The range might be from 10 percent more ($2.2 million) to 10 percent less ($1.8 million), subject to all the literature and evidence that can be mustered in justification, together with a proper gut feeling.

A Final Important Note In the end, logic and common sense must prevail. Any final valuation amount must be fine-tuned to be acceptable to all parties to avoid conflict. When a business is bought and sold in the real world, sooner or later a real price (the real fair market value) is struck and the deal is made.

In my experience, more closely held businesses have changed hands at a price arrived at using something like the six-step method above than by any other method.

TWO REAL-LIFE SAMPLE VALUATIONS

The following two valuations are taken from the office files of Blackman, Kallick and Co., Ltd. (BK). All names, locations, and other data were changed to prevent identification of the client. These cases were chosen to be a guide, not to be a how-to-do-it bible. Neither is a complete formal valuation proposal, but both contain excerpts that illustrate specific concepts of valuation.

For a complete valuation proposal, see Appendix A (which sets out a valuation proposal, except for financial statements, as it actually appears when provided to BK clients).

Capsule Valuation for Purposes of Discussion of Proposed Offers to Purchase Company

This first valuation is not a full-fledged valuation, but was requested by a client company for discussion purposes by its board of directors who were evaluating which of two preliminary offers(one from a private investor and the other from a publicly traded company) to purchase the company might be considered further.

The formula approach was used for the purpose of considering the merits of the offer from the private investor, and the *multiple of earnings approach* (using comparable publicly traded corporations) was used for purposes of considering the merits of the offer from the publicly traded company.

This capsule valuation is set out to illustrate that there is no one valuation method that is appropriate to use in every situation. Actually, in practice, it is just the reverse: different valuation methods must be used for different purposes, even if for the same company.

Often an appraiser is called upon to develop a short presentation for discussion purposes only. This example offers a format that accomplishes this purpose. Read the material under Discussion Outline and follow each step under the Capsule Valuation.

THE SUCCESS CORPORATION
Valuation for Purpose of Sale
May, 19

DISCUSSION OUTLINE

I. Formula Approach
    A. Determine adjusted book value
       1. Book value (net assets)
       2. Divide net assets as to:
          a. Operations
          b. Investments
       3. Add(subtract) items where book value is not true value of operating assets
          a. LIFO inventory reserve
          b. Fair market value of building in excess of depreciated basis

        c. Income tax effect
           i). on above
           ii). S Corporation status
    B. Determine reasonable rate of return
        1. Monetary
        2. Risk
    C. Determine excess profit over a reasonable rate of return (goodwill)
    D. Capitalize goodwill
    E. Add goodwill to adjusted book value of operating assets
    F. Set range and price
    G. Add investment net assets at fair market value
II. Multiple of Earnings Approach
    A. Determine value of earnings by reference to comparable companies
    B. Set price and range
    C. Add investment net assets at fair market value

CAPSULE VALUATION

I. Formula Approach
    A. Determine value of earnings by reference to comparable companies
        1. Book value
           (net assets) $8,800,00
        2. Divide net assets

	a) Operations	b) Investments
	$ 3,440,000	$5,360,000

        3. Add (subtract)
           items

a) LIFO inventory reserve	1,400,000
b) Building (to increase book value to appraisal value)	1,000,000
c) Tax effect	
i) Above items	
(A) LIFO	(720,000)
(B) Building	(200,000)
ii) S Corporation (see note 1)	(1,120,000)
ADJUSTED BOOK VALUE	$ 3,840,000

    B. Determine reasonable rate of return (after tax)
        1. Monetary
           Tax-frees available in market from $7\frac{1}{2}$–$9\frac{1}{2}$ percent. Use
           average after-tax.   8%

2. Risk (see note 2)
    a) Unit sales decreasing
    b) Product is almost indestructible (small reorder)
    c) Cashless society
    d) Lawsuit   5%
        REASONABLE RATE OF RETURN (after-tax)   13%

C. Determine excess profit over a reasonable rate of
    return
    1. Adjusted book value $3,840,000
    2. Reasonable rate of return   13%
    3. Reasonable return (line 1 × 2) $ 499,200
    4. Operating income (last year-end after adjust-
        ments for tax effect)   1,004,000
    5. Excess profit (goodwill) $ 504,800

D. Capitalize goodwill
    1. Excess profit $ 504,800
    2. Reasonable monetary rate
        of return (after-tax)   8%
    3. Reasonable monetary rate
        of return (pre-tax)   16%
    4. Multiplication factor   100/16
        Capitalized goodwill $3,155,000

E. Adjusted book value $3,840,000
    Capitalized goodwill   3,155,000
    Total $6,995,000
    Rounded $7,000,000

F. Set price and range   −10%   +10%
    1. Price $7,000,000 $7,000,000
    2. Range −/+ 10%   700,000   700,000
    Value of operating assets   6,300,000   7,700,000
    (see note 4)
G. Add investments   5,360,000   5,360,000
    (see notes 3 & 4)
    TOTAL VALUE $11,660,000 $13,060,000

II. Multiple of Earnings Approach
    A. Determine value of earnings by reference to comparable compa-
        nies

		Price/earnings ratio per *Wall Street Journal* on date		
1.	Burroughs	11		
2.	NCR	8		
3.	Sperry Rand	10		
4.	Pitney Bowes	10		
	AVERAGE	10		

			−10%	+10%
B.	Set price and range			
	1. Operating income (last year-end after adjustment for tax effect)		$ 1,004,000	$ 1,004,000
	2. Above at multiple of 10		$10,040,000	$10,040,000
	3. Range −/+ 10%		(1,004,000)	1,004,000
	Value of operating assets (see note 4)		9,036,000	11,044,000
C.	Add investments (see note 4)		5,360,000	5,360,000
	TOTAL VALUE		$14,396,000	$16,404,000

NOTE 1: Since an S corporation pays no tax, an adjustment must be made to book the tax liability that would be shown for a regular taxpaying corporation.

NOTE 2: The four items listed all have a negative impact on future profits, hence increase the risk.

NOTE 3: The business has investments with a fair market value of $5,360,000 that are not used in the operations of the business. The income from these investments is not included in the operating income at C.4.

NOTE 4: No matter what method is used to value an operating business that might be sold, it must be tested against what the seller will pay. Hence, only a range for discussion or negotiation purposes is established above. Investments, on the other hand, will change hands at dollar-for-dollar value based on fair market value on the date of closing.

Comparison of Comparable Valuation Approach to Capitalized Excess Earnings Approach

This valuation illustrates the pitfalls of the comparable method. As will be seen in the excerpts from the valuation that follows, the appraiser used two methods to determine the final valuation number: the comparable method and the capitalized excess earnings method. Its purpose was for valuing a minority stock interest in the company that was to be sold to the company's ESOP (see Chapter 13).

The client in this case wanted advice as to the validity of a valuation report from an appraiser that used the comparable approach. The client is founder, CEO, and chairman of the board of the company. The company is a wholesale and retail distributor of diesel, gasoline, and other petroleum products and currently has annual sales in excess of $25 million.

The client was dissatisfied with the results of the comparable valuation. He did not feel that any of the publicly traded companies used were anywhere near comparable to his closely held business.

The reasons for the client's apprehension could be found in the appraiser's report itself. In justifying its use of comparables, the report concluded that the closely held company was larger, had a stronger liquidity position, had a stronger working capital position, had a stronger leverage position, had a stronger profitability position, and stronger asset management relative to the 400 companies in the composite industry it was compared to. One can imagine the client already scratching his head in bewilderment.

The appraiser went on to state that the company was smaller than, had a comparable liquidity position to, had a comparable leverage position to, had a comparable profitability position to, had a stronger asset management than, and weaker revenue growth than four publicly traded companies selected as being comparable. The client became disturbed when the above factors led the appraiser to conclude that the closely held company was a higher investment risk than the comparables and should be sold at a discount five percent below the weighted average of the publicly traded stock.

The only criterion that directly connected the closely held company with the four publicly traded companies was that they too were engaged substantially in the sale and distribution of petroleum and petroleum products.

Was the client justified in lacking confidence in the comparability conclusions? In his eyes, the appraisal was unreliable because the appraiser had unwittingly made a case against the closely held company being comparable to any other company—publicly traded or otherwise—in the process of justifying the use of the comparable approach.

The client favored the capitalized excess earnings approach because it gave weight to the goodwill (excess earnings) attached to his particular business. He felt this approach did justice to the aspect of his business that sets it apart from others—his own ownership and management.

The final valuation figure in the appraisal was reached by weighting the results of each valuation approach. Even though the client felt strongly biased against the use of the comparable approach, we convinced him that it could not be ignored or the valuation could be subject to attack by other parties interested in the ESOP. We also pointed out to him that the final results reached by each method were close enough so that none need be regarded as far off the mark. Therefore the weighted average was close to the final result reached by the capitalized excess earnings approach alone.

Following are the exhibits to the valuation. They are for illustration only, and the reader is reminded that they were the work of another appraiser. [This author does not favor the use of comparables for this particular valuation, though their use was unavoidable.] However, the example is the work of an experienced appraiser who has excellent credentials and technique. The presentation is well done. Follow the flow of the data closely. You are the judge: based on what you have learned thus far, decide whether you agree or disagree with the logic or conclusions of the valuation.

LISTING OF EXHIBITS

Exhibit   1—Conclusion of Total Fair Market Value as of September 30, 1985.

Exhibit A–1—Market Comparison Approach Indication of Value as of September 30, 1985.

Exhibit A–2—Calculation of Net Income Figures for the Periods Indicated.

Exhibit A–3—Calculation of Current-Year's Weighted Average Price/Earnings (P/E) Multiple.

Exhibit A–4—Calculation of Last Two-Years' Weighted Average Price/Earnings (P/E) Multiple.

Exhibit A–5—Calculation of Last Three-Years' Weighted Average Price/Earnings) (P/E) Multiple.

Exhibit A–6—Determination of Weighting Factors Applicable to Comparable Public Companies.

Exhibit A–7—Public Companies' Comparative Financial Statistics.

Exhibit A–8—Synopses of Comparable Public Companies.

Exhibit B–1—Capitalized Excess Earnings Approach Indication of Value as of September 30, 1985.

Exhibit B–2—Weighted Average After-Tax Net Earnings for the period September 30, 1981—September 30, 1985.

Exhibit B–3—Weighted Average Net Tangible Assets Used in Business for September 30, 1981—September 30, 1985.

Exhibit B–4—Computation of Industry Median Return on Net Worth.

Exhibit B–5—Schedule of Adjusted net Tangible Assets as of September 30, 1985.

Exhibit C–1—Comparative Summary Income Statements.*

Exhibit C–2—Comparative Summary Balance Sheets.*

Exhibit C–3—Comparative Financial Analysis.*

Exhibit C–4—Comparative Industry Statistics.*

   * These Exhibits are not reproduced in this text. They are listed here to indicate to the reader other documents used in the valuation.

EXHIBIT 1

Royal Oil, Inc.
Conclusion of Total Fair Market Value As of September 30, 1985

Approach	Exhibit no.	Value	Weighting factor (Note ˙)	Weighted value
Market comparison	A-1	$2,323,200	.4	$ 929,280
Capitalized excess earnings	B-1	$2,464,740	.6	$1,478,840

Total fair market value as of September 30, 1985 — $2,408,120

Total number of common shares outstanding as of September 30, 1985 — 127,820

Fair market value per common share outstanding as of September 30, 1985 — $18.85

Note: In accordance with the observations and disclosures made throughout this report with regard to the applicability, nature, and reliability of the approaches utilized to value a minority interest in the Capital Stock of Royal Oil, Inc., it is our opinion that the above weighting factors yield a fair and reasonable value for said interest in the company as of September 30, 1985.

The accompanying report is an integral part of this Exhibit.

Author's Comment: A common and acceptable method of valuation is to use two methods (sometimes, but rarely more) of valuing a company. The results of the two methods are then averaged or weighted (as above) to arrive at the final fair market value.

A discount is not taken because in theory the ESOP provides a market place for the closely held stock.

EXHIBIT A-1

Royal Oil, Inc.
Market Comparison Approach Indication of Value As of September 30, 1985

	Net income (Exhibit A-2)	Multiple (Exhibits A-3, A-4, and A-5)	Indicated value	Weighting factor*	Weighted value
Current-Year Indication					
Net income for the twelve months' ended September 30, 1985, with current-year's weighted average P/E	$262,280	10.9	$2,858,850	.50	$1,429,430
Two-Year Average Indication					
Average net income for the fiscal years' ended 1984 and 1985, with two-year weighted average P/E	$192,960	8.8	$1,698,050	.25	$ 424,510
Three-Year Average Indication					
Average net income for the fiscal years' ended 1982 through 1985, with three-year weighted average P/E	$148,970	12.6	$1,877,020	.25	$ 469,260
Market comparison approach indication of value (to Exhibit 1)					$2,323,200

* *Note:* In accordance with the observations and disclosures made throughout this report and in consideration of the trend in net income, it is our opinion that the above weighting factors yield a realistic fair market value for Royal Oil, Inc. as of September 30, 1985.

EXHIBIT A–2

Royal Oil, Inc.
Calculation of Net Income Figures for the Periods Indicated

Fiscal years ended September 30	Last two-years' net income	Last three-years' net income
1983	—	$ 61,000
1984	$123,640	123,640
1985	262,280	262,280
	$385,920	$446,920

1984 Net income = $262,280 (To Exhibit A–1)

Two-year average net income for the period October 1, 1983
   through September 30, 1985:

   $385,920 divided by 2 = $192,960 (To Exhibit A–1)

Three-year average net income for the period October 1, 1982
   through September 30, 1985:

   $446,920 divided by 3 = $148,970 (To Exhibit A–1)

The accompanying report is an integral part of this Exhibit.

Author's Comment: Why are three years used rather than the usual
five years? The reason is that the above income of Royal Oil, Inc. is
to be compared to the income of the Public Companies and four
years or more is considered to be too remote.

EXHIBIT A-3

Royal Oil, Inc.
Calculation of Current-Year's Weighted Average
Price/Earnings (P/E) Multiple

Company	Ratio*	Weighting factor (Exhibit A-6)	Weighted ratio
Comparable Co. A	11.1	6	66.6
Comparable Co. B	NM	NA	NM
Comparable Co. C	13.7	4	54.8
Comparable Co. D	8.0	2	16.0
Totals	32.8	12	137.4

Range   8.0–13.7

Median 11.1

Mean   10.9

Current-year's weighted average P/E: 137.4 ÷ 12 = 11.5
Reduced multiple applied to Royal Oil, Inc.: 11.5 – 5% = 10.9
   (To Exhibit A–1)

*The indicated price/earnings multiple for the current year's average is derived by dividing the average of each company's high market price and low market price for the nine months ended September 30, 1985 by each company's respective earnings for 1985 as reported in Standard & Poor's Corporation's *Security Owner's Stock Guide,* October 1, 1985 edition.

NM = Not meaningful

NA = Not applicable

The accompanying report is an integral part of this Exhibit.

Author's Comment: The note above uses two logical approaches to minimize the impact of market price fluctuations—(1) using only the last 9 months of the public companies high-low market price, and (2) averaging those 9 months. Whether the result obtained is logical is left to the reader. To help in this decision, ask and answer this question: Would the buyers and sellers of closely held businesses you know, buy or sell based on this kind of information?

EXHIBIT A–4

Royal Oil, Inc.
Calculation of Last Two-Years' Weighted Average
Price/Earnings (P/E) Multiple

Company	Ratio*	Weighting factor (Exhibit A–6)	Weighted ratio
Comparable Co. A	8.5	6	51.0
Comparable Co. B	NM	NA	NM
Comparable Co. C	10.9	4	43.6
Comparable Co. D	8.7	2	17.4
Totals	28.1	12	112.0

Range 8.5–10.9

Median 8.7

Mean   9.4

Two-year weighted average P/E: 112.0 ÷ 12 = 9.3
Reduced multiple applied to Royal Oil, Inc.: 9.3 – 5% = 8.8
  (To Exhibit A–1)

*The two-year average price/earnings multiple is derived by dividing the average of each company's high market price and low market price for the years 1984 and 1985 by each company's respective earnings for each year. The two years are summed and the total is then divided by 2 to obtain the two-year average P/E multiple.

NM = Not meaningful

NA = Not applicable

The accompanying report is an integral part of this Exhibit.

EXHIBIT A–5

Royal Oil, Inc.
Calculation of Last Three-Years' Weighted Average
Price/Earnings (P/E) Multiple

Company	Ratio*	Weighting factor (Exhibit A–6)	Weighted ratio
Comparable Co. A	6.9	6	41.4
Comparable Co. B	24.3	6	145.8
Comparable Co. C	9.0	4	36.0
Comparable Co. D	8.1	2	16.2
Totals	48.3	18	239.4

Range 6.9–24.3

Median 8.6 (9.0 + 8.1 = 17.1 ÷ 2)

Mean 12.1

Three-year weighted average P/E: 239.4 ÷ 18 = 13.3
Reduced multiple applied to Royal Oil, Inc.: 13.3 – 5% = 12.6
  (To Exhibit A–1)

*The three-year average price/earnings multiple is derived by dividing the average of each company's high market price and low market price for the years 1983, 1984 and 1985 by each company's respective earnings for each year. The three years are summed, and the total is then divided by 3 to obtain the three-year average P/E multiple.

The accompanying report is an integral part of this Exhibit.

Author's Comment: Company B shows a ratio of 24.3, which is way out of the ratio of all the other companies. Also company B was not used in Exhibits A–3 or A–4. Do you think the use of Company B for one year helps value Royal Oil, Inc. Maybe this explains the 5% "Reduced Multiple Applied to Royal Oil, Inc."

EXHIBIT A-6

Royal Oil, Inc.

Determination of Weighting Factors Applicable to Comparable Public Companies

Comparable public companies	Size (A)	Financial performance (B)	Product line (C)	Combined factor (A + B + C)
Comparable Co. A	1	2	3	6*
Comparable Co. B	1	2	3	6*
Comparable Co. C	2	1	1	4*
Comparable Co. D	0	1	1	2*
Totals	4	6	8	18

*(To Exhibits A-3, A-4, and A-5)

Note: We have identified the above listed public companies as comparable to the non-public subject entity Royal Oil, Inc. for the reasons outlined in the explanation of the Market Comparison Approach. We have further identified three key classifications of comparability in order to calculate a combined weighting factor for each of the public companies. These weighting factors, when applied to the Price/Earnings multiples of the respective public companies enables one to accentuate those public companies most similar to Royal Oil, Inc. in terms of Size, Financial Performance, and Product Line. The public companies were weighted under each of the three comparability classifications by the following ranking: zero—not comparable, one—slightly comparable, two—comparable, or three—highly comparable. These combined weighting factors represent our opinion of each public company's relative similarity to Royal Oil, Inc. premised upon information contained primarily in Exhibits A-7 and A-8 in this report.

The accompanying report is an integral part of this Exhibit.

EXHIBIT A-7

Royal Oil, Inc.

Public Companies' Comparative Financial Statistics

Statistics and ratios*	Comparable company A	B	C	D	Range	Royal Oil, Inc.	Subject comparability
Fiscal years ended	10/31/84	1/31/85	7/31/85	12/31/84		9/30/85	
Size ($ Million)							
Revenue	$327.2	$186.8	$61.4	$5,393.0	$61.4–5,393.0	$26.8	Smaller
Total assets	$ 60.1	$ 74.0	$25.7	$4,644.5	$25.7–4,644.5	$ 4.3	Smaller
Net worth	$ 40.4	$ 32.5	$ 7.1	$1,422.0	$ 7.1–1,422.0	$ 1.5	Smaller
Liquidity ratios							
Current ratios	3.0	1.6	1.1	1.0	1.0–3.0	1.5	Low range
Working capital turnover	8.1	23.5	NM	NM	8.1–23.5	23.6	Above range
Leverage ratio							
Total liabilities to equity	0.3	1.3	2.6	2.3	0.3–2.6	1.9	Mid range
Profitability ratios							
Net profit to:							
Sales	2.3%	0.2%	0.8%	2.9%	0.2–2.9%	1.0%	Low range
Equity	18.5%	1.0%	7.0%	10.9%	1.0–18.5%	17.3%	High range
Total assets	12.5%	0.4%	2.0%	3.3%	0.4–12.5%	6.1%	High range
Activity ratio							
Asset turnover	5.4	2.5	2.4	1.2	1.2–5.4	6.2	Above range
Growth index**							
Revenues	NA	1.1	2.3	1.8	1.1–2.3	1.1	Above range

*Based on latest available annual report.

**Most recent year's revenues divided by revenues four years prior.

NA = Not available

NM = Not meaningful

The accompanying report is an integral part of this Exhibit.

EXHIBIT A-8

Royal Oil, Inc.
Synopses of Comparable Public Companies

Comparable Co. A
The Company mainly engages in crude oil and petroleum products supply and marketing. The Company was incorporated in Bermuda in 1980, and its corporate headquarters are located in Bermuda.

Comparable Co. B
Company, through its subsidiaries, is engaged in the wholesale sale of residential fuel oil and the distribution of gasoline and petroleum products to stations, some of which are operated by the Company. These stations sell at retail company-distributed gasoline, motor oil, lubricants, etc., under the company's proprietary brand name Power Test, or under other brand names. At January 31, 1984, the company distributed gasoline to 436 stations in New Jersey, Connecticut, Pennsylvania, Massachusetts, and New York. It owned 245 and leased 173 stations, 290 of which were leased or subleased to others.

Comparable Co. C
Company retails natural gas in northwest Tennessee. They obtain the natural gas from East Tennessee Natural Gas Company. Wholly owned subsidiary, Holston Oil, Inc., markets a full line of Texaco Petroleum products in its seven-county service area in northeast Tennessee.

Comparable Co. D
Company, mainly through wholly owned Texas Eastern Transmission Corp., and Transwestern Pipeline Company, transports and sells at wholesale natural gas. It also explores for and produces oil and gas, produces and sells petroleum, sells at retail and wholesale liquified petroleum gas, operates a petroleum product pipeline, performs chemical process research, development and engineering, explores for uranium, and develops commercial real estate.

Author's Comment: Elsewhere in the report, it says Royal Oil, Inc. "is a wholesale and retail distributor of diesel, gasoline, and other petroleum products in" one of the western states. "It currently has two locations . . . and revenues totaling in excess of $25 million." The appraiser did a terrific job of finding companies that are as comparable as possible given the size and business makeup of Royal Oil, Inc.

EXHIBIT B–1

Royal Oil, Inc.

Capitalized Excess Earnings Approach Indication of Value as of September 30, 1985

Average net tangible assets used in business for the period 1980–1984 (Exhibit B–3)		$1,136,890
(a) Industry rate of return at 10.0% (Exhibit B–4)	$113,690	
(b) Average net income for the period 1981–1985 (Exhibit B–2)	$208,920	
Excess earnings (b – a)		$ 95,230
Capitalized at 15% ($95,230 ÷ .15)		$ 634,870
Add adjusted net tangible assets at September 30, 1985 (Exhibit B–5)		$1,829,870
Capitalized excess earnings indication of value (to Exhibit 1)		$2,464,740

The accompanying report is an integral part of this Exhibit.

Author's Comment: The "industry rate of return"—10% as used above—is usually the best rate to use. But beware. If the industry rate of return is much higher or lower than the return for typical closely held businesses or other typical investments (say AAA bonds and U.S. Treasuries plus 2 to 4 points for the added risk of a closely held business), then use of the rate may give a false value. Use a typical rate (as described in the preceding sentence) instead. Caution is also required when an industry rate is unusually high or low due to temporary market conditions. For example, the industry rate of return for companies like Royal Oil, Inc. is only 5.7%. See Exhibit B–4.

EXHIBIT B–2

Royal Oil, Inc.

Schedule of Adjustments to After-Tax Net Earnings and Calculations of Average Adjusted Earnings for the Period September 30, 1981–September 30, 1985

Fiscal years ended September 30	Net income	Add (Less): LIFO effect*	Add: discretionary contribution**	Adjusted earnings
1981	$226,740	$ -0-	$ 90,420	$ 317,160
1982	90,810	42,690	59,680	193,180
1983	61,000	(5,260)	-0-	55,740
1984	123,640	(23,630)	6,670	106,680
1985	262,280	41,040	68,540	371,860
Totals	$764,470	$54,840	$225,310	$1,044,620

Average adjusted net income for the period 1981–1985: $1,044,620 ÷ 5 = $208,920
    (To Exhibit B–1)

*The inventory of gasoline, oil, accessories, etc., is accounted for by the last-in, first-out (LIFO) method, which was adopted by the Company in 1979. When compared to the first-in, first-out (FIFO) method, the effect of LIFO is to reduce income before taxes in a year of rising prices. Conversely, in a year of falling prices, LIFO will show greater income before taxes than FIFO. In our analysis, we have adjusted net income by the after-tax effect (assumed to be 33%) of any LIFO adjustment in order to restate income on a FIFO basis.

**Adjustments to the net income of Royal Oil, Inc. were made to reflect the average after-tax effect (assumed to be equal 33%) of contributions to the Company's Employee Stock Ownership Plan, which are of a discretionary nature.

The accompanying report is an integral part of this Exhibit.

EXHIBIT B-3

Royal Oil, Inc.
Average Net Tangible Assets Used in Business for the Period
September 30, 1980–September 30, 1984

Fiscal years ended September 30	Total assets	Less: total liabilities	Net tangible assets
1980	$ 2,941,500	$ 2,177,500	$ 764,000
1981	3,318,600	2,304,000	1,014,600
1982	3,717,500	2,576,700	1,140,800
1983	3,760,200	2,441,800	1,318,400
1984	3,663,480	2,216,840	1,446,640
Totals	$17,401,280	$11,716,840	$5,684,440

Average net tangible assets for the period September 30, 1980–September 30, 1984:
$5,684,440 ÷ 5 = $1,136,890 (to Exhibit B–1)

Note: In accordance with generally accepted valuation techniques, greater weighting has been accorded the more recent net tangible assets of the Company.

Author's Comment: Note that the determination of these asset figures use the beginning of the period, as opposed to the end of the period. Why? Because this represents the net assets invested to start with. Remember, the rate of earnings are always based on the initial investment rather than the ending investment.

The accompanying report is an integral part of this Exhibit.

EXHIBIT B-4

Royal Oil, Inc.
Computation of Industry Median Return on Net Worth

	RMA & profit before taxes to net worth (Notes 1 & 2)	Assumed % tax rate	RMA & profit after taxes to net worth	Weighting factor (Note 2)	Weighted average % profit after taxes to net worth	Weighting factor (Note 1)	Weighting % profit to net worth
Fuel Oil (Note 1–A)							
Upper quartile	23.9%	50%	12.0%	25%	3.0%		
Median quartile	11.1%	50%	5.6%	50%	2.8%		
Lower quartile	1.7%	50%	0.9%	25%	0.2%		
					6.0%	50%	3.0%
Petroleum products (Note 1–B)							
Upper quartile	20.5%	50%	10.3%	25%	2.6%		
Median quartile	10.4%	50%	5.2%	50%	2.6%		
Lower quartile	1.8%	50%	0.9%	25%	0.2%		
					5.4%	50%	2.7%
							5.7%

(See Author's Comment)

Note 1: Robert Morris Associates' Annual Statement Studies, 1984 Edition; Asset Size $1,000,000–$10,000,000; Industry Classifications:
(A) Wholesalers–Fuel Oil, SIC #5172, 168 companies reporting
(B) Wholesalers–Petroleum Products, SIC #5171, 232 companies reporting

Note 2: The figures are not average, but depict the upper quartile, median and lower quartile figure in each case. These figures were calculated by, first, arraying all the numerical values of that ratio in order of the strongest to the weakest ratio. The figure which falls in the middle of the list of ratio values is the median. The figure halfway between median and the weakest is the third quartile. Ratios presented in this fashion preclude the undue influence of extreme ratio values which would result if merely an "average" ratio figure were presented. Also, and more importantly, they give the analyst some idea of the "spread" or range of ratio values in each case. This might be made even clearer by realizing that the total spread between its first and third quartiles by definition includes the middle 50% of the companies represented. Ratio values greater than the third quartile, and less than the first quartile, therefore, rapidly begin to approach "unusual" values. Consequently, to consider these factors appropriately, the median ratio has been weighted at 50% while the upper and lower quartiles have been weighted at 25% each for purposes of these computations.

Author's Comment: Although the "Weighting % profit to net worth" computed above is 5.7%, the rate used in Exhibit B–1 is 10%, without any additional explanation as to why. However, see author's comment on Exhibit B–1.

The accompanying report is an integral part of this Exhibit.

EXHIBIT B–5

Royal Oil, Inc.
Schedule of Adjusted Net Tangible Assets as of September 30, 1985

Net tangible assets as of September 30, 1985		$1,517,020
Add: independent appraisal of fair market value of the following corporate assets*	$385,000	
Total net book value of appraised assets	$ 72,150	
Total fair market value in excess of net book value as of September 30, 1985**		$ 312,850
Adjusted net tangible assets as of September 30, 1985 (to Exhibit B–1)		$1,829,870

* The independent appraisal of fair market value was made by Real Estate Appraisal, Inc. as of May 8, 1983. It is management's opinion that this appraisal is still valid.

** During the fiscal year ended September 30, 1985, the building became fully depreciated.

The accompanying report is an integral part of this Exhibit.

PART 2
Particulars of Valuation

CHAPTER 8
Putting a Value on Goodwill and Other Intangibles

Goodwill is one of those terms that many people use but few can define precisely. In too many sales and purchases of privately held businesses, the buyer and seller hammer out a price for the business, and almost matter-of-factly, as a last-minute string to be tied in a pretty bow, allocate a portion of the price to "goodwill." Usually, one or both of the parties do so ignorant of the disastrous tax consequences that will attach to at least one of the parties to the transaction. That's because the income tax laws usually make valuation of goodwill a zero-sum game between buyer and seller, in which one party's tax savings is the other party's tax liability.

DEFINITION OF GOODWILL

A good working definition of the term *goodwill* is the difference between the value of a business' net assets—both tangible and intangible, but excluding goodwill—and the price that a willing buyer would pay for the business as a whole. Generally, this difference reflects the expectation that a business will maintain customer patronage, and as a result, will generate a reasonable rate of return after the buyer assumes ownership. It is a value that comes from the favorable reputation arising out of an established, well-known, and well-conducted business.

Goodwill is inseparable from the business, which means it cannot be sold separately. It is assumed that goodwill can be transferred to the buyer.

TAX TREATMENT OF GOODWILL AND OTHER INTANGIBLES

Goodwill is a two-sided tax coin. In the purchase and sale of a business, goodwill is a capital asset to the seller and a nondepreciable asset to the buyer. Accordingly, sellers benefit by putting a larger value on goodwill, increasing their capital gains, while buyers benefit by putting a smaller value on goodwill, allowing them to allocate more of the total purchase price to depreciable assets.

The tax treatment of other intangible assets, however, can be more favorable than goodwill. If it can be determined that a particular intangible asset has a limited useful life that can be estimated with reasonable accuracy and has a cost basis separate and distinct from goodwill, a buyer can deduct this asset via depreciation or amortization.

Examples of intangible assets are patents and copyrights, trademarks and trademark names, trade secrets, contracts and licenses, and mass assets such as customer lists and subscription lists.

WHY ALLOCATION OF PRICE TO GOODWILL AND OTHER INTANGIBLES IS NECESSARY

The competing tax interests of the buyer and seller make it necessary to spell out in the sale agreement the precise portion of the purchase price that is allocable to each asset. Why? Because if it is not done, both the IRS and the courts will take it upon themselves to do so. Not only that, but once involved they will concern themselves with other matters, such as going-concern value and valuation of covenants not to compete.

Generally, the courts have respected the efforts of buyers and sellers to reconcile their competing tax interests regarding such items as recapture of prior depreciation and investment tax credits, assignments of income, and allocation of ordinary income versus capital gain regarding goodwill, covenants, not to compete, and going-concern value. To be acceptable, the parties' allocation must be realistic. Also, the ultimate value assigned to the particular asset concerned should not be drastically raised or lowered in relationship to actual value to produce favorable results.

The IRS has declared that, while it is not bound by contractual allocations, it will respect them unless they are devoid of economic substance and defy the realities of the transaction. In other words, the IRS will nix the contract allocation if it thinks the parties were motivated by tax avoidance.

GOING-CONCERN VALUE

The IRS has in recent years successfully argued that an operating business possesses an asset separate from goodwill and other intangibles—*going-concern value*. Going-concern value must be recognized, goes the IRS argument, when acquired assets are assembled in an ongoing operating business. It is that element of value adhering to an assembled and established plant doing business and earning money, and does not apply to one not so established.

The courts describe going-concern value as the ability of a business to continue to function and generate income without interruption as a consequence of a change in ownership and management. Note how closely that definition corresponds with the goodwill definition of continuation of customer patronage.

Like goodwill, going-concern value is not depreciable. The significance of this is that the IRS will alternatively argue the presence of both goodwill and going-concern value in the assets of a business, hoping to score with either or both arguments. Unfortunately, this strategy has worked.

For example, in *VGS Industries* (68 TC 563; 1977), the IRS unsuccessfully argued for goodwill but was successful in arguing going-concern value. The court rejected goodwill because of the business' highly competitive industry (indicating no assurance of continued customer patronage) and lack of excess earnings.

Defining going-concern value as the ability of the business to continue to function and generate income without interruption as a consequence of a change in ownership, the court reasoned as follows:

> The combined business operations acquired by New Southland [the buyer] had in place and operational the Crupp and Rogerslacy Refineries, a terminal, a gas pipeline, six bulk plants and service stations, and various other necessary equipment in addition to a source of supply for crude oil and gasoline and the Southland trade name. Moreover, the Southland operations were able to survive and make a profit in a highly competitive industry during a time when many small refineries were unable to break even without the application of the foreign oil import quota. The business acquired by New Southland was more than a mere collection of assets. It was rather a viable, functioning, and going concern capable of generating a profit, and New Southland acquired a valuable property right as a result.

If the company was able to generate a profit, why was that not classified as goodwill? The difficulties involved in distinguishing between goodwill and going concern are illustrated by the *VGS* case. It appears that the courts treat goodwill as *demonstrated* earning power, while going-concern value is *potential* earning power. Either way, the buyer is stuck with a nondepreciable asset.

In *Concord Control, Inc.* (35 TCM 1345; 1976), the buyer purchased all of the assets of another company for $3.8 million. In order to head off a minority shareholder suit disputing the sales price, an independent appraisal of all tangible assets was made. The sales price was 89.5 percent of the appraisal value, with $1 set aside for all other assets. The buyer allocated the entire purchase price to tangible assets based upon the sales contract. The IRS allocated over $1 million of that price to goodwill.

The Tax Court rejected the goodwill contention of the IRS, mostly because the business' largest customer was lost after the sale. The buyer heaved a sigh of relief:

> A precondition to the possession of transferable goodwill is a finding that the seller's business is of such a nature as to provide the purchaser with the expectancy of both continuing excess earning capacity and competitive advantage of continued patronage. Excess earning capacity in and of itself is insufficient to demonstrate the transfer of goodwill. . . . Here K-D (the sold business) at the time of the sale was engaged in a industry fraught with a high degree of competition and little customer loyalty. . . . The loss (of K-D's largest customer) . . . amply demonstrates that the [buyer] had no reasonable expectancy of continued customer patronage flowing from its purchase of K-D.

However, the court then took off into the tax law stratosphere by fashioning a nondepreciable asset where none had existed before. To the buyer's chagrin, the court found that going-concern value of $335,000 was purchased by the buyer in the form of assets whose value was increased due to their existence as an integral part of an ongoing business.

As in the *VGS* case, the Tax Court distinguished going-concern value as potential earning capacity as opposed to goodwill as demonstrated earning power:

> Notwithstanding our conclusion that petitioner acquired no goodwill in connection with its purchase of K-D, it clearly did acquire an ongoing business that *was earning money*, had a trained staff of employees, had a product line presently ready for sale, and equipment ready for immediate use.

In the more recent case of Curtis Noll Corp. (44 TCM 288; 1982), a business was purchased for $3.2 million. The Tax Court found no going-concern value because inventory with a high turnover rate was a major part of the businesses' assets (which meant competitors could easily spring up by simply investing in inventory) and tangible operating assets were a small part of the business' total assets. But guess what?

The Tax Court found goodwill to be present because:

- the buyer succeeded to a well-established business,
- the buyer acquired the seller's favorable reputation built over 60 years of operations,
- recent profits were on the upswing,

- the buyer acquired company names, personnel, store leases, advertising and good store locations, and
- the business had been in business for 60 years, indicating a record of competitive pricing and good customer relations.

What these cases concerning going-concern value illustrate is that no matter how hard the buyer and seller try to avoid it, the value of an operating business will always contain an intangible nondepreciable asset, be it goodwill or going-concern value, at least if the courts or the IRS have anything to say about it.

GOODWILL AS MEASURED BY EARNINGS POWER

Goodwill is most easily measured by excess earnings power. However, excess earnings power is *indicative* of goodwill, not goodwill itself. Excess earnings over and above a reasonable rate of return could be attributable to extraordinary efforts or talents of key employees or the owner, nonrecurring windfalls, special customer relationships (such as captive supplier situation), or extraordinary market conditions.

On the other hand, the courts rarely find goodwill without excess earnings. Excess earnings power is a signal that goodwill is probably present. The reasons for the excess earnings is then determined, and usually attributed to goodwill. And remember, a court that refuses to find goodwill because of lack of excess earnings may still find going-concern value.

What is the standard way to measure excess earnings? That depends on your perspective. If you are the IRS, the so-called *gap* or *subtraction method* is used. The advantage to this method is simplicity. Take the net fair market value of all assets and compare that to the price paid for the business. The difference is goodwill, or going-concern value, if appropriate.

However, in my experience, the average buyer and seller consider a fair rate of return in determining goodwill. Here is the more realistic and most often used method of valuing goodwill:

1. Calculate a normal rate of return for the net assets of the business.
2. Compare the normal rate of return with the actual rate of return of the business.

3. If there is an excess of the actual over the normal rate, capitalize that difference by an appropriate factor.
4. The amount determined, if any, is the goodwill of the business.

Does this formula sound familiar? Look back to Chapter 3 to the section on ARM-34. It comes from there and is now comprehensively set forth in Revenue Ruling 69–609 (see Appendix B). The IRS says that this formula should be used only if there is no better basis for goodwill calculations. What this means is that the IRS will recognize its use only when it produces a larger value for goodwill. For the purposes of buying and selling in the real world, it is one of several good valuation methods.

The use of the earnings approach method of valuation precludes any additional calculation for goodwill. The earnings approach will determine whether excess earnings are present in a business, and whether an appropriate premium should be paid for it. That premium, however, usually includes the price tag for goodwill. The ARM-34 method is another way to calculate that same premium, and use of both methods should result in approximately the same goodwill amount.

When determining a normal rate of return and an appropriate capitalization rate, the skill and experience of the appraiser come to the forefront. In fact, resort to comparable businesses may be necessary, as well as an industry survey of reasonable rates of return.

COVENANTS NOT TO COMPETE

Often, when a buyer plans to continue a business as it is, he or she needs reassurance that the seller will not immediately set up a rival shop carrying on the same trade or business. To prevent this possibility, the buyer, as part of the sales transaction or agreement, will require the seller to covenant (promise), that he or she will not do so. A covenant not to compete is not an asset of the business, but is a condition of sale for which the seller receives consideration.

The tax consequences of such a covenant are as follows: the seller recognizes ordinary income, and the buyer can amortize the cost of the covenant over its life.

Unlike goodwill and going-concern value, where the buyer is the tax loser, here it is the seller who wishes to allocate the smallest possible amount to the covenant. Usually, where there is goodwill, a covenant not to compete is also present, to protect the buyer's investment in that goodwill. Normally, in the sales negotiations, there is a trade-off between buyer and seller concerning the tax consequences of the two items.

ALLOCATION ISSUES CONSIDERED BY THE COURTS

Several issues have arisen in the courts regarding the allocation of value in a sales price to intangibles such as goodwill, going-concern value, and covenants not to compete. There are three allocation situations that usually are considered in a court case:

1. where no allocation has been made and the IRS imposes its own allocation,
2. where an incorrect allocation is made ignorant of the tax consequences and the slighted party petitions for more favorable tax treatment, or
3. where the IRS considers the buyer and seller to have made inconsistent allocations for tax purposes.

An example of the IRS imposing its own allocation occurred in *Illinois Cereal Mills, Inc.* (46 TCM 1001; 1983). A purchase agreement did not contain an allocation of the purchase price, $240,000, among the various intangible assets acquired by the buyer. Those intangible assets included goodwill, a trademark, technical data, and customer lists. The purchase agreement also contained a five-year covenant not to compete. The buyer attempted to claim on his tax return that the entire purchase price was allocable to a covenant not to compete. The IRS claimed that the business as a whole was indivisible and that no allocation was possible.

The Tax Court made an allocation. It assigned a 20 percent value of $48,000 to the covenant not to compete (amortizable by the buyer), 10 percent applicable to the technical data, and the remaining 70 percent to goodwill and the other intangible assets (all found to be nondepreciable).

An example of an incorrect allocation being made ignorant of the tax consequences and an illustration of the court-created "strong-proof rule," occurred in *Stryker Corporation* (44 TCM 1020; 1982). There the buyer attempted to reallocate a larger portion of the purchase price of a business to a covenant not to compete. The buyer and seller had signed a separate no-competition agreement which contained a $1,000 price tag for a covenant not to compete. The buyer claimed the entire purchase price on his income tax return as paid for the covenant not to compete. Of course, the IRS disallowed all but the $1,000 evidenced in the separate agreement.

The Tax Court used the "strong-proof rule" to rule against the buyer. The strong-proof rule places heavy emphasis on the intention of the parties at the time the sales contract is entered into. That intention is best evidenced by the sales contract. Unless the party wanting to change the allocation contained in the sales contract can come up with strong proof that that allocation is not what the parties wanted, the court will not change it.

The strong-proof rule is the biggest obstacle a taxpayer faces if he or she makes a mistake in allocation in the sales contract. In the *Stryker* case, the court would not allow an allocation for the covenant not to compete over the agreed $1,000.

An example of the IRS considering the buyer and seller to have made inconsistent allocations for tax purposes usually involves the buyer and seller having hammered out a sales contract agreeable to both, including its tax consequences, and the IRS then dragging them into court for a reallocation that results in a higher overall tax on the transaction. Suppose in negotiation the buyer was unable to allocate as much as he or she wanted to depreciable assets, being stuck with a high nondepreciable goodwill amount, but in return was able to have a large amount of the purchase price allocated to an amortizable covenant not to compete. The other side of the same coin would be that the seller would realize more capital gain on the goodwill allocation but more ordinary income on the covenant not to compete.

When filing their tax returns, the temptation would be great for the buyer to assign a higher amount to the covenant than that agreed upon and a lower amount for the goodwill. The opposite would be true for the seller. The IRS would step in in such a situation and attempt to reduce the tax benefit to one or both parties. In a confusing irony, to correct taxpayers' inconsistent reporting, the IRS is allowed to take a position toward one party that is inconsistent with its position toward the other party.

This is what happened in *Jacques B. Wallach* (44 TCM 1002; 1982). In that case, buyer and seller agreed to a $330,000 purchase price for a medical laboratory business, and the sale took place. However, for tax purposes the buyer reported the transaction as a purchase of stock for $14,500 and a purchase of a covenant not to compete for $315,000. The seller reported the same transaction as a sale of his stock in the business for the $330,000 total. As reported, the buyer could maximize amortization of the purchase price, and the seller could maximize capital gains.

The IRS' inconsistent position taken towards the taxpayers' inconsistent reporting was this: It told the seller that $315,500 of the purchase price was allocable to a covenant not to compete (resulting in ordinary income) and told the buyer that none of the purchase price was allocable to the covenant not to compete (no amortization). Of course, the IRS couldn't have it both ways, but this case is a good illustration of how the IRS hedges its bets with a shotgun approach to revenue collecting.

The court nailed the buyer. First, it held that none of the purchase price was allocable to the covenant not to compete. Second, it held that $315,500 of the purchase price was allocable to goodwill. The seller had the capital gain; the buyer a nondepreciable asset in the same amount. The IRS won either way the court ruled: the court only decided whose goose was to be cooked.

What these cases teach is that in the purchase and sale of a privately held business, allocation of the purchase price to the business' nontangible assets can make or break the deal from the viewpoint of the buyer or the seller, or both. No allocation, or an incorrect allocation, can cost more in tax liability and court and attorney fees in the long run than any short-term benefits seemingly derived in sales negotiation by either party. True, the buyer and seller are natural adversaries when it comes to negotiating the total value of the business, but they would be better served to cooperate on the issue of allocation for tax purposes.

One final point: The buyer can buy insurance, in a sense, to prevent an IRS reallocation battle. How? Specify a specific dollar amount for goodwill in the sales contract and another specific amount for going-concern value. The seller won't mind; he or she will get a capital gain. Interestingly, the higher the premium paid—the more allocated to goodwill and going-concern value—the more likely the IRS will nod its approval.

CHAPTER 9
Valuation Discounts

The first part of this book deals with determining the fair market value of a privately held business. In most cases, the final value determined by using the various valuation methods and approaches is not really the final value that will be used by the appraiser. A further adjustment is needed to reach the final real fair market value that reflects the unique position of a privately held business. This adjustment is known as a *discount*. The valuation figure determined by the appropriate valuation method usually must be discounted to reflect the fact that a stock interest in a closely held business is not as easily marketable, for a variety of reasons, as that of a publicly traded corporation.

THE REAL FAIR MARKET VALUE

In order to value any business for tax purposes two distinct steps are required:

First. Value the business using the factors and approaches set out in the first part of this book

Second. Subtract an appropriate discount from the value determined in the first step in order to arrive at the *real fair market value*. The real fair market value is the number that will be submitted to the IRS, court, or other entity. There are two discounts that should be considered:

1. discount for general lack of marketability, and
2. discount for minority interest

Discount for General Lack of Marketability

Here is a simple way to illustrate the concept of discounting a valuation figure because of a general lack of marketability of shares of a privately held business:

Take a stack of stock certificates representing shares in a publicly traded corporation. The morning newspaper gives yesterday's stock market value at $1 million. A call to a broker will bring $1 million, less commissions, in cold cash in four business days.

Now take $1 million worth of Closc Fam Co. just valued by the appropriate methods described in this book. Is it worth $1 million? Maybe.

Somebody out there, when found, will pay the million—over maybe five
to seven years (plus interest at 10 percent, maybe, on the unpaid balance).
But the $1 million of Close Fam Co. stock is *not* going to bring a real
million dollars in cash or equivalent on the valuation data.

Intuition tells you a discount is in order. Why and how much? That is
the subject of this chapter.

The justification for a discount for a lack of marketability was stated
by the court in *Central Trust* as follows:

> It seems clear, . . . that an unlisted closely held stock of a corporation
> such as Heekin, in which trading, is infrequent and which therefore lacks
> marketability, is less attractive than a similar stock which is listed on an
> exchange and has ready access to the investing public.

Besides a general lack of marketability, shares of privately held corporations can be rendered unmarketable because of various restrictions on
their sale or transfer.

Recent valuation cases provided substantial discounts to the stock's
value for nonmarketability and other inhibiting factors. In *Estate of Arthur
F. Little, Jr.* (TCM 1982–26, CCH Dec. 38729–M), the Tax Court allowed
a total discount of 60 percent for shares of restricted stock of a publicly
held company. The court allowed a 35 percent discount for sales restrictions, a 15 percent discount for an irrevocable two-year voting proxy
agreement, and a 0 percent discount for shares that were held in escrow.

In *William T. Piper, Sr. Est.,* (72 TC No. 88, CCH Dec. 36, 315), the
court allowed a total discount of 64 percent for stock of a corporation that
owned publicly traded securities and rental property. The court allowed a
discount of 35 percent for lack of marketability, 17 percent for relatively
unattractive investment portfolios, and another 12 percent for possible
stock registration cost.

The IRS considers the discount for lack of marketability as only one
factor to be considered in valuing a business. The IRS frowns upon the use
of arbitrary discount percentages (see Revenue Ruling 77–287 in Appendix
B).

Discount for Minority Interests

The definition of a *minority interest* is control of less than 50 percent of the
shares of a corporation.

The discount for a minority interest in a privately held business
results from the unenviable position of the minority shareholder. The
holder of 15 percent (or any other minority interest) of the stock of a

closely held corporation cannot determine the dividend he or she will get, cannot get hired at a salary of his or her choosing, cannot compel a sale of the corporation, and many other unfortunate "cannots." Most importantly, minority shareholders are helpless if they want to cash in their interest in the corporation. No buyer will pay the 15 percent minority shareholder 15 percent of the total value of the whole corporation for that interest, because the buyer would be under the same disability. It necessarily follows that in the marketplace, this 15 percent interest cannot be sold for a price equivalent to 15 percent of the intrinsic value of the whole corporation. Normally, it will bring only some reduced price. That reduced price represents a discount.

To summarize, minority shareholders' problems are threefold:

1. Their interest lacks liquidity. Minority shareholders can get out of their position only if (a) the company goes public, (b) the business is sold or merged, or (c) they sell their shares to either the company or to fellow stockholders.
2. Their interest lacks current yield. Most privately held businesses don't declare dividends, and minority shareholders are powerless to compel them.
3. Their interest lacks control. Minority shareholders are powerless to affect the management and operations of the business. Their interests are at the mercy of the majority shareholder.

The Internal Revenue Service's position toward minority discounts is stingy, as is to be expected. While conceding that the discount is usually appropriate, the IRS almost always attempts to reduce its size. And in Revenue Ruling 81-253 (see Appendix B) it refuses to allow minority discounts for gift tax purposes when privately held stock is gifted between family members and the family as a whole owns a controlling interest. This position is at odds with court decisions that allow minority discounts in intrafamily transfers of privately held stock.

For instance, in *Estate of Bright* (658 F.2d 999, CA-5 1981), the appellate court refused to value half interest in a controlling block of 55 percent of a privately held corporation as half of a controlling interest, ruling instead that it was a 27.5 percent minority interest.

In *Estate of Andrews* (79 TC 938; 1982), the court applied both a discount for lack of control (minority interest) and for lack of marketability despite the fact that all shares of a privately held business were held by a decedent and his brothers. Citing the *Bright* case, the *Andrews* court held that a decedent's shares should not be valued as though the only hypothetical "willing buyer" would be a family member. To say that the only market for the decedent's shares would be a family member would violate the rule of Regulation 20.2031–1b regarding hypothetical willing buyers and sellers.

Most recently, the case of *Propstra* vs. *U.S.* (82–2 USTC 13, 475, CA–9; 1982), the Ninth Circuit Court of Appeals let it be known that only legislation would change its position on intrafamily minority discounts:

> We are unwilling to impute to Congress an intent to have "ownership of unity" principles apply to property valuations for estate tax purposes. . . . Fair market value [is defined] as the price at which property would change hands between a willing buyer and a willing seller, neither being under any compulsion to buy or sell and both having reasonable knowledge of relevant facts. By no means is this an explicit directive from Congress to apply the unity of ownership principles to estate valuations. In comparison, Congress has made explicit its desire to have unity of ownership or family attribution principles to apply in other areas of Federal tax law. In the absence of similarly explicit directives in the estate tax area, we shall not apply these principles when computing the value of assets in the decedent's estate. . . .
>
> Defining fair market value with reference to hypothetical willing-buyers and willing-sellers provides an objective standard by which to measure value. . . . The use of an objective standard avoids the uncertainties that would otherwise be inherent if valuation methods attempted to account for the likelihood that estates, legatees, or heirs would sell their interests together with others who hold undivided interests in the property. Executors will not have to make delicate inquiries into the feelings, attitudes, and anticipated behavior of those holding undivided interests in the property in question. Without an explicit direction from Congress we cannot require executors to make such inquiries.
>
> Not only would these inquiries require highly subjective assessments, but they might well be boundless. In order to determine whom the legatee or heir might collaborate with when selling his or her property interest, one would have to consider all the owners.

Despite these cases, the IRS is determined to fight minority discounts in intrafamily transfers of stock of privately held family businesses. The IRS pattern in this type of behavior is to stubbornly stick to its position until the U.S. Supreme Court rules one way or another on the issue.

Minority Interest vs. Lack of Marketability

Courts have a tendency to lump the discount for lack of marketability and the discount for minority interest together, as was the case in *Central*

Trust (see Appendix C). In practice, that is usually what happens when a business is bought and sold. Both discounts deal in lack of marketability, but for different reasons. The discount for minority interest is concerned with the minority shareholder's lack of control over the corporation's affairs. The discount for lack of marketability is concerned with the marketability of shares of a privately held business as compared to a comparable publicly traded corporation. However, the discount for lack of marketability applies to both minority and majority (controlling) interests in the corporation.

Some courts still make a distinction between the two discounts. The Tax Court distinguished the two as follows:

> In their arguments neither petitioner [taxpayer] nor respondent[IRS] clearly focuses on the fact that two conceptually distinct discounts are involved here, one for the lack of marketability and the other for lack of control. The minority shareholder discount is designed to reflect the decreased value of shares that do not convey control of a closely held corporation. The lack of marketability discount, on the other hand, is designed to reflect the fact that there is no ready market for shares in a closely held corporation. Although there may be some overlap between these two discounts in that lack of control may reduce marketability, it should be borne in mind that even controlling shares in a non-public corporation suffer from lack of marketability because of the absence of a ready private placement market and the fact that flotation costs would have to be incurred if the corporation were to publicly offer its stock.

The IRS is wary of making a distinction between the two discounts because it thinks that multiple discounts result in a larger overall total discount percentage. It tells its appeals officers to use a lower capitalization rate in the valuation process to reflect any appropriate discount or discounts. Remember, the lower the capitalization rate, the higher the multiple; the higher the multiple, the higher the value. (See *IRS Valuation Guide for Income, Estate, and Gift Taxes,* Federal Estate and Gift Tax Reporter (CCH), no. 115, part II, October 14, 1985, p. 86.)

HOW BIG A DISCOUNT?

Once it has been determined that a discount is in order, how big should it be? When negotiating a sale, a buyer will shoot for a higher discount, and the seller a lower one, if any. In tax disputes, the IRS will attempt to downplay the discount issue, while the taxpayer might use a discount to directly reduce the valuation and taxes.

Historically, no one, including the courts, has ever questioned the validity of the theory that a minority interest, or any interest subject to a market disability, must be discounted in value. The dispute always arises over the *size* of the discount. Historically, the discounts granted by the courts have almost invariably been in a low range of 5 percent to 15 percent.

Now the courts are yielding. In the past few years, the courts have tended to recognize higher discounts. Discounts of 40 percent to 50 percent, once unheard of, have been granted. (See "Minority Discounts Beyond Fifty Percent Can Be Supported," 59 *Taxes* 97, February 1981 and "Nonmarketability Discounts Should Exceed Fifty Percent," 59 *Taxes* 25, January 1981; both articles by George Arneson.) Even an IRS valuation expert employed a discount of 50 percent for illiquidity, along with the taxpayer's valuation expert, in *Estate of Ernest E. Kirkpatrick,* 34 TCM 1490 (1975).

The size of lack of marketability discounts, on the average, are smaller than those for minority interests. This is because the courts feel that in many instances a lack of marketability can be remedied (through a public flotation offering, for example), while a minority interest has no way of improving itself short of conversion to a controlling interest through the purchase of additional stock.

The IRS considers the determination of the size of a discount an arbitrary process that is subject to dispute, just like the overall process of valuing the privately held business. One school of thought holds that an appraiser should expect that any discount percentage will be disputed by the IRS. To counter this, as in any bargaining position, the appraiser should aim high on the discount percentage, but no higher than reason will support. This author, on the other hand, believes in another school of thought: Take the discount that the facts and circumstances call for: then fight like a tiger for your position if the IRS dares to challenge. (See Chapter 16 for the Tax Court's position on unreasonable valuation claims.)

Generally, lack-of-marketability discounts of 15 percent to 35 percent, and minority-interest discounts of 35 percent to 50 percent can be appropriate. Total discounts of over 50 percent are becoming more prevalent. Of course, the facts and circumstances of each case will determine the amount of the discount percentage. However, the recent trend upward in discounts no longer leaves the appraiser who takes a justifiable 50 percent or more discount feeling like he or she will be attacked, and likely overwhelmed, by other parties to the valuation.

Determining the size of a lack-of-marketability discount can be a simple matter of calculating the public offering expenses or "flotation costs" necessary to creating a public market for a stock. (See discussion on flotation costs in Appendix A, example 4.)

Determining the value of a minority interest usually involves three steps:

1. Determine the overall value of the business.
2. Determine the value of the minority shareholder's interest by determining the percentage interest in the overall value.
3. Apply the discount percentage to the minority shareholder's value.

CONCLUSIONS

Considering the number of plausible and possible discounts reaching 50 percent or more, getting oneself into a minority position in a privately held business makes a lot of sense for estate and gift tax purposes. And if the courts keep up their support for minority discounts in transfers of stock of privately held family corporations, obtaining a minority position through intrafamily sales can give a privately held business owner the best of both worlds—retention of control of the business within the family and maximization of tax savings.

Discounts should never be taken arbitrarily to arrive at the valuation objective of the party requesting the valuation. When the IRS is involved, such irresponsible values are subject to severe penalties. (See Chapter 16.)

CHAPTER 10
Restrictive Agreements

Like it or not, the day comes when all successful business owners must transfer their controlling interest in the fruit of their live's labors—their privately-held business. The transfer might take place because of their disability, retirement, or desire to move on to something more challenging, but let there be no doubt about it, the transfer will take place—if not during life, then certainly after death. Concerning ownership succession, restrictive agreements can kill three birds with one stone for the owners of a privately held business. If properly drafted, a restrictive agreement can do the following for owners:

1. ensure the orderly transfer of their controlling interest in the business to whomever they desire, without an interruption in the business' operations,
2. freeze the value of the owners' controlling interest for estate and gift tax purposes, avoiding the necessity to break up and sell part of the business to pay any tax liability, and
3. avoid the necessity of a valuation of the owners' interest for estate and gift tax purposes.

TYPES OF RESTRICTIVE AGREEMENTS

There are three types of restrictive agreements.

First, and most important from a valuation standpoint, are *buy-sell agreements*. In the context of a privately held business, this agreement says that upon the happening of some event, the shareholder's death, for example, a shareholder's interest in the business must be sold either to the remaining shareholders or back to the business.

A second type of restrictive agreement is an *option agreement,* where the privately held business owner grants an option to purchase his or her controlling interest in the business at a given price, exercisable at the will of the optionee, also upon the happening of an event, such as death. The existence of the option would preclude the owner from selling to someone else. Unlike the buy-sell agreement, only the owner is under an obligation to sell if conditions are met and the optionee makes a demand. The optionee is under no obligation to exercise the option.

The third type of restrictive agreement is called a *right of first refusal.* This agreement says that if the owners of the business want to sell their controlling interest, they must first offer it to a specified party at a specified price. If the offer is refused, the owners are then free to sell to whomever they desire. In this instance, neither the owner nor prospective buyer is under an obligation to sell or buy.

This chapter discusses the first type of restrictive agreement—the buy-sell agreement. Only this type of agreement is capable of killing the three birds with the one stone. The option agreement and the right of first refusal agreement can serve as methods for transferring controlling interest but with less certainty for tax planning purposes. Why? Because the people who can exercise the option or who have the right of first refusal can walk away from the agreement, by not exercising their right to buy. That leaves the owner off the hook and able to sell to someone else. As a practical matter, because the owner is not locked into a fixed price, these agreements are not recognized for tax purposes. However, it is the mutual obligation between the parties of the buy-sell agreement that locks in the price and makes it an excellent tax and financial planning tool.

TYPES OF BUY-SELL AGREEMENTS

Buy-sell agreements, as discussed in Chapter 2, can be broken down into three types:

1. The *redemption agreement* obligates the privately held corporation to buy the shareholder's interest upon the happening of any one of a list of specified events. The most commonly named events are death, disability, retirement, or termination of employment.
2. The *cross-purchase agreement* obligates the remaining shareholders to purchase the interest.
3. The *combination agreement* does one of two things. It either gives the remaining shareholders the option to buy the shares with the corporation obligated to purchase what the shareholders don't, or vice versa.

FUNCTION OF BUY-SELL AGREEMENTS

Buy-sell agreements are an excellent way to make sure that the termination of a shareholder's interest in the business does not create problems for the terminating shareholder, remaining shareholders, and the business. It creates a market for the terminating shareholder's interest, and in the case of his or her death, fixes the value of his or her interest for estate tax purposes.

The provision in the buy-sell agreement that requires the transfer of the terminating shareholder's interest to other shareholders or the corporation protects the corporation's existence as a going concern. It prevents the transfer of the interest to parties whose goals are inimical to present management or who would force a liquidation. The remaining shareholders are spared anxiety and apprehension over the business' future. Present employees are assured that there will not be wholesale or radical changes that could make their positions tenuous.

Finally, the successful drafting and implementation of a buy-sell agreement can make an appraisal of the business' value unnecessary. (See the steps in the valuation process listed in Chapter 7.)

Defeating the Estate Tax

A properly drafted and implemented buy-sell agreement can fix the estate tax value of a deceased shareholder's interest in a privately held corporation. In Chapter 2, four general requirements are listed to achieve the value freeze. Actually, they can be broken down further into six specific requirements:

1. The price stated in the agreement must be fixed or determined according to a valid valuation formula. For the deceased's estate, the fixed price will cause less trouble from an estate planning prospective. However, if the shareholders want to have appreciation in the stock considered to determine the final price—the usual case—a formula should be used. When hammering out the agreement, the interests of a deceased shareholder's estate must be weighed against those of the surviving shareholders or the corporation. When the shareholders are closely related, lower estate tax liability means lower basis for the purchasers of the stock which, in turn, means higher capital gain upon future sale, and vice versa. If the shareholders are not related, the price becomes an economic force; the selling stockholder wants the highest possible price, and the estate tax becomes a secondary consideration.

2. The estate of the deceased shareholder must be obligated, under the agreement, to sell the deceased's stock to the corporation or the shareholders at the agreement price. There does not have to

be an actual purchase of the shares by either of those two parties, as in the case of an option agreement, but failure to do so may be held as evidence that the stock is not worth the agreement price.

3. The agreement must state that the deceased can not sell his or her interest while alive to a third party without first offering the shares to the corporation or the remaining shareholders at the agreement price. The offer cannot be a right of first refusal which has the same price and terms as that offered to the third party. Such a right would be an escape hatch to lower the price for estate tax purposes. The offer must be at the agreement price.

4. The agreement price cannot be lower than the fair market value of the stock at the time the agreement is entered into. This requirement makes it mandatory for the shareholders to enter into the agreement as early as possible to avoid the IRS including appreciation in the value of the stock. An agreement entered into solely for the purpose of freezing the par or book value of a dying shareholder's interest shortly before his or her death will not do the trick.

5. The agreement must have what is called in tax parlance a *bona fide* business purpose. The courts have ruled, and the IRS reluctantly agrees, that preservation of management control, be it family or other, is a *bona fide* business purpose for a buy-sell agreement. So is a desire to prevent disruption of the business' operation.

6. The sixth requirement is that the agreement's *raison d'etre* (reason for existence) cannot be "testamentary," i.e., to beat the estate tax. In the words of the IRS, the agreement "must not be a tax avoidance device for passing a decedent's shares to the natural objects of his bounty for less than full and adequate consideration." Usually, if a *bona fide* business purpose exists, there is no tax avoidance. However, as is discussed below, this is changing. *Bona fide* business purpose is no guarantee that tax avoidance will not be found in the agreement.

IRS' Position on Buy-Sell Agreements.   The IRS doesn't say what a valid buy-sell agreement is, because it is not in the business of telling taxpayers how to beat the estate tax and lower government revenues. However, it does say what will not pass muster. For example, in Regulation 20.2031–2(h), it states:

Securities subject to an option or contract to purchase. Another person may hold an option or contract to purchase securities owned by the decedent at the time of his death. The effect, if any, that is given to the option or contract price in determining the value of the securities for estate tax purposes depends upon the circumstances of the particular case. Little weight will be accorded a price contained in an option or contract under which the decedent is free to dispose of the underlying securities at any price he chooses during his lifetime. Such is the effect, for example, of an agreement on the part of a shareholder to purchase whatever shares of stock the decedent may own at the time of his death. Even if the decedent is not free to dispose of the underlying securities at other than the option or contract price, such price will be disregarded in determining the value of the securities unless it is determined under the circumstances of the particular case that the agreement represents a bona fide business arrangement and not a device to pass the decedent's shares to the natural objects of his bounty for less than an adequate and full consideration in money or money's worth.

The IRS' position as stated above seems to say that the *bona fide* business agreement and testamentary tax avoidance device test are mutually exclusive—if an agreement is one it can't be the other.

Chapter 2 contains an explanation of a new IRS tactic: use of the gift tax to attack buy-sell agreements.

The Courts and Buy-Sell Agreements. While the IRS has chosen to leave taxpayers guessing as to what agreements will or will not pass muster, the courts have stepped in to fill the void. The six requirements listed earlier in this chapter derive from requirements fashioned over the years by the courts.

The general rule on buy-sell agreements is as follows:

It now seems well-established that the value of property may be limited for estate tax purposes by an enforceable agreement which fixes the price to be paid therefor, and where the seller if he desires to sell during his lifetime can receive only the price fixed by the contract and at his death his estate can receive only the price theretofore agreed on. (*Wilson* v. *Bowers,* 57 F.2d 682.)

Most of the litigation surrounding buy-sell agreements centers on the dichotomy between *bona fide* business purpose and testamentary device, and on whether the presence of one eliminates the possibility of the presence of the other (i.e., whether the two concepts are mutually exclusive).

The IRS usually attacks buy-sell agreements as testamentary devices with the taxpayer contending that it had a *bona fide* business purpose. The courts are not in full agreement that these two positions are mutually exclusive. Here are two cases that illustrate this point.

In *Estate of Bischoff* (69 TC 32; 1977), the court followed the mutually exclusive rule. That case involved a partnership interest subject to a buy-sell agreement. The partnership held stock in a family business. Here is the court's reasoning in upholding the price set in the buy-sell agreement as the value of the decedent's stock for estate tax purposes:

> We are convinced that the members of F.B. Associates and Frank Brunckhorst Co. entered into their respective partnership agreements in order to assure their continuing ability to carry on the pork processing business without outside interference, including that of a dissident limited partner. In order to accomplish this objective, restrictive buy-sell provisions were incorporated into the partnership agreements. The F.B. Associates agreement maintained ownership and control of F.B. Associates in the Bischoff and Brunckhorst families and in turn maintained ownership and control of Boar's Head and its sister corporation within those two families, and the Frank Brunckhorst Co. in the Bischoff, Brunckhorst, and Weiler families. We therefore conclude that the buy-sell provisions were grounded on legitimate business considerations. . .
> Having found such a purpose for both the F.B. Associates and Frank Brunckhorst Co. partnership buy-sell provisions and since the partnership provisions provided for a lifetime and after-death restrictions, we conclude that the value of the decedents' interests in F.B. Associates and Frank Brunckhorst Co. is the amount provided for and paid under the buy-sell provisions of the partnership agreement.

The IRS raised numerous objections to the buy-sell agreement in *Bischoff*. It argued that the partnership interests did in fact pass to the natural objects of the decedents' bounty, i.e., the interests passed to their children. The four partners were almost certain to predecease the children partners. Besides that, the children were only passive partners.

The *Bischoff* court did not disagree with these IRS contentions. It merely held that the legitimate business purpose of maintaining family control of the family business negated any testamentary intent in the buy-sell agreement.

In the case of *St. Louis County Bank* (674 F.2d 1207 CA–8 1982), the appellate court held that the existence of a *bona fide* business purpose in a buy-sell agreement did not negate the need for the taxpayer to also prove that the agreement was not a testamentary device. Instead of finding the two positions mutually exclusive, the court found that the taxpayer had to prove that the agreement (1) had a *bona fide* business purpose, and (2) was not a testamentary device.

The facts of the case were these: The decedent held a majority interest in a privately held moving and storage business. All the other shareholders were members of the decedent's family. A buy-sell agreement among the shareholders and the corporation gave surviving shareholders and the corporation the option to purchase a deceased shareholder's shares under a formula price based on the company's average annual earnings. At the time the agreement was entered into, the agreement price was close to the fair market value of the shares. Subsequently, however, the company's business changed from a profitable operating company to a real estate investment company. Losses mounted yearly. Under the agreement price formula the stock's price fell to zero.

One shareholder died and the agreement was not used. Upon the death of a second shareholder, the corporation invoked the agreement and redeemed the second deceased shareholder's shares for free, at the zero-formula price.

Although the appellate court found a legitimate business purpose for the buy-sell agreement (preservation of family ownership), three disturbing facts led it to hold that the agreement was testamentary device: (1) all of the parties to the agreement were related, (2) although the book value of the decedent's shares was $200,000, the agreement formula price was $0, and (3) the deceased had suffered two heart attacks at the time the agreement was executed.

The difference in the decisions in *Bischoff* and *St. Louis County Bank* seem to hinge on the health problems of the deceased. In *Slocum* (256 F. Supp. 753; 1966), failing health was also held as a reason for the court to find testamentary intent in an agreement. However, compare the opposite result in *Estate of O.B. Littick* (see Chapter 2) where the fact that the deceased had terminal cancer at the time of the execution of the buy-sell agreement was disregarded by the court in upholding its *bona fide* business purpose.

In summary, if the six requirements listed earlier in this chapter are satisfied, a buy-sell agreement should pass muster. Be aware, however, that the failing health of one party to the agreement, especially in a privately held family business situation, could lead to close scrutiny by the IRS and a probable attack on the value of the deceased's shares for estate tax purposes.

If the price in the agreement is set by formula, that formula should use one of the valuation methods or approaches listed in this book. For example, if a company is profitable, the earnings approach might be used. If the company is unprofitable or, as in the *St. Louis County Bank* case, has major nonoperating assets, a book value formula might be used.

A must regarding buy-sell agreements is that when a situation arises in which the agreement can be invoked (such as the death of one of the parties), it *must* be invoked. Failure by the parties to the agreement to exercise their purchase rights under the agreement (and take as a beneficiary under the will) is a red flag to the IRS that the agreement is a testamentary device and that the agreement price is below the actual value of the stock. This is again an instance when the interests of the surviving parties are pitted against those of the deceased's estate.

Finally, a bit of advice: enter into a buy-sell agreement as soon as possible, particularly when all the parties are in good health. Many of the tax problems mentioned in this chapter can thereby be avoided.

CHAPTER 11
Recapitalizations

In recent years, the most popular valuation-freezing tool for estate tax purposes has been the recapitalization. Unfortunately, the effectiveness of the recapitalization has been put in doubt because its desired estate tax results have become hotly contested by the IRS. Planning in this area has become increasingly treacherous. Some practitioners have begun to look elsewhere to obtain the results previously sought from recapitalizations. However, there is still a place for the recapitalization to fulfill the needs of the privately held business owner.

THE GENIUS OF DR. SALSBURY

The history of the recapitalization as an estate planning tool begins with the ingenuity of Dr. Joseph Salsbury. In 1946, Dr. Salsbury undertook a recapitalization of his privately held business, Salsbury Laboratories. Here's what he did. The only class of common stock in the company was canceled, and the shareholders were issued instead new preferred and common stock. The preferred stock received a six-cents-a-share fixed dividend with any excess being paid to the new class of common stock. The voting structure of the company after the recapitalization was as follows: one vote per share for the 690,000 shares of preferred and 27,290 shares of common stock. The voting control of the company was fixed in the preferred stock. The preferred stock was issued to the shareholders in the same proportions as the canceled old common. Dr. Salsbury, having 54 percent of the old common, received 54 percent of the preferred and retained control of the company. The new common stock, with minimal voting power, was issued to the doctor's wife and children.

As a result, Dr. Salsbury achieved the dream of the estate planner. He retained control of the company, froze the value of the company in the preferred stock, enabled his wife and children to share in any future appreciation in the company's worth, and avoided any gift tax on the issuance of the new common to his family.

The fruits of Dr. Salsbury's planning acumen were harvested when he died in 1967. At his death, he held voting control over a privately held business worth $13 million. However, he only owned preferred stock in that company that was eventually valued by the Tax Court for estate tax purposes at $514,000. In other words, $12.5 million worth of the business was not included in his estate and therefore escaped the estate tax. Keep in mind that Dr. Salsbury also managed to avoid the gift tax during his lifetime, and the magnitude of his accomplishment can be appreciated. He saved over $7 million in taxes (See *Estate of Salsbury,* TCM 1975–333). If only it were that easy today.

DEFINITION OF A RECAPITALIZATION

Technically, a recapitalization is a reorganization or reshuffling of a corporation's capital structure under Section 368 (a)(1)(E) of the Internal Revenue Code. If properly carried out, there is no gain or loss recognized by the shareholders or the corporation. It involves the cancellation of old and the issuance of new classes of stock.

RECAPITALIZATION SCENARIO

Following is a scenario that illustrates the actual situation of thousands of closely held business owners all over the United States. This author hears the story again and again in his office: he does more valuation for recapitalizations than for all other valuation purposes combined. You should change the facts as necessary to fit your own circumstances.

One point must be kept in mind: a recapitalization always uses a second class of stock, usually preferred stock.

The Scenario

Let's illustrate the use of preferred stock in the recapitalization of a job-bership. Joe Jobber is 61 years old, married, and has two children. He owns 1,000 shares, which is 100 percent, of Rich Corporation's common stock. He acquired these shares in 1960 when he incorporated his sole proprietorship. The fair market value of the corporation is $1 million.

His wife, let's call her Mother, does not participate in management. Nor does Joe's youngest child, who we will call Daughter. Daughter is married to an engineer, who will never be active in the corporation. Joe's oldest child, who we will call Son, has been employed by Rich Corporation for about 15 years and is now almost in complete control of operations. Joe's objectives and problems can be summarized in four statements.

One

Joe doubts that his estate will have the cash to pay any substantial amount of estate tax. Most of his wealth is tied up in Rich Corporation, which has land, buildings, and equipment. The inventory and receivables seem to grow incessantly. It is doubtful whether he or the corporation could accumulate any large amount of cash. Joe would like to freeze the value of his estate at its current level.

Two

Joe wants to stay in control of the corporation as long as he lives. He would like control to pass to his son upon his death.

Three

Joe would like Mother to have adequate support, after his death, assuming that she survives him.

Four

After Mother's death, Joe would like his estate to be divided equally between his son and his daughter. It is important to Joe that Son's control of Rich Corporation not be disturbed after his death. Although Joe would like Daughter to receive the same value as Son, Joe does not want her to be able to interfere in the management of the business.

After several meetings, Joe decides upon a recapitalization. To accomplish the recapitalization, Rich Corporation will issue three classes of stock in exchange for all of Joe's old 1,000 common shares. This exchange is tax free.

After the exchange this is the way Joe's new stock holdings will look:

Stock	Shares	Value
Voting Common	90	$ 90,000
Preferred		
Nonvoting	900	900,000
Voting	1,000	10,000
TOTAL VALUE		$1,000,000

Since most of the value of the corporation is in the nonvoting preferred, Joe is free to gift the voting common without incurring any current gift taxes. Assume that Joe makes a gift of 45 shares to his son and an equal gift to his daughter. If Joe has never made any other taxable gifts before, the $90,000 would be free of any immediate tax cost.

The most important objective accomplished is that 100 percent of the future growth of Rich Corporation will belong to Joe's children. The value of the business has been frozen for estate tax purposes.

HOW RECAPITALIZATION SOLVES PROBLEMS

The nonvoting preferred stock would be retained by Joe Jobber, to provide for Mother's support after his death via dividend payments or possibly by a complete redemption. Let's examine a variation. A portion of these shares could be used to equalize Daughter's shares of Joe's estate if Son had been given all or a larger proportion of the voting common at the inception of the recapitalization.

Let's clarify this variation. Often what is done in such a recapitalization is to give the son who is active in the business all of the shares of the common growth stock with none going to the daughter. In such a case, if Joe is typical, he will want Daughter to receive an amount equal to that Son received. This can be accomplished by leaving the nonvoting preferred to Daughter following a life estate to Mother. In any event, it can be seen that a tremendous amount of flexibility is available with either Son or Daughter taking a current interest in the future growth or a delayed interest via Joe's will.

One more point should be made—a clause in Joe's will should leave the 1,000 voting preferred shares to his son. Thus, Joe has been able to maintain control during his life and, at death, pass control to his son. Since these shares are worth $10,000, an equal gift might be left to Daughter in Joe's will.

VARIATIONS

The objectives, financial goals, and family requirements are as varied as the number of business owners in the United States.

The best news about a recapitalization is its *total flexibility*. A recapitalization can be tailored to fit the financial and family needs of each particular privately held or family held business.

RECAPITALIZATION CHECKLIST

Here is a checklist of the steps to be undertaken to implement the recapitalization:

1. A plan of recapitalization should be adopted by the board of directors of the corporation and approved by the shareholders. A copy of the plan should be submitted with the corporation's tax return for the year in which the recapitalization takes place.
2. The articles of incorporation of the company should be amended to allow for the issuance of the new classes of stock and the cancellation of the old. (Reg. 1–368–3(a).)
3. Cancel the old stock and issue the new shares. This involves the valuation of the stock canceled and the stock issued because they must be approximately equal in value. The valuation issue is discussed in detail below.
4. Be able to show a legitimate business purpose for the recapitalization, such as increasing the shareholding of a younger generation, providing incentives to key employees, minimizing difficulties in transferring the business so as not to damage ongoing operations, and so on. (See Letter Ruling 8213027.)

VALUATION PROBLEMS

Three valuation problems are present in a recapitalization: valuation of the preferred stock, valuation of the common stock, and valuation of the company as a whole. Before the recapitalization, the total value of the company is usually contained in one class of old common stock. After the capitalization, that same total value must be contained in the sum of the value of the new common and new preferred.

The IRS attacks Dr. Salsbury's invention by attempting to show a lesser value for the preferred stock at the time of the recapitalization and a higher value for the common stock. If there is substantial value assigned to the common stock, the owner of the old common is deemed to have gifted the new preferred to its recipient in the amount of its value, and a gift tax results.

For example, if the old common stock had a value of $10 million, and the value of the new preferred is determined to be $9 million, the holder of the old common is deemed to have gifted the $1 million to the recipients of the new common.

At the death of the preferred shareholder, the IRS will attempt to show that the preferred stock has all the characteristics of common stock and should be treated as such, carrying with it any appreciation in the company's value since the recapitalization. This results in a higher estate tax. The valuation experts attempting to keep intact the spirit of Dr. Salsbury must walk a minefield to avoid these dangers.

REVENUE RULING 83–120

This ruling is now the main weapon in the IRS' arsenal in attacking recapitalizations. It is reproduced in full in Appendix B. Basically, it sets out factors to be considered in valuing the preferred and common stock issued in the recapitalization. When considering these factors remember this: a decrease in the value of the preferred stock increases the value of the common stock and the gift tax liability connected with the common, and an increase in the value of the preferred stock has the opposite effect. Following is a summary of the factors listed in the ruling:

1. *Preferred Stock*
   a. *Yield.* What is the yearly or cumulative payout of the preferred stock? The absence of a cumulative provision on the preferred lowers its value, because dividends not paid are lost permanently. The presence of the cumulative features will increase the preferred stock's value, but it partially defeats the freeze because it increases the preferred shareholder's estate at the dividend rate. Only if the company appreciates in value above that rate is the purpose of the freeze fulfilled. Not only that, but what taxpayer is willing to incur the higher lifetime income tax liability on the cumulative dividend in order to save estate taxes after death?
   b. *Convertibility.* Establishing a ratio for the conversion of the preferred stock to a certain number of shares of common stock can substantiate the purported value of the preferred. For example, a 1:1 conversion rate would help establish the preferred stock at its par value.
   c. *Put Option.* Obligating the company to buy the stock at its stated par value when the shareholder exercises a put can produce the same result as the conversion factor.
   d. *Dividend Yield Rate.* A dividend rate on the preferred stock

that is lower than the rate on preferred of a comparable publicly traded company means the par value of the stock is overstated. A higher rate means it is understated.

e. *Dividend-paying Capacity.* The capacity of the company to pay the dividend yield provided for in the preferred stock is indicative of the stock's value. Can the company pay the preferred dividends yearly at the stated rate? The earnings history of the company is important as a determining factor of future capability. Here a regression analysis (See examples 3 and 4 in Appendix A) could be useful. If it is determined that the company cannot cover its dividend-paying obligation, the value of the preferred stock must be less than par. This factor makes it imperative for the company to pay the dividends in the years immediately following the recapitalization to establish a history of dividend-paying capacity. Otherwise the IRS will up the estate tax, claiming that the recapitalization plan never intended to pay the preferred dividends, making it easier to portray the preferred stock as common stock in disguise.

f. *Liquidation Preference.* The IRS will also look at the ability of the company to pay a full liquidation preference. This is measured at the time of the recapitalization by the ratio of the excess of the fair market value of the company's assets over liabilities.

g. *Voting Rights.* Voting rights increase the value of preferred stock. If the preferred shareholder has a controlling interest that value is increased even more. Most of the value of preferred stock is attained by the retention of controlling interest.

NOTE: The value of the preferred stock can exceed its par value when the holder of these shares has voting control (IRS Technical Advice Memorandum 8510002, 11/26/84).

2. *Common Stock*
   a. *Right to Future Appreciation.* The main factor considered by the IRS to give value to the common stock is the right to receive any future appreciation in the value of the company. Such a right "usually warrants a determination that the common stock has substantial value."
   b. *Subordinated Liquidation Preference.* The fact that the common stock's liquidation preference is subordinated to that of

the preferred may lower the value of the common if it is
determined that the company does not have the capacity to
cover the preferred liquidation preference.

c. *General Valuation Factors*. The common stock should also
be valued according to the general valuation principles of
Revenue Ruling 59–60.

3. *Company*

The valuation of the company itself can be accomplished by
the appropriate method under the principles outlined in this
book. Discounts for lack of marketability and minority interests are also appropriate.

SUMMARY

As can be seen from the preceding discussion of recapitalizations, the
general valuation skills described in various chapters in this book should
be used to fight the IRS in its efforts to impose a gift tax at the time of the
recapitalization or a larger estate tax at the death of the preferred shareholder. The recapitalization is just one valuation-freeze tool. Buy-sell
agreements can fulfill the same function from a control and an estate
planning viewpoint. In all likelihood, the IRS will continue its attack on
recapitalizations, attempting to make an effective estate planning tool too
costly to undertake in terms of time, money, and hassle.

If you are contemplating a recapitalization, read Chapter 12.

CHAPTER 12
Preferred Stock

Most of the valuation techniques described in this book that apply to common stock of the privately held business also apply to the valuation of preferred stock. There are no set rules, regulations, or case laws specifically applicable to preferred stock valuation. However, many of the factors listed in Revenue Ruling 83–120 (see Chapter 11 and Appendix B) for valuing preferred stock in recapitalizations have been individually used by the courts for valuation purposes.

Preferred stock issued in a recapitalization also carries with it hidden income tax traps that can result in ordinary income to the preferred stock shareholder. There problems are discussed in this chapter.

COURT CASES

A typical preferred stock valuation case is *FX Systems Corp.* (79 TC 957; 1982). The taxpayer corporation purchased assets of another corporation with cash, a promissory note, 500 shares of its series–A preferred stock, and 500 shares of its series–B preferred stock. The corporation claimed a basis in the assets equal to their fair market value. The IRS claimed that the assets should be valued according to what their cost was—the property (cash, promissory note, and preferred stock) given in exchange therefore. Since the value of the cash and promissory note was easily ascertainable, the bone of contention was the value of the preferred stock. Convertibility and the redemption price of the preferred stock was the court's benchmark in reaching its decision:

> Furthermore, the record indicates that the preferred stock that petitioner issued to Ferroxcube was worth nowhere near the amount that petitioner would have us find. The series A and series B preferred stock issued to Ferroxcube was redeemable by petitioner for a total price of $100,000. To accept petitioner's position, we would have to find that such preferred stock had a value of $652,180. We find it difficult to believe that stock worth $652,180 would be redeemable for only $100,000. Although petitioner maintains that the conversion privilege that accompanied the series B preferred stock was of considerable value, the record clearly shows that the conversion privilege could not account for this discrepancy. At the time of the sale, 345,000 shares of the petitioner's common stock were outstanding and another 40,000 had been subscribed, while the series B preferred stock issued to Ferroxcube was only convertible into 22,500 shares of common stock. Moreover, if anything, the record indicates that at the time of the sale 22,500 shares of petitioner's common

stock were worth considerably less than the $50,000 redemption price of the series B preferred stock issued to Ferroxcube.

The court found the preferred stock to be worth only $100,000 for both series, which was $147,000 less than contended by the taxpayer.

In *Estate of Von Hajke* (79–1 USTC 13,290), the court agreed with the estate's valuation because of the difficulties that would be caused by the redemption of the deceased shareholder's preferred stock. The deceased had the right to have her stock redeemed at a $1,000 par value. The estate set the value of the stock at $675. The IRS contended that the redemption price was the stock's value because the deceased shareholder held a controlling interest in the company and could have used her controlling interest to compel a redemption at that price.

The court disagreed:

> In my opinion, Mr. Johnston (the IRS expert) failed to give sufficient attention to the problems (of) a redemption. . . . Although a majority shareholder, under the by-laws and certificates of incorporation, would have the power to elect a board of directors, it does not follow that he would have the right to demand that the board redeem the stock (*U.S. v.Byrum*, 408 U.S. 125; 1972). . . . Moreover, I believe that the government failed to consider other difficulties that might be encountered if the redemption of the preferred stock were accomplished. The board of directors owes a fiduciary duty to the minority shareholders which precludes it from acting against the interests of the minority shareholders. A redemption of the preferred stock would likely require liquidation of a substantial portion of the corporation's assets, including some low-basis blocks of stock, which would produce a large capital gains tax liability offensive to the minority shareholders. . . . In addition, a recapitalization might effect a "squeeze-out" of the minority shareholders and result in litigation. Such litigation is a proper matter to consider in valuing the stock.

The *Von Hajke* case illustrates the point that valuation considerations applicable to common stock can also be used to value preferred stock.

Sometimes the attributes of preferred stock taken by itself would call for a lower value. However, if the preferred shareholder is also a common stock shareholder, certain situations require that the common and preferred holdings be valued as a block because a combination of the features of both classes of stock in the hands of the shareholder increases the combined value. For example, suppose the preferred had dividend and liquidation preference, but no voting rights, which were embodied in the common shares. This was the situation in *Estate of Lee* (69 TC 860; 1978), where the court valued the deceased shareholder's interest in a company, embodied in both preferred and common shares, as a whole. Here's the court's reasoning:

> The common and preferred stock each had negative features which would detract from their fair market value if sold separately. The preferred shares entitled their owner to a claim in liquidation or redemption to all the assets then owned plus all subsequent appreciation up to $10 million. The common shareholders had no prospect of realizing any monetary return from corporation assets for some time, yet had control over their management. In combination, however, the preferred and common shares entitled their owners to all the positive benefits while negating the detriments. As experts for both respondent and petitioner testified, the normal approach would be to market the preferred and common shares as a block.

As is evident from these cases, the valuation of preferred shares is even a more arbitrary process than the valuation of the privately held business as a whole. Similar to the valuation process in recapitalization set out in Revenue Ruling 83–120, after the value of the business as a whole is reached, the capital structure of a company often requires that the two component parts of that total valuation amount be calculated in a zero-sum game. The more value to common, the less to preferred, and vice versa. Below is a list of the most common attributes of preferred stock that might affect its value:

1. Is it nonconvertible or convertible to other securities in the capital structure of the company?
2. Is it noncumulative or cumulative regarding the payment of dividends?
3. Does it possess voting rights, and if so can the exercise of those rights affect the management and operations of the company?
4. Does it possess a liquidation preference with regard to the company's assets?
5. Can it be redeemed at a set price (does it possess a *call* feature)?
6. Is it subordinate or superior to other classes of preferred stock?
7. Does it possess a right to share in the earnings and profits of the corporation?
8. Does it possess other rights contingent on the happening of some event?

These are traits that affect the value of the preferred shares, and consequently, the value of the common shares of the corporation. The same process exists for the common shares. Listing the attributes of common shares can increase or decrease the value of those shares and consequently affect the value of the preferred shares.

RECAPITALIZATION PROBLEMS

Excess Redemption Premium

Although a recapitalization is tax-free, certain features of the preferred stock can cause problems. One problem arises upon the issuance of the preferred stock and the other upon the subsequent sale of it

Under Section 305, in a recapitalization where the corporation issues preferred stock that must be redeemed on the shareholder's death at a price that exceeds 110 percent of the issue price, the excess is treated as a distribution taxable as ordinary income that is received ratably over the life of the shareholder. For example, suppose the issue price of preferred stock is $100, and the stock must be redeemed at $140. The excess of $30 (110 percent × $100 = 110; $140 − $110 = $30) is deemed to be received by the shareholder over his or her life expectancy. Actuarial tables determine that estimated lifetime. If the shareholder had a remaining life expectancy of 20 years, he or she would be deemed to receive $1.50 a year per share as ordinary income over that 20 year period. (Reg. 1.305–5(b)(2)).

The same regulation states that redemption premiums above the 110 percent safe harbor may be nontaxable if shown to reasonable. A redemption premium is reasonable if it is in the nature of a penalty for the premature redemption of the preferred stock. For example, a shareholder receives the preferred stock in the expectation that it will provide income for a number of years. If, however, the stock is immediately redeemable at any time at the option of the corporation, the shareholder is deprived of the assurance that the income stream will continue. Therefore, if the corporation issues the preferred stock at a premium above the 110 percent in order to compensate the shareholder for the uncertainty of how long he or she will hold the preferred stock, no ordinary income will result on the distribution of the stock to the shareholder in the recapitalization. Therefore, a redemption premium in excess of 110 percent of issue price should always be accompanied by a "call" option exercisable by the corporation.

See Revenue Ruling 83–119 in Appendix B for a thorough explanation of how Section 305 affects the issuance of preferred stock redeemable at a premium above its issue price.

Section 306 Taint

A second problem that accompanies the issuance of preferred stock in a recapitalization is that it can be classified as Section 306 stock. Section 306 stock is preferred stock that is issued with respect to common stock and is received by the shareholder as a nontaxable stock dividend at the time the corporation has earnings and profits. The problem with Section 306 preferred stock arises when it is redeemed, sold, or transferred. The amount received for the Section 306 preferred stock is an ordinary income distribution to the extent that the fair market value of the stock was covered by the earnings and profits of the corporation on the date it was distributed. In this case, that would be the date of the recapitalization.

However, the Section 306 taint is removed from the stock upon the death of the shareholder. If one of the purposes of the recapitalization is to allow the owners of the business to remain in control until their death, the Section 306 taint is no problem since it will disappear when they die. In addition, as a general rule, the preferred stock received by the owner of the recapitalized corporation is free of the Section 306 taint if the owner receives only preferred stock (none of the common) in the recapitalization.

CHAPTER 13
Employee Stock Ownership Plans (ESOPs)

The valuation of stock contributed to and distributed from an Employee Stock Ownership Plan (ESOP) is of critical importance. Unfortunately, there is little guidance for the valuation process in case law or legislation. All that is stated in those sources is that if the valuation is done improperly, there will be Hades to pay by the closely held corporation sponsoring the ESOP. But before explaining that, a discussion of what an ESOP is and how it functions is in order.

DEFINITION AND OPERATION OF AN ESOP

An ESOP is a qualified defined-contribution plan, which is similar to a typical profit-sharing plan but is designed to invest primarily in the employer's stock or securities. Technically, an ESOP can be either a stock bonus plan or a combination stock bonus and money-purchase pension plan.

Here's an overview of a common method of using an ESOP. At the time that the ESOP is adopted, an Employee Stock Ownership Trust (ESOT) is established by the employer. In this chapter, there is no significant difference between the terms ESOP and ESOT. The ESOT invests in the employer's stock or securities. The ESOT can acquire the employer's stock from the employer company's shareholders, the employer corporation, or both. It can get the cash for the purchase either by a direct deductible contribution from the employer or by borrowing the money from a bank. Subsequent contributions to the ESOT, which are used to pay off principal and interest on funds borrowed to purchase employer stock, are deductible as made.

The ESOT, with all the rights and benefits of a shareholder, holds the stock for the benefit of participating employees. The stock is distributed to the participants when they are eligible to receive it, upon retirement, disability, or death. Usually, the ESOT or the corporation repurchases the distributed stock from the employees. It is this flow of stock "to, from, and back" to the trust or corporation, combined with very favorable tax breaks applicable to ESOPs, that make the ESOP an interesting planning tool.

The Tax Reform Acts of 1984 and 1986 further sweetened ESOPs with a number of new tax breaks, including the following:

1. *Payment of Estate Tax Liability by an ESOP*: An ESOP can assume a shareholder's estate tax liability connected with employer stock in exchange for the transfer of that stock to the

ESOP by the estate. The ESOP steps into the estate executor's shoes and is eligible for 4 percent interest and five-year deferral of principal available to pay the estate tax.

2. *Tax-deferred Rollover on Sale of Stock to an ESOT*: Shareholders can defer recognition of gain on the sale of their closely held stock to the ESOT. This deferral is available if (1) the sale proceeds are reinvested in "qualified replacement property" within 3 months before and 12 months after the sale, and (2) the ESOT controls at least 30 percent of the employer's stock immediately after the sale, and (3) none of the securities acquired by the ESOT in the rollover transaction are allocated to the selling shareholders. However, they can still participate in the ESOP if other employer securities are subsequently allocated to them.

3. *Reduced Estate Tax Value:* Stock of the closely held business owned by a deceased shareholder that is sold to an ESOT will enjoy a 50 percent reduction in value for estate tax purposes.

One significant disadvantage of an ESOP is that it dilutes the control and ownership of the present stockholders, including the controlling shareholder.

FIDUCIARY DUTIES

The danger inherent in the valuation of employer securities contributed to an ESOP is that the Pension Reform Act of 1974 imposed upon the fiduciary or trustee running the ESOP a duty to run the plan solely in the interest of the plan participants and beneficiaries. This means that when buying employer securities for the ESOP or purchasing them back from plan participants, the trustee must do so with care, skill, and diligence, paying as little as possible for the contributed shares and purchasing the shares back from participants at their fair market value.

A plan fiduciary who violates this fiduciary duty is personally liable to compensate the ESOP or others for any losses suffered because of his or her mistakes in dealing in the ESOP's employer stock. In many cases, the trustee is somehow affiliated (stockholder, officer, employee) with the employer corporation, especially in the case of a privately held business.

VALUATION PROBLEMS

If the ESOT trustee causes the ESOT to purchase employer stock at a price greater than its fair market value, the purchase can be a violation of the trustee's fiduciary duties.

If the employer corporation contributes stock to the ESOT and claims a deduction for the contribution greater than the fair market value of the stock, the deduction will be disallowed by the amount of the excess claimed. Worse yet, an excise tax can be imposed upon the principal shareholder or employer who sells stock to an ESOT at greater than fair market value.

If a plan participant sell shares back to the ESOT or the employer corporation at a put option priced at less than its fair market value, the participant may have a cause of action against the ESOT or the employer.

An interesting case that illustrates these principles is *Donovan* v. *Cunningham* (716 F.2d 1455, CA–5; 1983). In that case, the issue was whether the ESOT trustees had caused the ESOT to purchase employer stock from the employer corporation's sole shareholder for more than its fair market value.

The trustees had obtained an appraisal of the value of the stock from an independent appraiser, which is a statutory requirement for ESOP purchases. The secretary of labor, who had brought the suit against the trustees for their alleged violation of labor laws pertaining to ESOPs, disagreed with the appraisal report.

First, he claimed in his suit that the report was not updated and was made a considerable time before the purchases took place. He claimed that the report needed to be updated to take into account the impact of the ESOP on the value of the company stock and to reflect the difference between the actual operating results of the company following the appraisal and those that had been projected in the appraisal report itself.

Second, the secretary argued that the valuation in the appraisal should have been discounted to account for the ESOP's purchasing only a minority interest in the employer corporation. It must be admitted that this conclusion is a blow. Many commentators have maintained that no discounts should be taken when valuing ESOP stock: after all, the ESOT provides a marketplace for the stock. This case punctures this time-accepted logic.

The appellate court ruled for the secretary, holding:

> Under [legislation], as well as at common law, courts have focused the inquiry under the "prudent man" rule on a review of the fiduciaries'

independent investigation of the merits of a particular investment rather than on the evaluation of the merits alone. As a leading commentator has put it, the test of prudence is one of conduct and not a test of the result of the performance of the investment. The focus of the inquiry is how the fiduciary acted in his selection of the investment and not whether his investment succeeded or failed.

By this standard, the appellate court found the appraisal report to be lacking, because it failed to identify the facts and assumptions that justified its final valuation figure. Not only that, but the trustees failed to determine whether the appraisal report still had validity at the time of the purchases.

The lesson of this case is that a mistake in valuation methodology—or a failure to heed the lessons contained in this book—can be costly from a legal standpoint when valuations are done for ESOPs. As the *Donovan* court admonished, "valuations must be made in good faith and based on all relevant factors for determining the fair market value of securities." Be careful and thorough! The secretary of labor is watching you!

CHAPTER 14
Redemptions

One of the asset-freezing tools mentioned in Chapter 2 is the redemption. Valuation methods and approaches are usually necessary in the context of a redemption of shares of a privately held business, because a price must be set at which the shares are to be redeemed. The typical valuation problems and issues are inherent in the redemption of stock of the privately held business owner. This chapter does not discuss those issues per se, but is rather an explanation of what redemptions are and how they are used. The following discussion should give the reader a better appreciation of the valuation problems discussed elsewhere in this book, which often use the redemption as an example (see the *FX Systems Corp.* and *Estate of Von Hajke* cases in Chapter 12).

THE BASICS

A redemption occurs when a corporation uses its property to acquire its own stock from one or more stockholders. It is immaterial whether the redeemed stock is canceled, retired, or held as treasury stock. The term "property" includes money, securities, and other property (Section 317).

The vital question really is this: "Will the tax treatment to the redeeming stockholder be ordinary income or capital gain?"

The Internal Revenue Code provides a clear answer—Section 302. If the redemption qualifies as a sale or exchange, the excess of the proceeds over the taxpayer's basis will be a capital gain. If the redemption does not qualify, the entire amount of the proceeds will be a dividend. Of course, the amount of the dividend is limited to the earnings and profits (usually the same as retained earnings) of the corporation at the time of the redemption. The Code provides four redemption methods of attaining capital gain treatment:

1. Complete redemption,
2. Substantially disproportionate redemption,
3. Redemptions not essentially equivalent to a dividend, and
4. Certain redemptions involving railroad stock or bankruptcy situations.

Following are examples of the results in a typical situation where the corporation redeems part or all of the controlling shareholder's stock and the remaining shareholder is unrelated:

Example 1

Joe Founder owns 70 percent of the stock; the other 30 percent is owned by an unrelated business associate. The corporation J.F. Inc. is worth $1,000,000. J.F. Inc. redeems 10 percent of Joe's stock for $100,000. Joe is hung with a $100,000 dividend. (Becaust it is not a "complete redemption" and flunks the complex requirements of a "substantially disproportionate redemption.")

Example 2

J.F. Inc. redeems all of Joe's stock for $700,000. Joe's profit is a capital gain.

The redemption price may be paid in a lump sum or in installments. If paid in installments (or otherwise eligible), the redeeming stockholder may elect the installment method.

COMPLETE REDEMPTION (STOCKHOLDERS RELATED)

The Rule

Section 302(b)(3) provides for capital gains treatment when a shareholder terminates *his or her entire stock interest owned* by means of redemption. This means *ALL* of the stock owned by the redeeming shareholder. That sounds easy enough. In practice, however, the rule is complex and can result in a dividend.

Examples of the Rule in Operation

Facts

The percent of stock of Corporation C owned and the relationships between stockholders are as indicated. All stock has been owned for 12 years.

Stockholders	Percent owned
Related	
F (father)	40%
W (F's wife)	20
S (F's son)	10
D (F's daughter)	20
M (unrelated manager)	10
Total	100%

Problem

Situation 1: F desires to have *ALL* of his shares redeemed by C, together with *ALL* the shares owned by W, S, and D. C will redeem for cash. F will stay on the payroll as president of C.

Situation 2: Same as situation 1, except F alone will redeem.

Result: Capital Gain?

Situation 1: Yes! Per Revenue Ruling 76–524, F has terminated his entire stock interest, actual and constructive. The word ''constructive'' means the shares owned by W, S, and D.

Situation 2: Yes, no, or maybe—the answer depends on more facts. In particular, F must satisfy one of two requirements under Section 302 (c) to receive capital gains treatment: (1) avoid the ''attribution rules'' of Section 318(a), or (2) meet the five ''additional requirements.''

ATTRIBUTION RULES

The attribution rules apply to both complete redemptions and substantially disproportionate redemptions [Section 302(c)].

Effect of the Rules

Complete Redemption. Although the attribution rules are applicable, complete redemption of the stock of a particular family is not only practical but should be an integral part of the tax planning of every closely held family corporation. This is made possible by Section 302(c)(2), which allows waiver of the family attributions rules. (See following discussion under "Additional Requirements.")

Substantially Disproportionate Redemption.   As a practical matter, this type of redemption will never attain capital gain treatment when the stockholders are related by attribution. The arithmetic just does not work out, until all the interests of all the related family stockholders are redeemed.

The Rules

The attribution rules simply say that a shareholder will have attributed to his or her shares of stock owned by someone else if he or she is related to that someone else.

Example

A owns 55 percent of the stock of X Co., his wife owns 30 percent, and his 15-year-old son owns 15 percent. Since everyone is related, everyone owns 100 percent of the stock under the attribution rules.

The rules are not as complex as they appear; however, they must be precisely understood to work effectively with complete and substantially disproportionate redemptions.
All the rules are detailed in Section 318(a).
The following example illustrates the most important rules.

Example

The stock of C Co. is owned as follows:

Stockholder	Percent owned
F (founder)	65%
W (F's wife)	15
B (F's brother)	20
Total	100%

Situation 1: B redeems all his shares.
Result: Okay for capital gains treatment; attribution rules do not apply to siblings.
Situation 2: W redeems all her shares.
Result: Yes, capital gains treatment applies. The family attribution rules can be waived, assuming all the additional requirements are met.
Situation 3: B dies. F is the sole beneficiary of B's estate. B's executor has C redeem the 20 percent owned by the estate pursuant to a buy-sell agreement between F, B, and C.
Result: Disaster! The redemption will be treated as a dividend. The shares owned by B's estate are attributed to F. Neither the estate nor F can take advantage of the waiver rule (additional requirements).

Note

The result would be the same if W died and was substituted for B in this fact situation.

ADDITIONAL REQUIREMENTS

The attribution rules are avoided if the following five conditions are met under Section 302(c)(2) (often called the "waiver rule"). The first three conditions must always be met.

1. Immediately after the redemption, the redeeming stockholder must have no interest in the corporation as an officer, employee, or director. It is okay to be a creditor.

Example

F sells all his stock to C for $250,000—$50,000 in cash, plus a series of 10 notes of $20,000 each, payable over 10 years and secured by the assets of the corporation.
Result: Capital gain.

Exception

Here's a practical exception supported by a revenue ruling. Dad and his children, Bob and Charles, own 100 percent of Big Corp. Dad retires, and Big redeems all of his shares by a cash payment equal to the value of his stock. Bob and Charles assume all responsibility for operating Big. Under an unfunded preexisting written agreement between Dad and Big, Dad starts to receive a lifetime pension of $1,000 per month. The payments are not dependent upon Big's future earnings. Nor is Dad's claim to the payments subordinated to the claims of Big's general creditors. At retirement, Dad's life expectancy was 18 years.

The pension agreement is Dad's only continuing relationship with Big. The ruling says that this relationship does not constitute a prohibited interest. In addition, the payment to Dad for his stock is a complete redemption entitled to capital gain treatment. (Revenue Ruling 84–135)

2.   Within 10 years from the date of redemption, the redeeming stockholder must not acquire an interest in the corporation, other than as a creditor or by bequest or inheritance. An interest includes a position as an officer, employee, or director.

Example

F receives and accepts a gift of shares in C Co. five years after the redemption. The redemption will be considered a retroactive dividend back to the date of the redemption.

A purchase of shares by F would give the same result.

An inheritance from W would be okay.

3.   An agreement is filed by the redeeming stockholder (or an executor per Revenue Ruling 77–93) agreeing to notify the IRS of any acquisition described in condition 2 above and agreeing to retain the necessary records.

NOTE: The agreement must be in the form of a separate signed statement attached to a timely filed return for the year in which the redemption occurred [Reg. 1.302–4(a)].

4.   The redeemed stock shouldn't be acquired within the 10 years before redemption from a family member whose stock would be attributed to the redeeming stockholder under attribution rules.

Example

> F, 100 percent stock owner, gives his son, S, 10 percent of his stock in 1972. S redeems his 10 percent stock interest in 1977. The redemption is a dividend.

5. No person within the scope of the attribution rules should obtain stock from the redeeming stockholder within the 10-year period prior to the redemption unless such stock was also redeemed in the same transaction.

Example

> All stockholders are related under the attribution rules. Percentage of ownership and dates acquired appear below. The last three stockholders acquired their shares from F by gift. In 1985, all shares owned by F, W, and D are redeemed. S is now sole shareholder.

		Date acquired situation	
Stockholder	Percent owned	A	B
F (father)	80	1950	1950
W (F's wife)	10	1965	1965
S (F's son)	5	1965	1977
D (F's daughter)	5	1978	1978

> *Situation 1:* The redemption is a capital gain. Although D's stock does not meet the 10-year rule, it was redeemed in the same transaction with F.
> *Situation 2:* The redemption will be treated as a dividend. S did not own his stock for 10 years.

Exception

> If the redemption did not have a tax-avoidance motive, capital gains treatment will result even if the 10-year rule is violated.

Example 1: Add to situation B—in 1985, F has an unexpected disabling stroke. The doctor tells him to retire forever and move to a warmer climate.

Example 2: The corporation will redeem all of W's stock. She made gifts of stock (shortly before the redemption) to S, who will remain a shareholder and assume major management responsibility (Letter Ruling 8147169).

Example 3: A couple gave stock to their three children. Immediately following the gift, to shift control and majority ownership to one son and his immediate family, the corporation will redeem all the stock of the son's two sisters, who will each receive a 50 percent ownership in real property as tenants in common, plus interest-bearing notes (Letter Ruling 8147185).

DOES YOUR CORPORATION OWN APPRECIATED PROPERTY?

Quite often a family-controlled corporation owns property that has appreciated substantially over the years. Although the corporation may be rich in terms of appreciated property (in the form of vacant land, improved real estate, or something else), there may be no cash with which to redeem a retiring or selling founder.

A neat trick is having the redeeming stockholder (using a complete redemption) exchange stock for the appreciated property. *Result:* The corporation treats the transaction just like a sale to a stranger: the stockholder walks off with both a capital gain and the appreciated property. Where real estate is involved, the stockholder can lease the property back to the corporation.

HOW TO GET APPRECIATED PROPERTY OUT OF THE PRIVATELY HELD CORPORATION

Example

Stock redemptions can be used to take money or property out of a corporation at capital-gains rates. Consider this scenario. Assume Old

Corp. owns free and clear land and a building that originally cost $300,000. Its reduced tax basis, due to depreciation, is $100,000, and because of appreciation and inflation, the property is now worth $500,000. Mother, the founder of the corporation, owns 40 percent of the stock, while the other 60 percent is owned by members of her immediate family. Mother wants to retire. Her 40 percent of the stock is worth $500,000. The corporation exchanges the real estate for Mother's stock.

Here are the tax consequences:

1. The corporation realized a $400,000 profit—$500,000 value less $100,000 basis—just as if the corporation had sold the property. Except for depreciation recapture, the entire profit gets favorable capital gains treatment.
2. Mother has a capital gain equal to the difference between the $500,000 real estate value and her tax basis for the stock.
3. Mother can now turn around and lease the real estate to the corporation at a fair rental.
4. Best of all, Mother can depreciate the real estate (the building only, but not the land) just as if she had purchased it for $500,000.

Additional Tax-Saving Hints

1. If the property is worth less than the stock being redeemed, the corporation can pay the difference in cash or in notes to be paid over a period of time.
2. An installment election may be available to the stockholder.
3. If the property to be used for the redemption is worth more than the stock, a mortgage can be put on the property sufficient to reduce its net value to the value of the stock being exchanged.

CAUTION: If the property is subject to a mortgage (say $250,000) and its tax basis (say $150,000) is less than the liability, the difference ($100,000) is taxable income to the corporation [Section 311 (c)].

4. If the only appreciated property available for the exchange is needed in the operation of the business, the property can still be exchanged for the stock. Simultaneously with the exchange, the corporation should lease the property back from the stockholder. The exchange must be made at fair market value (FMV) and the

lease at fair rental. An expert appraiser should be used to fix the FMV—both of the stock and the real estate—and the rent.

5. Any appreciated property can be used. However, it may not be practical to use personal property subject to a large amount of depreciation recapture. Appreciated securities owned by the corporation can be used. Real estate subject to a substantial amount of depreciation recapture should not be used. Always, but always, make a projection of the tax impact on both the corporation and the stockholder.

COMMENT: Not only does this method remove future growth of the family corporation's stock from the founder's estate, but the rent (or dividends or interest in the case of securities) also provides a flow of income.

With the property out of the corporation, it is no longer subject to the claims of corporate creditors. Many founders find this last accomplishment reason enough to use this method.

How to Plan Ahead

These favorable tax results are accomplished by the tandem use of two sections of the Code plus a revenue ruling:

1. Section 302(b)(3) for a complete redemption gives the stockholder capital gains.
2. Section 311(d) gives the corporation capital gains, except for any depreciation recapture.
3. A shareholder's interest may be deemed terminated under Section 302(b)(3) despite a leaseback of the same property distributed in redemption (Revenue Ruling 70–369).

Example

The owner's wife plays no role in the corporation other than as a 20 percent shareholder. If the corporation buys her out, the gain is considered a capital gain. There is no dividend. And since the wife became a stockholder at the inception of the corporation, she does not have to wait 10 years to get capital gains treatment. The 10-year rule only applies to a transfer of stock.

SUMMARIZING WHEN AND WHY TO TAKE APPRECIATED PROPERTY OUT OF THE CORPORATION

This maneuver—distributing appreciated property—makes the most sense taxwise in two situations:

1. At the corporate level. The corporation has a large carryforward loss, and the gain to the corporation (on the appreciated property distribution) will be offset (all or in part) by the carryforward.
2. At the stockholder level.
   a. Capital loss carryforward. Just like the corporation situation outlined above, all or part of the gain on the redemption might be wiped out by the carryforward.
   b. Other reasons.
      (1) The owner wants the property out of the grasp of corporate creditors.
      (2) The future depreciation (an ordinary deduction) of the property in the hands of the stockholder could provide a real estate tax shelter.
3. After retirement, the founding stockholder will have a source of income.
4. An appreciating asset is removed from the corporation for estate purposes. Assume the founder takes appreciating real estate.
   a. These are the tax goodies the family gets: income sheltered by depreciation during the founder's life, an income-tax-free raised basis (to the property's fair market value) at the founder's death, and the ability of the heirs to depreciate the property all over again using the raised basis as a new cost at the founder's death.
   b. The real estate can be left to members of the family who do not work for the family corporation.

HINT: It is important to make a projection (for each year, carried out for 10 years or more) showing the tax consequences and cash flow for the corporation and for the redeeming stockholder.

The projections will give you the information needed to determine whether taking the appreciated property out of the corporation via a complete redemption is a "go" or a "no-go".

b. The real estate can be left to members of the family who do not work for the family corporation.

HINT: It is important to make a projection (for each year, carried out for 10 years or more) showing the tax consequences and cash flow for the corporation and for the redeeming stockholder.

The stockholder, in most cases, would use the old (useful life) method of depreciation rather than Accelerated Cost Recovery System (ACRS).

The projections will give you the information needed to determine whether taking the appreciated property out of the corporation via a complete redemption is a "go" or a "no-go".

CHAPTER 15
Gifts and Charitable Contributions

The primary advantage of an annual gift program, which is one way of freezing the value of and transferring ownership and control of a privately held business, is its simplicity. It can work very well to transfer a small business. Unfortunately, the larger the size of a privately held business, the less efficient the sole use of a gift program becomes. For larger businesses, the use of a gift program in combination with other asset-freezing transfer tools, such as redemptions and recapitalizations, is necessary. This chapter explains the important technical aspects of a combination gift-giving program and when combination plans should be used. The potential estate and gift tax liability that accompanies such freeze and transfer plans demand that the business valuation be exact.

Another form of gift-giving, the making of tax-deductible charitable contributions of closely held stock to exempt organizations, creates a reversal of the valuation game between privately held business owners and the IRS. Owners want to maximize their deductions so they push for the highest possible value for their contributed stock, while the IRS' interest is to value the stock as low as possible. These strategies are discussed in this chapter.

HOW THE GIFT TAX WORKS

Before going into the specifics of a stock-gift program, an overview of the gift tax structure as a whole is helpful in understanding the problems involved

Before 1977, because the gift tax rates were lower than the estate tax rates, it was often tax-wise to gift the entire value of the closely held business' stock in order to escape the potentially higher estate tax liability.

But Congress slammed the door: the estate and gift taxes are now one unified transfer tax. Even though the gift tax is imposed during life, at death all transfers made during life as gifts and all transfers made at death are added up and the total is subject to one unified transfer tax (misleadingly called the estate tax) using one schedule of tax rates (see Appendix E). There are certain tax breaks, such as the $10,000 annual exclusion for the gift tax, and the unified credit that can be used to reduce the unified transfer tax. That may sound simple, but the way it works in practice makes it appear as if the gift tax and the estate tax are two different animals. Here is a simplified explanation beginning with the $10,000 annual exclusion.

THE $10,000 ANNUAL EXCLUSION

Before going into the intricacies of how the gift tax works, let's begin with basics. First let's define the two people involved in a gift. The *donor* is the person who makes (gives) the gift. The *donee* is the person who receives it. An unmarried (single) donor can give up to $10,000 per year per donee without incurring any gift tax. In other words, as long as a donor does not give $10,000 or more to any one person, these gifts are tax-free.

If a donor is married, the annual exclusion can be doubled to $20,000 (Section 2513). This is accomplished when the spouse of the donor consents to the gifts. The result is a split gift, which means that each spouse is considered for gift tax purposes to have made half the gift. This allows each spouse individually to use the $10,000 exclusion, which results in a total $20,000 exclusion.

Example 1: Unmarried (Single) Taxpayer

Joe Bachelor makes a $9,000 gift to his nephew, Steve. Since the $9,000 gift is less than the $10,000 annual exclusion, Joe pays no gift tax.

Example 2: Married Taxpayer

Joe marries Sue. He makes an $18,000 gift to Steve, and Sue consents. Because the $18,000 split gift is less than the $20,000 combined annual exclusion for Joe and his wife, they pay no gift tax.

Any year in which a taxpayer makes more than a $10,000 gift, a gift tax return must be filed. Both Joe and Sue must file a gift tax return even though neither incurred any gift tax liability.

TAXABLE GIFTS

What happens if a donor makes a gift or gifts in one year that are more than the annual exclusion? The excess is considered a "taxable gift" on which a gift tax might have to be paid—a "gift tax payable" is created.

Example 3: Unmarried (Single) Taxpayer

Joe makes a $50,000 gift to Steve. After deducting the $10,000 annual exclusion, Joe is considered to have made a taxable gift of $40,000 ($50,000 − $10,000).

Example 4: Married Taxpayer

Joe marries Sue. With Sue's consent, they make a split gift to Steve of $50,000. The taxable gift made by each of them is determined as follows:

	Total	Split Joe	Split Sue
Gift	$50,000	$25,000	$25,000
Less—annual exclusion	20,000	10,000	10,000
Taxable gift to Steve	$30,000	$15,000	$15,000

The annual exclusion is calculated on a per donee basis. In other words, Joe could give $10,000 (or $20,000 with the split-gift) each to an infinite number of people tax free. For example, if single he could give away $100,000 a year tax-free, $10,000 apiece to 10 individuals.

In examples 3 and 4, the fact that a taxable gift has been made does not necessarily mean that a gift tax must be paid in cash. However, once the gift exceeds the annual exclusion, the resulting taxable gift creates a potential gift tax liability—a gift tax payable. Fortunately, all or a portion of this liability can be snuffed out by using the unified credit. Simply put, the gift tax payable can be "paid" (up to a point) by using the unified credit instead of cash.

UNIFIED CREDIT

A gift tax payable is created for each year a taxable gift is made. The amount of the gift tax payable can be reduced dollar for dollar by the available unified credit.

For each dollar of estate or gift tax liability snuffed out, an equivalent (corresponding) amount of gifts or an equivalent amount of a taxpayer's gross estate is shielded from tax by an exemption (see the schedule that follows). For 1987, if a taxpayer has a taxable estate of $600,000, the estate tax liability is $192,899. Or if a taxpayer makes a taxable gift of $600,000, the tax payable is $192,800. However, up to $192,800 in those taxes can be eliminated by the unified credit, which shields up to $600,000 (the equivalent amount) of taxable gifts and the estate from the single transfer tax.

The $600,000 amount applies to the sum total of lifetime and death transfers. What isn't used during a taxpayer's lifetime to shield gifts is available to shield the estate. To put it another way, the amount of the unified credit used against the gift tax payable effectively reduces the amount of the unified credit available against the estate tax.

For example, if the taxpayer makes only $300,000 in taxable gifts during his or her lifetime and shields that amount with the unified credit, enough of the credit would remain to shield $300,000 of the estate.

The amount of the unified credit depends on the year the gift is made or the year of death:

Year of gift or death	Unified credit	Exemption equivalent
1984	$ 96,300	$325,000
1985	121,800	400,000
1986	155,800	500,000
1987 and after	192,800	600,000

The taxpayer must use the unified credit to "pay" as much gift tax payable as possible. There is no choice (Rev. Rul. 79–398, 1979–2 CB 338).

During a taxpayer's lifetime, the unified credit can be used in conjunction with the annual exclusion to escape paying any cash gift tax.

Example 5: Unmarried (Single) Taxpayer

Take the same facts as Example 3, where Joe makes a $50,000 gift which resulted in a $40,000 taxable gift after the $10,000 annual exclusion. Joe can use the unified credit to negate the gift tax payable (8,200) and shield the $40,000 taxable gift from the gift tax.

The gift-splitting provision in Section 2513 also makes it possible to double the unified credit. This allows each spouse to shield (avoid paying any gift tax payable in cash) an exemption equivalent amount of $600,000 in lifetime gifts—or $1,200,000 for a married couple.

Example 6: Married Couple

Take the facts of Example 4, in which Joe and Sue make a split gift of $50,000 to Steve. They use their combined $20,000 annual exclusion, leaving a $30,000 taxable split gift. Each is responsible for the gift tax payable on his or her $15,000 portion of the split gift. The gift tax payable on a $15,000 taxable gift is $2,800. Both can use their unified credit to pay their $2,800 gift tax payable; combined they can use their unified credits to pay $5,600 in gift taxes payable. This shields the remaining $30,000 of the gift to Steve.

In examples 5 and 6, note that if the same $50,000 gift is made by a single taxpayer and married taxpayers who split the gift, the married taxpayers pay $2,600 less in taxes and use up less of their unified credit.

HOW THE GIFT TAX IS CALCULATED

Let's recap. A taxpayer can make tax-free gifts each year up to the $10,000 annual exclusion amount. Anything above that is a taxable gift, upon which is imposed a gift tax payable. A unified credit can be used to offset ("pay") up to $192,000 in gift taxes payable, shielding an exemption equivalent of up to $600,000 in taxable gifts. If the gift exceeds the amount of the annual exclusion and the exemption equivalent of the unified credit, the gift tax payable on the excess must be paid in cash. A gift tax return must be filed whenever a taxable gift is made.

The amount of the unified credit used to "pay" the gift tax on taxable gifts (1) effectively reduces the amount of the credit that can be used to shield a taxpayer's estate from the estate tax, and (2) actually reduces the amount of the unified credit that can be used to shield future taxable gifts. Theoretically, all $192,800 of the credit could be used in one year to shield a $600,000 taxable gift. But then there would be no credit to "pay" gift taxes payable on future taxable gifts or to protect the taxpayer's estate.

With all that in mind, here's an overview of how the gift tax is calculated. The gift tax applies to all taxable gifts made during the donor's lifetime. At the end of each year in which a taxable gift is made, a gift tax is imposed. (See the tax-rate schedule in Appendix E.) That tax is determined by four steps:

1. Add up all taxable gifts made by the donor in his or her lifetime, including the year in question, and then apply the uniform estate

and gift tax rate schedule to that amount. The result is tentative tax (1); say, for example, $14,200.

2. Add up all the taxable gifts made by the donor in his or her lifetime, not including the year in question, and apply the uniform rate to that amount. The result is tentative tax (2); say $6,200.

3. Subtract tentative tax (2) from tentative tax (1). The result is the gift tax payable for the year in question, or $8,000 ($14,200 − 6,200).

4. The taxpayer cannot pay the gift tax payable in cash until he or she uses up the unified credit to "pay" the gift tax payable for the year. The amount of the unified credit available for the year is reduced by the amount of the unified credit used in previous years. Once the unified credit is exhausted, any additional gift tax payable must be paid in cash.

Example 7: Unmarried (Single) Taxpayer

In 1987, George, who has made no previous lifetime gifts, makes a $50,000 gift to his cousin, Fred. This results in a $40,000 taxable gift ($50,000 − $10,000 annual exclusion). Since there were no previous lifetime transfers, George's gift tax payable for 1987 on the $40,000 under the uniform rate schedule is $8,200, and is "paid" by using a portion of the $192,800 unified credit.

In 1988, George makes another gift of $50,000 to Fred, resulting in a taxable gift for 1988 of $40,000. George's gift tax for 1988 is determined as follows: First, George's tentative tax (1) is $18,200, determined by applying the uniform rate schedule to $80,000 (his total lifetime taxable gifts, including 1988). Second, his tentative tax (2) is $8,200, determined by applying the uniform rate schedule to $40,000 (his total lifetime gifts not including 1988). His gift tax payable for 1988 is tentative tax (1) minus tentative tax (2), or $10,000. Again, George must "pay" by using his unified credit against this amount.

What happens if George keeps making yearly gifts in the same amount? The total lifetime transfers will keep adding up, pushing subsequent gifts into higher and higher rate brackets.

HOW THE ESTATE TAX IS CALCULATED

The transfer tax is unified because when Joe dies and it comes time to figure his estate tax, (1) all taxable gifts made during his lifetime are added to his gross estate, and (2) any gift tax Joe actually paid in cash (not including those "paid" by the unified credit) in his life is subtracted from his estate tax.

Example 8: Unmarried (Single) Taxpayer

(A)   Joe dies in 1992. He leaves a gross estate of $1,000,000. Taking into account the lifetime gifts he made in example 7 (on which he paid no cash gift tax), his estate tax liability is calculated as follows:

Gross estate	$1,000,000
Add: Lifetime taxable gifts	80,000
Taxable transfers	$1,080,000
Tentative tax (see Appendix E)	$ 378,600
Minus: Gift taxes paid in cash	0
Gross estate tax	$ 378,600
Minus: Unified credit	192,800
Net estate tax (to be paid in cash)	$ 185,800

(B)   Suppose that Joe made lifetime taxable gifts of $1,000,000, and shielded $600,000 of that amount with the unified credit. That would mean he paid a cash gift tax of $153,000 on the $400,000 excess. (The tax of $1,000,000 is $345,800, as shown in Appendix E). After deducting the $192,800 unicredit, the cash-gift-tax payment is $153,000. If he has a gross estate of $80,000, his estate tax liability is calculated as follows:

Gross estate	$ 80,000
Add: Lifetime taxable gifts	$1,000,000
Taxable transfers	$1,080,000
Tentative tax (same as above)	$ 378,600
Minus: Gift taxes paid in cash	153,000
Gross estate tax	$ 225,600
Minus: Unified credit	192,800
Net estate tax (to be paid in cash)	$ 32,800

Add the $32,800 estate tax to the $153,000 gift tax paid in cash by Joe during his life, and you come up with the same total tax paid in cash in A as in B, $185,800. This is proof of the unified nature of the estate and gift taxes. Whether Joe transferred wealth by gift or at his death, he eventually ended up paying the same amount of tax.

PUTTING IT ALL TOGETHER

By using the annual exclusion and the unified credit, a good part of the unified transfer tax can be avoided. How? By gifting enough property during one's lifetime to reduce the remaining estate so it is protected by the unified credit.

Let's put all of this into the context of the closely held business owner. For example, if Joe Entrepreneur is single, he would want to gift enough of his stock during his lifetime, using $10,000 annual exclusions, so that the remaining value of his business in his estate would be protected by the unified credit. As noted earlier, unless Joe begins the gift program early in life, or unless his business is small, he probably can't protect his entire business and other assets from the unified estate and gift tax.

Now let's put this into the context of real life. Many privately held business owners are married, have children, and want to pass their businesses on to the next generation. Here's where a gift program can become a tax hero.

For example, within a week, Joe Entrepreneur—if he is married and has two children—could transfer $80,000 of his business tax-free. How? Suppose on December 27 of Year 1 he and his wife make split gifts of stock worth $20,000 to each of the children. Using the annual exclusion, $40,000 worth of stock gifts can be made tax-free in Year 1. Suppose also that a week later on January 3rd of Year 2, Joe and his wife make the exact same split gifts to the children. Because the gift tax is imposed on an annual basis, this second set of gifts would also be tax-free, courtesy of another $40,000 of annual exclusions. In the space of one week, Joe transferred a substantial part of his business. If Joe continued this gift-program over a 10-year period, he could transfer $400,000 of his business tax-free.

Not only that, but gift-splitting could allow Joe to shield up to $1,200,000 of his business from the gift tax, over and above the annual exclusions.

GIFTS OF APPRECIATED PROPERTY: PRIVATELY HELD STOCK

Property that is likely to appreciate over time (like stock in a privately held corporation) is the perfect gift to be made to members of a younger generation. Future appreciation is revoked from the donor's estate without any tax cost.

CONTROL OF THE CORPORATION

Although the founder would like to transfer the ownership of the stock, so that it will be removed from his or her estate, he or she might not want to transfer control to his or her children. At least three circumstances always require attention:

- The children are minors.
- Although adult children are active in the business, they are not capable of managing (or, as is often the case, the management ability of one or more of the adult children is a matter of fierce family disputes), and the founder wants to hang in there.
- Adult children are not active in the business and could not (even if given the opportunity) make intelligent voting decisions to direct management.

These problems can usually be solved by the founder

- putting the stock into a trust,
- issuing nonvoting stock, or
- always keeping enough stock to stay in control.

STOCK IN TRUST

Only gifts of a "present interest" can benefit from the $10,000 annual exclusion. A present interest is an "unrestricted right to immediate use, possession, or enjoyment of property or the income from property." [Reg. 25.2503–3(b)]. If the stock is put in trust, and represents a future interest (the beneficiary can only get benefits from the trust in future years), the $10,000 annual exclusion is lost. The goal then is to convert the gift into a gift of a present interest under section 2503. The use of a so-called *Crummey* provision can accomplish this goal. This provision arises from the case of *Crummey* v. *Commissioner* (397 F.2d 82; CA–9, 1968). A *Crummey* trust is one in which a beneficiary has the right to demand distributions from the trust in the same year in which the gift is made to the trust. That right to demand distributions makes the gift of stock to such a trust a present interest eligible for the exclusion. The IRS has indicated in Revenue Ruling 73–405 that it will recognize the *Crummey* powers provision as creating a present interest for gift tax purposes, even if the right to demand distribution cannot be practically exercised because the minor beneficiary has no appointed guardian.

LIMITATIONS

Lifetime gifts alone can seldom fulfill the goals of the privately held business owner. This is simply a matter of the relatively small amount of the $10,000 annual exclusion and the fact that most businesses are worth more than the $600,000 exemption equivalent. Even when these amounts are doubled for a married taxpayer, many business owners still cannot escape the unified transfer tax. Because of this, gifts—in an overall financial plan to transfer the stock of a privately held business—are used in combination with other methods.

COMBINATIONS

The principal goal of using gifts in combination with other transfer tools is to shift income to lower-bracket family members and to allow the future appreciation of the privately held business to accrue to the younger shareholders, while reducing the elders' estate.

On the other hand, the owners of the business, although desiring that the transfer tools be put in place, do not want to negate their ability to control and run the business' operations during their lifetime or before their voluntary retirement.

Following are some tools, which, when properly used in conjunction with a gift program, are capable of achieving these goals of the business owner: (1) defeating the estate and gift taxes, (2) transferring control of the business, and (3) retaining control for the owner during his lifetime or until he retires. But be careful: not all of the tools are designed to achieve all of the goals.

GIFTS AND INSTALLMENT SALES

The use of an installment sale of stock in conjunction with a gift program can freeze the value of the gifted property. If the owner's stock interest in the privately held business has appreciated significantly, the use of the installment method is tax-wise, especially if the business has good future prospects or property used in the business (such as land) will continue its appreciation.

If the purchasers of the stock are cash-poor in any year, the annual gift tax exclusion can be used to allow the seller to forgive up to $10,000 per year in installment payments from the buyers (that is, the buyer would not have to pay the amount forgiven). That's because if property is exchanged for less than its full value, the deficit between its fair market value and its price is regarded as a gift from the seller to the buyer. Here's how it works:

> Joe Owner controls 100 percent, or $200,000 of Company X stock. Over a 10-year period, Joe could gift the stock to his two sons incurring no gift tax liability. Or he could sell the stock on the installment method, with $10,000 payments over 10 years, utilizing the gift tax exclusion to forgive payments in years the sons were unable to make payments. A word of caution: the forgiveness should not be assumed or evidenced in the installment note. The IRS could regard the entire sale as a gift in the year the sale is made if it is.

What is accomplished is that the property is out of the owner's estate, and the future appreciation accrues to the heirs. Keep in mind that the spousal gift-splitting provisions could allow up to $20,000 per year per donee to be transferred to the two sons, or $40,000 of stock per year. If used in combination with an installment sale without any forgiveness, a substantial amount of a business can be transferred over a couple of years while ensuring the owner an income stream from the installment sale. The individual facts and circumstances of each privately held business owner's situation will dictate what percentages of the business should be transferred either by gift or sale.

GIFTS AND REDEMPTIONS

Use of the gift and installment sale method along with a complete redemption can also effect the transfer and freeze. Part of the owner's interest can be gifted and sold, while the balance can be redeemed by the corporation, effectively putting the donee/purchasers in control of the corporation as the sole shareholders. (See Chapter 14 for the correct use of redemptions for capital gains treatment to the owner redeeming stock.) This combination is especially effective if the future owners cannot afford to buy the entire business at once.

GIFTS AND RECAPITALIZATIONS

In Chapter 11, the valuation problems of a recapitalization are discussed, particularly the valuation of the common and preferred stock issued in the

recapitalization and the gift tax consequences attached to the valuation of
the common stock.

VALUATION OF GIFTS OF STOCK

The valuation of gifts of privately held stock is determined by the IRS
under the same principles applied to estate tax purposes (see Section
2512). However, this chapter is concerned with the gifting of minority
interests in stock that eventually add up to a controlling interest. In recognition of this fact, especially in a family business setting, the IRS in Revenue Ruling 81–253 (see Appendix B) has made it clear that it will not allow
discounts for gift tax purposes on gifts of minority interests, while such
minority discounts are allowable for estate tax purposes. Instead, for valuation purposes in determining a gift tax liability, the entire value of the
company is determined and then multiplied by the percentage of stock
gifted. (See also the *Albert C. Luce* case in Appendix C for a gift tax
valuation.)

CHARITABLE CONTRIBUTIONS AND DONATING
APPRECIATED PROPERTY

A corporation can deduct contributions or gifts made to or for the use of
exempt organizations in an amount up to 10 percent of its taxable income.
     Shareholders of a privately held corporation can make contributions
of stock and arrange to have the corporation redeem the shares from the
charitable organization without having the redemption proceeds taxed to
the shareholders.
     In the case of *Palmer* (62 TC 684; 1974), the controlling shareholder of
a privately held corporation donated stock to a charitable organization and
then caused the corporation to redeem the shares. The IRS claimed that
the contribution was actually a redemption of the shares by the shareholder, followed by a donation of the proceeds to the charity. The Tax
Court disagreed and let the transaction stand as it was. The shareholder
got the charitable contribution and was not taxed on the proceeds.
     Under Revenue Ruling 78–197, the IRS announced that it agreed with
the *Palmer* decision and would treat the arrangement as a gift of the stock
to the charitable organization. But caution is advised: the charitable orga-

nization must not be under an obligation to sell the shares back to the privately held corporation. If it is, redemption income will result to the donor.

Whether the corporation or the shareholder should make the contribution depends upon which is in the higher tax bracket and can make the best use of the deduction.

As mentioned before, gifts of appreciated property are tax-wise because they remove the appreciation from the donor's estate. Charitable contributions of appreciated property, such as stock in a privately held corporation, yield two tax benefits to the owner: (1) the estate tax reduction, and (2) an income tax deduction [see Section 170(e)]. The following example shows why this deduction has special additional income tax advantages:

> Jill Owner wants to make a $10,000 gift to charity. One share of stock in her privately held business has a basis of $2,000, but a fair market value of $10,000. Jill can make the $10,000 contribution in one of two ways:
>
> 1. She can sell the stock for $10,000 and give the proceeds to charity. If Jill is in the 50 percent tax bracket, she pays about $1,600 in capital gains tax. Her total tax savings is about $3,400—the $5,000 in taxes saved by deducting the $10,000 contribution minus the $1,600 paid in capital gains.
> 2. She can give the appreciated stock directly to the charity. The charity sells the stock and realizes a full $10,000 contribution. Jill gets a $10,000 deduction saving $5,000 in income taxes. Jill is in-pocket $1,600 more with this alternative. Why? Because the appreciated value (the $8,000 profit) escapes taxation when the stock is gifted to charity.

VALUATION OF CHARITABLE CONTRIBUTIONS

The larger the value determined for the contributed closely held stock, the larger the deduction. If this can be accomplished, fine and dandy. But be aware that the IRS could come right back with that same larger contribution valuation as past evidence of valuation for estate and gift tax purposes.

The following are recent cases in which the stock of closely held corporations were valued for the purpose of charitable contributions: *Paul W. Learner* (45 T.C.M. 922; 1983), *William E. Gatlin* (44 T.C.M. 945; 1982), and *Estate of Thomas L. Kaplin* (44 T.C.M. 660; 1982).

VALUATION OF STOCK CONTRIBUTED TO CHARITY: REPORTING REQUIREMENTS

As the example above shows, the amount of the charitable contribution deduction is equal to the fair market value of the property contributed on the date the contribution is made. In the case of stock of a privately held corporation, there are certain requirements a taxpayer must meet in order to substantiate the value of the stock claimed for the deduction. These requirements amount to a lot of paperwork.

The requirements must be met if the value claimed for the closely held stock is more than $10,000 ($5,000 in the case of all other property).

The main requirement is that the donor must obtain a formal appraisal from an independent appraiser to substantiate the value of the stock. The appraiser must submit to the taxpayer two documents: the appraisal itself and an appraisal summary. The appraisal summary must be attached to the income tax return on which the deduction is claimed.

The appraiser must be independent of the donor and the charitable organization and must be qualified to value stock in the particular closely held corporation.

The appraisal report cannot be made earlier than 60 days before the charitable contribution is made and must contain certain information describing the property contributed, the method by which the property was appraised, and the qualifications of the appraiser (see Regulation 1.170A–13T). (See Chapter 16 for penalties for incorrect appraisals.)

CHAPTER 16
Other Things You Should Know

This chapter addresses a number of issues not previously discussed, but important still to the valuation process.

THE IRS AND POSSIBLE VALUATION PENALTIES

The Tax Reform Act of 1984 gives the IRS a new club with which to punish taxpayers who might misvalue property, including a closely held business.

Valuation Overstatements (Section 6659)

If your income tax bill is underpaid by $1,000 or more because of an overvaluation of property, you can be hit with a penalty. Worse yet, the penalty is not deductible. The overvaluation must be 150 percent or more greater than the value finally determined to be correct. For example, if you claimed a $12,000 value and the IRS determines the value to be only $5,000 (240 percent more), you are hung for a penalty. There are two ways to determine the penalty, depending on the type of property involved.

Other Than Charitable Deduction Property

Ratio of claimed valuation to correct valuation (%)	Penalty percentage (%)
150 to 200	10
Over 200 to 250	20
Over 250	30

NOTE: An overstatement of adjusted basis caused by overvaluation (for example, valuation of property in an estate) is treated like a valuation overstatement.

Charitable Deduction Property. Penalty is a 30 percent addition to tax underpayment due to the valuation overstatement.
Charitable deduction property is any property contributed by an indi-

vidual, closely held corporation, or personal service corporation for which a charitable contribution has been claimed.

Example

> The IRS determines that the taxpayer owes an additional $2,000 in taxes after a downward adjustment of the property value claimed as a contribution deduction. The penalty is $600 (30 percent of $2,000).

Valuation Understatement (Section 6660)

The penalty applies if

1. The understatement is made on a federal estate or gift tax return,
2. Because of the understatement, there is a tax underpayment of $1,000 or more, and
3. The value of the property claimed on the gift or estate tax return is 66⅔ percent or less than the value finally determined.

NOTE: The penalty can be waived by the IRS if the taxpayer can show a reasonable basis for the claimed value and that the claim was made in good faith.

The penalty, which is based on the amount of tax underpayment, is determined as follows:

Ratio of claimed valuation to correct valuation	Penalty percentage (%)
Over 50%, but not over 66 ⅔%	10
Over 40%, but less than 50%	20
Less than 40%	30

Example

> Jill's $42,000 valuation on a gift tax return ends up being $100,000 (42 percent of correct value) after an IRS audit. This causes an additional tax of $25,000. Jill's penalty is $5,000 (20 percent of $25,000).

IMPLIED VALUATION PENALTIES IMPOSED BY THE COURTS

In Chapter 9 (under "How Big a Discount?"), it is stated that some appraisers take the position that since the IRS almost always will seek a higher value for the privately held business for tax purposes (except in the case of charitable contributions) it makes sense to contend a higher than justified discount in expectation that the compromise figure will be reached in negotiations with the IRS or in the courts.

But be forewarned: the Tax Court has let it be known that it is becoming increasingly fed up with this tactic, on the part of the taxpayer and the IRS. In order to stem this practice, the Tax Court sounded a warning in the case of *Buffalo Tool and Die Manufacturing Co.* v. *Commissioner* (74 T.C. 441; 1980), in which it stated:

> We are convinced that the valuation issued is capable of resolution by the parties themselves through an agreement which will reflect a compromise Solomon-like adjustment, thereby saving the expenditure of time, effort, and money by the parties and the Court—a process not likely to produce a better result. Indeed, each of the parties should keep in mind that, in the final analysis, the Court may find the evidence of valuation by one of the parties sufficiently more convincing than that of the other party, so that the final result will produce a significant financial defeat for one or the other, rather than a middle-of-the-road compromise which we suspect each of the parties expects the court to reach. If the parties insist on our valuing any or all of the assets, we will. We do not intend to avoid our responsibilities but instead seek to administer them more efficiently—a factor that has become increasingly important in light of the constantly expanding workload of the court.

The Tax Court's threat is clear: if the IRS and taxpayers continue jamming the courts with cases that should be resolved through negotiation, the court will make one or the other pay the total price. No compromise: one party's valuation will be thrown out, and the other's accepted as is. This either/or approach to contending valuations is not universally accepted by all the members of the Tax Court. The Tax Court in *Estate of Mark S. Gallo* (see Appendix C) reserved the right to itself to pick apart each of the contending valuations and fashion its own from their parts *a la carte*.

When contending with the IRS over valuation issues, don't count on the help of some third party, such as the courts, to reach a compromise. Be able to document and justify your valuation methods and amounts, and then fight like a wildcat for them. If you don't, you might catch the Tax Court in a foul mood and suffer the consequences.

UNBOOKED ASSETS AND LIABILITIES TO BE PAID OR RECEIVED OVER TIME

Sometimes the financial statements made available to the appraiser do not contain certain assets or liabilities. As a result, the book value of the company is overstated or understated. The profit and loss statement may suffer the same disability because of the unbooked asset or liability. For the purposes of the appraisal, such items should be booked to correct both the book value and the earnings. Usually, the items not reflected on the statements are contingent assets and liabilities. These must be estimated and reflected.

What about assets or liabilities that will be paid or received over some time period in the future—either fixed (say 5, 10, or 15 years) or variable (when the president of the company dies)? The amount, as well as the time frame, can be fixed or variable. In any event, reasonable assumptions must be made when the amount or time frame is uncertain and the contingent items must be reduced to a single hard number or, if appropriate, a range of numbers.

Following are some examples of what is likely to occur in practice.

Royalty Income (An Asset)

If the company is entitled to receive royalty income, the value of the income can be determined by preparing a schedule as follows:

Licensee name	Years left	Anticipated annual royalty	Present value factor*	Present value of future royalty
Luckey Co.	3	$100,000	2.4437	$244,370
Star Inc.	6	23,638	4.2305	100,000
Batt Co.	3	22,765	2.4437	55,630
Total present value of future royalties				$400,000
Less: taxes at 50%				(200,000)
After-tax value of future royalties				$200,000

*Select a present value factor, usually about the same percentage rate as prime or the before-tax rate of return earned by the company.

Deferred Compensation to Executives (A Liability)

A common nonbooked liability is the liability to key executives (or their heirs) that will become payable down the road, pursuant to a nonqualified deferred compensation agreement. Here is a sample of a typical schedule taken from an actual client's file covering two executives:

Details	Sam Goget	George Charger
1. Age	62	59
2. Deferred compensation per year before tax	$250,000	$100,000
3. Beginning payment date	Age 65	Age 65
4. Life expectancy for men who attain age 65	15 years	15 years
5. Number of years before executives reach age 65	3	6
6. Total number of years from present to end of life expectancy	18	21
7. Present value annuity factors for 18 and 21 years, respectively at 11%	7.7016	8.0751
8. Present value annuity factor for the number of years before executives reach age 65	2.4437	4.2305
9. Net present value annuity factor (line 7 minus line 8)	5.2579	3.8446
10. Deferred compensation per year after-tax (50% tax rate)*	125,000	50,000
11. Present value of deferred compensation liabilities (line 9 times line 10)	$657,238	$192,230
Total deferred compensation liability		$849,468

*Always use the tax rate applicable at the time of the valuation; 50% was the tax rate when the above was prepared.

EIGHT-STEP PER-SHARE VALUATION APPROACH

Often, when two or more factors are used to value a business, it is easier to reduce each factor to a value per share. Then the factor can be weighted as desired to arrive at the final per-share fair market value. The following shows an easy and organized way to make the computations.

The eight steps summarize the case of *Skove* v. *United States*, Report of Special Commissioner to the Court of Claims, May 26, 1967. This is a *formula approach*, according to most commentators. This author calls it a *combination approach* (book value and earnings).

Step	Per Share
1. Adjusted book value	$49.18
2. Earnings—five-year average weighted in favor of most recent years	7.58
3. Dividends paid—five latest years considered. Last year used.	1.00
4. Ratios—6 principal price-earning customers used at about 11 times earnings. $7.58 × 11 =	78.00
5. Dividend yield—principal customers based on average market prices $1 capitalized at 5.4%	18.50
6. Weighting of factors	

Factor	As above	Weight	Product
Earnings	$78.00	50%	$39.00
Dividend yield	18.50	30%	5.55
Book value	49.18	20%	9.83

Statistical fair market value	54.38

Less discounts:

7. Lack of marketability	15%	
8. Minority interest	10%	
Total	25%	

$54.38 × 25% =	13.58
Fair market value	$40.80

HOW TO TEST THE VALUATION RESULT

Often, logic alone dictates that the valuation is too high or too low. The appraiser must take another look. However, it is difficult to explain unsupported logic or a gut feeling to an adversary on the other side of the table, the IRS, or the courts.

There is a practical way to test a high or low valuation. The liquidation value of a business is the floor value of any valuation. No matter what method or combination of methods is involved, if it causes the valuation to dip below liquidation value, the result can be disregarded. So the mission becomes to determine liquidation value, and that becomes fair market value.

NOTE: At best, liquidation value is an estimated figure. It is determined by estimating what the amount of cash in hand would be if every asset on the company's balance sheet was sold. For this purpose, cash can mean "cash and notes." All the liabilities of the company and the cost of liquidating each asset (appraiser fees, real estate fees, brokerage commissions, legal and accounting fees, and so on) then must be subtracted from the total cash received to determine the net liquidation value.

If net liquidation is the floor—the test for a low valuation—is there a way to test the ceiling—a high valuation? Yes. Something a client told this author after returning from a valuation seminar provides a crude but effective explanation of the method. He said that the seminar instructor, with tongue in cheek, said this about the buyer's viewpoint: "I don't care what the seller wants for the business. The selling price is not all that important. Just let me set the terms." And those terms will depend upon how much cash the buyer has in hand. Those "terms" determine how the balance of the price is to be paid: amount of payments, over what period of time, interest rate, and so on. The point is that if the buyer can meet the terms (i.e., make the payments), the price isn't too high.

On the other hand, if the payments cannot be made out of the cash flow of the business being bought, the price is too high, or the terms forcing the high payments are too steep, or both. When valuing a business, one way to look at the transaction is through the eyes of a willing buyer. It is a three-step process:

1. Set down the most likely price and terms.
    a. Price
    b. Terms
        i. Amount down
        ii. Number of months or years to pay
        iii. Rate of interest
2. Make a cash flow projection considering the after-tax profit of the business being bought.
3. Vary the price, terms, and cash flow projections. Usually, at least three variations are required—best, most likely, and worst case.

Each projection should be carried out for as many years as is necessary to show that the business can (or cannot) meet the required payments and pay off the balance due.

Following is a sample taken from an actual client file. The client was trying to determine whether he could meet the payments for a proposed $3,000,000 purchase price. Here are projections for the first four years:

Projections for	Year 1	Year 2	Year 3	Year 4
Operating income (A)	$1,260,000	$1,050,000	$1,196,000	$1,242,000
Interest expense				
To seller (B)	217,879	187,256	153,257	115,510
To bank (C)	315,000	295,504	287,617	273,437
Total interest	532,879	482,760	440,874	388,947
Taxable income	727,121	567,240	755,126	853,053
Less: income tax (D)*	363,560	283,620	377,563	426,526
Net income (E)	363,561	283,620	377,563	426,527
Add: depreciation	100,000	100,000	100,000	100,000
Net cash available (F)	463,561	383,620	477,563	526,527
Principal to seller (B)	277,886	308,509	342,508	380,255
Principal to bank (C)	$ 185,675	$ 75,111	$ 135,055	$ 146,272

1. Actually, six projections were made using various assumptions. The above projection was considered the most likely.

2. The buyer, our client, was buying only the assets of the seller. The purchase price was $2,200,000. The terms were no money down, 72 equal monthly payments including principal and interest with interest at 10.5 percent per annum on the unpaid balance. Our client is a leader in the industry and is very substantial; thus the no-money down terms.

3. It was estimated that a $3,000,000 loan was needed from the bank to finance the additional sales volume. The bank agreed to renew the loan as needed at a floating prime to be adjusted every three months. The above projection was prepared using a 10.5 percent (prime was 9.5 percent at the time) per annum interest rate on the unpaid balance. The projection assumes that the "Principal to Bank" (The bottom line of the projection) would reduce the principal balance due to the bank.

4. Every cash-flow projection must arrive at net income after taxes.

5. In order to arrive at Net Cash Available, depreciation must be added back. Under ordinary circumstances, amounts required for capital expenditures (buildings, plant, equipment) would be subtracted at this point. In this case, there is no provision for capital expenditures because our client could easily absorb all of the purchased increased sales in its present plant and equipment, which is already in place, by running an additional shift.

*(Same as handwritten on page 211)

The preceding projections show that the $2,200,000 purchase price passed the valuation test. But take another look at the numbers and recognize that the purchase really required a $5,200,000 investment (counting the $3,000,000 bank loan). Only the willingness of the bank to go along with an old customer made this purchase possible.

The ceiling valuation amount, in the practical sense, is the highest amount that will enable the company to pay for itself over a reasonable period of time out of its available cash flow. One caveat: approximately 20 percent to 40 percent of the available cash flow should be kept as a reserve for unforeseen contingencies. This is particularly true when buyers are buying a new business that will be their one and only business. If the buyer has an existing business that can subsidize any shortfall in the cash flow of the purchased business, the contingency reserve can be narrowed and in some cases, even eliminated.

OTHER FACTORS THAT CAN AFFECT PRICE (VALUATION)

Suppose that the fair market value has been determined using the appropriate methods as detailed in this book. Here are some factors that can raise or lower the price in an actual negotiation between a real buyer and a real seller:

Leverage vs. Cash

An all-cash transaction almost always produces a lower price. Installment sales should yield a higher price: the longer the term, assuming a market rate of interest, the higher the price is likely to be. Another general rule to keep in mind is that the more leveraged the transaction, the higher the purchase price.

Security to Seller

Often the seller does not want all cash. Why? All cash can cause a higher tax bill. So the seller wants two things: first, to string the payments out for a designated period of time, and, second, to have the maximum security possible to collateralize the note received for the noncash balance. The collateral might include the buyer's personal signature, the stock being purchased, or other assets of the buyer. As a rule, the greater the security, the lower the purchase price (value of the business). Put another way, the greater the amount of cash or security at the time of closing, the greater the discount on the valuation of the business.

Form of Sale

When the business is appraised for the purposes of sale, the form of the sale effects the ultimate price. There are two reasons for this: the tax effect and the assumption of liabilities. There are two basic forms (methods) of selling a corporate business: sell the stock (assume 100 percent) or sell the assets. Which method is the best way to buy a particular business for tax reasons is an important and complex subject and must be explored in-depth with the help of a tax expert.

In general, a sale of stock is preferred by sellers because (1) they simply pay capital gains tax on their profits, (2) all corporate liabilities are assumed by the buyer as the new owner of the corporation, and (3) they do not get taxed at the corporate level for depreciation recapture (ordinary income) when the corporation sells the assets.

On the other hand, buyers usually want to buy only the assets because they do not have to worry about corporate liabilities (known or unknown) and they get a new depreciation basis for the assets they purchase. Consider these facts together when there is an asset purchase: (1) sellers get stung for depreciation recapture (more taxes, reducing the after-tax profit) and (2) buyers can reduce their tax bill because of a larger depreciation deduction improving their after-tax cash flow. Both of these facts tend to increase the value of the company.

Amount of Interest

A rate of interest greater than the current market rate on the unpaid purchase price balance should lower the purchase price. The result is the opposite for a lower than market rate of interest. In general, if the interest rate charged is less than a current market rate, the tax law imputes a market rate of interest for tax purposes. This raises the interest and lowers the purchase price as far as the IRS is concerned.

The "How-Much-Can-I-Pay" Formula (or How to Test Your Valuation)

The highest price any buyer should pay for a business should be controlled by the "How-much-can-I-pay" formula. This formula tests the price according to these criteria: is it a price at which the company has the ability to pay for itself, with a reasonable cushion for a margin of error, over a reasonable length of time. The formula can be reduced to numbers by taking the following steps:

1. After the initial cash payment at closing, determine the time frame over which payments should be made (usually 5 to 10 years) to pay off the balance due. If the cash flow will not retire the debt, the price paid is too high or the terms must be renegotiated.
2. Project the net available cash for the time frame selected (see the cash-flow sample earlier in this chapter). Make sure to add back depreciation to the after-tax profit and deduct required capital expenditures.
3. Allow 60 percent to 80 percent of the net available cash for debt retirement, the balance (20 percent to 40 percent) should be considered a reserve to handle the cash needed for the unexpected.

AND IN CONCLUSION

Now you are ready to go forth and conquer the valuation world. And as I have been telling my clients for years, "If you have any questions—call me."

APPENDIX A
Sample Valuations

Example 1 A-1

APPENDIX A
CONTENTS

EXAMPLE 1
Valuation Methods: (1) Adjusted book value and
(2) combination of book value and earnings capacity.
Comment: Company earns *more* than a fair rate of return on its net operating assets.

EXAMPLE 2
Valuation Methods: combination of adjusted book
value and earning capacity.
Comments: Company earns *less* than a fair rate of return on its net operating assets and has substantial nonoperating assets.

EXAMPLE 3
Calculation method: Adjusted book value.
Comment: Company owns substantial real estate used in operations but does not make a fair rate of return on its net operating assets.

EXAMPLE 4
Valuation Methods: (1) Comparables and (2) net asset value.
Comment: This is a company that indeed can be valued (and, in fact, was valued) by the comparable method.

This appendix contains excerpts of valuations that the author has compiled. The excerpts have been chosen to illustrate certain valuation methods and particular circumstances. They should give you flavor of valuation techniques. They also act as reference material for sections in the main text of the book. Only selected portions of the valuations are shown, and they have been edited for book presentation and to protect the identity of the client.

Example 1

A-3

VALUATION EXAMPLE 1. ADJUSTED BOOK VALUE AND COMBINATION OF BOOK VALUE AND EARNING CAPACITY

(This company earns more than a fair rate of return on its net assets.)

Purpose of Valuation

This valuation has been requested to enable the 51 percent controlling shareholder brother of the company to buy out his 49 percent minority shareholder sister. The purpose of the valuation is to value the sister's interest to determine whether the brother's buyout offer of $2,205,000 is reasonable. The brother operates the business. The sister is a passive owner.

Brief Description of Company

The company (XYZ for our purposes), founded in the mid-1940s, is a metal stamping factory producing spare parts for radios, televisions, autos, appliances, and computers. Its largest customer, accounting for 10 percent in annual sales, is Sting computers. XYZ has four sales representatives to service its customers nationwide. It has one class of common stock (owned in the proportions stated above) and no preferred stock.

Methods of Valuation

The following two methods of valuation are used to determine the fair market value of XYZ:

Method I   Adjusted Book Value
Method II   Combination of Book Value and Earning Capacity

The higher amount produced by either Method I or Method II is the fair market value of the company as of July 31, _____.

An updated version should be considered when current fiscal financial statements become available.

Method I: Adjusted Book Value. Method I considers assets that have appreciated in determining fair market value. The machine presses used by XYZ have fair market values that materially exceed their book values. Accordingly, the book value of the company is adjusted as follows:

Book value of assets as of 7/31/_____	(Exhibit 1)*	$3,034,923
Add: Fair market value of machine presses	$2,660,000	
Less: Book value of machine presses	(1,298,324)	1,361,676
Total Adjusted Book Value of Assets as of 7/31/_____		$4,396,599

    * Exhibit 1 is the balance sheet of XYZ and is not included in this book.

Method II: Combination of Book Value and Earning Capacity. Method II combines the earning capacity and book value of XYZ to determine the fair market value. In calculating the earning power of XYZ, net income should be adjusted, net of taxes, over a five-year period ended July 31, _____ to reflect the following facts:

1. Inventories are stated at cost under the last-in, first-out (LIFO) method of accounting. The LIFO method suggests that the higher-prices, current-year inventory purchases are still in ending inventory, resulting in a higher cost of goods sold. Consequently, net income should be adjusted to reflect inventory under the first-in, first-out method of accounting.
2. XYZ owns a 7 percent interest in two limited partnerships. Since the valuation is done on the earning power of *operating* assets, the losses generated by the limited partnerships should not be used in calculating net income.
3. For four years of the five years under review, the salary of John Winter, the president, remained somewhat consistent—ranging from $136,000 to $171,000. However, for year 2, his salary was $322,800. Net income for the period should be adjusted to reflect a more reasonable compensation amount.

(See Exhibit 3, which details the above three income statement adjustments.)

Example 1   **A-5**

Method II Computation		
Weighted average after-tax earnings (Exhibit 4)		$ 557,950
Weighted average annual net assets (Exhibit 5)	$2,483,934	
Fair rate of return	× 15%	372,590
Excess earnings attributed to goodwill		185,360
Capitalization rate of excess earnings		× 4
Capitalized excess earnings		741,440
Plus: book value of XYZ assets as of 7/31/__ (Exhibit 1)		$3,034,923
Fair market value of XYZ		$3,776,363

SUMMARY

Based on using the higher fair market value between Method I and Method II, the sister's interest can be valued at $2,154,334 ($4,396,599 × 49%). However, since XYZ is a privately-held company and her ownership interest is less than 50%, the initial value of her interest of $2,154,334 should be adjusted to reflect its lack of marketability as follows:

49% of fair market value of	$2,154,334
Discount factor (1—20%)	× 80%
Fair market value of 49% ownership interest	$1,723,467
Let's say	$1,725,000

NOTE

This valuation excludes two limited partnership interests owned by the company. When this is taken into consideration, the offer to purchase the sister's 49% interest in XYZ for $2,205,000 is reasonable and fair.

   It should also be pointed out that the price offered by the brother for the company's operations is viewed as a cash price (either lump sum or, more likely, a down payment and the balance to be paid over time plus a reasonable rate of interest on any unpaid balance). Any rate of interest lower than one point below prime would be considered a reduction of the price.

VALUATION OF GOODWILL

This valuation also contains a good example of calculating goodwill. Under the Method II computation, the weighted average of annual net assets is multiplied by a fair rate of return. The weighted average after-tax earnings of the company itself are then compared to that result and the difference is attributed to goodwill. The rate of return of XYZ was actually 22% ($557,950 divided by $2,483,934). The calculation for goodwill is another method of calculating the premium that should be attached to XYZ's value because it earns more than a fair rate of return on its adjusted book value.

EXHIBIT 3

Adjustments to Financial Statement Net Income for Five Years

	Year 1**	Year 2	Year 3	Year 4	Year 5
Net income (loss) (Exhibit 2)*	$265,709	$544,713	$622,648	$ (59,507)	$297,910
Excess of FIFO over LIFO	212,450	239,067	262,169	226,038	351,429
Partnership loss	—	—	63,622	532,460	100,000
Salary adjustment ($322,800–$160,000)	—	162,800	—	—	—
Total adjustments	212,450	401,867	325,791	758,498	451,429
Less tax effect	50%	50%	50%	50%	50%
	106,225	200,934	162,896	379,249	225,715
Total adjustments after tax effect	106,225	200,934	162,896	379,249	225,715
Net income after adjustments	$371,934	$745,647	$785,544	$319,742	$523,625

*Exhibit 2 is XYZ's Profit and Loss Statement, and is not included in this example.

**Year 1 is the most recent year.

EXHIBIT 4

Weighted Average of XYZ After-Tax Earnings for Five Years

Year	Weight	Adjusted after-tax earnings (Exhibit 3)	Total
1	3	$371,934	$1,115,802
2	2	745,647	1,491,294
3	2	785,544	1,571,088
4	1	319,742	319,742
5	1	523,625	523,625
			5,021,551
			÷ 9
Weighted average after-tax earnings			$ 557,950

EXHIBIT 5

Weighted Average of XYZ Book Value of Assets for Five Years

Year	Weight	Book value of assets	Total
1	3	$3,034,923	$ 9,104,769
2	2	2,769,214	5,538,428
3	2	2,224,501	4,449,002
4	1	1,601,852	1,601,852
5	1	1,661,359	1,661,359
			22,355,410
			÷ 9
Weighted average book value of assets			$ 2,483,934

Example 2   A-9

VALUATION EXAMPLE 2. COMBINATION METHOD OF ADJUSTED BOOK VALUE AND EARNING CAPACITY

(This company earns less than a fair rate of return on its net operating assets.)

Purpose of Valuation

This valuation determines the fair market value of 48 shares (representing an 18.25 percent interest) of J-R Tool Inc.'s common stock as of December 31, 198_____ .

The 48 shares are in a trust for numerous grandchildren. The shares will be distributed to the grandchildren upon termination of the trust in one year, on December 31, 198_____ .

The valuation involves a small minority interest in a corporation that has a rate of return on its operating assets below a fair or industry average rate.

Brief Description of Company

J-R Tool was founded in the mid 1940s. It is a tool and die/metal stamping job shop producing metal parts tailored to specific customer needs.

J-R Tool has historically used a high percentage of its profits to purchase nonoperating assets such as Treasury bills, certificates of deposit, and marketable securities. Appropriate adjustments are made for these assets of the business that are not being used in operations.

There is one class of common stock and no preferred stock. A 32 percent block of the common stock (from which the 18.25 percent interest comes) is held in trust for 28 grandchildren of the owner/founder (now deceased). The owner/founder's son owns 17 percent of the stock. The remaining 51 percent of the stock of J-R Tool is owned by 12 individuals whose ownership interests range between 4 and 8 percent.

Method of Valuation

A combination of the earnings capacity and adjusted book value methods is used to determine the fair market value of J-R Tool, Inc. as of December 31, 198_____ . This methodology requires several steps.

Step 1. Determination of adjusted book value.

	Operating assets	Nonoperating assets	Total
Book value (Exhibit 5)	$1,033,584	$1,035,288	$2,068,872
Adjustments			
Building (Note 1)	50,000		50,000
Securities (Note 2)		(2,400)	(2,400)
Adjusted book value	$1,083,584	$1,032,088	$2,116,472

Note 1: Management estimates that the value of real estate is $50,000 greater than its book value.

Note 2: The $2,400 downward adjustment reflects management's determination that the actual market value of the marketable securities as of 12/31/8_ was $2,400 less than book value. The actual market value of these non-operating assets should be redetermined for any purchase of stock after the valuation date.

Step 2. Determination of the fair market value of operating assets.

Weighted average of earnings from operating assets (Exhibit 4)		$ 107,615
Adjusted book value of operating assets	$1,083,584	
Fair rate of return including risk (Note)	× 18%	195,045
Negative earnings capacity		(87,430)
Capitalized at 25% ($87,430 × 4)		$(349,720)
Add: adjusted book value as of 12/31/8_		1,083,584
Value before discounts		$ 733,864

Note: The fair rate of return is the sum of two elements—a return available in the market-place as of December 31, 198_ without much risk in the range of 13%, plus an additional rate of 5% for the risk inherent in the business in which the operating assets are used.

An easy way to understand the theory of earnings capacity is to ask *how much would someone pay to earn $107,615 considering the type of investment that requires an 18 percent return because of the risk?* The answer would be $597,861 (because $597,681 × 18 percent equals $107,615). This valuation method is commonly used to value securities, like long-term bonds. However, the $733,864 value is preferred because if the earnings capacity had been positive, as opposed to the negative figure, it would have been capitalized at 25 percent. This method is used to value a going business.

Example 2 A-11

Step 3. Discount for general lack of marketability.
The current economic environment of the tool and die/metal stamping industry is not on solid ground. A company's continued earnings stream and ability to increase sales depend on whether the manufacturer can satisfy its customers' demands for "state of the art" products.

Many of J-R Tool's customers are, or will soon be, advanced technology companies. These "high-tech" companies need nonmetal products to use for computers, circuits, semiconductors, and so on.

If J-R Tool does not update and convert its equipment to facilitate plastic injection molding and powered metal processing, the company will subsequently lose business to its competition. In fact, sales to one of its major customers have already sharply declined, because J-R Tool does not have the capacity to supply parts for that customer's new typewriters.

Considering the economic environment, would a willing purchaser pay the value before discounts as shown for a tool and die/metal stamping company that has machinery and processes that are not up-to-date? It would be safe to assume that a reasonable purchaser would pay only a lesser value.

The buyer, if in fact one could be found to buy this type of business in this uncertain business climate for tool and die/metal stamping companies, would be able to negotiate a discount for general lack of marketability.

Value before discounts	$733,864
Discount for general lack of marketability—20%	146,773
Fair market value of operating assets	$587,091

Comment: In some cases the fair market value of a business as an ongoing operating concern is less than its liquidating value. If liquidating value is higher than the fair market value, it should be used. No attempt has been made herein to determine a liquidating value, which requires an extensive investigation and analysis to determine the losses that would be incurred in selling the assets and dismantling the going operations.

Operating assets (as above)	$ 587,091
Nonoperating assets (as adjusted above)	1,032,888
Total fair market value	$1,619,979
Shares to be valued	× 18.25%
Fair market value of these shares ($1,619,979 × .1825)	$ 295,646
Let's say	$ 300,000

Taking into consideration the data made available and the company's general lack of marketability, a $300,000 offer to purchase an 18.25 percent interest in J-R Tool would be fair and reasonable if the entire company was being sold (100 percent of all stock). However, if only the minority interest were to be the subject of the sale, an additional substantial discount (perhaps has high as 33 percent) for such a minority interest should be considered.

EXHIBIT 3

J-R Tool, Inc.

Adjustments to Financial Statement Net Income for the Years Ending December 31, 198_

	Year 1**	Year 2	Year 3	Year 4	Year 5
Net income (Exhibit 2)*	$189,953	$76,979	$197,777	$181,153	$253,566
Nonoperating income					
Interest	56,672	70,632	96,718	43,386	39,250
Dividends	30,875	17,799	7,026	5,402	5,319
Gain on sale of marketable securities	6,749	4,288	—	—	—
Total nonoperating income	94,296	92,719	103,744	48,788	44,569
Less—dividend exclusion	(26,244)	(15,129)	(5,972)	(4,592)	(4,521)
Net taxable nonoperating income	68,052	77,590	97,772	44,196	40,048
Approximated tax rate	50%	20%	50%	50%	50%
Approximated tax on nonoperating income	34,026	15,518	48,886	22,098	20,024
Total nonoperating income after-tax effect	60,270	77,201	54,858	26,690	24 545
Net income minus nonoperating income	$129,683	$ (222)	$142,919	$154,463	$229 021

*Exhibit 2, The Profit and Loss Statement of J-R Tool, Inc., is not shown.

**Year 1 is the most recent year.

EXHIBIT 4

Weighted Average of J-R Tool, Inc. Net Income for the Five Years Ended December 31, 198_

Year	Weight	Net income minus nonoperating income (Exhibit 3)	Total
1	5	$129,683	$ 648,415
2	4	(222)	(888)
3	3	142,919	428,757
4	2	154,463	308,926
5	1	229,021	229,021
	15		1,614,231
			÷ 15
Weighted average of net income			$ 107,615

EXHIBIT 5

J-R Tool, Inc.
Book Value of Operating Assets for the Year Ended December 31, 198_

December 31, 198_ book value of assets (Exhibit 1)*		$2,068,872
Less nonoperating assets:		
Cash and equivalents	601,510	
Certificates of deposit and treasury bills	205,903	
Marketable securities	276,584	
CSV of life insurance	51,291	
	1,135,288	
Cash needed for operations	(100,000)	
Total nonoperating assets	1,035,288	
		(1,035,288)
Total December 31, 198_ book value of operating assets		$1,033,584

*Exhibit 1, the Balance Sheet, is not shown.

Example 3 A-15

VALUATION EXAMPLE 3: ADJUSTED BOOK VALUE METHOD

The following valuation is unique because it calls for the valuation of a 50 percent interest in a privately held business. Is the shareholder's controlling interest glass half empty or half full? Does he control the company? If he does, a premium attaches to his stock. If he doesn't, a discount for not having control is in order. Since the purpose of the valuation is determination of estate tax liability, the shareholder takes the position that it is not a controlling interest and is therefore entitled to a discount.

This example contains a large excerpt of the valuation text but very little of the supporting financial data. Aside from the discount issue, you should be aware of several other unusual points considered in the valuation text:

1. The method of valuation selected and the reasons therefore
2. The larger discount given to the nonvoting common stock over the voting stock, and again, the reasons therefore
3. Why the value of the common stock was reduced by the par value of the preferred stock rather than the fair market value of the preferred
4. Treatment of the contingent liability for compliance with EPS regulations
5. Treatment of the after-tax effect for various adjustments, and in particular, the difference in after-tax treatment between fixed assets to be retained in the business and fixed assets to be sold

Purpose of Valuation

The purpose of this valuation is to determine the fair market value of the 50 percent interest in two classes of common stock of Ewing Enterprises, Inc., owned by Jason Ewing at the date of his death April 15, 1986. The results of the valuation are to be used to determine the estate tax value under section 2031 of the Internal Revenue Code.

Brief Description of Business

Ewing Enterprises was founded in the late 1920s by the father of the present owners. It began as a gasoline and heating oil wholesaler and expanded to acquiring and building service stations. Ewing Enterprises sells its products primarily through its service stations and ARCO and Shell stations. It also sells products to wholesale and commercial accounts through card-lock sales outlets identified as "Gulf Goods."

The company has made numerous real estate investments for petroleum and nonpetroleum use. It still owns property not being used in business operations. The deceased was co-owner with his brother, Cliff Ewing, until his death.

As of April 15, 1986, Ewing Enterprises, Inc.'s capital structure consisted of the following:

Class	Authorized shares	Outstanding shares
Class A—voting common stock	25,000	18,538
Class B—nonvoting common stock	25,000	18,538
Nonvoting preferred stock	3,000	2,596

On April 15, 1986, Jason Ewing owned 9,269 shares of Class A Voting Common Stock and 9,269 shares of Class B Nonvoting Common Stock. His brother Richard Ewing owns the remaining shares of the common stock.

Ewing Enterprises, Inc. experienced a substantial operating loss in 1985. The major oil companies have been highly price competitive in Ewing's dominant marketing areas. The outlook for the near term indicates that this competitive condition will remain unchanged.

Ewing Enterprises, Inc.'s operations may be divided into three categories:

1. retail service stations
2. wholesale operations
3. convenience store operations

The bulk of its operations is in the retail service station business.

Outlook for the Oil Industry

U.S. gasoline demand is projected to fall some 1 percent per year for the rest of the century.

Example 3 A-17

After the 1973 Arab oil embargo, the consumer's mind was on the availability, and marketing strategy was simply securing supplies. With current abundant supplies, the consumer is back in the driver's seat. A consumer can be selective with regard to price, product quality, service, and convenience. Accordingly, the marketing strategy has gone through a period of dramatic changes. Retailers have been forced to achieve cost-effectiveness and meet customer's needs for quality and convenience.

With price controls on gasoline and many long-term oil supply relationships gone, competition at the retail level is intense. In January 1981, President Reagan abolished price controls on domestic gasoline, allocations of crude products in time of scarcity, and the entitlement programs. This initially may have helped some independents, who turned quickly to the noncontract market for supplies to compete effectively with major integrated oil companies that were still tied to many long-established high-price contractual supply arrangements. However, with the drop in Saudi crude prices in March 1983 and with most of the other major integrated oil companies working out of their unfavorable contractual arrangements, the entire industry seems to be on an equal footing in 1986. This has hurt the independents, because some major integrated oil companies have operated their retail operations at a loss to compete with them. Major companies with oil and gas production profits can absorb these losses; the independents cannot and are vulnerable to being pushed out of business. Margins (the equivalent of gross profit in other commercial businesses) on gasoline and oil have narrowed due to this competitive pressure. As a result, cost-effectiveness has become the high priority in marketing.

In addition to cost-effectiveness, retailers are paying increased attention to customers' demand for products and convenience. Marketing techniques include self-service electronic credit using card-lock devices, multiproduct dispensers, and more convenient dispensers. Moves designed to appeal to customers' desire include the combination gas station–convenience outlet, offering such items as milk, bread, and other fast-moving convenient items. Many stations also are being remodeled to project a uniform image quickly identifiable by brand-oriented customers, and stations are being equipped to emphasize the complete car-care concept. Innovation and change has become routine.

In summary, cost-effectiveness and appeal to consumer demand for products and convenience are the keys to survival in the highly competitive oil retailing environment.

Problems of Retail Service Stations

The primary problem in the retailing service station operations for Ewing Enterprises, Inc. has been the poor profit margin in the marketplace. As the major oil companies continue to battle for market share in its operating areas, profit margins probably will remain at low levels and only the most effective marketers will survive.

In 1985 and 1986, company management took various steps to reduce operating costs. Five unprofitable units were closed in 1985. In spite of these steps, operating costs remain high in relation to the gross profit potential. In addition, the company tried to reduce the volume of petroleum products purchased on an unbranded basis. Late in 1985, efforts were made with Shell, Mobil, Chevron, and Texaco to brand many of their service outlets. However, management has not been successful in this endeavor. Management intends to continue these steps in an attempt to reduce costs and improve profit margins; in addition, it will strive to reduce general and administrative overhead costs.

The wholesale operations have not received much management attention in the past. The company lacks information on its competitive price condition in relation to its competitors. Sales volume was down by 136 percent in 1985 (compared to 1984).

Management does not anticipate any significant progress in wholesale sales growth.

Ewing Enterprises, Inc. has only one convenience store. The store has experienced inadequate sales due to poor promotional, merchandising, and marketing efforts, However, there have been positive changes in recent months because of new merchandising and promotional programs. Company management has determined that the company should not be involved in the convenience store business in the near future. Management is attempting to lease the existing store operation to an operating chain.

In summary, Ewing Enterprises, Inc.'s future plan is to control costs and to meet consumer demands for products and convenience.

Analysis of Financial Statements

The following sources of information were used and relied upon for the valuation:

Example 3   **A-19**

1. Audited financial statements of Ewing Enterprises, Inc. for the periods ended December 31, 1981 through December 31, 1985.
2. Unaudited and unadjusted financial statements for the four-month period ended April 30, 1986.
3. *U.S. Industrial Outlook for 1986.*
4. Standard and Poor's *Industry Surveys.*
5. *Industrial Norms and Key Business Ratios, 1985–1986,* Dun and Bradstreet.
6. *Mergers and Acquisitions* magazine.
7. *Almanac of Business and Industrial Financial Ratios.*
8. Information furnished by management of the company.
9. Other sources as cited in the body of this report.

Financial and statistical information from the above sources is deemed to the reliable. However, we make no representation as to our sources' accuracy or completeness and have accepted their information without further verification.

We reviewed audited financial statements for the years ended December 31, 1981 through 1985. The following observations are made concerning the company's position:

- Total assets have not increased during the period from December 31, 1981 to December 31, 1985. Total assets were $4,211,964 on December 31, 1981 and $4,299,674 on December 31, 1985. This tends to indicate that the company has not been growing during this period of time.
- Current assets have dropped significantly from $2,332,531 on December 31, 1981 to $1,462,066 on December 31, 1985. Current assets, as a percentage of total assets, have decreased from 55.38 percent in 1981 to 34.00 percent in 1985. On the other hand, fixed assets and investment in affiliates have increased from $2,782,806 on December 31, 1981 to $4,585,397 on December 31, 1985. This indicates that the company has been shifting its liquid assets to less liquid assets. Comparison of Ewing's Enterprises, Inc. to 1985–1986 industry ratios from Dun and Bradstreet indicates that the company's ratio of fixed assets to total assets is almost twice as large as the industry norm, while its current assets to total assets is just about 60 percent of the industry norm.
- Stockholders' equity has decreased slightly from $2,393,695 on December 31, 1981 to $2,312,743 on December 31, 1985. This indicates

that the company has not been profitable over the past several years. Its stockholders' equity to total assets as of December 31, 1985 (53.8 percent) compares favorably to the industry norm of 56.0 percent.

- Current liabilities have not changed significantly from $1,596,851 on December 31, 1981 to $1,279,457 on December 31, 1985, although current assets have dropped substantially over the same period.
- However, the industry norm for 1985 indicates that its current ratio of 1.14 in 1985 is within the lower industry quartile of 1.2.
- Net sales went up in 1982 but dropped back down to $38,120,188 in 1985, which is slightly higher than $35,702,248 in 1981. This indicates that the company has not increased its market share significantly.
- Its gross profit margin dropped from 8.08 percent in 1981 to 6.16 percent in 1982, with a steady improvement to 7.63 percent in 1985. This indicates that the company has been striving to improve cost-efficiency. However, the company still experienced operating losses in 1984 and 1985. The medium return on net worth for the lower industry quartile in 1985 was 5 percent.

In summary, the comparative financial analysis indicates the following:

- Limited sale growth has occurred over the past few years.
- The company has experienced poor profitability over the past few years. However, the poor profitability may be partially attributable to its relatively large amount of depreciation allowance from its high level of fixed asset investment in comparison to the industry norm.
- There are potential profits in the future, as the company's gross profit margin has improved modestly since 1982 in spite of competitive pressures.
- Even with a substantial investment in fixed assets, the company's ability to meet its current liabilities in 1985 remains adequate, as its current ratio of 1.14 is within the norm of the lower industry quartile of 1.2. Also, its stockholders' equity to total assets is close to that of the industry norm.
- Its asset composition deviates greatly from the industry norm, as its fixed asset investment is nearly twice as large as the industry norm in 1985. Economic goodwill might not be present due to the company's recent poor operating results. Nonetheless, its large investment in carefully selected real estate indicates a going business

Example 3 A-21

concern with a value over and above the book value reflected on the books of the business.

Specific Valuation Methods

We have considered four basic approaches toward valuing the 50 percent common stock ownership interest of Ewing Enterprises, Inc. as follows:

- net book value approach
- adjusted book value approach
- capitalized earnings approach
- market comparison approach

Selection of Valuation Techniques. We have considered all of the foregoing approaches and have selected the appropriate method to correspond to the specific circumstances of Ewing Enterprises, Inc. as of the valuation date. For various reasons discussed later, the value of Ewing Enterprises, Inc. has been determined on a going-concern basis with primary reliance on the adjusted net asset approach. Each method and the underlying philosophies are described in the following pages and considered in relation to the circumstances of the company.

Net Book Value Approach. The net book value approach (or *net equity method*) implies that a company is worth its accumulated retained earnings or deficit plus its original capitalization. There have been litigated cases where either the Internal Revenue Service or the taxpayer contended that the fair market value of stock approximated its book value. The courts in all such cases generally rejected the contention that book value approximated the fair market value of capital stock.

The primary reason the net book value approach is not relied upon as a good method of ascertaining the fair market value of Ewing Enterprises, Inc. is the substantial real estate owned by the company. The real estate has appreciated substantially and its fair market value is substantially higher than its original cost less accumulated depreciation.

Adjusted Book Value Approach One of the key inherent weaknesses of the net book value method, namely, that historical cost-based asset value may bear very little relationship to market value, is overcome in the adjusted net book value approach.

The adjusted book value method requires that all assets be evaluated to determine their true economic value. Fixed assets are appraised at a figure approximating their market value as opposed to depreciated cost.

This approach is used in cases (e.g., in bankruptcy proceedings) where the assets are actually to be liquidated following their acquisition. This method also is appropriate in those entities where economic goodwill is not present but whose assets are collectively employed in such a way as to produce a going concern and contain a value over and above what is recorded on the books of the business. This approach is applicable to companies having erratic or depressed earnings which are inadequate to provide a fair return on the value of the net tangibile assets employed. In theory, the value of all assets, less all outstanding liabilities, provides an indication of the fair market value of ownership equity.

In Revenue Ruling 59–60, the IRS also indicates that the net asset value can be the primary consideration for valuing closely held investment or real estate holding companies.

Because of the depressed earnings of Ewing Enterprises, Inc. from 1983 through 1985, coupled with its relatively large real estate holdings, we believe that the adjusted net book value approach should be relied upon for determining the fair market value of the company.

Capitalized Earnings Approach.   Conceptually, the capitalized earnings approach determines the fair market value of an ongoing business enterprise based on its earnings capacity. This approach is based on the theory that an investment (i.e., net tangible assets) will yield a return sufficient to recover its initial cost and to justly compensate the investor for the inherent risks of ownership. This approach is often used to arrive at a value for a company that reflects the company's goodwill due to its earnings in excess of the industry norm.

What constitutes a reasonable return on net tangible assets can best be answered by referring to Revenue Ruling 68–609, which states:

> The percentage of return on the average annual value of tangible assets used should be the percentage prevailing in the industry involved at the date of valuation

The median return on net worth for the gasoline service station industry as compiled by Dun and Bradstreet for 1985–1986 was 5 percent for the lower industry quartile. The median return on net worth of all companies in the sample was 17.5 percent.

From 1983 through 1985, Ewing Enterprises, Inc. experienced losses.

Example 3   **A-23**

Thus its past losses tend to indicate that the company does not have goodwill (i.e., excess earnings) that can be quantified currently. Although future earnings are to be used for earnings capitalization, past earnings are usually the guide for determining future earnings. In this regard, Revenue Ruling 59–60 states, "Prior earnings records usually are the most reliable guide as to the future expectancy." In view of past losses, the company's future earnings are uncertain. Accordingly, we believe that the capitalized earnings approach should not be relied upon to value the company, as the capitalization of losses would produce an unrealistic negative value.

Market Comparison Approach. The market comparison approach involves selecting public companies that are in the same or similar businesses and using their price-earnings multiples as a guide in determining the value of the subject company. Price-earnings multiples established in active trading represent the market's fair rates of return on the investment. They are considered as being reliable indicators of the fair capitalization rates for the subject company, as appropriately adjusted for the risk factors associated with the subject company.

Finding price-earnings multiples of comparable publicly traded companies is a more difficult task than might be imagined. Often, finding even one listed company comparable to a closely held company is no easy task. In fact, such a comparable company might not exist. Moreover, Ewing Enterprises, Inc. has been experiencing losses over the past years. Applying price-earnings multiples to Ewing Enterprises, Inc. would create a negative value to the company as a whole. Accordingly, using price-earnings multiples of publicly traded companies would not be meaningful.

Computations of Adjusted Net Asset. As indicated previously, we believe that the adjusted net asset approach should be relied upon in determining the value of Ewing Enterprises, Inc. This approach involves adjusting the company's net assets from a book value basis to an approximation of market. We made the following adjustments to the assets:

1. Convert investments and securities to approximate market value from cost. Some of the adjustments, for investments in privately held companies, are based on company management's estimations.
2. Convert inventory from LIFO to FIFO by using the shareholders' equity as computed under the FIFO method by the company's independent certified public accountants.

3. Markup fixed assets to an approximation of market value. The adjustments are based on an appraisal of these assets.

4. Incorporate the approximate after-tax loss during the period from January 1, 1986 to April 30, 1986. This adjustment is a rough approximation based on unaudited financial statements provided by company management. Such an adjustment is necessary to account for the change in net assets from the audited financial statements as of December 31, 1985 to April 30, 1986, the month prior to the death of Jason Ewing.

5. Proceeds received by the corporation as the beneficiary of Jason Ewing's life insurance policy.

6. Company management's estimate of costs to comply with regulations of the U.S. Environmental Protection Agency (EPA) regarding protection and clean-up costs on gas pumps and underground tanks. The company has engaged a consultant to make an independent study regarding such costs.

The computations of the adjusted net assets of Ewing Enterprises, Inc. as of April 15, 1986, as shown in Exhibit D is $3,982,969.

Valuation of Common Stock Interest.   Since our purpose is to value the common stock, it is necessary to determine how much of the $3,982,969 adjusted net asset value is allocable to the common stock interest.

As of April 15, 1986, the company had 2,596 shares of outstanding nonvoting preferred stock. The preferred stock is callable at $100 par value, with a 5 percent cumulative dividend rate.

Revenue Ruling 83–120, 1983–2CB 170 provides guidance to the valuation of preferred stock. It states that the most important factors to be considered in determining the value of preferred stock are its yield, dividend coverage, and protection of its liquidation preference.

The ruling also states that the dividend yield determines whether the preferred stock has a value equal to its par value. It specifically states the following:

> Whether the yield of the preferred stock supports a valuation of the stock at par value depends in part on the adequacy of the dividend rate. The adequacy of the dividend rate should be determined by comparing its dividend rate with the dividend rate of high-grade publicly traded preferred stock. A lower yield than that of high-grade preferred stock indicates a preferred stock value of less than par. In addition, whether the preferred stock has a fixed dividend rate and is nonparticipating influences the

Example 3 A-25

value of the preferred stock. . . . A publicly traded preferred stock for a company having a similar business and similar assets with similar liquidation preferences, voting rights, and other similar terms would be the ideal comparable for determining yield required in arms length transactions for closely held stock. Such ideal comparables will frequently not exist. In such circumstances, the most comparable publicly-traded issues should be selected for comparison and appropriate adjustments made for differing factors.

In short, the valuation method for preferred stock is to capitalize the annual dividend at a market rate equal to the rate of returns from similar grade marketable securities and then make appropriate adjustments for variations.

The ruling is essential for the determination of the fair market value of the preferred stock. However, it is not our objective here to value the preferred stock. Our goal is to determine the portion of the adjusted net asset value that is allocable to the common stock interest. A prudent investor planning to purchase only the common stock would allocate the adjusted net asset value to the preferred stock at the par value, as the preferred stock is callable at par and has a liquidation preference at par. A preferred stock having a market value less than its par value does not necessarily mean that the value attrition would increase the portion of the adjusted net asset value allocable to the common stock. Accordingly, the adjusted net asset value allocable to the common stock should be determined by accounting for the preferred stock at its par value, as follows:

Adjusted net asset value (Exhibit D)	$3,982,969
Less: Amount allocated to preferred stock at $100 par value per share	(259,600)
Adjusted net asset value allocable to the two classes of common stock	$3,723,369
Shares of common stock outstanding	37,076
Adjusted net asset value per share of common stock	$ 100.43

DISCOUNT FOR GENERAL LACK OF MARKETABILITY AND NONCONTROLLING INTEREST

The adjusted net asset value figure of $3,723,369 allocable to common stock is a value based on intrinsic factors (i.e., the aggregate values of the underlying assets). Since Ewing Enterprises, Inc. is a closely held business, a discount for general lack of marketability is appropriate. The lack of marketability discount concept recognizes the fact that closely held stock interests are less attractive and have fewer potential purchasers than similar publicly traded stock.

The principle of a discount for lack of marketability has been stated as follows:

> It seems clear . . . that an unlisted closely held stock of a corporation . . ., in which trading is infrequent and which therefore lacks marketability, is less attractive than a similar stock which is listed on an exchange and has ready access to the investing public.
> *Central Trust Co.,* 305 F2d 393 (CtCl 1962)

If the owners of closely held stocks should try to list a block of such securities on a stock exchange for sale to the public, they would probably have to make the offerings through underwriters. There would be costs for registering nonpublicly traded stocks with the Securities and Exchange Commission (SEC), involving (among other fees), the expense of preparing a prospectus. In addition, the underwriters themselves would receive commissions. The actual costs of such an offering can range from 10 percent to 25 percent of the selling price to the public.

Another support for the amount of discount for lack of marketability is provided by transactions in letter stocks. A letter stock is identical in all respects to the freely traded stock of a public company, except that it is restricted from trading on the open market for some period. The duration of the restriction varies from one situation to another. Since marketability is the only difference between the letter stock and its freely tradable counterpart, the differences in prices between letter stock transactions and open market transactions in the same stock provide some evidence about the price spread the market placed between a readily marketable security and its otherwise identical counterpart that is subject to certain marketability restrictions.

In a major study done by the SEC on institutional investor actions, one of the topics was the amount of discount at which transactions in restricted stock (letter stock) took place, as compared to the prices of otherwise identical but unrestricted stock on the open market. The study, "Discounts Involved in Purchases of Common Stock" [in U.S. 92d Congress, 1st Session, House, *Institutional Investor Study Report of the Securities and Exchange Commission*, Washington, D.C.: U.S. Government Printing Office (March 10, 1971), 5:2444–2456. (Document No. 92–64, Part

Example 3   **A-27**

5], shows the amounts of discounts on letter stock transactions by four market categories:

1. New York Stock Exchange
2. American Stock Exchange
3. Over-the-Counter (reporting companies)
4. Over-the-Counter (nonreporting companies)

A reporting company is a publicly traded company that must file forms 10-K, 10-Q, and other information with the SEC. A nonreporting company is a company that is publicly traded OTC but is not subject to the same reporting requirements.

The study shows that the discounts on the letter stocks were the least for NYSE listed stocks, but increased, in order, for ASE listed stocks, OTC reporting companies, and OTC nonreporting companies. For OTC nonreporting companies, the largest number of restricted stock transactions fell in the 30 to 40 percent discount range. Slightly over 56 percent of the OTC nonreporting companies experienced discounts greater than 30 percent on the sale of their restricted stock. A little over 30 percent of the OTC reporting companies experienced discounts over 30 percent, and over 52 percent experienced discounts over 20 percent.

Another study on marketability discounts for closely held business interests was done by J. Michael Maher ["Discounts for Lack of Marketability for Closely Held Business Interests," *Taxes* (September 1986), pp. 562–71]. The study involves a comparison of price paid for restricted stocks with the market prices of their unrestricted counterparts. The study shows that "the mean discount for lack of marketability for the years 1969–73 amounted to 35.43 percent." Maher then makes an interesting second computation, eliminating the top 10 percent and the bottom 10 percent of purchases to remove especially high- and low-risk situations; the result was almost identical with a mean discount of 34.73 percent.

Maher concludes,

> The result I have reached is that most appraisers underestimate the proper discount for lack of marketability. The results seem to indicate that this discount should be about 35 percent. Perhaps this makes sense because by committing funds to restricted common stock, the willing buyer (a) would be denied the opportunity to take advantage of other investments, and (b) would continue to have his investment at the risk of the business until the shares could be offered to the public or another buyer is found.

The 35 percent discount would not contain elements of a discount for a minority interest because it is measured against the current fair market value of securities actively traded (other minority interests). Consequently, appraisers should also consider a discount for a minority interest in those closely held corporations where a discount is applicable.

Recent cases in valuation provided substantial discounts for non-marketability and other inhibiting factors. In *Estate of Arthur F. Little, Jr.* [TCM 1982–26, CCH Dec. 38729(M)], the Tax Court allowed a total discount of 60 percent for shares of restricted stock of a publicly held company. The court allowed a 35 percent discount for sales restrictions, a 15 percent discount for an irrevocable two-year voting proxy agreement, and a 10 percent discount for shares that were held in escrow.

In *William T. Piper, Sr. Est.* (72 TC No. 88 CCH Dec. 36,315), the court allowed a total discount of 64 percent for stock of a corporation which owned publicly traded securities and rental property. The court allowed a discount of 35 percent for lack of marketability, 17 percent for relatively unattractive investment portfolios, and another 12 percent for possible stock registration costs.

In *Estate of Mark S. Gallo* [TCM 1985–363, CCH Dec. 42241(m)], the Tax Court allowed a discount of 36 percent for general lack of marketability.

Of particular interest is the *Estate of Ernest E. Kirkpatrick* [CCH Dec. 33,524(M), 34 TCM 1490 (1975)]. In this case, the court found per-share value without mentioning discount. However, expert witnesses for both the IRS and the taxpayer used a 50 percent discount to reflect the stock's lack of marketability and minority interest.

In addition to the general lack of marketability as discussed above, the 50 percent interest in common stock owned by Jason Ewing does not represent a controlling interest in the company. An acquisition of such interest does not afford a potential purchaser the power to fully influence management and day-to-day business operations. An acquisition of a 50 percent interest may afford a greater discount than a mere discount for the general lack of marketability. Put another way, the value of a noncontrolling interest (50 percent or less) is lower than the per-share value of an interest in the same company that would have control (more than 50 percent).

The extent to which any restriction on marketability and inhibiting factors reduce the value of a specific stock is determined based on facts and circumstances. In view of the depressed earnings of Ewing Enterprises, Inc. over the recent past years, the noncontrolling block of stock,

Example 3

A-29

and the general lack of marketability factors, a 30 percent discount is appropriate for the valuation of the 50 percent voting common stock owned by Jason Ewing. An additional 10 percent discount is appropriate for the valuation of the other 50 percent nonvoting common stock owned by Jason Ewing. This additional 10 percent discount accounts for the nonvoting privileges of the stock. As held in *Estate of Arthur F. Little, Jr.*, the Tax Court allows a 15 percent discount for an irrevocable two-year voting proxy agreement.

Applying the discounts, the value per share of the two classes of common stock are as follows:

	Class A voting	Class B nonvoting
Adjusted net asset value per share	$100.43	$100.43
Less: discount for general lack of marketability, noncontrolling interest, and depressed earnings—30%	(30.13)	(30.13)
Discount for nonvoting privilege—10%	—	(10.04)
Adjusted net asset value per share after discount	$ 70.30	$ 60.26

Conclusion

Based on the information and analyses summarized in this report, it is our opinion that, as of April 15, 1986, the fair market value of each of the two classes of common stock held by Jason Ewing is as follows:

	Common stock		
	Class A voting	Class B nonvoting	Total
Value per share	$ 70.30	$ 60.26	
Number of shares held	9,269	9,269	
Total value	$651,611	$558,550	$1,210,161

Statement of Limiting Conditions

In accordance with recognized professional ethics, the fee for this service is not contingent upon our conclusion of value, and neither Blackman,

Kallick and Company, Ltd. nor any of its employees has a present or intended financial interest in the Company.

Financial and statistical information is from sources we deem reliable. However, we make no representation as to our sources' accuracy or completeness and have accepted their information without further verification.

The opinion of value expressed herein is valid only for the stated purpose and date of the appraisal. The fair market value of Ewing Enterprises, Inc. was determined for estate tax valuation purposes.

Future services regarding the subject matter of this report, including, but not limited to, testimony or attendance in court shall not be required of Blackman, Kallick and Company, Ltd., unless previous arrangements have been made in writing.

Neither all nor any part of the contents of this report shall be conveyed to the public through advertising, public relations, news, sales, mail, direct transmittal, or other media without the prior written consent and approval of Blackman, Kallick and Company, Ltd.

EXHIBIT D

Ewing Enterprises, Inc.
Computations of Adjusted Net Assets as of April 15, 1986

Description		Amount
1. Total stockholders' equity as of December 31, 1985 (per audited statements)		$2,312,743
2. After-tax adjustment to retained earnings from LIFO to FIFO inventory method		
a. Retained earnings under LIFO	$1,924,982	
b. Retained earnings under FIFO	1,941,867	
Adjusted increase in retained earnings		16,885
3. Investments in affiliates		
a. Westar fueling (partnership)—approximate increase in earnings from 1/1/86 to 4/30/86 from unadjusted statements		
Earnings as of 4/30/86	$ 80,374	
Earnings as of 12/31/85	54,173	
Increase	$ 26,201	
50% interest		13,101*
b. Atlas petroleum (corporation)—approximate increase in after-tax earnings from 11/1/85 to 4/31/86 as provided by management		3,526
4. Investment in securities		
a. Port of Naples—$100,000		(16,821)
b. Atlantic Resources—272 shares		1,349

Example 3   **A-31**

EXHIBIT D (*Continued*)

c. The Gasahol Corp.—100 shares		(171)
d. Allied Oil of California—711.9047 shares		10,337

5. Fixed assets: land, buildings, equipment and leasehold improvements
  a. Owned properties to be kept.

Estimated fair market value	$2,090,000	
Net book value as of 12/31/85	1,079,199	
Increase		1,010,801

  b. Owned properties intended to be sold.

Estimated selling price	$1,780,000	
Net book value as of 12/31/85	566,359	
Increase		1,213,641*

  c. Improvements and equipment on leased properties to be abandoned

Estimated salvage value	$ 32,000	
Net book value	89,987	
Decrease		(57,987)*

  d. Improvements and equipment on leased properties to be used until lease expiration

Estimated value	$ 186,323	
Net book value	186,323	
Adjustments		-0-
e. Equipment in storage		(15,509)

6. Approximate loss from January 1, 1986 to April 30, 1986—per unadjusted statement   (149,000)*
7. Life insurance proceeds—Jason Ewing   100,000
8. Management's estimated costs to comply with EPA regulations

$10,000 before-tax per operating site for 22 sites	(220,000)*
9. Cumulative income tax effects	(239,926)
Adjusted net asset value as of April 15, 1986	$3,982,969

Notes: See accompanying pages for notes relating to the computations of adjusted net asset value.

*Each of these items affect the taxable income of the Company. All are reflected in the $239,926 opposite "9. Cumulative Income Tax Effect." The item in 5.b., $1,213,641 is included in 9. at capital gain rates; note that this property is "Intended to be Sold," hence the estimated profit is reduced by taxes to arrive at the "Adjusted Net Asset Value." On the other hand, the item at 5.a. "Owned Property to be Kept," does not have its increase of $1,010,801 reduced by potential capital gains tax. See "Notes . . ." immediately following for a more detailed explanation.

Notes to Computations of Adjusted Net Assets

Investments in Affiliates. Adjustments for investments in affiliates were based on respective affiliate management's representations that the shareholder's equity approximates the fair market value of such affiliates. We relied upon such representations without verification. The net adjustment to Westar Fueling involves the determination of the approximate after-tax earnings for the period between January 1, 1986 to April 30, 1986. Increase in capital contribution to Tri-Met Fueling during the same period is not adjusted, as it involves a mere shifting of funds.

Fixed Asset Mark-up. Adjustments to fixed assets represent company management's appraisal of fair market value of the fixed assets. Company management represented that they are knowledgeable in the determination of market value of these types of fixed assets. Appraisals by independent appraisers usually are obtained and preferred. We relied upon management's valuation as accurate and reliable and have no reason to believe that these valuations should not be used.

Vehicles, Furniture, and Fixtures. No adjustments were made to vehicles and furniture and fixtures ($493,165 and $168,667, respectively) as shown on the 12/31/85 balance sheet, as company management represented that their net book values fairly reflected the fair market value of these assets.

Other Fixed Assets. In adjusting the net book value of other fixed assets to fair market value, we divided the fixed assets into four separate categories:

- Real properties (and improvements and equipment thereon) owned and to be kept by the company indefinitely.
- Real properties (and improvements and equipment thereon) owned by the company but which management intends to dispose of.
- Real properties leased by the company and on which the company management intends to continue to operate businesses over the lease terms.
- Real properties leased by the company and which the company management intends to abandon.

Example 3   A-33

Real Properties Owned and to Be Kept.   In adjusting net book value to fair market value for real properties owned and to be kept by the company, no adjustments are provided for potential trapped-in income taxes related to the appreciation. Although such an adjustment could be proper, the courts have on various occasions rejected such an adjustment. In *Edwin A Gallum* [1974–284 TCM (CCH) p. 1320], U.S. Tax Court rejected an adjustment for potential capital gains tax. It states,

> In arriving at our determination we have rejected the argument of [taxpayer] that a discount should be allowed for a potential capital gains tax that would result if the investment portfolio were to be liquidated. The record does not establish that the management of the portfolio had any immediate plans to liquidate the investment portfolio. Furthermore, it is possible that the management at some time in the future may dispose of certain or all of the investment assets without incurring a capital gains tax. Under these circumstances, such a discount is not appropriate. See Estate of Frank A Cruikshank (Dec. 15, 1941), 9 T.C. 162 (1947); Estate of Alvin Thalheimer (Dec. 32, 714(M)), T.C. Memo. 1974–203.

The court's position seems to be based on the fact that the taxpayer had no intention to liquidate its investment holding at the time of the valuation. Although the court has denied an adjustment for capital gains tax, a trapped-in capital gains tax is a liability that arguably should be recognized. Support for this position is found in the American Institute of Certified Public Accountants official guidelines for the preparation of personal financial statements, where assets with unrealized appreciation are adjusted to market value. They unequivocally take the position that any upward adjustment to market value must be accompanied by a deduction for the related capital gains tax. The text of the AICPA position is this:

> An accrual for income taxes on net unrealized appreciation (the difference between the tax basis of the net assets and estimated value) is required in the presentation of the estimated value column in personal financial statements. This accrual is necessary because the estimated values cannot generally be realized without incurring taxes.
> —AICPA, *Audits of Personal Financial Statements* (New York, 1968), p. 5.

Real Properties Owned and to be Sold.   For real properties and related equipment to be sold by the management, we adjusted the value to account for potential income tax effects. We believe such an adjustment is

EXHIBIT D (*Continued*)

proper since management's intention is to dispose of the assets. The fact that management intends to sell is distinguishable from the Edwin A. Gallum case.

Improvements and Equipment on Leased Properties to be Abandoned. Since management's intention is to abandon such assets, a potential investor would not be willing to pay for shares of stock whose intrinsic value includes the full net book value of such assets. A payment of its full net book value would result in an inherent immediate loss in the stock investment. Accordingly, improvements and equipment are adjusted downward to reflect the after-tax losses from intended abandonment.

Other Improvements and Equipment of Leased Properties. Company management represents that the net book value of these improvements and equipment approximates the fair market value.

Equipment in Storage. Equipment with a total net book value of $40,509 was in storage and not being utilized. Management estimated the fair market value of these idle assets to be $25,000. No income tax effects are given to the downward adjustments since management does not intend to dispose of these assets in the near future. No income tax effect adjustment was given in accordance with the argument as suggested by the Tax Court in *Edwin A. Gallum*.

After-Tax Loss from January 1, 1986 to April 30, 1986. The approximate tax loss is based on unaudited and unadjusted financial statements as of April 30, 1986. We did not verify the accuracy of such information.

Compliance with EPA Regulations. The estimated after-tax costs to comply with the EPA regulations were provided by company management. The company is conducting a study on the costs for EPA compliance. Company management expects that the study will be completed in November 1986. Adjustments to the estimated compliance costs should be made if the study indicates any major differences in compliance costs.

Cumulative Income Tax Effects. The cumulative income tax effects are computed as follows:

Example 3   **A-35**

Exhibit D (Continued)

a. Approximate increase in earnings from Westar Fueling	$ 13,101
b. Increase in value on owned properties intended to be sold	1,213,641*
c. Decrease in value on improvements and equipment on leased properties to be abandoned	(57,987)
d. Approximate loss of Ewing Enterprises, Inc. from 1/1/86 to 4/30/86	(149,000)
e. Estimated costs to comply with EPA regulations	(220,000)
Cumulative increase in value subject to income tax effects	$ 799,755
Approximate tax rate*	30%
Cumulative Income Tax Effects	$ 239,926

*Almost all of this amount would be taxable as a long-term capital gain (the law as it existed at the time the above valuation was prepared). Always use the tax rate applicable at the time of the valuation.

Example 4   A-37

VALUATION EXAMPLE 4. COMBINATION METHOD—COMPARABLES AND NET ASSET VALUE FOR RECAPITALIZATION

This next valuation uses a combination method based on two approaches: comparables and net asset value. The purpose of the valuation was to value common and preferred stock to be issued under a Section 368(a)(1)(e) recapitalization. Because of the size of the company being valued and to protect the identity of the client, some facts concerning the company and actual dates involved have been changed.

Business History and Industry Outlook

J.J.Bean, Inc. was founded in 1939 by J.J.Bean, the principal shareholder. It was incorporated in Massachusetts and specialized in the manufacture of tailored sportcoats. Its main production facilities are located at 15th and Fenway Street, Beantown, Massachusetts.

Over the years, J.J. Bean, Inc. branched out into other apparel under the leadership of its founder. It began to manufacture women's apparel in 1960.

J.J.Bean, Inc. presently produces men's tailored sportcoats, suits, slacks, sweaters, and assorted sportswear. Its ladies division produces women's jackets, pants, blouses, and other assorted articles. In 198_____, menswear accounted for about 60 percent of the total sales, while womenswear accounted for the remaining 40 percent. Tailored clothing continues to be the solid base of the business. In menswear, it is about 70 percent; in womenswear, 45 percent.

J.J. Bean, Inc. is noted as a slacks specialist and is one of the largest slacks makers in the country in its price range. ALso, it is well known for in-stock service, maintaining substantial inventories to handle customers' at-once orders.

J.J.Bean, Inc.'s various menswear divisions have approximately 50 representatives throughout the country and the womenswear division has approximately ten. Sales are made to major department stores and specialty stores throughout the country. The number of active accounts is approximately 4,500.

J.J.Bean, Inc. has four wholly-owned subsidiaries:

- Pan Am Sporting Corp.
- J.J. Spooling Co., Inc.

- J & R Clothing, Inc.
- J. J. Bean Underwear, Inc.

Total current employment by J. J. Bean, Inc. and subsidiaries is approximately 1,800 people.

Except for fiscal years ended September 198_____ and 198_____, the company has experienced growth under the leadership of J. J. Bean. He has been the key driving force in the business. He devotes 12 or more hours a day to operating the business. He personally manages the day-to-day operations of the sales, styling, and design offices, while Phillip Dalmas (present and shareholder) manages the production facilities.

J.J. Bean is a businessman and designer, as well as an advertising pro. He formulates the strategic plans of the company and makes all major business and personnel decisions. He directs and oversees the development and design of all new product lines, such as the company's latest additions of women's specialty wear and men's specialty merchandise. It was J. J. Bean who spearheaded the company's drive to become one of the first companies producing women's specialty clothing.

J.J. Bean also personally selects and purchases the fabric for the company's products. He also decides on the price range of the company's product lines.

J. J. Bean shapes the company's image by formulating all its marketing and promotional campaigns. He also coordinates with licensees in developing national advertising campaigns. He was instrumental in developing the new, successful "plentiful" and "up-beat style" advertising approach which greatly benefited the licensees.

J. J. Bean single-handedly builds up the company's clientele. He is the driving force in developing a binding and lasting relationship with all clients by dealing with them personally. He constantly entertains, assists, and nurtures the clients. He also maintains personal relationships with clients.

J. J. Bean, Inc. has four classes of stock authorized and outstanding. The current outstanding shares are as follows:

Class of stock	Number of shares outstanding
Common stock	
Class A voting	10.00
Class B nonvoting	124.00
Preferred stock	
Class A nonvoting	500.00
Class B nonvoting	2,375.00

Example 4 A-39

J.J. Bean owns 100 percent of the outstanding voting common stock. He also owns a number of shares of nonvoting common stock and class B preferred stock.

No public sale of any stock has occurred over the past five years.

The apparel industry is considered a risky and highly volatile industry. Although apparel represents a necessity of life, both for protection against the elements and for reasons of social decency, most clothing purchases can be postponed indefinitely.

The basic analysis (dated December 198_____) from Standard & Poor's *Industry Surveys* stated that 198_____ was a record year for the number of bankruptcies in the apparel industry. It indicated that the number of bankruptcies was twice or even three times as high as the previous year. In addition, the unemployment rate for apparel workers hit 18.4 percent in April 198_____, the highest postwar level since the record 19.3 percent registered in March 1975.

The current analysis (dated April 21, 198_____) from Standard & Poor's *Industry Surveys* indicated that the apparel industry was soft in 198_____ but is in a rebound. Members of the industry attributed the rebound to improved retail sales. However, they cautioned that price promoting by retailers was partly responsible for the retail sales growth.

The Value Line *Investment Survey* (dated September 9, 198_____) also stated that retail clothing sales grew by 18.7 percent adjusted for inflation in the second quarter of 198_____. The improved retail clothing sales in the second quarter of 198_____ would have translated into improved sales for the manufacturers in subsequent quarters when retailers rebuild their inventories. This delayed effect thus should have caused an upsurge in manufacturing sales in the third quarter of 198_____ since retailers had been operating with extremely lean inventories during the early part of 198_____. As Value Line stated in its report, "retailers have significantly stepped up their buying for the fall season, providing an additional fillup to bookings that were already on an uptrend as a result of storekeepers' need to rebuild their bare bones inventories."

Notwithstanding the encouraging industry forecast, Value Line also cautioned unforeseeable problems:

> Besides the usual caveat having to do with surprise changes in the economy, there's one particularly applicable to the apparel industry: As we move through a new year, overall industry estimates tend to be reduced. That's because in a high-style industry, some of the participants are likely to stray off the path of current fashion, thereby losing a portion of profitability, even falling into the red. There's no way our analysts can spot a backfiring fashion line until the industry is in season.

Sales volume of J.J. Bean, Inc. and subsidiaries was $69.5 million for fiscal year ended September 30, 198_____ and dropped down to $65.8 million the next year. Management estimated that the sales volume for the next fiscal year would be slightly less than $60 million. Management indicated that its peak sales period is between April and September.

Despite the encouraging industry news and the improved clothing sales in the second quarter of 198_____ announced by Value Line, J. J. Bean, Inc. still experienced a drop of more than $5 million in sales for fiscal year 198_____ compared to the preceding year.

Management attributed the decline in sales over the past two years to increasingly keen competition. One noticeable source of competition came from overseas. In 198_____, the value of apparel imports rose 9.2 percent to $7.1 billion at wholesale. Over the past few years, imports have risen at a faster rate than has overall U.S. consumption of apparel and footwear, a pattern that is not expected to change in the future. Foreign-made clothing is estimated to account for one out of every four garments sold in the United States.

In particular, imports from Mainland China grew 47 percent during 1984. Recently, China and the U.S. entered into a new five-year textile agreement which allows the Chinese an average annual growth of 3.5 percent in textile sales in the U.S. Presently, the exact details of the agreement are not available. Management indicated that the new agreement could have an adverse impact on the company, although the magnitude of any such impact cannot be ascertained at the present time.

Management stated that it does not anticipate or foresee any real growth in its sales volume. It stated that its main goal is to maintain its current market share. Management indicated that its most likely sales volume for next year would be within the range of $50–60 million.

In summary, the industry forecast is encouraging. J.J. Bean, Inc., however, has not experienced the sales rebound mentioned in the forecast. Its sales volume for fiscal year 198_____ (just ended) is the lowest over the last three years.

Seemingly, the increasingly keen competition overshadows the daylight of the industry forecast for J. J. Bean, Inc. and its subsidiaries.

Comparative Approach to Valuation

Selection of Comparable Corporations   In searching for comparable corporations for the purpose of valuing J. J. Bean, Inc. and subsidiaries

Example 4 A-41

(herein referred to as J. J. Bean, Inc.), both financial and nonfinancial characteristics were considered. Factors considered in the selection process included these:

- Business activities;
- Competitive standing in terms of the company's reputation, depth of management, and growth rate;
- Profitability in terms of net income to sales; and
- Corporate capital structure (i.e., long term debt to total equity).

Financial ratios were also developed to determine the operating and financial posture of J. J. Bean, Inc. in comparison to the selected comparable companies.

Five publicly held companies were initially selected as possible comparables from a candidate list of over 15 corporations that are in the apparel industry. The other corporations were not selected because their product lines are quite different from those of J. J. Bean, Inc. (Appendix A [not shown in this book] provides a partial listing of corporations.) Subsequent examination of corporate financial information resulted in further elimination of two of the five companies: Philips Van Heusen and Oxford, Inc.

Philips Van Heusen was eliminated because its overall operating performances (i.e., percent of net income to net sales and rate of return on total assets) were comparatively lower than those of J. J. Bean, Inc. and the other four public companies over the five-year period under review. Its capital structure (i.e., percentage of long term debt to total equity) was also materially different from that of J. J. Bean, Inc.

Oxford, Inc. was also excluded because of its substantial sales to two principal customers. J. C. Penney Co. and Sears, Roebuck & Co. accounted for 20 percent and 12 percent of its sales, respectively, in fiscal year 198_____ .

The three publicly held corporations selected as the best possible comparable corporations are (1) Hartmarx (formerly Hart, Schaffner and Marx), (2) Palm Beach, Incorporated, and (3) Cluett, Peabody.

Business Summary of Selected Comparables Following is a business overview of the three companies selected as comparables.

1. *Hartmarx*. Hartmarx is the leading diversified manufacturer and retailer of men's and women's apparel. Its main emphasis is on quality and fashion. Through a recent acquisition, it is expanding into the low-markup market for men's suits and sportcoats.

Its product lines include suits, sportcoats, slacks, outercoats, rainwear, and sportswear. Men's apparel is manufactured under such high-quality labels as Hart Schaffner & Marx, Hickey Freeman, Society Brand, and Austin Reed of Regent Street.

The company also operates specialty stores. About two thirds of the clothing sold in the specialty stores is produced by its manufacturing division. Its manufacturing operations accounted for 74 percent of its net profit in 198_____; its retailing activities accounted for the remaining profit.

2. *Palm Beach, Incorporated*. Palm Beach manufactures a diversified line of apparel with concentration on brand names. The Palm Beach name is used in men's tailored clothing, blazers for men, and tailored clothing and blazers for boys. Other clothing labels include Evan-Picone, Gant, Haspel, Pierre Cardin, and John Weitz. Palm Beach sells directly to department stores and clothing specialty stores.

Palm Beach is the smallest of the three companies selected. However, Palm Beach has experienced relatively rapid growth over the past few years.

3. *Cluett, Peabody*. Cluett, Peabody manufactures a diversified line of apparel. It owned eight retail stores until their recent sales in July. Manufacturing accounted for 91 percent of its profit and retailing accounted for 4 percent of profit in 198_____. The remaining 5 percent of its profit was derived from the licensing of trademarks and patents. Its Shoeneman division produces men's and women's suits and sportcoats and a line of designer clothing under the Halston name. Other apparel manufactured includes men's dress, sport, and knit shirts, jackets, sweaters, underwear, sportswear, and hosiery.

The three companies selected are larger and more diversified than J. J. Bean, Inc. These differences, however, should not deter them from being considered as comparable to J. J. Bean, Inc.

Rarely will two companies be identical. If unduly restrictive criteria were set for the selection of comparable companies, it would be virtually impossible to find a comparable. This would render the comparative approach to valuation virtually meaningless. In *Estate of Ethyl L. Goodrich* TCM 1978-248, CCH Dec 35250(M), taxpayer rejected certain companies as comparables of a newspaper publishing company that was being valued because these companies had (1) much smaller or larger revenues,

Example 4   **A-43**

(2) policies of growth through corporate acquisition (instead of only internal growth), or (3) revenues from activities other than newspaper publishing. The U.S. Tax Court stated that such a selection process "was too selective and excluded companies that in our view are of probative value in the determination of the value of the Central Newspapers stock."

The size differential and product diversification of the comparables selected indicate that they are less risky than J. J. Bean, Inc. from the investment standpoint. These differences can be reasonably accounted for in arriving at the value of J. J. Bean, Inc. The use of larger and more diversified companies as comparables is acceptable. A case in point is *Sol Koffler*, TCM 1978-159, CCH Dec 35119(M), wherein the comparable company selected for the valuation of a luggage manufacturing company was the largest luggage manufacturer in the United States. In addition, it also manufactured and sold furniture, toys, and small computers. The company was accepted as a comparable with adjustments made to account for the dissimilarities.

The three comparables are reasonably similar to the business activities conducted by J. J. Bean, Inc., as all specialize in good quality men's clothing. They all manufacture men's suits and sportcoats. In particular, Hartmarx is the leader in quality men's suits and blazers. It is a more integrated operation than J. J. Bean, Inc., as it has its own sales outlets. Its sales outlets provide a greater visibility of its products and facilitate the marketing of its products. Being the leader in quality clothing with a well integrated operation, many potential investors would view its operations as a benchmark of excellence. Its stock value and price-earnings ratio would likely represent the starting point for a potential buyer to determine the price for a less established and less integrated apparel manufacturer like J. J. Bean, Inc.

Financial Analyses   To determine the operating and financial posture of J. J. Bean, Inc. in comparison to the three selected comparable companies, certain ratios were computed to determine growth, profitability, and financial stability.

1. *Sales Growth.* J. J. Bean, Inc. and Palm Beach, Inc. have been growing at a comparatively rapid pace. Hartmarx and Cluett, Peabody experienced comparatively less growth. This disparity is attributable to the fact that Hartmarx and Cluett, Peabody are substantially larger and have reached the point where the relative growth rate would be low.

Palm Beach's sales were about seven times that of J.J. Bean, Inc. over the past five years. The average annual growth for both over this five-year period was around 20 percent. The following table shows the growth status (Year 1 is the most recent year):

	Annual sales growth % from previous year					
	Year 5	Year 4	Year 3	Year 2	Year 1	Annual average
J.J. Bean, Inc.	7.5	35.5	36.3	26.1	(5.4)	20.0
Palm Beach	13.1	39.0*	25.9	21.8	(1.3)	19.7
Hartmarx	6.8	3.9	6.9	20.8*	5.7	8.8
Cluett, Peabody	(2.3)	16.6*	9.9	10.6	5.9	8.1

*Reflects mergers and acquisitions.

2. *Profitability*. Over the past five years, the percentage of net income to gross revenue of J. J. Bean, Inc. climbed from 2.3 percent in Year 5 to 3.2 percent in Year 3, but then dropped to 0.7 percent in Year 1. Palm Beach's net income percentage declined steadily from 5.9 percent in Year 5 to 1.9 percent in Year 1. Hartmarx moved steadily upward from 3.0 percent to 3.7 percent. Cluett, Peabody fluctuated between 2.1 percent and 3.3 percent.

Net income as a percentage of gross revenue shows the average rate of profit earned on each dollar of revenue received. J. J. Bean, Inc. and Palm Beach each demonstrated a relatively poor trend on this performance measure. J. J. Bean, Inc. lacked income stability; while Palm Beach was on a downward trend because of marginal or poor performance by some of its operating divisions. Hartmarx and Cluett, Peabody performed relatively better in terms of income stability. The following table shows the relationship of net income to revenue:

	% of Net income to revenue					
	Year 5	Year 4	Year 3	Year 2	Year 5	Average
J.J. Bean, Inc.	2.3	2.3	3.0	3.2	0.7	2.30
Palm Beach	5.9	4.2	3.5	2.7	1.9	3.64
Hartmarx	3.0	3.3	3.3	3.4	3.7	3.34
Cluett, Peabody	3.3	2.6	2.1	2.6	2.7	2.66

An analysis of rate of return (i.e., net income over average total assets) also shows that the profitability of J. J. Bean, Inc. has

Example 4   **A-45**

been unstable. Its rate of return on assets climbed from 8.6 percent in Year 4 to 11.2 percent in year 3, but then dropped dramatically to 2.3 percent in Year 1. The following table shows the rate of return on assets:

	Rate of return (%)				
	Year 4	Year 3	Year 2	Year 1	Average
J.J. Bean, Inc.	8.6	11.2	11.2	2.2	8.3
Palm Beach	9.6	7.4	6.0	4.1	6.8
Hartmarx	6.1	6.0	6.3	7.0	6.4
Cluett, Peabody	4.8	4.7	6.0	5.4	5.2

As the table indicates, J. J. Bean, Inc. experienced a relatively high rate of return except for Year 1. A closer examination, however, reveals that its high rate of return was attributable to its low level of current assets. J. J. Bean, Inc. has been financing its accounts receivable externally by factoring, thereby reducing its asset base. The comparable companies basically financed their accounts receivable internally. Should J. J. Bean, Inc. have financed its outstanding accounts receivable internally, its rate of return on assets would be appreciably lower.

3. *Financial Position.* J. J. Bean's financial position is less secure than that of the comparable companies. The following tables show the current ratio and the quick asset ratio of the respective companies:

	Current ratio					
	Year 5	Year 4	Year 3	Year 2	Year 1	Average
J.J. Bean, Inc.	1.58	1.56	1.56	1.69	1.99	1.67
Palm Beach	2.7	2.2	1.8	1.7	2.9	2.26
Hartmarx	3.3	3.4	2.7	2.3	2.6	2.86
Cluett, Peabody	3.5	3.3	3.6	3.0	3.3	3.34

	Quick asset ratio			
	Year 3	Year 2	Year 1	Average
J.J. Bean, Inc.	.21	.11	.17	.16
Palm Beach	.70	.67	1.27	.88
Hartmarx	1.15	1.02	1.19	1.12
Cluett, Peabody	1.55	1.20	1.33	1.36

Undoubtedly, the low level of current assets was due to the external financing of accounts receivable. A review of the accounts receivable records indicates a severe cash shortage. J. J. Bean, Inc. has been continuously receiving advances from its factoring company in excess of its outstanding accounts receivable balance. In April 198_____, total advances from the factoring company were $11.6 million in excess of its outstanding accounts receivable.

In summary, J. J. Bean, Inc. has experienced sales growth in most, but not all, recent years. Such growth, however, was not unique, as Palm Beach also experienced a good rate of growth. It does not now appear likely that J. J. Bean, Inc. will continue its past growth, since its sales volume stagnated in the range of $60 million in Year 2 and Year 1, and it is projected that next year sales will also be at this same level.

The profit margin (i.e., net income as a percentage of revenue) of J. J. Bean, Inc. has been fluctuating over the last few years. It moved to a high of 3.2 percent in Year 3 and then dropped down to .7 percent in Year 2. Its profit margin has been highly volatile compared to that of Hartmarx and Cluett, Peabody. Except for Year 3, its profit margin was also consistently less than that of Palm Beach.

The unstable profit margin of J. J. Bean, Inc. was partially attributable to its high level of external financing of accounts receivable. Its earnings potential is relatively sensitive to the movement of market interest rates.

The financial position of J. J. Bean, Inc. has been weak in relation to the comparables. It has experienced cash flow problems and has repeatedly required advances from its factor company (lender) in excess of its outstanding accounts receivable in order to continue to finance its production and maintain inventory levels.

Nonfinancial Analyses. Besides the financial differences (as discussed above) between J. J. Bean, Inc. and the comparables, nonfinancial characteristics must also be considered. These main nonfinancial characteristics are diversification and depth of management. The apparel industry is sometimes classified as a relatively high-risk industry. This risk can be reduced through sound management practices and broad-based diversification.

Although J. J. Bean manufactures different lines of products, its main concentration is in slacks and sweaters. Furthermore, its products are manufactured only under one brand name label. The manufacturing opera-

Example 4   A-47

tions of the comparables are much more diversified in terms of product lines and name labels. For example, Hartmarx has about 19 brand-name labels for men's suits and blazers.

Having one brand name label makes J. J. Bean, Inc. more susceptible to the problems of "off-price retailing." Off-price retailing has been a serious problem for J. J. Bean, Inc., as its products have continuously and unseemingly appeared in discount stores. The discount stores sell the products at off-price (i.e., at a substantially lower price). Hence, consumers would purchase the products at discount stores at substantial savings instead of paying a full price at department stores and specialty stores. Some department and specialty stores would, in turn, stop purchasing and carrying the products or would only purchase the products at a lower price. Off-price retailing thus has the effect of dissipating the value and reputation of the products. This ultimately affects the profitability of the products.

While off-price retailing is an industry-wide problem, medium price-range products such as those of J. J. Bean, Inc. are more susceptible to the problem. With only one name label, the profitability of J. J. Bean, Inc. could be seriously impaired should its name label dissipate in value due to off-price retailing.

Although J. J. Bean, Inc. has been successful, its success is solely the result of the work of its founder, J. J. Bean. J. J. Bean is paramount to the company's success and reputation. He is personally involved in almost every facet of the company operations; he personally (1) purchases the fabrics, (2) develops advertising and promotional campaigns, (3) formulates pricing, (4) services and entertains clients, and (5) makes all major business decisions. In essence, the company is faced with thin management.

In summary, J. J. Bean, Inc. is less attractive than the selected comparables from investment and business standpoints because of thin management and the lack of diversification in products and name labels.

Price-earnings Multiples.   To establish a value for J. J. Bean, Inc., a price-earnings ration must be determined by analyzing the respective ratios of the comparables. In connection with the determination of an appropriate price-earnings ratio, the U.S. Tax Court has stated:

> In times of wide speculation and resulting fluctuations in the stock market, we are extremely doubtful that the price at which a stock is traded on the exchange on any particular day is a true reflection of what an investor would pay for the stock if he was looking primarily to the

historical earnings of the corporation to determine a fair price. We believe such an investor would give more weight to price-earnings ratios of comparable stocks during each of the years under consideration in determining a multiple that he can apply to the historical earnings of a corporation whose stock he is buying to determine the price he would pay for that stock.

—*Estate of Oakley J. Hall*, TCM 1975–141, CCH Dec. 33198(M).

The present stock market has been extremely bullish. The stock market began one of its greatest rallies in stock prices in 50 years in August 198_____. The Dow Jones Industrial Average climbed from about 800 in August to 1248.30 on June 16, 198_____—a gain of about 448.30 points.

No bull market in modern history has gotten off to as strong a start as the current one, as the following table illustrates:

Bull market	*Gain after 10 months
Aug. '21–Sep. '29	34%
June '32–Mar. '37	34
Apr. '42–May '46	47
June '49–Aug. '56	33
Oct. '57–Aug. '59	22
June '62–Feb. '66	33
Oct. '66–Nov. '68	31
May '70–Jan. '73	44
Oct. '74–Sep. '76	41
Mar. '78–Nov. '80	14
Aug. '82	59

*Based on S&P composite index of 500 stocks (402 stocks in 1921–29 calculation).

In light of the unprecedented bullishness of the market, it is inappropriate to rely entirely on the current price-earnings ratios to determine the fair market value of J. J. Bean, Inc. The proper price-earnings ratio for a buyer of a closely held business should be a normative amount free from excessive, exaggerated, or depressed price factors.

If a potential buyer relies unequivocally on the current price-earnings ratio, he could be faced with a disastrous result. As a matter of fact, the bullish sentiments had taken a disastrous toll on some unwary investors. The bullish sentiments attracted many companies to go public. Enthusias-

Example 4 A-49

tic investors in some of these companies faced a murderous dive in their investments, as illustrated by the following table:

Stock	Offering price	High bid	Current bid	Change from offering
Fortune Systems	$22.00	$22.50	$ 9.37	– 57%
Victor Tech.	17.50	22.12	7.50	– 57
U.S. Telephone	14.00	26.62	6.50	– 53
Amgen	18.00	18.00	8.00	– 56
Kolff Medical	12.50	12.50	7.12	– 43
Micro D	16.00	16.75	9.25	– 42
Activision	12.00	12.62	8.75	– 27
Wicat	18.00	20.00	12.50	– 31
Integrated Genetics	13.00	13.00	9.00	– 31
Gtech	13.25	13.25	10.12	– 24
Damon Biotech	17.00	17.50	12.00	– 30
Biogen	23.00	24.25	14.50	– 37
Zymos	12.50	12.75	9.50	– 24

Source: New Issues Ft. Lauderdale, Fla., published in the *Chicago Tribune.*

An article in the *Chicago Tribune*, September 24, 198_____, also suggested a less than bullish sentiment in the future from the chief investment officer of one of the nation's leading banks. The article stated that the investment officer "thinks the Dow could tumble to 1,000–1,050 range. That's about a 200–250 point drop."

As the Tax Court has articulated in *Estate of Oakley J. Hall*, a potential buyer of a closely held operating business would consider the price earnings ratio of comparable stocks over a number of years in determining a price multiple and the price he would pay for the business. In arriving at an appropriate price-earnings ratio, the following factors deserve consideration:

1. The unweighted average price-earnings ratio for the three comparable companies over a 5 year period is 6.20. (See Schedule 1 for computations.)
2. A weighted average of price-earnings ratios over the same period is 6.82. The weighted average approach is a form of "exponential smoothing" (a standard statistical procedure used for time-series data), giving greater weights to the ratios of the more recent periods. (See Schedule 2 for computations.)

3. The June 10, 198_____ issue of Value Line *Investment Survey* projected the average price-earnings ratio for the three-year period, 198_____ to 198_____, for the entire apparel industry to be about 9.0. This projected price-earnings ratio is close to the industry composite ratio of 8.3 in 198_____, the period before the current market rally. This indicates that the current inflated price-earnings ratio is a temporary phenomenon. It also projected that the average annual price-earnings ratio for Palm Beach (a selected comparable that was relatively similar to J. J. Bean, Inc. in terms of growth rate and earnings stability) would come back down to 7.5 for the three-year period indicated above.

4. Available information on two recent acquisitions of apparel manufacturers indicates that the price-earnings multiple paid for these acquisitions was about 5.5. In April 198_____, Leslie Fay, Inc. went private for approximately 5.4 times of earnings. Leslie Fay is a manufacturer of women's apparel such as sportswear, sweaters, and dresses.

    In December 198_____, Hartmarx acquired Kuppenheimer Manufacturing Co., Inc. for about $28.8 million. Based on available information, it is estimated that the price-earnings ratio for the acquisition was about 5.6. Kuppenheimer manufactures men's low-price suits and sportcoats and operates 41 retail discount outlets.

No single prescribed formula or mathematical average may be applied to arrive at a price-earnings ratio. After considering the Value Line projections, the price-earnings ratios over a $5\frac{1}{2}$ year period, and two recent apparel acquisitions, a 7.0 earnings multiple would be a generous estimate of the price which a potential buyer would pay, given the past movement of market price-future earnings ratios and anticipation of future movement thereof.

Earnings Projections. Once the price-earnings ratio is determined, it is necessary to determine the earnings potential of J. J. Bean, Inc. An important factor affecting the future earnings of J. J. Bean, Inc. is the prime interest rate, since its earnings are relatively sensitive to the movement of interest rates.

As of August 198_____, the prime interest rate stood at 11 percent. Presently, there is a good deal of uncertainty among investors about the

Example 4   **A-51**

future behavior of interest rates. An officer of a large money-management firm indicated that there is a strong possibility that the prime rate will advance to 12 percent (*Chicago Tribune*, August 21, 198_____). An August report, issued by the U.S. Congressional Budget Office, indicated that the federal deficits could total about $200 billion in each of the next several fiscal years of Congress and the Reagan administration does not agree on deficit reduction actions. The projected deficits could result in ''possibly higher interest rates and slower economic growth.'' In an article in *The Wall Street Journal* on August 22, 198_____, two economists interviewed were concerned with the budget dispute and indicated that the deficit problems would put a crimp on interest-sensitive business sectors. Also, respected observers like the Nobel Laureate Milton Friedman, have looked at the tremendous surge in the money supply that began in August 198_____ and concluded that a return to rapid inflation is inevitable.

J. J. Bean, Inc. experienced good sales growth for the three-year period from 198_____ to 198_____. However, it is unlikely that growth pattern can be sustained. Sales volume was at $69.5 million for fiscal year 198_____ and dropped down to $65.9 million for 198_____. For the six months ended March 31, 198_____, J. J. Bean, Inc. experienced net sales of $26 million. Although general economic forecasts for the apparel industry indicate a sales recovery for 198_____, management anticipated that the sales volume would be slightly less than the $60 million level for fiscal year ended September 30, 198_____. Thus, the company's sales volume has been declining two years in a row. Its sales volume has dropped by about 13.7 percent since 198_____. Management attributed the sales reduction to the increasingly keen competition.

Management estimated that the most likely sales volume for next year would be around the $50–$60 million level. Management does not anticipate any real growth in the future. Management also indicated that sales reduction is possible due to the recent five-year textile agreement between China and the U.S, which allows the Chinese an average annual growth of 3.5 percent in textile sales in the U.S. Management indicated that the new agreement could have an adverse impact on the company, although the magnitude of any such impact cannot be ascertained at the present time.

Given the continuing sales reduction for the two years ended in 198_____, it is management's view that future sales volume will most likely be at the $60 million level. Taking into account the uncertainty of future interest rates, annual earnings will most likely be in the range of $1.3 million.

The $1.3 million earnings are determined after considering the following analyses:

1. *Regression Analysis*: Regression analysis is a mathematical technique which expresses earnings as a function of sales volume. In the present case, this technique was used to project the earnings potential associated with the expected future sales volume.

    Operating results for six years were used as the basic data for projecting the earnings potential. (See Schedule 3 for information.) Six years of data were used so that periods of high as well as low prime interest rates are included in the data base. (In Year 6 in Schedule 3, the prime rate was only 6.8 percent). Given a projected sales volume of $60 million for the future years, earnings of about $1.3 million are computed using regression analysis. To test the reasonableness of the projection, the earnings for Year 1 in Schedule 3 were projected at $1,329,582 for the anticipated $60 million sale volume. Management's estimate of net earnings after-tax for this year was also about $1.3 million. Thus, the regression-based earnings projection compares very favorably to the actual (projected) results reported by the management, lending credibility to the regression model.

2. *Simple Average of Earnings:* Since the sales volumes for Years 2, 3, and 4 in Schedule 3 are around the $60 million level, a simple average of the earnings for these years was computed to provide insight about the future earnings at the projected sales level of $60 million. An average computation can be helpful it is applied judiciously. The simple average of the three-year's earnings is $1,302,519. (See Schedule 4 for computations.)

3. *Weighted Average of Earnings:* Instead of a simple average, a weighted average for the same three-year period would provide an average earnings of $1,301,889. The earnings for Year 1 are given twice as much weight as the previous years because the present conditions probably more closely resemble the future. (See Schedule 4 for computations.)

Comparative Value Based on Comparables. Applying a price-earnings ratio of 7.0 to a projected annual earnings of $1.3 million, the comparative value per share of common stock of J. J. Bean, Inc. is determined as follows:

Example 4   A-53

Projected annual earnings		$1,300,000
Number of shares of common stock outstanding:		
Class A Voting	10	
Class B Nonvoting	124	
	134	
Projected annual earnings per share of voting or nonvoting stock		$ 9,701
Price-earnings multiple		7.0
Comparative value per share		$ 67,907

Comparative values for the voting common stock and nonvoting common stock are as follows:

	Common stock	
	Voting	Nonvoting
Comparative value per share	$ 67,907	$ 67,907
No. of shares outstanding	10	124
Total comparative value	$679,070	$8,420,468

NOTE: The only difference between the voting common stock and the nonvoting stock is the yoting rights.

Discount Adjustments. The comparative value per share of common stock is based on the implicit assumption that ownership of the common stock of J. J. Bean, Inc. entails the same risk as ownership of the common stock of the comparables selected. However, the risk involved in investing in an actively traded corporation is less than that of purchasing a company for which there is no ready market.

As discussed in the earlier part of this report, J. J. Bean, Inc. differs from the comparables in the following respects:

- size differential
- less product and name label diversification
- thin management
- weak financial position

In addition, the stock of J. J. Bean, Inc. lacks marketability since it is not publicly traded and could not be marketed easily. To account for these differences, a reasonable discount must be provided. In an article entitled "Nonmarketability Discounts Should Exceed Fifty Percent," 59 *Taxes* 25 (1981), the author suggests that a discount of 50 percent or more for closely held corporations should be applied. The author offered a reasonable basis for arriving at a 50 percent discount.

A possible step in determining a nonmarketability discount is to consider the public offering expenses or "flotation costs" necessary to create a hypothetical market for a closely held company. Such costs range from 5 percent for large offerings to 20 percent for smaller offerings based on aggregate offer price, as shown below:

Cost of flotation for offerings to general public through securities dealers

Size of issue ($ millions)	No.	Compensation (percent of gross proceeds)	Other expenses (percent of gross proceeds)
Under– .5	43	13.24	10.35
.5– .99	227	12.48	8.26
1.0– 1.99	271	10.60	5.87
2.0– 4.99	450	8.19	3.71
5.0– 9.99	287	6.70	2.03
10.0– 19.99	170	5.52	1.11
20.0– 49.99	109	4.41	.62
50.0– 99.99	30	3.94	.31
100.0–499.99	12	3.03	.16
Over –500.0	0	—	—
Total/averages	1,599	8.41	4.02

Source: "Cost of Flotation of Registered Issues, 1971–1972," Securities and Exchange Commission, December, 1974 at 9.

The SEC in its report also noted that, in addition to costs shown above, there was noncash compensation in the form of warrants or portions in many instances. It stated that "such compensation has been prevalent among small equity issues, but during 'hot issues' periods it has been prevalent among equity issues across all issues size strata. As a practical matter, valuation of these arrangements is not possible." Many closely held companies would most likely require such additional noncash compensation, and in appraising the cost to market such securities, these noncash items should be provided for.

While flotation costs provide a reasonable judgment of the cost of

Example 4 A-55

creating a public market for the stock being valued, other factors (such as size differential, business diversification, thin management, and financial position) must also be considered to give full effect of the privately held company in comparison to the publicly held companies.

An IRS study published in the "IRS Valuation Guide for Income, Estate, and Gift Taxes"[CCH Federal Estate and Gift Taxes, No. 264 Part II (5/11/82)], demonstrated the need for discount of size differentials. The study encompassed all manufacturing and merchandising corporations having their common stock traded or quoted on the New York Stock Exchange as of February 28, 1957. The following statistics are provided by the IRS:

Market price of outstanding stocks and long-term debts		No. of companies of this size	Price/earning ratios on basis of:	
Minimum value	Maximum value		Latest years earnings	5-Year average earnings
$ 1,000,000	$ 4,999,999	17	11.51	12.26
5,000,000	9,999,999	36	8.95	10.10
10,000,000	24,999,999	131	9.78	11.35
25,000,000	49,999,999	118	10.40	11.76
50,000,000	99,999,999	119	11.18	13.74
100,000,000	499,999,999	156	12.84	15.91
500,000,000	or more	51	16.13	18.56

The table indicates discount for size differential as much as 45 percent [i.e., $1 - (8.95 - 16.13)$] based on the latest year's earnings. The IRS states this:

This tendency seems to be quite logical, however, in view of the practical consideration which most investors follow when making their buy and sell decisions. For one thing, the most successful companies gradually become the largest companies and in many cases become the leaders in their particular industries. Their very success and consequent size is ample evidence to the investing public that each of these enterprises has the ability to meet and survive competition and also has the ability to develop and grow either from internal expansion of its plant and products or by means of mergers. High quality management is ordinarily a prime requisite in such firms and with such the investing public is likely to place greater confidence in these corporations. Certainly, the securities of such corporations are better known to the public and become by the same fact more marketable. Any of these reasons could account for the greater interest, popularity, and consequent higher ratio of price to earnings. Regardless of the underlying causes, however, it is apparent that a genuine and easily discernible trend exists with respect to the size of the corporate enterprise and the price-earnings ratios which it displays.

Recent cases in valuation provided substantial discounts for non-marketability and other inhibiting factors. In *Estate of Arthur F. Little, Jr.* [TCM 1982–26, CCH Dec. 38729(M)], the Tax Court allowed a total discount of 60 percent for shares of restricted stock of a publicly held company. (Restricted stock is stock of a publicly held company that is subject to certain sales restrictions.) The court allowed a 35 percent discount for sales restrictions, a 15 percent discount for an irrevocable two-year voting proxy agreement, and a 10 percent discount for shares that were held in escrow.

In *William T. Piper, Sr. Est.* [72TC No. 88, CCH Dec. 36,315], the court allowed a total discount of 64 percent for stock of a corporation which owned publicly traded securities and rental property. The court allowed a discount of 35 percent for lack of marketability, 17 percent for relatively unattractive investment portfolios, and another 12 percent for possible stock registration costs.

In *Sol Koffler* [TCM 1978–159], the taxpayer gifted common stock of a luggage manufacturing company, American Luggage Works, Inc. (ALW). The comparable selected for valuation was the largest luggage manufacturer in the U.S. It was also a diversified company engaged in the manufacture and sale of furniture, toys, and small computers, which accounted for about 25 percent of the net sales.

The dissimilarities between J. J. Bean, Inc. and its selected comparables resemble that of the *Sol Koffler* case in the following respects:

- thin management
- lack of product diversification
- failure to pay dividends to common stockholders
- nonmarketability

In *Sol Koffler*, the U.S. Tax Court provided a total discount of 60 percent or more to account for the differences between ALW and the comparable selected, as follows:

> Using Samsonite as a comparative, we think substantial discounts would be required in arriving at a price-earnings ratio for ALW: at least 15 percent for ALW's thin management; at least 30 percent for ALW's lack of diversification, its outmoded manufacturing facilities, its limit to the

Example 4   **A-57**

domestic market, its failure to pay any dividends since 1951, and its domination by a single family; and an equal discount for the fact that the ALW stock was not publicly traded and could not be easily marketed.

In view of the circumstances surrounding J. J. Bean, Inc., a discount of 35 percent is reasonable for the voting common stock. An additional 5 percent should be added to the nonvoting common stock because of its absence of voting rights. In *Estate of Arther F. Little* [TCM 1982–26, CCH Dec. 38729(M)], the U.S. Tax Court accepted a 15 percent discount for the loss of voting privilege of common stock because of an irrecoverable two-year proxy executed by the decedent.

Applying the discount as determined, the value of the common stock is as follows:

	Common Stock	
	Voting	*Nonvoting*
Discount for nonmarketability, thin management, weak financial position, lack of diversification, etc.	35%	35%
Discount for nonvoting privilege	—	5%
Total discount	35%	40%
Comparative value after discount	$441,400	$5,052,380
Comparative value per share	$ 44,140	$ 40,745

Net Asset Value of Underlying Assets

Revenue Ruling 59–60 states that "the appraiser will accord primary consideration to earnings when valuing stocks of companies which sell products or services to the public." It states that net asset value should be a primary consideration for valuing closely held investment or real estate holding companies. According to Revenue Ruling 59–60, net asset value should be given minimum weight in the valuation of an operating company such as J. J. Bean, Inc.

The position expressed in Revenue Ruling 59–60 is fully supported by other authorities. For example, Judge Learned Hand stated in *Borg* v. *International Silver Co.* [11F. 2d 147, 152 (2nd Cir. 1925)] that "Everyone knows that the value of shares in a commercial or manufacturing company depends chiefly on what it will earn."

Authorities on valuation also commented that earnings, not net asset value, are the ultimate factor in valuing operating businesses. In *The Financial Policy of Corporations* [5th ed., The Ronald Press, 1953], A.S. Dewing, an authority in valuation, takes the position squarely and openly that the ultimate and final controlling criterion of the value of a going business is earning power:

> The businessman, frankly, is interested neither in the engineer's appraisal of physical property, according to some arbitrary rule of unit values, nor in the accountant's report of past expenditures. He is interested primarily in the past earning capacity of the business so far as this can throw light on the future earnings in his hands. He is buying earning capacity and not physical assets.

In the *Estate of Oakley J. Hall*, the U.S. Tax Court also indicated that the net asset value approach plays a minor role in the valuation of an operating business. The court stated;

> We have not overlooked the fact that [the operating business] had a book value of $3,422,000 at September 30, 1967, but we deem it quite unlikely that such a value could have been realized if the company had been liquidated; furthermore, there was no indication in the evidence that there was any intent to liquidate the company at the time of decendent's death.

In summary, the net asset value approach can be a meaningful technique for valuing an investment or real estate holding company. But it has some conceptual limitations for valuing a vigorous operating company such as J. J. Bean, Inc. Nonetheless, the net asset value of the business must be determined since courts have given this value some consideration. As the U.S. Tax Court stated in *Estate of Woodbury G Andrews* [79 TC No. 58, CCH Dec. 39523],

> Certainly, the degree to which the corporation is actively engaged in producing income rather than merely holding property for investment should influence the weight to be given to the values arrived at under the different approaches but it should not dictate the use of one approach to the exclusion of all others.

Computations of Net Asset Value. Net asset value represents the fair market value of the net assets (fair market value of all assets less liabilities) underlying the stock of the corporation. Pursuant to section 5(b) of Reve-

Example 4   **A-59**

nue Ruling 59–60, the net asset value (before discount adjustments) of J. J. Bean, Inc. as of September 30, 198_____ was determined at about $9.6 million, as follows:

Shareholder's equity as of March 31, 198_	$8,656,863
Adjustments:	
Add: (1) After-tax LIFO reserve	850,000
(2) Estimated after-tax earnings for the 6 months ended 9/30/8_	1,200,000
(3) Approximated value of net assets from dormant corporation that merged into J. J. Bean, Inc.	700,000
Minus: (1) Present value of estimated after-tax deferred compensation to officers and executives	(1,849,468)
Net asset value as of September 30, 198_ before discount	$9,557,395

Valuation authorities have suggested that book value of assets shown on the balance sheet may be adjusted to reasonably reflect their market value when the net asset value approach is used. Revenue Ruling 59–60 also suggests that in "computing the book value per share of stock, assets of the investment type should be revalued on the basis of their market price and the book value adjusted accordingly." This means that investment assets (i.e., assets not utilized in the trade of business of the corporation) held by either an investment or an operating company would be revalued at their market value. However, physical assets used in the trade of business (i.e., operating assets such as building and machinery) would not be revalued or adjusted. The approach advocated by the revenue ruling seems logical for an operating company, since the primary emphasis is on earnings and the actual value of operating assets could not be realized without ceasing operations and liquidating the business.

Adjustments may also be made to reflect elements that do not appear on the balance sheets. Items requiring consideration are intangible assets and deferred or contingent liabilities.

An examination of the balance sheet of J. J. Bean as of March 31, 198_____ indicates that only one adjustment to the book value of assets is necessary: adjustment for the LIFO Reserve. The book value of the fixed assets should approximate their net realizable value.

As of September 30, 198_____, the original costs of the land and building improvements were $2,428,145, with accumulated depreciation of only $258,005. The land and buildings are located in a deteriorated neighborhood where vandalism and crime are not an uncommon occurrence. An appraisal conducted as of October 20, 198_____ indicated that the property had a remaining useful life of probably no greater than 20 years. The appraisal report also stated that the general industrial market would find the property to be somewhat limited in flexibility of use primarily because of its design, size, and age. In view of the circumstances, it is unlikely that the property would command a value substantially higher than the book value.

Examination of financial statements and other financial records also revealed that certain assets and liabilities not presented in the balance sheet must be accounted for to reflect the net asset value of the company. These undisclosed assets and liabilities are discussed below.

Corporate Merger. During fiscal year ended September 30, 198_____, a corporation wholly owned by J. J. Bean was merged into J. J. Bean, Inc. The net asset value of the merged corporation was estimated by management at about $700,000.

Deferred Compensation to Officers. J. J. Bean, Inc has entered into various deferred compensation agreements with its key officers and executives. In general, the agreements state that the corporation shall pay the employee a sum of $_____ yearly to commence in equal monthly installments at age 65 and continuing during the employee's lifetime.

If the employee should die after age 65 before receiving installment payments over a 10-year period, payments will continue to be made by the corporation for the remainder of the 10-year period to a beneficiary designated by the employee. The agreements are binding on the corporation and its successor.

The compensation, although deferred to the future, represents a true liability of the corporation. A. G. Cox, an actuarial consulting firm, made the determination of this liability. The after-tax deferred compensation amount is $1,849,468.

Allocation of Net Asset Value. The net asset value computed above represents the value of both common stock and preferred stock as a whole. Accordingly, the net asset value must be allocated to each class of stock outstanding. The amount of net value allocable to the preferred stock would be the liquidation preference amount. The remaining value would be allocated to the two classes of common stock. The net asset value for each share of common stock was determined to be $69,178, as follows:

Example 4   **A-61**

Net asset value before discount	$9,557,395
Less: amount allocated to preferred stock at $100 per share of liquidation preferences	(287,500)
Net asset value allocable to common stock	$9,269,895
Net asset value per share of common stock ($9,269,895—134 shares)	$ 69,178

Net asset value for each class of common stock would be $691,780 for Class A voting stock and $8,578,072 for Class B nonvoting stock. Computations are as follows:

	Class A voting	Class B nonvoting
Net asset value per share	$ 69,178	$ 69,178
No. of shares outstanding	10	124
Total net asset value before discount	$691,780	$8,578,072

Discount Adjustments for Net Asset Value.   As discussed in the Comparative Approach to Valuation section, a discount must be provided for an interest held in a closely held business. Applying the discount factors presented in the Comparative Approach to Valuation section, the total value of the common stock under the net asset value approach would be $5,596,528, as follows:

	Class A voting	Class B nonvoting
Net asset value after discount	$449,660	$5,146,868
Value per share	$ 44,966	$ 41,507

Dividend-paying Capacity

Dividend-paying capacity is identified in Revenue Ruling 59–60 as one factor to be considered in valuing a closely held business. In determining dividend-paying ability, liquidity is an important consideration. A relatively profitable company may be illiquid as funds are needed for fixed assets and working capital.

J. J. Bean, Inc. has not paid any dividends to its common stock shareholders over the years. Based on its financial history, J. J. Bean, Inc. has limited capacity to pay dividends. It has been continuously obtaining operating funds from a factoring company in excess of its outstanding accounts receivable balance. Any dividend payment to shareholders would exacerbate the present cash problems. As a practical matter, J. J. Bean, Inc. has a nominal value based on its dividend-paying capacity.

Valuation of Preferred Stock

Revenue Ruling 83-120 (IRB 1983–33, 8, August 15, 1983) provides guidance to the valuation of preferred stock. It states that the most important factors to be considered in determining the value of preferred stock are its yield, dividend coverage and protection of its liquidation preference.

The ruling also states that the dividend yield determines whether the preferred stock has a value equal to its par value. It specifically states the following:

> Whether the yield of the preferred stock supports a valuation of the stock at par value depends in part on the adequacy of the dividend rate. The adequacy of the dividend rate should be determined by comparing its dividend rate with the dividend rate of high-grade publicly traded preferred stock. A lower yield than that of high-grade preferred stock indicates a preferred stock value of less than par. In addition, whether the preferred stock has a fixed dividend rate and is nonparticipating influences the value of the preferred stock . . . A publicly traded preferred stock for a company having a similar business and similar assets with similar liquidation preferences, voting rights, and other similar terms would be the ideal comparable for determining yield required in arms length transactions for closely held stock. Such ideal comparables will frequently not exist. In such circumstances, the most comparable publicly traded issues should be selected for comparison and appropriate adjustments made for differing factors.

In short, the valuation method for preferred stock is to capitalize the annual dividend at a market rate equal to the rate of returns from similar grade marketable securities and then make appropriate adjustments for variations.

Example 4 A-63

Classes of Preferred Stock. J. J. Bean, Inc. has two classes of preferred stock outstanding. Presently, there are 500 shares of Class A preferred stock and 2,375 shares of Class B preferred stock outstanding. The features of these preferred stocks are as follows:

	Preferred stock	
Stock features	Class A	Class B
Par value	$100	$100
Annual dividend rate	8%	10%
Liquidation preferences	$100	$100
Callable amount	$100	$105

In addition, both classes of stock are nonparticipating, noncumulative, nonconvertible, and nonvoting. These classes of stock are not a particularly attractive investment because of their callable and noncumulative features.

Comparative Value After Adjustments. Cluett, Peabody is the only comparable company whose preferred stock was publicly traded in September 198_____. This preferred stock was priced to yield 5.6 percent. However, this stock is far from comparable to either class of J. J. Bean, Inc.'s preferred stock. The Cluett, Peabody stock is cumulative and convertible into common stock. Because of the convertible feature, a lower yield is provided. J.J. Bean, Inc.'s preferred stock should provide a higher yield because of the nonconvertible and callable features. Adjustments to account for the nonconvertibility feature using Cluett, Peabody as a comparable, while possible, are difficult and possibly unsound. It would be more appropriate to search for other preferred stock as possible comparables.

The search for comparable preferred stock was extended to other companies in the apparel industry. However, no preferred stock that was traded to yield a rate of return of around 12–13 percent. (Appendix I [not shown in this book] provides a listing of public utility preferred stocks.)

In view of the lack of comparable preferred stock in the apparel industry, the search was extended to the public utility sector. In September, high-grade preferred stocks in selected public utility companies were traded to yield a rate of return of around 12–13 percent. (Appendix I [not shown in this book] provides a listing of public utility preferred stocks.)

Given the dividend yield from selected stock of public utility companies, the preferred stock with features similar to those of J. J. Bean, Inc.

should be priced to earn a dividend yield of at least 12 percent. At a dividend yield of 12 percent, the value of the preferred stock would be as follows:

	Number of shares	Price per share to yield 12%	Total value
Class A	500.00	$66.70	$ 33,350
Class B	2,375.00	83.30	197,838
			$231,188

The value of the preferred stock as indicated above represents value of high-grade publicly traded stock. Due to J. J. Bean, Inc.'s thin management, weak financial position, and lack of marketability, the value should be discounted by at least 35 percent. Accordingly, the fair market value of the preferred stock of J. J. Bean, Inc. would be $150,286, as follows:

	Preferred stock	
	Class A	Class B
Value before discount	$33,350	$197,838
Discount	35%	35%
Value after discount	$21,680	$128,606
Value per share	$ 43.36	$ 54.15

Summary Statements

The common stock of J. J. Bean, Inc. was valued based on three approaches: comparative value, net asset value, and dividend-paying capacity. Although the dividend-paying capacity approach provides a much lower value for J. J. Bean, Inc., the comparative value approach and the net asset value approach should be given the greatest weights in determining the value of J. J. Bean, Inc. Both the comparative value approach and the net asset value approach provide approximately the same after-discounted values. The comparative value approach provides a total value of

Example 4   **A-65**

$5,493,780, while the net asset value approach gives a total value of $5,596,528. Given the close proximity of the values between the two methods, the value of the common stock as of September 30, 198_____ would clearly be within the price range of $5.5 to $5.6 million. Accordingly, the fair market value of the two classes of common stock should be $5,493,780, divided as follows:

	Common Stock	
Voting	Nonvoting	Total
$441,440	$5,052,380	$5,493,780

SCHEDULE 1

J.J. Bean, Inc.
Simple Average of Price-Earnings Ratios of Selected Comparables

Company	Year 6	Year 5	Year 4	Year 3	Year 2	Year 1
Hartmarx	5.9	4.9	4.8	6.1	6.3	10.67
Palm Beach	4.1	4.6	4.9	7.4	7.7	11.73
Cluett, Peabody	5.8	5.8	5.8	5.8	6.7	9.28
Totals	15.80	15.30	15.50	19.30	20.70	31.68
Averages per period	5.26	5.10	5.16	6.43	6.90	10.56
Simple average weighted factor	1	1	1	1	1	.50
Simple average per period	5.26	5.10	5.16	6.43	6.90	5.28
Simple average over the 5 1/2 year period	$(5.26 + 5.10 + 5.16 + 6.43 + 6.90 + 5.28) \div 5.5 = 6.20$					

Source: The Value Line Investment Survey
Standard & Poor's Standard NYSE Stock Reports
Standard & Poor's Stock Guide

SCHEDULE 2

J.J. Bean, Inc.
Weighted Average of Price-Earnings Ratios of Selected Comparables

Company	Year 6	Year 5	Year 4	Year 3	Year 2	Year 1
Hartmarx	5.9	4.9	4.8	6.1	6.3	10.67
Palm Beach	4.1	4.6	4.9	7.4	7.7	11.73
Cluett, Peabody	5.8	5.8	5.8	5.8	6.7	9.28
Totals	15.80	15.30	15.50	19.30	20.70	31.68
Averages per period	5.26	5.10	5.16	6.43	6.90	10.56
Weighted factor	1	2	3	4	5	3
Weighted average per period	5.26	10.20	15.48	25.72	34.50	31.68
Weighted average over the 5 1/2 year period	$(5.26 + 10.20 + 15.48 + 25.72 + 34.50 + 31.68) \div 18 = 6.82$					

Source: The Value Line Investment Survey
Standard & Poor's Standard NYSE Stock Reports
Standard & Poor's Stock Guide

Example 4   **A-67**

SCHEDULE 3

J. J. Bean, Inc.
Regression Analysis* of Earnings Potential

Year	Net sales	Net earnings
3	$65,806,459	$ 453,531
4	69,505,067	2,154,026
5	55,075,549	1,650,668
6	40,371,493	882,124
7	29,783,391	671,006
8	27,689,397	473,569

Projections	Given net sales**	Projected earnings	Index of correlation
Year 2	$60 million	$1,320,582	.35
Year 1 (including projected earnings of year 2 in the data base)	$60 million	$1,320,582	.37

**Net Sales as projected by management.

*(It is not the author's wish to burden the reader with the complex mathematical formulas involved in regression analysis. Suffice it to say, regression analysis is a mathematical formula that attempts to determine the future behavior of one factor, such as earnings in Schedule 3 above, by charting its past behavior in relation to another factor, such as net sales above.

Look at the relationship between net sales and earnings from years 3 to 8, with year 3 being last year or the most recent year. During that time, a change in net sales either up or down would produce a change in net earnings in a similar direction. By using a mathematical formula to analyze the relation between net sales and earnings, a projection is made as to what earnings will be next year (Year 2), and the following year (Year 1), given a certain amount of net sales, in our case $60 million. The Index of Correlation tells what percentage of the change in projected earnings is due to the given amount of net sales—for example, from Year 3 to Year 2 it is .35 or 35%.)

SCHEDULE 4

J. J. Bean, Inc.
Average Earnings for Three-Year Period Fiscal Years Ended 9/30/8_ to 198_

Year	Net earnings	Weighted factor	Weighted earnings
1	$1,300,000*	2	$2,600,000
2	453,531	1	453,531
3	2,154,026	1	2,154,026
Totals	3,907,557		5,207,557
Simple average	$1,302,519		
Weighted average			$1,301,889

*Earnings as estimated by management for year 1.

APPENDIX B
Revenue
Rulings

CONTENTS

IRS REVENUE RULINGS

A.R.M. 34, C.B. 2, 31 (1920)   **See Revenue Rul. 65-192**

Rev. Rul. 59-60, 1959-1 C.B. 237   **B-5**

> (Note: This ruling is modified and amplified by various revenue rulings following in Appendix B: Rev. Rul. 65-193, Rev. Rul. 77-287, Rev. Rul. 80-213, and Rev. Rul. 83-120.)
> This is the oldest and still the most important of IRS rulings on the valuation of privately held businesses. It is discussed in length in Chapter Three.

Rev. Rul. 65-192, 1965-2 C.B. 259*   **B-13**

> This ruling makes the methods and factors used in Rev. Rul. 59-60 applicable to valuations for income tax purposes, and all other tax purposes. It also restricts the use of the formula approach set out in A.R.M. 34 (See Chapter Three) to the valuation of intangible assets, and only if there is no better valuation method available.

Rev. Rul. 65-193, 1965-2 C.B. 370   **B-17**

> This ruling modifies Rev. Rul. 59-60 to conform with Rev. Rul. 65-192 regarding use of the formula approach contained in A.R.M. 34 in the valuation of intangible assets of a privately-held business.

Rev. Rul. 68-609, 1968-2 C.B. 327   **B-19**

> This ruling summarizes and updates the changes made to Rev. Rul. 59-60 regarding the use of the formula approach contained in A.R.M. 34 in valuing the intangibles assets of a privately-held business.
> This ruling makes the methods and approaches of Rev. Rul. 59-60 applicable to the valuation of business interests of any and all types, including partnerships and proprietorships.

*Contains full text of A.R.M. 34, C.B. 2, 31 (1920)

Rev. Rul. 77-287, 1977-2 C.B. 319   B-21

This ruling provides guidelines for valuation of shares of stock (to determine the appropriate discount) of a privately-held business where the shares are subject to some restriction under the Federal securities laws.

Rev. Rul. 78-367, 1978-2 C.B. 249   B-27

This ruling involves the valuation of stock of a privately-held business for purposes of the gift tax. It states that the valuation should take into account the effects of a public announcement of a merger of the privately-held business into a larger publicly-traded corporation.

Rev. Rul. 79-7, 1979-1 C.B. 294   B-29

This ruling states that when a person transfers a minority interest of stock in a privately-held business while retaining a majority interest, and the transferred minority interest is includible in his estate upon death, the minority interest and the retained majority interest are valued as one block of stock for estate tax purposes.

Rev. Rul. 81-15, 1981-1 C.B. 457   B-31

This ruling was issued in reaction to the Supreme Court decision in *Byrum*, 408 U.S. 125 (1972). That case concluded that where a decedent transferred in trust the stock of a privately-held business, the retention of certain rights by the decedent over the disposition of the stock did not make the stock includible in his estate.
The IRS in Rev. Rul. 67-54 had come to the opposite conclusion under circumstances similar to *Byrum*. Rev. Rul. 67-54 is revoked.

Rev. Rul. 81-253, 1981-2 C.B. 187   **B-33**

This ruling disallows minority discounts for gifts of all the stock of a privately-held business given by the controlling shareholder to members of his family. Each family member received a minority interest. Each minority interest must be valued the same as if it were part of a controlling interest held by one member of the family.

Rev. Rul. 83-119, 1983-2 C.B. 57   **B-37**

This ruling says that where preferred stock issued as part of a recapitalization must be redeemed at 110% of its issue price when the holder dies, the 10% excess can be treated as a distribution, which could be a taxable dividend, deemed to be received ratably over the life of the shareholder receiving the preferred stock in the recapitalization.

Rev. Rul. 83-120, 1983-2 C.B. 170   **B-43**

This ruling sets forth guidelines for the valuation of common and preferred stock issued in a recapitalization (See Chapter Eleven).

REVENUE RULING 59-60

SECTION 2031.—DEFINITION OF GROSS ESTATE

26 CFR 20.2031–2: Valuation of stocks and bonds. Rev. Rul. 59–60
(Also Section 2512.)
(Also Part II, Sections 811 (k), 1005, Regulations 105, Section 81.10.)

> In valuing the stock of closely held corporations, or the stock of corporations where market quotations are not available, all other available financial data, as well as all relevant factors affecting the fair market value must be considered for estate tax and gift tax purposes. No general formula may be given that is applicable to the many different valuation situations arising in the valuation of such stock. However, the general approach, methods, and factors which must be considered in valuing such securities are outlined.
> Revenue Ruling 54–77, C.B. 1954–1, 187, superseded.

SECTION 1. PURPOSE.

The purpose of this Revenue Ruling is to outline and review in general the approach, methods and factors to be considered in valuing shares of the capital stock of closely held corporations for estate tax and gift tax purposes. The methods discussed herein will apply likewise to the valuation of corporate stocks on which market quotations are either unavailable or are of such scarcity that they do not reflect the fair market value.

SEC. 2. BACKGROUND AND DEFINITIONS.

.01 All valuations must be made in accordance with the applicable provisions of the Internal Revenue Code of 1954 and the Federal Estate Tax and Gift Tax Regulations. Sections 2031(a), 2032 and 2512(a) of the 1954 Code (sections 811 and 1005 of the 1939 Code) require that the property to be included in the gross estate, or made the subject of a gift, shall be taxed on the basis of the value of the property at the time of death of the decedent, the alternate date if so elected, or the date of gift.

.02 Section 20.2031–1(b) of the Estate Tax Regulations (section 81.10 of the Estate Tax Regulations 105) and section 25.2512–1 of the Gift Tax Regulations (section 86.19 of Gift Tax Regulations 108) define fair market value, in effect, as the price at which the property would change hands between a willing buyer and a willing seller when the former is not under any compulsion to buy and the latter is not under any compulsion to sell, both parties having reasonable knowledge of relevant facts. Court decisions frequently state in addition that the hypothetical buyer and seller are assumed to be able, as well as willing, to trade and to be well informed about the property and concerning the market for such property.

.03 Closely held corporations are those corporations the shares of which are owned by a relatively limited number of stockholders. Often the entire stock issue is held by one family. The result of this situation is that little, if any, trading in the shares takes place. There is, therefore, no established market for the stock and such sales as occur at irregular intervals seldom reflect all of the elements of a representative transaction as defined by the term "fair market value."

Sec. 3. Approach to Valuation.

.01 A determination of fair market value, being a question of fact, will depend upon the circumstances in each case. No formula can be devised that will be generally applicable to the multitude of different valuation issues arising in estate and gift tax cases. Often, an appraiser will find wide differences of opinion as to the fair market value of a particular stock. In resolving such differences, he should maintain a reasonable attitude in recognition of the fact that valuation is not an exact science. A sound valuation will be based upon all the relevant facts, but the elements of common sense, informed judgment and reasonableness must enter into the process of weighing those facts and determining their aggregate significance.

.02 The fair market value of specific shares of stock will vary as general economic conditions change from "normal" to "boom" or "depression," that is, according to the degree of optimism or pessimism with which the investing public regards the future at the required date of appraisal. Uncertainty as to the stability or continuity of the future income from a property decreases its value by increasing the risk of loss of earnings and value in the future. The value of shares of stock of a company with very uncertain future prospects is highly speculative. The appraiser must exercise his judgment as to the degree of risk attaching to the business of the corporation which issued the stock, but that judgment must be related to all of the other factors affecting value.

.03 Valuation of securities is, in essence, a prophesy as to the future and must be based on facts available at the required date of appraisal. As a generalization, the prices of stocks which are traded in volume in a free and active market by informed persons best reflect the consensus of the investing public as to what the future holds for the corporations and industries represented. When a stock is closely held, is traded infrequently, or is traded in an erratic market, some other measure of value must be used. In many instances, the next best measure may be found in the prices at which the stocks of companies engaged in the same or a similar line of business are selling in a free and open market.

Sec. 4. Factors To Consider.

.01 It is advisable to emphasize that in the valuation of the stock of closely held corporations or the stock of corporations where market quotations are either lacking or too scarce to be recognized, all available financial data, as well as all relevant factors affecting the fair market value, should be considered. The following factors, although not all-inclusive are fundamental and require careful analysis in each case:

(a) The nature of the business and the history of the enterprise from its inception.

(b) The economic outlook in general and the condition and outlook of the specific industry in particular.

(c) The book value of the stock and the financial condition of the business.

(d) The earning capacity of the company.

(e) The dividend-paying capacity.

(f) Whether or not the enterprise has goodwill or other intangible value.

(g) Sales of the stock and the size of the block of stock to be valued.

(h) The market price of stocks of corporations engaged in the same or a similar line of business having their stocks actively traded in a free and open market, either on an exchange or over-the-counter.

.02   The following is a brief discussion of each of the foregoing factors:

(a) The history of a corporate enterprise will show its past stability or instability, its growth or lack of growth, the diversity or lack of diversity of its operations, and other facts needed to form an opinion of the degree of risk involved in the business. For an enterprise which changed its form of organization but carried on the same or closely similar operations of its predecessor, the history of the former enterprise should be considered. The detail to be considered should increase with approach to the required date of appraisal, since recent events are of greatest help in predicting the future; but a study of gross and net income, and of dividends covering a long prior period, is highly desirable. The history to be studied should include, but need not be limited to, the nature of the business, its products or services, its operating and investment assets, capital structure, plant facilities, sales records and management, all of which should be considered as of the date of the appraisal, with due regard for recent significant changes. Events of the past that are unlikely to recur in the future should be discounted, since value has a close relation to future expectancy.

(b) A sound appraisal of a closely held stock must consider current and prospective economic conditions as of the date of appraisal, both in the national economy and in the industry or industries with which the corporation is allied. It is important to know that the company is more or less successful than its competitors in the same industry, or that it is maintaining a stable position with respect to competitors. Equal or even greater significance may attach to the ability of the industry with which the company is allied to compete with other industries. Prospective competition which has not been a factor in prior years should be given careful attention. For example, high profits due to the novelty of its product and the lack of competition often lead to increasing competition. The public's appraisal of the future prospects of competitive industries or of competitors within an industry may be indicated by price trends in the markets for commodities and for securities. The loss of the manager of a so-called "one-man" business may have a depressing effect upon the value of the stock of such business, particularly if there is a lack of trained personnel capable of succeeding to the management of the enterprise. In valuing the stock of this type of business, therefore, the effect of the loss of the manager on the future expectancy of the business, and the absence of management-succession potentialities are pertinent factors to be taken into consideration. On the other hand, there may be factors which offset, in whole or in part, the loss of the manager's services. For instance, the nature of the business and of its assets may be such that they will not be impaired by the loss of the manager. Furthermore, the loss may be adequately covered by life insurance, or competent management might be employed on the basis of the consideration paid for the former manager's services. These, or other offsetting factors, if found to exist, should be carefully weighed against the loss of the manager's services in valuing the stock of the enterprise.

(c) Balance sheets should be obtained, preferably in the form of comparative annual statements for two or more years immediately preceding the date of appraisal, together with a balance sheet at the end of the month preceding that date, if corporate accounting will permit. Any balance sheet descriptions that are not self-explanatory, and balance sheet items comprehending diverse assets or liabilities, should be clarified in essential detail by supporting supplemental schedules. These statements usually will disclose to the appraiser (1) liquid position (ratio of current assets to current liabilities); (2) gross and net book value of principal classes of fixed assets; (3) working capital; (4) long-term indebtedness; (5) capital structure; and (6) net worth. Consideration also should be given to any assets not essential to the operation of the business, such as investments in securities, real estate, etc. In general, such nonoperating assets will command a lower rate of return than do the operating assets, although in exceptional cases the reverse may be true. In computing the book value per share of stock, assets of the investment type should be revalued on the basis of their market price and the book value adjusted accordingly. Comparison of the company's balance sheets over several years may reveal, among other facts, such developments as the acquisition of additional production facilities or subsidiary companies, improvement in financial position, and details as to recapitalizations and other changes in the capital structure of the corporation. If the corporation has more than one class of stock outstanding, the charter or certificate of incorporation should be examined to ascertain the explicit rights and privileges of the various stock issues including: (1) voting powers, (2) preference as to dividends, and (3) preference as to assets in the event of liquidation.

(d) Detailed profit-and-loss statements should be obtained and considered for a representative period immediately prior to the required date of appraisal, preferably five or more years. Such statements should show (1) gross income by principal items; (2) principal deductions from gross income including major prior items of operating expenses, interest and other expense on each item of long-term debt, depreciation and depletion if such deductions are made, officers' salaries, in total if they appear to be reasonable or in detail if they

seem to be excessive, contributions (whether or not deductible for
tax purposes) that the nature of its business and its community position require the corporation to make, and taxes by principal items,
including income and excess profits taxes; (3) net income available
for dividends; (4) rates and amounts of dividends paid on each class
of stock; (5) remaining amount carried to surplus; and (6) adjustments to, and reconciliation with, surplus as stated on the balance
sheet. With profit and loss statements of this character available,
the appraiser should be able to separate recurrent from nonrecurrent
items of income and expense, to distinguish between operating income
and investment income, and to ascertain whether or not any line
of business in which the company is engaged is operated consistently
at a loss and might be abandoned with benefit to the company. The
percentage of earnings retained for business expansion should be
noted when dividend-paying capacity is considered. Potential future
income is a major factor in many valuations of closely-held stocks,
and all information concerning past income which will be helpful
in predicting the future should be secured. Prior earnings records
usually are the most reliable guide as to the future expectancy, but
resort to arbitrary five-or-ten-year averages without regard to current trends or future prospects will not produce a realistic valuation.
If, for instance, a record of progressively increasing or decreasing
net income is found, then greater weight may be accorded the most
recent years' profits in estimating earning power. It will be helpful,
in judging risk and the extent to which a business is a marginal operator, to consider deductions from income and net income in terms of
percentage of sales. Major categories of cost and expense to be
so analyzed include the consumption of raw materials and supplies
in the case of manufacturers, processors and fabricators; the cost of
purchased merchandise in the case of merchants; utility services;
insurance; taxes; depletion or depreciation; and interest.

(e) Primary consideration should be given to the dividend-paying
capacity of the company rather than to dividends actually paid in
the past. Recognition must be given to the necessity of retaining
a reasonable portion of profits in a company to meet competition.
Dividend-paying capacity is a factor that must be considered in an
appraisal, but dividends actually paid in the past may not have any
relation to dividend-paying capacity. Specifically, the dividends paid
by a closely held family company may be measured by the income
needs of the stockholders or by their desire to avoid taxes on dividend
receipts, instead of by the ability of the company to pay dividends.
Where an actual or effective controlling interest in a corporation is
to be valued, the dividend factor is not a material element, since the
payment of such dividends is discretionary with the controlling stockholders. The individual or group in control can substitute salaries
and bonuses for dividends, thus reducing net income and understating
the dividend-paying capacity of the company. It follows, therefore,
that dividends are less reliable criteria of fair market value than other
applicable factors.

(f) In the final analysis, goodwill is based upon earning capacity.

The presence of goodwill and its value, therefore, rests upon the excess of net earnings over and above a fair return on the net tangible assets. While the element of goodwill may be based primarily on earnings, such factors as the prestige and renown of the business, the ownership of a trade or brand name, and a record of successful operation over a prolonged period in a particular locality, also may furnish support for the inclusion of intangible value. In some instances it may not be possible to make a separate appraisal of the tangible and intangible assets of the business. The enterprise has a value as an entity. Whatever intangible value there is, which is supportable by the facts, may be measured by the amount by which the appraised value of the tangible assets exceeds the net book value of such assets.

(g) Sales of stock of a closely held corporation should be carefully investigated to determine whether they represent transactions at arm's length. Forced or distress sales do not ordinarily reflect fair market value nor do isolated sales in small amounts necessarily control as the measure of value. This is especially true in the valuation of a controlling interest in a corporation. Since, in the case of closely held stocks, no prevailing market prices are available, there is no basis for making an adjustment for blockage. It follows, therefore, that such stocks should be valued upon a consideration of all the evidence affecting the fair market value. The size of the block of stock itself is a relevant factor to be considered. Although it is true that a minority interest in an unlisted corporation's stock is more difficult to sell than a similar block of listed stock, it is equally true that control of a corporation, either actual or in effect, representing as it does an added element of value, may justify a higher value for a specific block of stock.

(h) Section 2031(b) of the Code states, in effect, that in valuing unlisted securities the value of stock or securities of corporations engaged in the same or a similar line of business which are listed on an exchange should be taken into consideration along with all other factors. An important consideration is that the corporations to be used for comparisons have capital stocks which are actively traded by the public. In accordance with section 2031(b) of the Code, stocks listed on an exchange are to be considered first. However, if sufficient comparable companies whose stocks are listed on an exchange cannot be found, other comparable companies which have stocks actively traded in on the over-the-counter market also may be used. The essential factor is that whether the stocks are sold on an exchange or over-the-counter there is evidence of an active, free public market for the stock as of the valuation date. In selecting corporations for comparative purposes, care should be taken to use only comparable companies. Although the only restrictive requirement as to comparable corporations specified in the statute is that their lines of business be the same or similar, yet it is obvious that consideration must be given to other relevant factors in order that the most valid comparison possible will be obtained. For illustration, a corporation having one or more issues of preferred stock, bonds or debentures in addition to its common stock should not be considered to be directly comparable to one having only common stock outstanding. In like manner, a company with a declining business and decreasing markets is not comparable to one with a record of current progress and market expansion.

SEC. 5. WEIGHT TO BE ACCORDED VARIOUS FACTORS.

The valuation of closely held corporate stock entails the consideration of all relevant factors as stated in section 4. Depending upon the circumstances in each case, certain factors may carry more weight than others because of the nature of the company's business. To illustrate:

(a) Earnings may be the most important criterion of value in some cases whereas asset value will receive primary consideration in others. In general, the appraiser will accord primary consideration to earnings when valuing stocks of companies which sell products or services to the public; conversely, in the investment or holding type of company, the appraiser may accord the greatest weight to the assets underlying the security to be valued.

(b) The value of the stock of a closely held investment or real estate holding company, whether or not family owned, is closely related to the value of the assets underlying the stock. For companies of this type the appraiser should determine the fair market values of the assets of the company. Operating expenses of such a company and the cost of liquidating it, if any, merit consideration when appraising the relative values of the stock and the underlying assets. The market values of the underlying assets give due weight to potential earnings and dividends of the particular items of property underlying the stock, capitalized at rates deemed proper by the investing public at the date of appraisal. A current appraisal by the investing public should be superior to the retrospective opinion of an individual. For these reasons, adjusted net worth should be accorded greater weight in valuing the stock of a closely held investment or real estate holding company, whether or not family owned, than any of the other customary yardsticks of appraisal, such as earnings and dividend paying capacity.

SEC. 6. CAPITALIZATION RATES.

In the application of certain fundamental valuation factors, such as earnings and dividends, it is necessary to capitalize the average or current results at some appropriate rate. A determination of the proper capitalization rate presents one of the most difficult problems in valuation. That there is no ready or simple solution will become apparent by a cursory check of the rates of return and dividend yields in terms of the selling prices of corporate shares listed on the major exchanges of the country. Wide variations will be found even for companies in the same industry. Moreover, the ratio will fluctuate from year to year depending upon economic conditions. Thus, no standard tables of capitalization rates applicable to closely held corporations can be formulated. Among the more important factors to be taken into consideration in deciding upon a capitalization rate in a particular case are: (1) the nature of the business; (2) the risk involved; and (3) the stability or irregularity of earnings.

SEC. 7. AVERAGE OF FACTORS.

Because valuations cannot be made on the basis of a prescribed formula, there is no means whereby the various applicable factors in a particular case can be assigned mathematical weights in deriving the fair market value. For this reason, no useful purpose is served by taking an average of several factors (for example, book value, capitalized earnings and capitalized dividends) and basing the valuation on the result. Such a process excludes active consideration of other pertinent factors, and the end result cannot be supported by a realistic application of the significant facts in the case except by mere chance.

SEC. 8. RESTRICTIVE AGREEMENTS.

Frequently, in the valuation of closely held stock for estate and gift tax purposes, it will be found that the stock is subject to an agreement restricting its sale or transfer. Where shares of stock were acquired by a decedent subject to an option reserved by the issuing corporation to repurchase at a certain price, the option price is usually accepted as the fair market value for estate tax purposes. See Rev. Rul. 54–76, C.B. 1954–1, 194. However, in such case the option price is not determinative of fair market value for gift tax purposes. Where the option, or buy and sell agreement, is the result of voluntary action by the stockholders and is binding during the life as well as at the death of the stockholders, such agreement may or may not, depending upon the circumstances of each case, fix the value for estate tax purposes. However, such agreement is a factor to be considered, with other relevant factors, in determining fair market value. Where the stockholder is free to dispose of his shares during life and the option is to become effective only upon his death, the fair market value is not limited to the option price. It is always necessary to consider the relationship of the parties, the relative number of shares held by the decedent, and other material facts, to determine whether the agreement represents a bonafide business arrangement or is a device to pass the decedent's shares to the natural objects of his bounty for less than an adequate and full consideration in money or money's worth. In this connection see Rev. Rul. 157 C.B. 1953–2, 255, and Rev. Rul. 189, C.B. 1953–2, 294.

SEC. 9. EFFECT ON OTHER DOCUMENTS.

Revenue Ruling 54–77, C.B. 1954–1, 187, is hereby superseded.

REVENUE RULING 65-192

SECTION 1001.—DETERMINATION OF AMOUNT OF AND RECOGNITION OF GAIN OR LOSS

26 CFR 1.1001–1 : Computation of gain or loss.   Rev. Rul. 65–192

> The general approach, methods and factors outlined in Revenue Ruling 59–60, C.B. 1959–1, 237, for use in valuing closely-held corporate stocks for estate and gift tax purposes are equally applicable to valuations thereof for income and other tax purposes and also in determinations of the fair market values of business interests of any type and of intangible assets for all tax purposes.
>
> The formula approach set forth in A.R.M. 34, C.B. 2, 31 (1920), and A.R.M. 68, C.B. 3, 43 (1920), has no valid application in determinations of the fair market values of corporate stocks or of business interests, unless it is necessary to value the intangible assets of the corporation or the intangible assets included in the business interest. The formula approach may be used in determining the fair market values of intangible assets only if there is no better basis therefor available. In applying the formula, the average earnings period and the capitalization rates are dependent upon the facts and circumstances pertinent thereto in such case.

SECTION 1. PURPOSE.

The purpose of this Revenue Ruling is to furnish information and guidance as to the usage to be made of suggested methods for determining the value as of March 1, 1913, or of any other date, of intangible assets and to identify those areas where a valuation formula set forth in A.R.M. 34, C.B. 2, 31 (1920), as modified by A.R.M. 68, C.B. 3, 43 (1920), both quoted in full below should and should not be applied. Since it appears that such formula has been applied to many valuation issues for which it was never intended, the Internal Revenue Service reindicates its limited application.

SEC. 2. BACKGROUND.

A.R.M. 34 was issued in 1920 for the purpose of providing suggested formulas for determining the amount of March 1, 1913, intangible asset value lost by breweries and other businesses connected with the distilling industry, as a result of the passage of the 18th Amendment to the Constitution of the United States. A.R.M. 68 was issued later in the same year and contained a minor revision of the original ruling so that its third formula would be applied in accordance with its purpose and intent.

SEC. 3. STATEMENT OF POSITION.

.01 Although the formulas and approach contained in A.R.M. 34, were specifically aimed at the valuation of intangible assets of distilling and related companies as of March 1, 1913, the last two paragraphs of the ruling seemingly broaden it to make its third formula applicable to almost any kind of enterprise. The final sentences, however, limit the purpose of such formula by stating that "In * * * all of the cases the effort should be to determine what net earnings a purchaser of a business on March 1, 1913, might reasonably have expected to receive from it, * * *, "and by providing certain checks and alternatives. Also, both A.R.M. 34 and A.R.M. 68 expressly stated that such formula was merely a rule for guidance and not controlling in the presence of "better evidence" in determining the value of intangible assets. Furthermore, T.B.R. 57, C.B. 1, 40 (1919), relating to the meaning of "fair market value" of property received in exchange for other property, which was published before A.R.M. 34 and A.R.M. 68 and has not been revoked, set forth general principles of valuation that are consistent with Revenue Ruling 59–60, C.B. 1959–1, 237. Moreover, in S.M. 1609, C.B. III–1, 48 (1924) it was stated that "The method suggested in A.R.M. 34 for determining the value of intangibles is * * * controlling only in the absence of better evidence." As said in *North American Service Co., Inc.* v. *Commissioner*, 33 T.C. 677, 694 (1960), acquiescence, C.B. 1960–2, 6, "an A.R.M. 34 computation would not be conclusive of the existence and value of good will if better evidence were available * * *."

.02 Revenue Ruling 59–60 sets forth the proper approach to use in the valuation of closely-held corporate stocks for estate and gift tax purposes. That ruling contains the statement that no formula can be devised that will be generally applicable to the multitude of different valuation issues. It also contains a discussion of intangible value in closely-held corporations and some of the elements which may support such value in a given business.

Sec. 4. Delineation of Areas in Which Suggested Methods Will Be Effective.

.01 The general approach, methods, and factors outlined in Revenue Ruling 59–60 are equally applicable to valuations of corporate stocks for income and other tax purposes as well as for estate and gift tax purposes. They apply also to problems involving the determination of the fair market value of business interests of any type, including partnerships, proprietorships, etc., and of intangible assets for all tax purposes.

.02 Valuation, especially where earning power is an important factor, is in essence a process requiring the exercise of informed judgment and common sense. Thus, the suggested formula approach set forth in A.R.M. 34, has no valid application in determinations of the fair market value of corporate stocks or of business interests unless it is necessary to value the intangible assets of the corporation or the intangible assets included in the business interest. The formula approach may be used in determining the fair market values of intangible assets only if there is no better basis therefor available. In applying the formula, the average earnings period and the capitalization rates are dependent upon the facts and circumstances pertinent thereto in each case. See *John Q. Shunk et al.* v. *Commissioner*, 10 T.C. 293, 304–5 (1948), acquiescence, C.B. 1948–1, 3, affirmed 173 Fed. (2d) 747 (1949); *Ushco Manufacturing Co., Inc.* v. *Commissioner*, Tax Court Memorandum Opinion entered March 10, 1945, affirmed 175 Fed. (2d) 821 (1945); and *White & Wells Co.* v. *Commissioner*, 19 B.T.A. 416, nonacquiescence C.B. IX–2, 87 (1930), reversed and remanded 50 Fed. (2d) 120 (1931).

SEC. 5. QUOTATION OF A.R.M. 34.

For convenience, A.R.M. 34 reads as follows:

The Committee has considered the question of providing some practical formula for determining value as of March 1, 1913, or of any other date, which might be considered as applying to intangible assets, but finds itself unable to lay down any specific rule of guidance for determing the value of intangibles which would be applicable in all cases and under all circumstances. Where there is no established market to serve as a guide the question of value, even of tangible assets, is one largely of judgment and opinion, and the same thing is even more true of intangible assets such as good will, trade-marks, trade brands, etc. However, there are several methods of reaching a conclusion as to the value of intangibles which the Committee suggests may be utilized broadly in passing upon questions of valuation, not to be regarded as controlling, however, if better evidence is presented in any specific case.

Where deduction is claimed for obsolescence or loss of good will or trade-marks, the burden of proof is primarily upon the taxpayer to show the value of such good will or trade-marks on March 1, 1913. Of course, if good will or trade-marks have been acquired for cash or other valuable considerations subsequent to March 1, 1913, the measure of loss will be determined by the amount of cash or value of other considerations paid therefor, and no deduction will be allowed for the value of good will or trade-marks built up by the taxpayer since March 1, 1913. The following suggestions are made, therefore, merely as suggestions for checks upon the soundness and validity of the taxpayers' claims. No obsolescence or loss with respect to good will should be allowed except in cases of actual disposition of the asset or abandonment of the business.

In the first place, it is recognized that in numerous instances it has been the practice of distillers and wholesale liquor dealers to put out under well-known and popular brands only so much goods as could be marketed without affecting the established market price therefor and to sell other goods of the same identical manufacture, age, and character under other brands, or under no brand at all, at figures very much below those which the well-known brands commanded. In such cases the difference between the price at which whisky was sold under a given brand name and also under another brand name, or under no brand, multiplied by the number of units sold during a given year gives an accurate determination of the amount of profit attributable to that brand during that year, and where this practice is continued for a long enough period to show that this amount was fairly constant and regular and might be expected to yield annually that average profit, by capitalizing this earning at the rate, say, of 20 per cent, the value of the brand is fairly well established.

Another method is to compare the volume of business done under the trademark or brand under consideration and profits made, or by the business whose good will is under consideration, with the similar volume of business and profit made in other cases where good will or trade-marks have been actually sold for cash, recognizing as the value of the first the same proportion of the selling price of the second, as the profits of the first attributable to brands or good will, is of the similar profits of the second.

The third method and possibly the one which will most frequently have to be applied as a check in the absence of data necessary for the application of the preceding ones, is to allow out of average earnings over a period of years prior to March 1, 1913, preferably not less than five years, a return of 10 per cent upon the average tangible assets for the period. The surplus earnings will then be the average amount available for return upon the value of the intangible assets, and it is the opinion of the Committee that this return should be capitalized upon the basis of not more than five years' purchase—that is to say, five times the amount available as return from intangibles should be the value of the intangibles.

In view of the hazards of the business, the changes in popular tastes, and the difficulties in preventing imitation or counterfeiting of popular brands affecting the sales of the genuine goods, the Committee is of the opinion that the figure given of 20 per cent return on intangibles is not unreasonable, and it recommends that no higher figure than that be attached in any case to intangibles without a very clear and adequate showing that the value of the intangibles was in fact greater than would be reached by applying this formula.

The foregoing is intended to apply particularly to businesses put out of existence by the prohibition law, but will be equally applicable so far as the third formula is concerned, to other businesses of a more or less hazardous nature.   In the case, however, of valuation of good will of a business which consists of the manufacture or sale of standard articles of every-day necessity not subject to violent fluctuations and where the hazard is not so great, the Committee is of the opinion that the figure for determination of the return on tangible assets might be reduced from 10 to 8 or 9 per cent, and that the percentage for capitalization of the return upon intangibles might be reduced from 20 to 15 per cent.

In any or all of the cases the effort should be to determine what net earnings a purchaser of a business on March 1, 1943, might reasonably have expected to receive from it, and therefore a representative period should be used for averaging actual earnings, eliminating any year in which there were extraordinary factors affecting earnings either way.   Also, in the case of the sale of good will of a going business the percentage rate of capitalization of earnings applicable to good will shown by the amount actually paid for the business should be used as a check against the determination of good will value as of March 1, 1913, and if the good will is sold upon the basis of capitalization of earnings less than the figures above indicated as the ones ordinarily to be adopted, the same percentage should be used in figuring value as of March 1, 1913.

Sec. 6.   Quotation of A.R.M. 68.

Also for convenience, A.R.M. 68 reads as follows:

The Committee is in receipt of a request for advice as to whether under A.R.M. 34 the 10 per cent upon tangible assets is to be applied only to the net tangible assets or to all tangible assets on the books of the corporation, regardless of any outstanding obligations.

The Committee, in the memorandum in question, undertook to lay down a rule for guidance in the absence of better evidence in determining the value as of March 1, 1913, of good will, and held that in determining such value, income over an average period in excess of an amount sufficient to return 10 per cent upon tangible assets should be capitalized at 20 per cent.   Manifestly, since the effort is to determine the value of the good will, and therefore the true net worth of the taxpayer as of March 1, 1913, the 10 per cent should be applied only to the tangible assets entering into net worth, including accounts and bills receivable in excess of accounts and bills payable.

In other words, the purpose and intent are to provide for a return to the taxpayer of 10 per cent upon so much of his investment as is represented by tangible assets and to capitalize the excess of earnings over the amount necessary to provide such return, at 20 per cent.

Sec. 7.   Effect on Other Documents.

Although the limited application of A.R.M. 34 and A.R.M. 68 is reindicated in this Revenue Ruling, the principles enunciated in those rulings are not thereby affected.

———

Valuation of intangible assets of a business where separate appraisal of tangible and intangible assets may not be possible.   See Rev. Rul. 65–193.

REVENUE RULING 65-193

26 CFR 20.2031–2: Valuation of   Rev. Rul. 65–193
  stocks and bonds.
(Also Sections 1001, 2512; 1.1001–1, 25.2512–2.)

Revenue Ruling 59–60, C.B. 1959–1, 237, is hereby modified to delete the statements, contained therein at section 4.02(f), that "In some instances it may not be possible to make a separate appraisal of the tangible and intangible assets of the business. The enterprise has a value as an entity. Whatever intangible value there is, which is supportable by the facts, may be measured by the amount by which the appraised value of the tangible assets exceeds the net book value of such assets."

The instances where it is not possible to make a separate appraisal of the tangible and intangible assets of a business are rare and each case varies from the other. No rule can be devised which will be generally applicable to such cases.

Other than this modification, Revenue Ruling 59–60 continues in full force and effect. See Rev. Rul. 65–192.

REVENUE RULING 68-609

SECTION 1001.—DETERMINATION OF AMOUNT OF AND RECOGNITION OF GAIN OR LOSS

26 CFR 1.1001–1: Computation of gain or loss.   Rev. Rul. 68–609 [1]
(Also Section 167; 1.167(a)–3.)

The purpose of this Revenue Ruling is to update and restate, under the current statute and regulations, the currently outstanding portions of A.R.M. 34, C.B. 2, 31 (1920), A.R.M. 68, C.B. 3, 43 (1920), and O.D. 937, C.B. 4, 43 (1921).

The question presented is whether the "formula" approach, the capitalization of earnings in excess of a fair rate of return on net tangible assets, may be used to determine the fair market value of the intangible assets of a business

The "formula" approach may be stated as follows:

A percentage return on the average annual value of the tangible assets used in a business is determined, using a period of years (preferably not less than five) immediately prior to the valuation date. The amount of the percentage return on tangible assets, thus determined, is deducted from the average earnings of the business for such period and the remainder, if any, is considered to be the amount of the average annual earnings from the intangible assets of the business for the period. This amount (considered as the average annual earnings from intangibles), capitalized at a percentage of, say, 15 to 20 percent, is the value of the intangible assets of the business determined under the "formula" approach.

The percentage of return on the average annual value of the tangible assets used should be the percentage prevailing in the industry involved at the date of valuation, or (when the industry percentage is not available) a percentage of 8 to 10 percent may be used.

The 8 percent rate of return and the 15 percent rate of capitalization are applied to tangibles and intangibles, respectively, of businesses with a small risk factor and stable and regular earnings; the 10 percent rate of return and 20 percent rate of capitalization are applied to businesses in which the hazards of business are relatively high.

The above rates are used as examples and are not appropriate in all cases. In applying the "formula" approach, the average earnings period and the capitalization rates are dependent upon the facts pertinent thereto in each case.

The past earnings to which the formula is applied should fairly reflect the probable future earnings. Ordinarily, the period should not be less than five years, and abnormal years, whether above or below the average, should be eliminated. If the business is a sole proprietorship or partnership, there should be deducted from the earnings of the business a reasonable amount for services performed by the owner or partners engaged in the business. See *Lloyd B. Sanderson Estate* v. *Commissioner*, 42 F. 2d 160 (1930). Further, only the tangible assets entering into net worth, including accounts and bills receivable in

---

[1] Prepared pursuant to Rev. Proc. 67–6, C.B. 1967–1, 576.

excess of accounts and bills payable, are used for determining earnings on the tangible assets. Factors that influence the capitalization rate include (1) the nature of the business, (2) the risk involved, and (3) the stability or irregularity of earnings.

The "formula" approach should not be used if there is better evidence available from which the value of intangibles can be determined. If the assets of a going business are sold upon the basis of a rate of capitalization that can be substantiated as being realistic, though it is not within the range of figures indicated here as the ones ordinarily to be adopted, the same rate of capitalization should be used in determining the value of intangibles.

Accordingly, the "formula" approach may be used for determining the fair market value of intangible assets of a business only if there is no better basis therefor available.

See also Revenue Ruling 59–60, C.B. 1959–1, 237, as modified by Revenue Ruling 65–193, C.B. 1965–2, 370, which sets forth the proper approach to use in the valuation of closely-held corporate stocks for estate and gift tax purposes. The general approach, methods, and factors, outlined in Revenue Ruling 59–60, as modified, are equally applicable to valuations of corporate stocks for income and other tax purposes as well as for estate and gift tax purposes. They apply also to problems involving the determination of the fair market value of business interests of any type, including partnerships and proprietorships, and of intangible assets for all tax purposes.

A.R.M. 34, A.R.M. 68, and O.D. 937 are superseded, since the positions set forth therein are restated to the extent applicable under current law in this Revenue Ruling. Revenue Ruling 65–192, C.B. 1965–2, 259, which contained restatements of A.R.M. 34 and A.R.M. 68, is also superseded.

REVENUE RULING 77-287

Section 2031.—Definition of Gross Estate

26 CFR 20.2031-2: Valuation of stocks and bonds.
(Also Sections 170, 2032, 2512; 1.170A-1, 20.2032-1, 25.2512-2.)

Valuation of securities restricted from immediate resale. Guidelines are set forth for the valuation, for Federal tax purposes, of securities that cannot be immediately resold because they are restricted from resale pursuant to Federal securities laws; Rev. Rul. 59-60 amplified.

Rev. Rul. 77-287

SECTION 1. PURPOSE.

The purpose of this Revenue Ruling is to amplify Rev. Rul. 59-60, 1959-1 C.B. 237, as modified by Rev. Rul. 65-193, 1965-2 C.B. 370, and to provide information and guidance to taxpayers, Internal Revenue Service personnel, and others concerned with the valuation, for Federal tax purposes, of securities that cannot be immediately resold because they are restricted from resale pursuant to Federal securities laws. This guidance is applicable only in cases where it is not inconsistent with valuation requirements of the Internal Revenue Code of 1954 or the regulations thereunder. Further, this ruling does not establish the time at which property shall be valued.

SEC. 2. NATURE OF THE PROBLEM.

It frequently becomes necessary to establish the fair market value of stock that has not been registered for public trading when the issuing company has stock of the same class that is actively traded in one or more securities markets. The problem is to determine the difference in fair market value between the registered shares that are actively traded and the unregistered shares. This problem is often encountered in estate and gift tax cases. However, it is sometimes encountered when unregistered shares are issued in exchange for assets or the stock of an acquired company.

SEC. 3. BACKGROUND AND DEFINITIONS.

.01 The Service outlined and reviewed in general the approach, methods, and factors to be considered in valuing shares of closely held corporate stock for estate and gift tax purposes in Rev. Rul. 59-60, as modified by Rev. Rul. 65-193. The provisions of Rev. Rul. 59-60, as modified, were extended to the valuation of corporate securities for income and other tax purposes by Rev. Rul. 68-609, 1968-2 C.B. 327.

.02 There are several terms currently in use in the securities industry that denote restrictions imposed on the resale and transfer of certain securities. The term frequently used to describe these securities is "restricted securities," but they are sometimes referred to as "unregistered securities," "investment letter stock," "control stock," or "private placement stock." Frequently these terms are used interchangeably. They all indicate that these particular securities cannot lawfully be distributed to the general public until a registration statement relating to the corporation underlying the securities has been filed, and has also become effective under the rules promulgated and enforced by the United States Securities & Exchange Commission (SEC) pursuant to the Federal securities laws. The following represents a more refined definition of each of the following terms along with two other terms—"exempted securities" and "exempted transactions."

(a) The term "restricted securities" is defined in Rule 144 adopted by the SEC as "securities acquired directly or indirectly from the issuer thereof, or from an affiliate of such issuer, in a transaction or chain of transactions not involving any public offering."

(b) The term "unregistered securities" refers to those securities with respect to which a registration statement, providing full disclosure by the issuing corporation, has not been filed with the SEC pursuant to the Securities Act of 1933. The registration statement is a condition precedent to a public distribution of securities in interstate commerce and is aimed at providing the prospective investor with a factual basis for sound judgment in making investment decisions.

(c) The terms "investment letter stock" and "letter stock" denote shares of stock that have been issued by a corporation without the benefit of filing a registration statement with the SEC. Such stock is subject to resale and transfer restrictions set forth in a letter agreement requested by the issuer and signed by the buyer of the stock when the stock is delivered. Such stock may be found in the hands of either individual investors or institutional investors.

(d) The term "control stock" indicates that the shares of stock have been held or are being held by an officer, director, or other person close to the management of the corporation. These persons are subject to certain requirements pursuant to SEC rules upon resale of shares they own in such corporations.

(e) The term "private placement stock" indicates that the stock has been placed with an institution or other investor who will presumably hold it for a long period and ultimately arrange to have the stock registered if it is to be offered to the general public. Such stock may or may not be subject to a letter agreement. Private placements of stock are exempted from the registration and prospectus provisions of the Securities Act of 1933.

(f) The term "exempted securities" refers to those classes of securities that are expressly excluded from the registration provisions of the Securities Act of 1933 and the distribution provisions of the Securities Exchange Act of 1934.

(g) The term "exempted transactions" refers to certain sales or distributions of securities that do not involve a public offering and are excluded from the registration and prospectus provisions of the Securities Act of 1933 and distribution provisions of the Securities Exchange Act of 1934. The exempted status makes it unnecessary for issuers of securities to go through the registration process.

SEC. 4. SECURITIES INDUSTRY PRACTICE IN VALUING RESTRICTED SECURITIES.

.01 *Investment Company Valuation Practices.* The Investment Company Act of 1940 requires open-end investment companies to publish the valuation of their portfolio securities daily. Some of these companies have portfolios containing restricted securities, but also have unrestricted securities of the same class traded on a securities exchange. In recent years the number of restricted securities in such portfolios has increased. The following methods have been used by investment companies in the valuation of such restricted securities:

(a) Current market price of the unrestricted stock less a constant percentage discount based on purchase discount;

(b) Current market price of unrestricted stock less a constant percentage discount different from purchase discount;

(c) Current market price of the unrestricted stock less a discount amortized over a fixed period;

(d) Current market price of the unrestricted stock; and

(e) Cost of the restricted stock until it is registered.

The SEC ruled in its Investment Company Act Release No. 5847, dated October 21, 1969, that there can be no automatic formula by which an investment company can value the restricted securities in its portfolios. Rather, the SEC has determined that it is the responsibility of the board of directors of the particular investment company to determine the "fair value" of each issue of restricted securities in good faith.

.02 *Institutional Investors Study.* Pursuant to Congressional direction, the SEC undertook an analysis of the purchases, sales, and holding of securities by financial institutions, in order to determine the effect of institutional activity upon the securities market.

The study report was published in eight volumes in March 1971. The fifth volume provides an analysis of restricted securities and deals with such items as the characteristics of the restricted securities purchasers and issuers, the size of transactions (dollars and shares), the marketability discounts on different trading markets, and the resale provisions. This research project provides some guidance for measuring the discount in that it contains information, based on the actual experience of the marketplace, showing that, during the period surveyed (January 1, 1966, through June 30, 1969), the amount of discount allowed for restricted securities from the trading price of the unrestricted securities was generally related to the following four factors.

(a) *Earnings.* Earnings and sales consistently have a significant influence on the size of restricted securities discounts according to the study. Earnings played the major part in establishing the ultimate discounts at which these stocks were sold from the current market price. Apparently earnings patterns, rather than sales patterns, determine the degree of risk of an investment.

(b) *Sales.* The dollar amount of sales of issuers' securities also has a major influence on the amount of discount at which restricted securities sell from the current market price. The results of the study generally indicate that the companies with the lowest dollar amount of sales during the test period accounted for most of the transactions involving the highest discount rates, while they accounted for only a small portion of all transactions involving the lowest discount rates.

(c) *Trading Market.* The market

in which publicly held securities are traded also reflects variances in the amount of discount that is applied to restricted securities purchases. According to the study, discount rates were greatest on restricted stocks with unrestricted counterparts traded over-the-counter, followed by those with unrestricted counterparts listed on the American Stock Exchange, while the discount rates for those stocks with unrestricted counterparts listed on the New York Stock Exchange were the smallest.

(d) *Resale Agreement Provisions.* Resale agreement provisions often affect the size of the discount. The discount from the market price provides the main incentive for a potential buyer to acquire restricted securities. In judging the opportunity cost of freezing funds, the purchaser is analyzing two separate factors. The first factor is the risk that underlying value of the stock will change in a way that, absent the restrictive provisions, would have prompted a decision to sell. The second factor is the risk that the contemplated means of legally disposing of the stock may not materialize. From the seller's point of view, a discount is justified where the seller is relieved of the expenses of registration and public distribution, as well as of the risk that the market will adversely change before the offering is completed. The ultimate agreement between buyer and seller is a reflection of these and other considerations. Relative bargaining strengths of the parties to the agreement are major considerations that influence the resale terms and consequently the size of discounts in restricted securities transactions. Certain provisions are often found in agreements between buyers and sellers that

affect the size of discounts at which restricted stocks are sold. Several such provisions follow, all of which, other than number (3), would tend to reduce the size of the discount:

(1) A provision giving the buyer an option to "piggyback", that is, to register restricted stock with the next registration statement, if any, filed by the issuer with the SEC;

(2) A provision giving the buyer an option to require registration at the seller's expense;

(3) A provision giving the buyer an option to require registration, but only at the buyer's own expense;

(4) A provision giving the buyer a right to receive continuous disclosure of information about the issuer from the seller;

(5) A provision giving the buyer a right to select one or more directors of the issuer;

(6) A provision giving the buyer an option to purchase additional shares of the issuer's stock; and

(7) A provision giving the buyer the right to have a greater voice in operations of the issuer, if the issuer does not meet previously agreed upon operating standards.

Institutional buyers can and often do obtain many of these rights and options from the sellers of restricted securities, and naturally, the more rights the buyer can acquire, the lower the buyer's risk is going to be, thereby reducing the buyer's discount as well. Smaller buyers may not be able to negotiate the large discounts or the rights and options that volume buyers are able to negotiate.

.03 *Summary.* A variety of methods have been used by the securities industry to value restricted securities. The SEC rejects all automatic or mechanical solutions to the valuation of restricted securities, and prefers, in the case of the valuation of investment company portfolio stocks, to rely upon good faith valuations by the board of directors of each company. The study made by the SEC found that restricted securities *generally* are issued at a discount from the market value of freely tradable securities.

SEC. 5. FACTS AND CIRCUMSTANCES MATERIAL TO VALUATION OF RESTRICTED SECURITIES.

.01 Frequently, a company has a class of stock that cannot be traded publicly. The reason such stock cannot be traded may arise from the securities statutes, as in the case of an "investment letter" restriction; it may arise from a corporate charter restriction, or perhaps from a trust agreement restriction. In such cases, certain documents and facts should be obtained for analysis.

.02 The following documents and facts, when used in conjunction with those discussed in Section 4 of Rev. Rul. 59-60, will be useful in the valuation of restricted securities:

(a) A copy of any declaration of trust, trust agreement, and any other agreements relating to the shares of restricted stock;

(b) A copy of any document showing any offers to buy or sell or indications of interest in buying or selling the restricted shares;

(c) The latest prospectus of the company;

(d) Annual reports of the company for 3 to 5 years preceding the valuation date;

(e) The trading prices and trading volume of the related class of traded securities 1 month preceding the valuation date, if they are traded on a stock exchange (if traded over-the-counter, prices may be obtained from the National Quotations Bureau, the National Association of Securities Dealers Automated Quotations (NASDAQ), or sometimes from broker-dealers making markets in the shares);

(f) The relationship of the parties to the agreements concerning the restricted stock, such as whether they are members of the immediate family or perhaps whether they are officers or directors of the company; and

(g) Whether the interest being valued represents a majority or minority ownership.

SEC. 6. WEIGHING FACTS AND CIRCUMSTANCES MATERIAL TO RESTRICTED STOCK VALUATION.

All relevant facts and circumstances that bear upon the worth of restricted stock, including those set forth above in the preceding Sections 4 and 5, and those set forth in Section 4 of Rev. Rul. 59-60, must be taken into account in arriving at the fair market value of such securities. Depending on the circumstances of each case, certain factors may carry more weight than others. To illustrate:

.01 Earnings, net assets, and net sales must be given primary consideration in arriving at an appropriate discount for restricted securities from the freely traded shares. These are the elements of value that are always used by investors in making investment decisions. In some cases, one element may be more important than in other cases. In the case of manufacturing, producing, or distributing companies, primary weight must be accorded earnings and net sales; but in the case of investment or holding companies, primary weight must be given to the net assets of the company underlying the stock. In the former type of companies, value is more closely linked to past, present, and future earnings while in the latter type of companies, value is more closely linked to the existing net assets of the company. See the discussion in Section 5 of Rev. Rul. 59-60.

.02   Resale provisions found in the restriction agreements must be scrutinized and weighed to determine the amount of discount to apply to the preliminary fair market value of the company. The two elements of time and expense bear upon this discount; the longer the buyer of the shares must wait to liquidate the shares, the greater the discount. Moreover, if the provisions make it necessary for the buyer to bear the expense of registration, the greater the discount. However, if the provisions of the restricted stock agreement make it possible for the buyer to "piggyback" shares at the next offering, the discount would be smaller.

.03   The relative negotiation strengths of the buyer and seller of restricted stock may have a profound effect on the amount of discount. For example, a tight money situation may cause the buyer to have the greater balance of negotiation strength in a transaction. However, in some cases the relative strengths may tend to cancel each other out.

.04   The market experience of freely tradable securities of the same class as the restricted securities is also significant in determining the amount of discount. Whether the shares are privately held or publicly traded affects the worth of the shares to the holder. Securities traded on a public market generally are worth more to investors than those that are not traded on a public market. Moreover, the type of public market in which the unrestricted securities are traded is to be given consideration.

SEC. 7.   EFFECT ON OTHER DOCUMENTS.

Rev. Rul. 59-60, as modified by Rev. Rul. 65-193, is amplified.

REVENUE RULING 78-367

Section 2512.—Valuation of Gifts

26 CFR 25.2512-2: Stocks and bonds.

Valuation; closely held securities. The valuation, for purposes of section 2512 of the Code, of stock in a closely held company should take into account a proposed merger of the company with a publicly owned corporation.

Rev. Rul. 78-367

Advice has been requested concerning the value of corporate stock for purposes of section 2512 of the Internal Revenue Code of 1954, under the circumstances described below.

Three shareholders, *A*, *B*, and *C*, each owned a one-third interest in *X* corporation. These same individuals each owned a 20 percent interest in *Y* corporation, a publicly owned company. Their shares in *Y* corporation, taken together, were a majority interest.

In January 1975 the two companies publicly announced an intention to merge *X* corporation with *Y* corporation. The merger was subject to the formulation of a detailed agreement regarding the consideration to be exchanged, and subject to the approval of the stockholders of both corporations.

Two months after the announcement, *A* made a gift of some of the *X* corporation stock to *D*. In March 1976, all details concerning the merger were finally completed and the merger effected shortly thereafter. The shareholders of *X* corporation received one share of *Y* corporation stock in ex-change for each share in *X* that they held. Prior to the merger, there had been no sales of *X* corporation stock.

The question presented is whether the proposed merger should be considered in the valuation of the gift of the *X* stock.

Section 2512 of the Code provides that a gift shall be taxed on the basis of the value of the property on the date of the transfer. Section 25.2512-1 of the Gift Tax Regulations states the following general rules:

> * * * The value of the property is the price at which such property would change hands between a willing buyer and a willing seller, neither being under any compulsion to buy or to sell, and both having reasonable knowledge of relevant facts. . . . All relevant facts and elements of value as of the time of the gift shall be considered. * * *

Section 25.2512-2(f) of the regulations provides the following guidelines for valuation of corporate securities for which actual sales are lacking:

> (f) *Where selling prices or bid and asked prices are unavailable.* If the provisions of paragraphs (b), (c), and (d) of this section are inapplicable because actual sale prices and bona fide bid and asked prices are lacking, then the fair market value is to be determined by taking the following factors into consideration:
> (1) In the case of corporate or other bonds, the soundness of the security, the interest yield, the date of maturity, and other relevant factors; and
> (2) In the case of shares of stock, the company's net worth, prospective earning power and dividend-paying capacity, and other relevant factors.

Some of the "other relevant factors" referred to in subparagraphs (1) and (2) of this paragraph are: the good will of the business; the economic outlook in the particular industry; the company's position in the industry and its management; the degree of control of the business represented by the block of stock to be valued; and the values of securities of corporations engaged in the same or similar lines of business which are listed on a stock exchange. However, the weight to be accorded such comparisons or any other evidentiary factors considered in the determination of a value depends upon the facts of each case. * * *

Rev. Rul. 59-60, 1959-1 C.B. 237, as modified by Rev. Rul. 65-193, 1965-2 C.B. 370, and as amplified by Rev. Rul. 77-287, 1977-2 C.B. 319, outlines some methods and factors to be considered when valuing shares of stock on which market quotations are unavailable. Although nine representative factors are discussed, the ruling advises that *all* relevant factors affecting fair market value should be considered.

In the present case, no share of *X* corporation stock had been sold prior to the date of the gift. The announcement of the merger two months before, as well as the preliminary decision to merge, did not attempt to fix the consideration to be exchanged. The value of the stock, for purposes of the merger, was not finally agreed upon until one year after the gift.

The concept of "fair market value"

is premised on a hypothetical sale in which both the prospective buyer and seller have reasonable knowledge of the facts. See *Estate of Reynolds v. Commissioner,* 55 T.C. 172, 195 (1970), acq., 1971-2 C.B. 2.

The standards set by the regulations and Rev. Rul. 59-60, as modified and amplified, reflect the reality of the market place. A prospective seller would inform a prospective buyer of all favorable facts in an effort to obtain the best possible price, and a prospective buyer would elicit all the negative information in order to obtain the lowest possible price. In this arm's length negotiation, all relevant factors available to either buyer or seller, known to both, provide a basis on which the buyer and seller make a decision to buy or sell and come to an agreement on the price.

Accordingly, the valuation of the stock of *X* as of the date of the gift should take into account the effects of the public announcement of the merger and all information covering the status of the merger negotiations available to the buyer and seller.

REVENUE RULING 79-7

Section 2035.—Transactions in Contemplation of Death [As in Effect Prior to 1977]

26 CFR 20.2035-1: Transactions in contemplation of death.
(Also Section 2031; 20.2031-1.)

Valuation; transfer in contemplation of death; stock of closely held corporation. An individual who owned a controlling stock interest in a closely held corporation transferred a minority stock interest that was included in the individual's gross estate as a transfer in contemplation of death. The minority interest transferred and the stock retained by the individual until death are treated as one block of shares in determining the value of the stock interest includible in the gross estate.

Rev. Rul. 79-7

ISSUE

Whether the interest in a closely held corporation that is includible in the decedent's gross estate under section 2035 of the Code should be valued as a minority interest in the corporation, under the circumstances described below.

FACTS

The decedent, A, owned 600 shares of the common stock of X corporation, a closely held corporation. The 600 shares represented sixty percent of the outstanding stock of X corporation. In 1974, two years prior to death, A transferred 300 shares to B, A's child, in a transfer that was determined to have been made in contemplation of death.

The stock transferred by A was therefore includible in A's gross estate under section 2035 of the Code. In addition, the 300 shares A owned outright at the time of death were included in the gross estate under section 2033 of the Code.

LAW AND ANALYSIS

Section 20.2031-2(f) of the regulations provides that in determining the value of a decedent's stock interest in a closely held corporation for purposes of the federal estate tax, consideration should be given to the degree of control of the corporation represented by the block of stock to be valued. The question presented in the instant case is whether the 300 shares of X corporation stock included in the decedent's gross estate under section 2035 of the Code is to be valued as a minority interest in the corporation, without reference to the stock interest included in the decedent's gross estate under section 2033.

Rev. Rul. 59-60, 1959-1 C.B. 237, sets forth guidelines for the valuation of shares of capital stock of a closely-held corporation. Both section 20.2031-2(f) of the regulations and Rev. Rul. 59-60, state that the determination of value of such closely-held stock is to be made with reference to a range of factors in the absence of an established "market" in the shares. It is assumed that there is no established "market" for closely-held corporate stocks. See Rev. Rul. 59-60, cited above.

At the time of A's death, section 2035(a) of the Code provided that the gross estate shall include the value of any interest in property transferred by the decedent (except in the case of a bona fide sale for an adequate and full consideration in money or money's worth) in contemplation of death. Section 20.2035-1(e) of the Estate Tax Regulations provides that the value of an interest in transferred property includible in a decedent's gross estate under section 2035 is the value of the interest as of the applicable valuation date, determined in accordance with section 2031 of the Code and the regulations thereunder.

Underlying the provisions of section 2035 of the Code is the intent to prevent the avoidance of the estate tax by taxing inter vivos gifts made as substitutes for testamentary transfers as if they were testamentary transfers. *Milliken v. United States,* 283 U.S. 15 (1931). Consequently, the value of property included in the decedent's gross estate under section 2035 should be treated, for purposes of the estate tax, in the same manner as it would have been if the transfer had not been made and the property had been owned by the decedent at the time of death. *Humphrey's Estate v. Commissioner,* 162 F. 2d 1 (5th Cir. 1947). *Ingleheart v. Commissioner,* 77 F. 2d 704 (5th Cir. 1935) ; Rev. Rul 76-235, 1976-1 C.B. 277.

In the situation presented here, the stock interest in *X* corporation transferred by *A* to *B* represented a minority interest in the corporation. However, pursuant to the court's decisions in *Humphrey's Estate* and *Ingleheart,* the value of the stock included in the gross estate under section 2035 of the Code should be taxed as if the decedent had retained the stock until death. If *A* had not transferred the 300 shares, then a total of 600 shares of stock would have been included in *A*'s gross estate under section 2033. That block of shares would represent a controlling interest in *X* corporation and would be valued, in accordance with Rev. Rul. 59-60, cited above, taking into account the controlling interest the shares represent.

HOLDING

The 300 shares of *X* corporation stock includible in *A*'s gross estate under section 2033 of the Code, and the 300 shares includible under section 2035, are to be treated as 1 block of 600 shares of stock for purposes of determining whether the stock includible in *A*'s gross estate represents a minority or majority interest in *X* corporation. Under these circumstances, the inclusion of the 300 shares of stock under section 2035 of the Code will have the same tax effect as if the decedent had retained the 300 shares until death.

The conclusion of this ruling would be the same under section 2035 of the Code as amended by the Tax Reform Act of 1976 for that amendment merely eliminated the requirement that the transfer be in contemplation of death. The purpose of the statute, as amended, remains the same as it was prior to modification.

REVENUE RULING 81-15

Section 2036.—Transfers With Retained Life Estate

26 CFR 20.2036-1: Transfers with retained life estate.

Stock transferred in trust; retained power. In view of the *Byrum* decision and the enactment of section 2036(b) of the Code, Rev. Rul. 67-54 is revoked.

Rev. Rul. 81-15

ISSUE

The Internal Revenue Service has been asked to reconsider Rev. Rul. 67-54, 1967-1 C.B. 269, in view of the Supreme Court decision in *United States v. Byrum,* 408 U.S. 125 (1972), 1972-2 C.B. 518, and the enactment of section 2036(b) of the Internal Revenue Code.

FACTS

In Rev. Rul. 67-54, the decedent transferred assets to a corporation which issued nonvoting preferred stock and debentures, for the full current value of the assets transferred. The corporation also issued 10 shares of voting and 990 shares of nonvoting common stock. The decedent transferred the 990 shares of nonvoting stock in trust for the benefit of his children. The trust owned the 990 shares at the date of decedent's death. Under the terms of the trust, the trustee could not dispose of the stock without the consent of the decedent. Under an alternative fact situation, the grantor designated himself as trustee.

Rev. Rul. 67-54 concludes that the decedent has retained control of the corporate dividend policy through retention of the voting stock and, thus, has retained the right to determine the income from the nonvoting stock. The decedent has also retained control over the disposition of the nonvoting stock, either as trustee or as a result of the restrictions on the trustee's power to dispose of the stock. The ruling holds that the decedent's retention of the right to control income and the restriction on disposition amount to a transfer whereby the decedent has retained for life or for a period which in fact did not end before death the right to designate the persons who shall enjoy the transferred property or income therefrom. Therefore, the property is includible in decedent's gross estate under section 2036(a)(2) of the Code.

Rev. Rul. 67-54 also holds that, pursuant to section 2031 of the Code, the value of the nonvoting shares included in the gross estate should reflect the additional value inherent in the closely held voting shares by reason of control of company policies.

LAW AND ANALYSIS

Section 2036(a)(2) of the Code provides that the value of the gross estate shall include the value of any interest in property transferred by a decedent if the decedent has retained for life the right, alone or in conjunction with any person, to designate the persons who shall possess or enjoy the property or the income therefrom.

In *United States v. Byrum,* the Supreme Court addressed the issue of includibility of transferred stock where the decedent had transferred the stock in trust, retaining the right to vote the transferred shares, the right to veto the sale or acquisition of trust property and the right to replace the trustee.

The court concluded that because of the fiduciary constraints imposed on corporate directors and controlling shareholders, the decedent "did not have an unconstrained *de facto* power to regulate the flow of dividends, much less the right to designate who was to enjoy the income." See *Byrum, supra* at 143.

Thus, *Byrum* overruled the proposition on which Rev. Rul. 67-54 was based; that is, that a decedent's retention of voting control of a corporation, coupled with restrictions on the disposition of the stock, is equivalent to the right to designate the person who shall enjoy the income.

Section 2036(b)(1), added by the Tax Reform Act of 1976, 1976-3 C.B. (Vol. 1) 1, as amended by the Revenue Act of 1978, section 702(i), 1978-3 C.B. (Vol. 1) 1, 165, provides that for purposes of section 2036(a) (1), the direct or indirect retention of voting rights in transferred stock of a controlled corporation shall be considered to be a retention of the enjoyment of transferred property.

The Senate Finance Committee Report relating to section 2036(b)(1) provides as follows:

The rule would not apply to the transfer of stock in a controlled corporation where the decedent could not vote the transferred stock. For example, where a decedent transfers stock in a controlled corporation to his son and does not have the power to vote the stock any time during the 3-year period before his death, the rule does not apply even where the decedent owned, or could vote, a majority of the stock. Similarly, where the decedent owned both voting and nonvoting stock and transferred the nonvoting stock to another person, the rule does not apply to the nonvoting stock simply because of the decedent's ownership of the voting stock. S. Rep. No. 95-745, 95th Cong., 2d Sess. 91 (1978).

The legislative history of section 2036(b) demonstrates that the rule of that section will not apply to the transfer of stock in a controlled corporation where the decedent could not vote the transferred stock. Thus, the effect of *Byrum* on Rev. Rul. 67-54 is not changed by the enactment of section 2036(b) of the Code.

HOLDING

In view of *United States v. Byrum,* and the enactment of section 2036(b) of the Code, Rev. Rul. 67-54 is revoked. However, the Service will continue to apply the general principles of valuation under section 2031, noted in the revenue ruling.

EFFECT ON OTHER REVENUE RULINGS

Rev. Rul. 67-54 is revoked.

REVENUE RULING 81-253

26 CFR 25.2512-1: Valuation of property; in general.

Valuation; stock; intrafamily transfers; minority discounts. Simultaneous gifts of one-third of the stock of a family controlled corporation to each of the donor's three children are not valued as minority interests for purposes of section 2512 of the Code.

Rev. Rul. 81-253

ISSUE

Whether minority discounts should be allowed in valuing for federal gift tax purposes three simultaneous transfers of all of the stock in a closely held family corporation to the donor's three children.

FACTS

The donor, *A*, owned all of the 90 outstanding shares of stock in corporation *X*, the sole asset of which is a parcel of real estate. On December 30, 1978, *A* made simultaneous gifts of one-third (30 shares) of the stock in *X* to each of *A*'s three children. On that date, the established fair market value of each share of *X* stock, if all the stock were sold together, was $100x per share.

At the time the gifts were made, there were no corporate bylaws or other instruments restricting the voting or disposition of corporate shares by any shareholder, and there were no negotiations underway for the disposition of the corporation's assets or the disposition of the shares in question before or subsequent to the date of the gifts. In addition there is no evidence of the kind of family discord or other factor that would indicate that the family would not act as a unit in controlling the corporation. The corporation still owns the parcel of real estate and *A*'s children still own the corporate shares.

LAW AND ANALYSIS

Section 2501(a)(1) of the Internal Revenue Code provides that a tax is imposed for each calendar quarter on the transfer of property by gift during such calendar quarter. Section 2512(a) provides that the value of the property at the date of the gift shall be considered the amount of the gift.

Section 25.2512-1 of the Gift Tax Regulations defines the value of property as the price at which such property would change hands between a willing buyer and willing seller, neither being under compulsion to buy or sell, and both having reasonable knowledge of relevant facts. The regulations provide that the value of a particular kind of property is not the price that a forced sale of the property would produce, and that all relevant facts and elements of value as of the time of the gift shall be considered.

Section 25.2512-2(a) of the regulations provides that the value of stocks and bonds is the fair market value per share or bond on the date of the gift. Section 25.2512-2(f) provides that the degree of control of the business represented by the block of stock to be valued is among the factors to be considered in valuing stock where there are not sales prices or bona fide bid and asked prices. See also Rev. Rul. 59-60, sections 4.01(g), 4.02(g), 1959-

1 C.B. 237.

The fair market value of a piece of property depends on the facts and circumstances. Section 3.01, Rev. Rul. 59-60, 1959-1 C.B. 237, *Messing v. Commissioner*, 48 T.C. 505, 512 (1967), *acq.* 1968-1 C.B. 2. Thus questions of valuation cannot be resolved by mechanical application of formulae and cases involving valuation can often be distinguished. Nonetheless, certain overriding legal principles to which each set of facts is applied govern valuation. *Powers. v. Commissioner*, 312 U.S. 259 (1941); *Maytag v. Commissioner*, 187 F.2d 962 (10th Cir. 1951).

Judicial authority is inconsistent regarding the correct legal principle governing the availability of a minority discount in the instant case. Therefore, this ruling is intended to state the Service's position.

Several cases have held or implied that no minority discount is available when the transferred stock is part of a family controlling interest. *Driver v. United States*, No. 73C 260 (W.D. Wis., Sept. 13, 1976); *Blanchard v. United States*, 291 F. Supp. 248 (S.D. Iowa, 1968); *Richardson v. Commissioner*, No. 95770 (T.C.M. 1943), *aff'd*, 151 F. 2d 102 (2d Cir. 1945), *cert. denied*, 326 U.S. 796 (1946); *Hamm v. Commissioner*, T.C.M. 1961-347, *aff'd*, 325 F.2d 934 (8th Cir. 1963), *cert. denied*, 377 U.S. 993 (1964). The Service will follow these decisions. Other cases have allowed a minority discount on similar facts. *Whittemore v. Fitzpatrick*, 127 F. Supp. 710 (D. Conn. 1954); *Obermer v. United States*, 238 F. Supp. 29, 34 (D. Hawaii, 1964); *Estate of Piper v. Commissioner*, 72 T.C. 1062 (1979); *Clark v. United States*, Civil Nos.

1308, 1309 (E.D.N.C., May 16, 1975); *Bartram v. Graham*, 157 F. Supp. 757 (D. Conn. 1957); *Estate of Lee v. Commissioner*, 69 T.C. 860 (1978), *nonacq.* 1980-2 C.B. 2; *Estate of Bright v. United States*, No. 78-2221 (5th Cir., Oct. 1, 1981). The Service will not follow these and similar cases.

It is the position of the Service that ordinarily no minority discount will be allowed with respect to transfers of shares of stock among family members where, at the time of the transfer, control (either majority voting control or de facto control) of the corporation exists in the family, *Dattel v. United States*, No. D.C. 73-107-S, (N.D. Miss., Oct. 29, 1975), *Cutbirth v. United States*, Civil No. CA-6-75-1 (N.D. Tex., June 16, 1976). However, when there is evidence of family discord or other factors indicating that the family would not act as a unit in controlling the corporation, a minority discount may be allowed. Although courts have recognized that where a shareholder is unrelated to other shareholders a minority discount may be available because of absence of control, *Estate of Schroeder v. Commissioner*, 13 T.C. 259 (1949), *acq.* 1949-2 C.B. 3, where a controlling interest in stock is owned by family members, there is a unity of ownership and interest, and the shares owned by family members should be valued as part of that controlling interest. This conclusion is based on an evaluation of the facts and circumstances that would affect the price received for the shares in a hypothetical sale. It is unlikely that under circumstances such as exist in the instant case, shares that are part of a controlling interest would be sold other than as a unit except to a family member in whose hands the shares would retain their control value because of the family relationship. Thus, where a controlling interest in stock is owned by a family, the value per share of stock owned by one family member is the same as stock owned by any other family member and is the same value that would exist if all the stock were held by one person.

HOLDING

No minority discount is allowable and the value of each share of stock for federal gift tax purposes is $100x$.

REVENUE RULING 83-119

Section 305.—Distributions of Stock and Stock Rights

26 CFR 1.305-5: Distributions on preferred stock.

Recapitalization; excess redemption premium; preferred stock. In a recapitalization where a corporation issues preferred stock that must be redeemed at the time of the holder's death at a price in excess of one hundred and ten percent of the issue price, the amount of the excess redemption premium is treated under section 305(c) of the Code as a distribution of stock within the meaning of section 305(b)(4). The redemption amount will be constructively received ratably over the holder's life expectancy.

Rev. Rul. 83-119

ISSUE

In a recapitalization where a corporation issues preferred stock that must be redeemed on the holder's death at the price in excess of one hundred and ten percent of the issue price, is the amount of the excess redemption premium treated, by reason of section 305(c) of the Internal Revenue Code, as a distribution with respect to preferred stock within the meaning of section 305(b)(4)? If so, when is this distribution deemed to be received?

FACTS

A domestic corporation, *X*, had outstanding 100 shares of common stock. *A* owned 80 shares of the *X* common stock and *B*, *A*'s child, owned the other 20 shares. *A* was actively engaged in *X*'s business as its president, and *B* was a key employee. *A* retired from the business and resigned as a director, officer, and employee of *X* with no intention to take part in the future activities of *X*. Pursuant to a plan of recapitalization for the purpose of transferring control and ownership of the common stock to *B* in conjunction with *A*'s retirement, a single class of nonvoting, dividend paying preferred stock (as defined in section 1.305-5(a) of the Income Tax Regulations) was authorized. There are no redemption provisions with regard to the preferred stock, except that on the death of a shareholder of the preferred stock, *X* is required to redeem the preferred stock from the shareholder's estate or beneficiaries at its par value of 1,000*x* dollars per share. On January 1, 1981, *A* had a life expectancy of 24 years determined by using the actuarial tables provided in section 1.72-9 of the regulations. On January 1, 1981, *A* exchanged 80 shares of common stock for 80 shares of preferred stock. Following this exchange, *A* held all of the preferred stock, and *B* held all of the common stock that *X* then had outstanding.

On the date of the exchange the *X* common stock surrendered had a fair market value of $1,000*x* dollars per share, and the *X* preferred stock had a par value of $1,000*x* dollars per share. The one-for-one exchange ratio resulted because the par value of the preferred stock was presumed to represent its fair market value. However, the fair market value of the preferred stock was only 600x dollars per share. See Rev. Rul. 83-120, page 170, this Bulletin, for factors taken into account in valuing common and preferred stock. Thus, A surrendered X common stock with a fair market value of 80,000x dollars (80 × 1,000x dollars) in exchange for X preferred stock with a fair market value of 48,000x dollars (80 × 600x dollars).

The exchange of all of A's X common stock for X preferred stock is a recapitalization within the meaning of section 368(a)(1)(E) of the Code. Under section 354, no gain or loss will be recognized to A with regard to the receipt of the preferred stock to the extent of its 48,000x dollars fair market value. However, the 32,000x dollars excess in the fair market value of the X common stock surrendered by A as compared to the fair market value of the preferred stock A received will be treated as having been used to make a gift, pay compensation, satisfy obligations of any kind, or for whatever purposes the facts indicate. Section 356(f) of the Code and Rev. Rul. 74-269, 1974-1 C.B. 87.

LAW AND ANALYSIS

Section 305(a) of the Code provides generally that gross income does not include the amount of any distribution of the stock of a corporation made by such corporation to its shareholders with respect to its stock, except as otherwise provided in section 305(b) or (c).

Section 305(b)(4) of the Code provides, in part, that section 305(a) will not apply to a distribution by a corporation of its stock, and the distribution will be treated as a distribution of property to which section 301 applies, if the distribution is with re-

spect to preferred stock.

Section 305(c) of the Code provides, in part, that the Secretary shall prescribe regulations under which a difference between issue price and redemption price will be treated as a distribution with respect to any shareholder whose proportionate interest in the earnings and profits or assets of the corporation is increased by the transaction. Section 1.305-7(a) of the regulations provides, under the authority of section 305(c), that an unreasonable redemption premium on preferred stock will be treated in accordance with section 1.305-5.

Section 1.305-5(b)(1) of the regulations provides that if a corporation issues preferred stock which may be redeemed after a specific period of time at a price higher than the issue price, the difference will be considered under the authority of section 305(c) of the Code to be distribution of additional stock on preferred stock (section 305(b)(4)) constructively received by the shareholder over the period of time during which the preferred stock cannot be called for redemption. However, section 1.305-5(b)(2) states that section 1.305-5(b)(1) will not apply to the extent that the difference between issue price and redemption price is a reasonable redemption premium, and that a redemption premium will be considered reasonable if it is in the nature of a penalty for the premature redemption of the preferred stock and if such premium does not exceed the amount the corporation would be required to pay for the right to make such premature redemption under market conditions existing at the time of issuance. Section 1.305-5(b)(2) also states that a redemption premium not in excess of 10 percent of the issue price on stock which is not redeemable for five years from the date of issuance shall be considered reasonable.

Section 1.305-7(a) of the regulations provides, in part, that a change in conversion ratio, a change in redemption price, a difference between redemption price and issue price, a redemption which is treated as a distribution to which section 301 applies, or any transaction (including a recapitalization) having a similar effect on the interest of any shareholder will be treated as a distribution to which sections 305(b) and 301 apply if (1) the proportionate interest of any shareholder in the earnings and profits or assets of the corporation deemed to have made such distribution is increased by such transaction, and (2) such distribution has the result described in paragraph (2), (3), (4), or (5) of section 305(b).

Section 1.305-3(e), Example (12), of the regulations illustrates a situation where section 305 does not apply to exchanges of stock in a recapitalization that is a "single and isolated transaction". However, section 1.305-7(c)(1) of the regulations provides that a recapitalization, whether or not an isolated transaction, will be deemed to result in a distribution to which section 305(c) of the Code and section 1.305-7 of the regulations apply, if, among other things, it is pursuant to a plan to periodically increase a shareholder's proportionate interest in the assets or earnings and profits of the corporation.

One element which is necessary to taxability under sections 305(b) and (c) is that there must be a distribution. Regarding this requirement, section 305(b) deals with actual distributions, and section 305(c) deems cer-

tain transactions which are not actual distributions to be distributions for section 305 purposes. Certain recapitalizations, even if isolated, are treated as distributions under regulations section 1.305-7(c). That is, an actual exchange of stock, even though clearly isolated, can be treated as a distribution if the exchange is pursuant to a larger plan to periodically increase a shareholder's proportionate interest. Section 1.305-5(c) of the regulations provides, "For rules for applying sections 305(b)(4) and 305(c) to recapitalizations, see section 1.305-7(c)". This means that section 1.305-7(c) of the regulations is the rule used to impose section 305(b)(4) and (c) of the Code on an exchange of stock which qualifies as a recapitalization. However, it does not mean that section 1.305-7(c) must be found to be applicable to a transaction in order for any deemed distribution which may result from the transaction to be subject to section 305(b)(4) and (c) and the regulations thereunder.

Although an exchange of stock in an isolated recapitalization would not in itself result in section 305(b) and (c) applicability, the terms of the preferred stock used in the exchange may result in this applicability. The difference between issue price and redemption price (section 1.305-7(a) of the regulations) and the fact that the stock cannot be called for redemption for a specific period of time (section 1.305-5(b) of the regulations) are the factors which combine to produce a deemed distribution. The imposition of tax results from the deemed distribution of additional preferred stock over the period the stock cannot be called or presented for redemption.

Section 1.305-5(d), Example (7), of the regulations describes the proper treatment of preferred stock issued pro rata to the holders of a corporation's common stock. The fair market value of the preferred stock immediately after its issuance was $50x$ dollars. The preferred stock is redeemable at the end of five years for $105x$ dollars per share. There is no evidence that a call premium in excess of $5x$ dollars per share is reasonable. The $50x$ dollars excess of the call premium ($55x$ dollars) minus the deemed reasonable premium ($5x$ dollars) is considered to be a distribution of additional stock on preferred stock to which sections 305(b)(4) and 301 of the Code apply. This $50x$ dollar excess is considered to be distributed to the shareholders ratably over the five year period.

In the present situation, X common stock was exchanged by A for X preferred stock. Since the exchange was not part of a plan to periodically increase a shareholder's proportionate interest, the recapitalization itself did not result in a deemed distribution. However, the preferred stock will be redeemed by X on the death of a shareholder at a price of $1,000x$ dollars per share. Since the preferred stock had a fair market value of $600x$ dollars per share on the date of issuance, the preferred stock has a redemption premium of $400x$ dollars per share. There is no evidence that a call premium in excess of $60x$ dollars was reasonable. Because (1) the X stock is closely held, (2) no public offerings are planned, (3) the X stock is held by members of a family group within the meaning of section 318(a), and (4) the stock is not readily marketable, it is presumed that, at the time of the exchange, the shareholders intended that A would not transfer the preferred stock, and, therefore, redemption would occur upon A's death. Although the exact duration of A's life is not yet known, A's life is "a specified period of time" within the meaning of section 1.305-5(b)(1) of the regulations. Because A has a life expectancy of 24 years, the $400x$ dollar redemption premium on the X preferred stock has substantially the same effect as a $400x$ dollar redemption premium payable at the end of a fixed term of 24 years.

HOLDING

The recapitalization in which X issues X preferred stock that must be redeemed on the shareholder's death at a price ($1,000x$ dollars) which exceeds the issue price ($600x$ dollars) results in the recipient, A, being deemed to receive a distribution of additional stock with respect to preferred stock, within the meaning of section 305(b)(4) of the Code, by reason of section 305(c), in the amount of $340x$ dollars ($400x$ dollars less a deemed reasonable redemption premium of $60x$ dollars) on each share of preferred stock. This amount will be constructively received ratably ($14.16x$ dollars per share per year) over A's life expectancy of 24 years, and will be treated as a distribution to which section 301 applies. If A should die earlier, any part of the $340x$ dollars per share not yet constructively received by A would be deemed received at the time of A's death.

26 CFR 1.305-5: Distributions on preferred stock.

Significant factors in deriving the fair market value of preferred and common stock received in certain corporate reorganizations. See Rev. Rul. 83-120, page 170.

26 CFR 5c.305-1: Special rules of application for dividend reinvestment in stock of public utilities.

T.D. 7897

TITLE 26.—INTERNAL
REVENUE.—CHAPTER 1, SUB-
CHAPTER A, PART 5c—TEMPO-
RARY INCOME TAX REGULA-
TIONS UNDER THE ECONOMIC
RECOVERY TAX ACT OF 1981

REVENUE RULING 83-120

Section 2512.—Valuation of Gifts

26 CFR 25.2512-2: Stocks and bonds.
(Also Sections 305, 351, 354, 368, 2031; 1.305-5, 1.351-1, 1.354-1, 1.368-1, 20.2031-2.)

Valuation; stock; closely held business. The significant factors in deriving the fair market value of preferred and common stock received in certain corporate reorganizations are discussed. Rev. Rul. 59-60 amplified.

Rev. Rul. 83-120

SECTION 1. PURPOSE

The purpose of this Revenue Ruling is to amplify Rev. Rul. 59-60, 1959-1 C.B. 237, by specifying additional factors to be considered in valuing common and preferred stock of a closely held corporation for gift tax and other purposes in a recapitalization of closely held businesses. This type of valuation problem frequently arises with respect to estate planning transactions wherein an individual receives preferred stock with a stated par value equal to all or a large portion of the fair market value of the individual's former stock interest in a corporation. The individual also receives common stock which is then transferred, usually as a gift, to a relative.

Sec. 2. BACKGROUND

.01 One of the frequent objectives of the type of transaction mentioned above is the transfer of the potential appreciation of an individual's stock interest in a corporation to relatives at a nominal or small gift tax cost. Achievement of this objective requires preferred stock having a fair market value equal to a large part of the fair market value of the individual's former stock interest and common stock having a nominal or small fair market value. The approach and factors described in this Revenue Ruling are directed toward ascertaining the true fair market value of the common and preferred stock and will usually result in the determination of a substantial fair market value for the common stock and a fair market value for the preferred stock which is substantially less than its par value.

.02 The type of transaction referred to above can arise in many different contexts. Some examples are:

(a) *A* owns 100% of the common stock (the only outstanding stock) of *Z* Corporation which has a fair market value of 10,500x. In a recapitalization described in section 368(a)(1)(E), *A* receives preferred stock with a par value of 10,000x and new common stock, which *A* then transfers to *A*'s son *B*.

(b) *A* owns some of the common stock of *Z* Corporation (or the stock of several corporations) the fair market value of which stock is 10,500x. *A* transfers this stock to a new corporation *X* in exchange for preferred stock of *X* corporation with a par value of 10,000x and common stock of corporation, which *A* then transfers to *A*'s son *B*.

(c) *A* owns 80 shares and his son *B* owns 20 shares of the common stock (the only stock outstanding) of *Z* Corporation. In a recapitalization described in section 368(a)(1)(E), *A* exchanges his 80 shares of common stock for 80 shares of new preferred stock of *Z* Corporation with a par value of 10,000x. *A*'s common stock had a fair market value of 10,000x.

SEC. 3. GENERAL APPROACH TO VALUATION

Under section 25.2512-2(f)(2) of the Gift Tax Regulations, the fair market value of stock in a closely held corporation depends upon numerous factors, including the corporation's net worth, its prospective earning power, and its capacity to pay dividends. In addition, other relevant factors must be taken into account. *See* Rev. Rul. 59-60. The weight to be accorded any evidentiary factor depends on the circumstances of each case. *See* section 25.2512-2(f) of the Gift Tax Regulations.

SEC. 4. APPROACH TO VALUATION—PREFERRED STOCK

.01 In general the most important factors to be considered in determining the value of preferred stock are its yield, dividend coverage and protection of its liquidation preference.

.02 Whether the yield of the preferred stock supports a valuation of the stock at par value depends in part on the adequacy of the dividend rate. The adequacy of the dividend rate should be determined by comparing its dividend rate with the dividend rate of high-grade publicly traded preferred stock. A lower yield than that of high-grade preferred stock indicates a preferred stock value of less than par. If the rate of interest charged by independent creditors to the corporation on loans is higher than the rate such independent creditors charge their most credit worthy borrowers, then the yield on the preferred stock should be correspondingly higher than the yield on high quality preferred stock. A yield which is not correspondingly higher reduces the value of the preferred stock. In addition, whether the preferred stock has a fixed dividend rate and is non-participating influences the value of the preferred stock. A publicly traded preferred stock for a company having a similar business and similar assets with similar liquidation preferences,

voting rights and other similar terms would be the ideal comparable for determining yield required in arms length transactions for closely held stock. Such ideal comparables will frequently not exist. In such circumstances, the most comparable publicly-traded issues should be selected for comparison and appropriate adjustments made for differing factors.

.03 The actual dividend rate on a preferred stock can be assumed to be its stated rate if the issuing corporation will be able to pay its stated dividends in a timely manner and will, in fact, pay such dividends. The risk that the corporation may be unable to timely pay the stated dividends on the preferred stock can be measured by the coverage of such stated dividends by the corporation's earnings. Coverage of the dividend is measured by the ratio of the sum of pre-tax and pre-interest earnings to the sum of the total interest to be paid and the pre-tax earnings needed to pay the after-tax dividends. *Standard & Poor's Ratings Guide*, 58 (1979). Inadequate coverage exists where a decline in corporate profits would be likely to jeopardize the corporation's ability to pay dividends on the preferred stock. The ratio for the preferred stock in question should be compared with the ratios for high quality preferred stock to determine whether the preferred stock has adequate coverage. Prior earnings history is important in this determination. Inadequate coverage indicates that the value of preferred stock is lower than its par value. Moreover, the absence of a provision that preferred dividends are cumulative raises substantial questions concerning whether the stated dividend rate will, in fact, be paid. Accordingly, preferred stock with noncumulative dividend features will normally have a value substantially lower than a cumulative preferred stock with the same yield, liquidation preference and dividend coverage.

.04 Whether the issuing corporation will be able to pay the full liquidation preference at liquidation must be taken into account in determining fair market value. This risk can be measured by the protection afforded by the corporation's net assets. Such protection can be measured by the ratio of the excess of the current market value of the corporation's assets over its liabilities to the aggregate liquidation preference. The protection ratio should be compared with the ratios for high quality preferred stock to determine adequacy of coverage. Inadequate asset protection exists where any unforeseen business reverses would be likely to jeopardize the corporation's ability to pay the full liquidation preference to the holders of the preferred stock.

.05 Another factor to be considered in valuing the preferred stock is whether it has voting rights and, if so, whether the preferred stock has voting control. See, however, Section 5.02 below.

.06 Peculiar covenants or provisions of the preferred stock of a type not ordinarily found in publicly traded preferred stock should be carefully evaluated to determine the effects of such covenants on the value of the preferred stock. In general, if covenants would inhibit the marketability of the stock or the power of the holder to enforce dividend or liquidation rights, such provisions will reduce the value of the preferred stock by comparison to the value of preferred stock not containing such covenants or provisions.

.07 Whether the preferred stock contains a redemption privilege is another factor to be considered in determining the value of the preferred stock. The value of a redemption privilege triggered by death of the preferred shareholder will not exceed the present value of the redemption premium payable at the preferred shareholder's death (i.e., the present value of the excess of the redemption price over the fair market value of the preferred stock upon its issuance). The value of the redemption privilege should be reduced to reflect any risk that the corporation may not possess sufficient assets to redeem its preferred stock at the stated redemption price. See .03 above.

SEC. 5. APPROACH TO VALUATION— COMMON STOCK

.01 If the preferred stock has a fixed rate of dividend and is nonparticipating, the common stock has the exclusive right to the benefits of future appreciation of the value of the corporation. This right is valuable and usually warrants a determination that the common stock has substantial value. The actual value of this right depends upon the corporation's past growth experience, the economic condition of the industry in which the corporation operates, and general economic conditions. The factor to be used in capitalizing the corporation's prospective earnings must be determined after an analysis of numerous factors concerning the corporation and the economy as a whole. *See* Rev. Rul. 59-60, at page 243. In addition, after-tax earnings of the corporation at the time the preferred stock is issued in excess of the stated dividends on the preferred stock will increase the value of the common stock. Furthermore, a corporate policy of reinvesting earnings will also increase the value of the common stock.

.02 A factor to be considered in determining the value of the common stock is whether the preferred stock also has voting rights. Voting rights of the preferred stock, especially if the preferred stock has voting control, could under certain circumstances increase the value of the preferred stock and reduce the value of the common stock. This factor may be reduced in significance where the rights of common stockholders as a class are protected under state law from actions by another class of shareholders, *see Singer v. Magnavox Co.*, 380 A.2d 969 (Del. 1977), particularly where the common shareholders, as a class, are given the power to disapprove a proposal to allow preferred stock to be converted into common stock. See ABA-ALI Model Bus. Corp. Act, Section 60 (1969).

SEC. 6. EFFECT ON OTHER REVENUE RULINGS

Rev. Rul. 59-60, as modified by Rev. Rul. 65-193, 1965-2 C.B. 370 and as amplified by Rev. Rul. 77-287, 1977-2 C.B. 319, and Rev. Rul. 80-213, 1980-2 C.B. 101, is further amplified.

APPENDIX C
Court
Cases

COURT CASES

CONTENTS

The court cases contained in this appendix were not selected to illustrate a certain valuation method or approach. They are here to give a feeling for the thought processes by which a court reaches its final valuation decision. It should be noted that the valuation area is like a wild, tropical forest...growing all the time. This appendix contains some of the best specimens.

The cases contain good examples of the issues that this book discusses concerning the valuation of privately-held business. However, rather than compartmentalize those specific topics, the reader should read each case as a whole from beginning to end to get an idea of the role that the courts reluctantly assume as final arbiters in valuation disputes between the IRS and the taxpayer.

The cases also should give the reader an idea of the multitudinous diversity of facts and law involved in each valuation dispute. No two cases are alike. And despite the huge body of case law upon which the courts can draw principles to justify their decisions, each case comes down to the court acting as an appraiser and givings its own opinion as to a proper valuation amount.

A final word: Remember the parable about the six blind men and the elephant? Each went up to an elephant and felt a different piece of the animal's anatomy, and each, based on his own separate exploration, described a completely different animal. They all were right in their conflicting descriptions, even though they failed to realize that their restricted observations were based upon the same beast. Just substitute the privately-held business for the elephant, and appraisers for the blind men, and you get an idea of how a court can disregard the opinions of some experts and accept those of others, even though each appraiser is valuing the same business, to come up with a valuation figure that is essentially a hybrid.

The Central Trust Company and Albert E. Heekin, Jr., Co-Executors of the Estate of Albert E. Heekin, Deceased v. The United States. Successor Executor and Trustee under the Will of Alma R. Heekin, Deceased v. The United States.

U.S. Court of Claims, Dkt. Nos. 196-58, 199-58, 200-58, 7/18/62.—(305 F. 2d 393.)

Thomas L. Conlan (Kyte, Conlan, Wulsin & Vogeler were on the briefs) for Plaintiffs in Dkt. No. 196-58. John W. Warrington, Cincinnati, Ohio (Graydon, Head & Ritchey were on the briefs), for Plaintiffs in Dkt. Nos. 199-58 and 200-58. Earl L. Huntington, with whom was Louis F. Oberdorfer, Asst. Attorney General, Dept. of Justice, Washington, D. C., for Defendant.

PER CURIAM: These cases were referred by the court, pursuant to Rule 45, to Saul Richard Gamer, a trial commissioner of the court, with directions to make findings of fact and recommendations for conclusions ot law. The commissioner has done so in a report filed April 17, 1962. Plaintiffs in case No. 196-58 filed their notice of intention to except to the commissioner's findings and recommendations on May 2, 1962, and on June 18, 1962, moved to withdraw this notice. Plaintiffs in case No. 199-58 and case No. 200-58 filed their notices to except to the commissioner's findings and recommendations on May 1, 1962, and on June 13, 1962, moved to withdraw these notices. On June 15, 1962, the defendant filed its reply advising the court that it had no objection to the withdrawal of the notices and on June 22, 1962, the court allowed plaintiffs' motions to withdraw the notices of intention to except in all three cases.

Plaintiffs in their motions to withdraw their notices of intention to except also moved, pursuant to Rule 46(a), that the court adopt the commissioner's report as the basis for its judgment in the cases. Defendant's reply filed June 15, 1962, concurred in these motions. Since the court agrees with the recommendations and findings of the commissioner, as hereinafter set forth, it hereby adopts the same as the basis for its judgment in these cases. Plaintiffs are therefore entitled to recover and judgment is entered to that effect. The amounts of recovery will be determined pursuant to Rule 38(c).

It is so ordered.

Opinion of the Commissioner

These suits are for the refund of federal gift taxes. They involve the common question of the value of shares of stock of the same company. A joint trial was therefore conducted.

On August 3, 1954, Albert E. Heekin made gifts totaling 30,000 shares of stock of The Heekin Can Company. The donor had formerly, for 20 years, been president of the Company and at the time of the gifts was a member of its board of directors. The gifts were composed of 5,000 shares to each of six trusts created for the benefit of his three sons, each son being the beneficiary under two trusts. Following his death on March 10, 1955, the executors of his estate filed a gift tax return in which the value of the stock was fixed at $10 a share. On October 28, 1957, however, they filed an amended gift tax return and a claim for refund, contending that the correct value of the Heekin Company stock on August 3, 1954 was $7.50 a share.

On October 25, 1954, James J. Heekin made gifts totaling 40,002 shares of Heekin Can Company stock. This donor, a brother of Albert E., had also formerly been, for 23 years, the president of the Company and at the time of the gifts was chairman of the board. The gifts were composed of 13,334 shares to each of three trusts created for the benefit of his three children and their families. Separate gift tax returns with respect to these (and other) gifts were filed by both James J. Heekin and his wife, Alma (who joined in the stock gifts), in which the value of the stock was similarly declared to be $10 a share. However, on January 21, 1958, James filed an amended gift tax return and a claim for refund, also contending that the correct value of the stock on October 25, 1954, was $7.50 a share, and on the same day, the executor of Alma's estate (she having died on November 9, 1955) filed a similar amended return and claim for refund.

On February 5, 1958, the District Director of Internal Revenue sent to James J. Heekin and the executors of the estates of Alma and Albert E. Heekin notices of deficiency of the 1954 gift taxes. Each of the three deficiencies was based on a determination by the Commissioner of Internal Revenue that the value of the Heekin Company stock on the gift dates was $24 a share.

Consistent with his deficiency notices, the District Director, on May 15, 1958, disallowed the three refund claims that had been filed, and in July 1958 payment was made of the amounts assessed pursuant to the deficiency notices. After the filing in August and September 1958 of claims for refund concerning these payments, the claims again being based on a valuation of $7.50, and the rejection thereof by the District Director, these three refund suits were instituted in the amounts of $169,876.19, $95,927.08, and $94,753.70 with respect to the Albert E. Heekin, James J. Heekin and Alma Heekin gifts, respectively, plus interest.

[*Nature of Business*]

The Heekin Can Company is a well-established metal container manufacturer in Cincinnati, Ohio. In 1954, the year involved in these proceedings, its principal business consisted of manufacturing two kinds of containers, its total production being equally divided between them. One is known as packer's cans, which are generally the type seen on the shelves of food markets in which canned food products are contained. The other is referred to as general line cans, which consist of large institutional size frozen fruit cans, lard pails, dairy cans, chemical cans, and drums. This line also includes such housewares as canisters, bread boxes, lunches boxes, waste baskets, and a type of picnic container familiarly known by the trade names of Skotch Kooler and Skotch Grill. On the gift dates its annual sales, the production of five plants, were approximately $17,000,000.

The Company was founded in 1901 in Cincinnati by James Heekin, the father of the donors Albert and James. In 1908, it built a six-story 250,000 square foot factory in Cincinnati, which is still its headquarters and one of its main operating plants, producing general line cans. In 1917 it acquired a plant in Norwood, a suburb of Cincinnati, which has since become entirely surrounded by the city, and entered the packer's can business. By 1954, it was a multistory plant with about 275,000 square feet, having grown irregularly throughout the years, one section having four floors, another three, and another only one.

In 1946, the Company branched out from Cincinnati and established a packer's can plant at Chestnut Hill, Tennessee, on property leased from and contiguous to the plant of its largest customer, which used the entire output of the Heekin plant. The cans were run by conveyor directly into the customer's packing plant.

In 1949, the Company built a 100,000 square foot plant in Springdale, Arkansas, to supply its customers in the Ozark area on a more competitive basis concerning freight costs, a large part of which, under the industry's freight-equalization practice, it had theretofore absorbed.

In 1952, the Company established it fifth plant, constituting an operation at Blytheville, Arkansas, similar to the one at Chestnut Hill, Tennessee. The plant was on leased property adjacent to the customer's plant, with the cans running directly into such plant. By 1954 this concept of installing can-making lines immediately adjacent to customers' packing plants was a recognized practice in the industry. Thus, the Company was progressively adapting itself to the modern practices of its industry.

From the beginning, the Heekin family has dominated the enterprise. James, the founder, was its president from 1901 to 1905. He was succeeded by his son, James J., one of the donors herein, who served as president for 23 years. In 1928, another son,

Albert E., another donor herein, then became president, serving for 20 years. He was succeeded in 1948 by still another son, Daniel M., who served for 6 years. In March 1954, Albert E. Heekin, Jr., the son of donor Albert E. and the grandson of the founder, succeeded to the presidency. A lawyer, he had served the Company up to 1950 as its legal counsel, joining the Company in that year as assistant to the president. On August 3, 1954, of the ten-member board of directors, eight were members of the Heekin family, five of whom were sons of the founder, and three his grandsons. Both donors were members of the board, James J. being chairman. On October 25, 1954, the board was similarly constituted, except for the death of one son in August. Despite this family domination, there was no indication on the gift dates that the enterprise was not capably managed or that salaries were in any way excessive.

On the gift dates, the Company had 254,125 shares of common stock outstanding, there being no restrictions on their transferability or sale. There was no other class of stock. Including the 70,002 shares involved in these cases, a total of 180,510 shares were owned by 79 persons who were related to James Heekin, the founder. Thus, the Heekin family owned approximately 71 percent of all of the outstanding stock. The remaining 73,615 shares were owned by 54 unrelated persons, most of whom were employees of the Company and friends of the family.

[Business Relations]

Six major customers accounted for almost one-half of Heekin's 1954 business. Relations with these important customers were long-standing and excellent. One of these customers, the Hamilton Metal Products Company, which placed over $2,000,000 worth of business with Heekin in 1954, and for whom Heekin manufactured the Skotch Kooler and Grill, had, prior to the gift dates, advised Heekin of its need for certain new products, and on August 3, 1954 (one of the gift dates), Heekin's board of directors authorized the expenditure of approximately $90,000 for new tooling and equipment at its Cincinnati plant for the manufacture of such products. Another major customer was the Reynolds Tobacco Company, which

placed almost $1,500,000 of business with Heekin in 1954 and with whom Heekin had dealt since 1908.

As indicated, freight costs play an important part in Heekin's business. These costs are significant in two aspects. One is the cost of transporting raw material to Heekin's plants. In this respect Heekin was quite favorably located. It has a dock on the Ohio River in Cincinnati, permitting it to take advantage of inexpensive water transportation of steel shipped from Pittsburgh, with a consequent advantage over some of its competitors in the same area who receive their raw materials by rail. The other important freight aspect is, as above noted, the cost of shipping the final product to the customer, and which factor motivated the establishment of its Springdale, Arkansas, plant. The Hamilton Metal Products Company was located only 25 miles from Cincinnati, giving Heekin an important freight advantage. And also, on August 3, 1954, Heekin's board of directors authorized the expenditure of about $650,000 for new tooling, machinery and equipment for its Norwood plant so that Heekin could enter the new field of manufacturing beer cans. At that time no other company in the Cincinnati area was engaged in the production of such cans, and Heekin concluded that, with the freight advantage it would have over its competitors in serving the brewers of the Cincinnati area, a profitable new source of business would be developed.

In 1954, favorable economic conditions generally prevailed in the can-manufacturing industry, and demand was at a record level. Indeed, this was the condition throughout the container and packaging industry, and optimism generally prevailed about the continuation of the then current high demand.

[Competitive Industry]

But Heekin had its problems too. It is a relatively tiny factor in a highly competitive industry dominated by two giants, the American Can Company and the Continental Can Company. In 1954, these two companies, each with over $600,000,000 of annual sales produced from 76 and 40 plants respectively, together accounted for about 75 percent of the country's total can sales. Three other can manufacturing companies, the National Can Corporation, the Pacific Can

Company, and Crown Cork & Seal Co., Inc., together made about 8 percent of the sales. Heekin, with its five plants, did a little less than 1 percent of the total business. Prices in the can-making industry are for practical purposes established by American and Continental. When they announce prices, Heekin goes up or down with them. Unable to compete on a price basis, Heekin strives to give its customers better personal service, which, because it is smaller and closer knit, it can frequently do.

[Age of Equipment]

Probably Heekin's major problem is the age, and the resulting relative inefficiency, of a large part of its plant and equipment, and its inability to finance a large-scale program of modernization. This again is in part a problem of its small size. The relatively small amounts it can use for this purpose are generated by retained earnings, and it has consequently fallen behind the giants of the industry in erecting efficient plants and installing modern, high-speed, automatic can-making lines. During the war, Heekin was unable to buy new equipment. However, such competitors as American, Continental, and Pacific manufactured their own can-making equipment and were able to forge ahead, and such equipment as Heekin was able to buy after the war from other companies could not match American and Continental's modern automatic packer's can equipment, which produced 500 cans a minute. Heekin's older packer's can equipment could turn out only about 300 cans a minute, and even the new equipment it was able to buy after the war could attain, with difficulty, speeds of only 400 cans a minute. In 1954, about 90 percent of Heekin's equipment had been acquired in the middle 1930's or prior thereto. In all its plants, the Company had 37 can-making lines, 11 of which were very old and still hand operated.

Similarly, Heekin's Cincinnati and Norwood multistory plants, which accounted for about 75 percent of Heekin's total 1954 production, were less efficient than modern, single-story buildings. The can-making business is primarily a material-handling one, requiring a rapid and efficient flow of large amounts of material through the plant, from the receipt of the raw materials to the shipment of finished products. In a single-story building, materials can freely be moved horizontally with fork-lift trucks and conveyors, whereas in its six-story Cincinnati and four-story Norwood plants, elevators are used for the vertical movement of materials, resulting in excessive labor and handling costs and more difficult production controls. The proceeds of a $3,000,000 long-term loan which Heekin secured in 1950 were for the most part not available for such a plant and equipment modernization program.

However, the competitive disadvantage of lack of modern equipment was reflected more on the packer's can phase of its business than on the general line cans, which are produced both by Heekin and its competitors on only semiautomatic equipment. Such equipment does not lend itself as readily to the speed and automation required with respect to packer's cans. Heekin's semiautomatic lines were capable of producing around 300 cans a minute.

[Unlisted Stock]

The Heekin stock was not listed on any stock exchange, and trading in it was infrequent. There was some such activity in 1951 and 1952 resulting from the desire of certain minority stockholders (the descendants of a partner of James Heekin, the founder) to liquidate their holdings, consisting of 13,359 shares. One individual alone had 10,709 shares. Arrangements were privately made in early 1951 by these stockholders with Albert E. Heekin and his son, Albert E. Heekin, Jr., to sell these holdings at the prearranged price of $7.50 a share. These shares were all sold, commencing March 22, 1951, and ending April 16, 1952, in 44 separate transactions, 35 of which took place in 1951 and 9 in 1952. No attempt was made to sell the shares to the general public on the open market. All sales were made to Heekin employees and friends of the Heekin family at such $7.50 price. Other than these 1951 and 1952 sales, the only sales of stock made prior to the gift dates consisted of one sale of 100 shares in 1953 by one Heekin employee to another, and one sale in 1954 of 200 shares, again by one Heekin employee to another, both sales also being made for $7.50 a share.

Against these background facts, the valuation question in dispute may be approached. Section 1000 of the Internal Revenue Code of 1939 (26 U. S. C. 1952 Ed., § 1000, 53 Stat. 144), the applicable statute, imposed a tax upon transfers of property by gift, whether in trust or otherwise. Section 1005 provided that "If the gift is made in property, the value thereof at the date of the gift shall be considered the amount of the gift."

Section 86.19(a) of the Regulations issued with respect thereto (Treasury Regulations 108, 8 Fed. Reg. 10858) defines such property value as the price at which the property "would change hands between a willing buyer and a willing seller, neither being under any compulsion to buy or to sell. * * * Such value is to be determined by ascertaining as a basis the fair market value at the time of the gift of each unit of the property. For example, in the case of shares of stock * * *, such unit of property is a share * * *. All relevant facts and elements of value as of the time of the gift should be considered." With respect to determining the fair market value per share at the date of the gift, subsection (c)·(6) stated that, if actual sales or bona fide bid and asked prices are not available, the value should be arrived at "on the basis of the company's net worth, earning power, dividend-paying capacity, and all other relevant factors having a bearing upon the value of the stock."

Further, a lengthy Revenue Ruling (54-77, 1954-1 Cum. Bull. 187), entitled "Valuation of stock of closely held corporations in estate tax and gift tax returns," was in effect at the time of these gifts which outlined "the approach, methods and factors to be considered in valuing shares of the capital stock of closely held corporations for estate tax and gift tax purposes." After warning in section 3 that fair market value, "being a question of fact," depends on the "circumstances in each case," and that "No formula can be devised that will be generally applicable to the multitude of different valuation issues arising in estate and gift tax cases," and that there is ordinarily "wide differences of opinion as to the fair market value of a particular" closely held stock, section 4 goes on to enumerate the following factors which "are fundamental and require careful analysis in each case": (1) the nature of the business and its history,

(2) the general economic outlook of business in general and the specific industry in particular, (3) the book value of the stock and the company's financial condition, (4) the company's earning capacity, (5) its dividend-paying capacity, (6) its goodwill, (7) such sales of the stock as have been made as well as the size of the block to be valued and (8) "the market price of stocks of corporations engaged in the same or similar line of business which are listed on an exchange." After discussing each factor in detail, the Ruling goes on to consider such matters as (a) the weight to be accorded the various factors, concluding that, in a product selling company, primary consideration should normally be given to the earnings factor, and (b) the necessity of capitalizing the earnings and dividends at appropriate rates.

There appears to be no dispute between the parties concerning the validity, or the propriety of applying the principles, of the Regulations and the Ruling to these cases. The dispute arises from the differences of opinion which are inherent in the Ruling's statement that "A sound valuation will be based upon all the relevant facts, but the elements of common sense, informed judgment and reasonableness must enter into the process of weighing those facts and determining their aggregate significance."

[Testimony of Experts]

Where, as in the present cases, the problem is the difficult one of ascertaining the fair market value of the stock of an unlisted closely held corporation, it is not surprising that, in assisting the court to arrive at an "informed judgment," the parties offer the testimony of experts. In such a situation, the opinions of experts are peculiarly appropriate. *Bader v. United States,* [59-1 USTC ¶ 11,865] 172 F. Supp. 833 (D. C. S. D. Ill.). At the trial, the taxpayers produced three experts, and the Government one.

One of plaintiffs' experts was the senior partner of a firm of investment bankers and brokers. He felt that the limited prior sales of the stock at $7.50 warranted the consideration of the other factors listed in the Revenue Ruling applicable to closely held corporations. There were four major factors which he considered in arriving at his conclusion. The first was book value.

Utilizing the Company's balance sheet as of December 31, 1954 (a date subsequent to the gift dates), the book value came to about $33 a share. In this connection he noted that the Company's financial position at that time was sound, with a ratio of current assets to current liabilities of about 4.3 to 1. However, principally because of the age and multistoried inefficiency of the Company's two main plants at Cincinnati and Norwood, he reduced the book value factor by 50 percent. The second factor was earnings. The Company's audited annual statements for 1952, 1953 and 1954, which he accepted without adjustment, showed that the average of its earnings for these 3 years was $1.77 a share. He felt that, in the case of this Company, a price earnings ratio of 6 to 1 would be appropriate, but, recognizing that this was the most important factor, he weighted it to give it double value. The third factor was dividend yield. In said 3 years, the Company paid an annual dividend of 50 cents. Accepting this figure as the dividend the Company would be likely to pay in the future, he concluded that an investor would look for a 7 percent yield on this stock, and capitalized it on that basis. The fourth factor was the prior sales at $7.50. Adding and weighting these figures, he derived a value of $10.50 a share. However, because the stock was not listed on any exchange, and was closely held, with sales being infrequent, he discounted that value by 25 percent to reflect the stock's lack of marketability, and came out with an ultimate valuation of $7.88 a share.[1] This is the value plaintiffs now rely on in these cases. This value was applied to the entire block of 70,002 shares and to both dates, a block which, he noted, would give a purchaser only a minority position. Considering the Revenue Ruling's suggestion to investigate "the market price of stocks of corporations engaged in the same or similar line of business which are listed on an exchange," this witness felt that there were no listed companies that could properly be compared with Heekin.

Plaintiffs' second expert, a certified public accountant who had experience in and was familiar with the principles involved in valuing stocks of closely held corporations, arrived at the somewhat higher valuations of $9.50 per share for the 30,000 shares given on August 3, 1954, and $9.65 for the 40,002 given on October 25, 1954. He recognized that the previous sales of the stock in 1951, 1952, 1953 and 1954 at $7.50 could not be determinative because, being all at the same selling price, they could not have reflected the month-to-month or year-to-year fluctuations of actual value, which was the problem herein involved. He concluded that that price was predicated primarily to give a yield of 6⅔ percent based on an annual dividend rate of 50 cents, which the Company had paid each year from 1946 through 1954, except for a 1½-year period in 1950 and 1951. In 1950, the Company suffered extraordinary losses and dividends were suspended, and in 1951, only 25 cents was paid. Accordingly, he considered the situation appropriate for the application of the principles enunciated in the Revenue Ruling.

In so doing, he too concluded that the four major factors to be considered were earnings, dividend yield, book value, and the price of the prior sales. As to earnings, he computed, from the Company's audited statements for the years 1950-54, without adjustment, average annual earnings of $1.68. Using the comparative method of calculating price-earnings ratios of listed companies in the same or similar business and then correlating such results to Heekin, he selected 11 leading corporations in the container industry (only two of which, American Can and Continental Can, were can companies), and computed their average price-

---

[1] *Book value* = $33.20, less 50%.................................... $16.60
Earnings = Average 3 years = 1.77; price to earnings ratio = 6:1 = $10.62. Weighted to two factors..................... 21.24
Dividends = To give yield of 7% at rate of 50¢ per annum, would have to sell at.................................... 7.14
Prior Sales 7.50

Total all factors.. 52.48
Divided by 5 to obtain weighted average............... 52.48 ÷ 5 = $10.50
Less 25% for lack of marketability.................................... 2.62

7.88

earnings ratio over the similar 5-year period at 10 to 1, with 1954 alone producing a ratio of 11.6 to 1 because of the rise in prices of container industry stocks in that year.[2] However, he capitalized Heekin's 5-year average earnings of $1.68 at an earnings multiple of only eight times which he considered appropriate for a "marginal" company like Heekin. Since this produced a value of $13.44 based only on earnings. as of December 31, 1954, due to his using the figures for the full year 1954, he adjusted the figure to August 3, 1954, the first gift date, by reducing the figure by 14.1 percent, a figure derived by calculating the general rise in a relatively large group of certain other industry stocks between August 3 and December 31. Thus, on the basis of earnings alone, he calculated a value of $11.55 as of August 3.

As to dividends, this witness then calculated Heekin's average for the 5 years ended December 31, 1954, at 35 cents per share and capitalized that figure at 6 percent, which he considered to be appropriate in Heekin's case in view of the 5-year average dividend yield of 5.1 percent for the 11 leading companies in the container industry which he used as comparatives, and the even higher returns, on a 5-year average basis, afforded by general groups of leading industrials during that period. Thus, on the basis of a 6 percent dividend yield alone, he calculated a value of $5.83.

Using as factors the value figures derived as described on the bases of price earnings ($11.55) and dividend yield ($5.83) ratios, together with a book value figure of $33.23 as of December 31, 1954, and a $7.50 figure as the price of the prior sales, the witness then weighted these four factor figures, giving the earnings and dividend factors 40

percent each (i. e. each figure multiplied by 4), and the book value and prior sales figure 10 percent each (i. e. each figure multiplied by 1). This total figure was then reduced by 15 percent to reflect the stock's lack of marketability (which was equated to the underwriting cost of floating 30,000 shares) which, after dividing by the weight factor (10), gave the market price as of August 3 as $9.37,[3] which he rounded out to $9.50.

Using the same criteria and method, the witness valued the 40,002 shares given on October 25, 1954, at the slightly higher price of $9.65, the price of listed stocks having generally risen between the two dates.

The taxpayers' third expert, a senior officer in a firm specializing in valuing the stocks of closely held corporations, came out with the still higher valuation of $11.41 per share on August 3, in blocks of 10,000 ($11.76 in a block of 30,000 shares). For the shares given on October 25, however, his value was only $9.40 per share in blocks of 13,334 shares ($9.47 in a block of 40,002 shares).

This witness also used the technique of selecting comparable companies traded on a national exchange, ascertaining, by a very comprehensive study, the relationship between their market prices and their earnings, "earnings paid out," and return on invested capital (to which he added long-term debt), and then correlating the data to Heekin. Unlike the other two experts, he did not accept the exact figures of the audited statements of annual earnings, but studied them with a view to detecting and eliminating abnormal and nonrecurring items of loss or profit in order to obtain a better picture of the Company's normal operation and of what an investor, therefore, might reasonably conclude the Company's future performance would be. With such adjustments and eliminations, he thus recast the Com-

---

[2] He noted that this 10-to-1 ratio was higher than the Dow-Jones average of 9.9 for 30 industrials, the Standard & Poor average of 9.3 for 50 industrials, and the Moody average of 9.7 for 125 industrials for the same 5-year period.

		Weight	*Total*
[3] Price earnings ratio	$11.55	4	$46.20
Dividend—35¢ capitalized at 6%	5.83	4	23.32
Stock sales	7.50	1	7.50
Book value	33.23	1	33.23
			110.25
Less 15%—amount for nonmarketability (flotation cost)			16.51
			93.74
Divided by factor 10			9.37

pany's earnings for the years 1949-1953. He selected eight companies in both the can and glass container fields to use as comparatives.

In calculating Heekin's earnings, the witness used a 5-year average, as adjusted. One of the adjustments was to the Company's abnormal profits in 1951 as a result of the Korean war, which he eliminated and reduced to more normal levels. Another was to eliminate, as abnormal and non-recurring, rather large losses the Company suffered in 1950, 1951 and 1952 as a result of the operations of a subsidiary which was liquidated. By applying a price-earnings ratio of 11.82, as derived from the comparative companies, he determined a value of the Heekin stock on August 3, based only on earnings, of $13.78 per share; a value based on earnings paid out (in which he included not ony dividends but also interest on long-term debt) on the capital invested in the business of $9.59 per share; and a value based on invested capital of $31.34 per share. To these three determinants of value, he added the fourth factor of $7.50 derived from the prior sales price. He too then weighted these figures, assigning a weight of 33⅓ percent each to the values based on earnings and earnings-paid-out, and 16⅔ percent each to the values based on invested capital and the prior stock sales. This gave a total weighted value of $14.26. He then too applied a 20-percent reduction for lack of marketability, which he also equated with flotation costs for blocks of 10,000 shares, resulting in the net figure of $11.41 as of August 3.[4]

The same technique produced a figure of $9.40 per share as of October 25, 1954, in blocks of 13,334 shares.[5] This lower valuation is attributable to the drop in the market prices of the comparative companies between August 3 and October 25, 1954. One of the comparatives (Pacific Can Company) which had been used for the August 3 valuation

was dropped since it enjoyed a rather atypical sharp rise after such date due to a proposed merger.

[Criticisms of Experts' Appraisals]

Various major criticisms can fairly be made of these three appraisals offered by plaintiffs. First, they all give undue weight as a factor to the $7.50 price of the prior stock sales. Almost all of these sales occurred in the relatively remote period of 1951 and early 1952. Only one small transaction occurred in each of the more recent years of 1953 and 1954. Such isolated sales of closely held corporations in a restricted market offer little guide to true value. *Wood, Adm. v. United States,* 89 Ct. Cl. 442; *First Trust Co. v. United States,* [59-1 USTC ¶ 11,843] 3 Am. Fed. Tax R. 2d 1726 (D. C. W. D. Mo.); *Drayton Cochran v. Commissioner,* 7 CCH Tax Ct. Mem. 325; *Schnorbach v. Kavanagh,* [52-1 USTC ¶ 10,836] 102 F. Supp. 828 (D. C. W. D. Mich.). In an evaluation issue, this court recently even gave little weight to the sale of shares on a stock exchange when the amount sold was "relatively insignificant." *American Steel Foundries v. United States,* Ct. Cl. No. 197-54, decided April 7, 1961 (slip opinion, p. 4). To the same effect is *Heiner v. Crosby,* [1 USTC ¶ 276] 24 F. 2d 191 (C. C. A. 3d) in which the court rejected stock exchange sales as being determinative and upheld the resort to "evidence of intrinsic value" (p. 194). Furthermore, the $7.50 price of the 1951 and 1952 sales evolved in early 1951 during a period when the Company was experiencing rather severe financial difficulties due to an unfortunate experience with a subsidiary which caused a loss of around $1,000,000, and when, consequently, the Company found itself in a depleted working capital position and was paying no dividends. Further, there is no indication that the $7.50 sales price evolved as a result of the usual factors taken into

Value based on earnings—13.78 @ 33⅓%...	$ 4.59
Value based on earnings paid out—9.59 @ 33⅓%...................................	3.20
Value based on invested capital—31.34 @ 16⅔%...................................	5.22
Value based on stock sales—7.50 @ 16⅔%..	1.25
100%	14.26
Less 20% for lack of marketability (flotation cost in blocks of 10,000 shares)....	2.85
Net value	11.41
Less 17.5% reduction if in a block of 30,000 shares........................	11.76

$9.47 per share in a block of 40,002 shares.

consideration by informed sellers and buyers dealing at arm's length. Fair market value presupposes not only hypothetical willing buyers and sellers, but buyers and sellers who are informed and have "adequate knowledge of the material facts affecting the value." *Robertson v. Routzahn,* [35-1 USTC ¶ 9124] 75 F. 2d 537, 539 (C. C. A. 6th); Paul, *Studies in Federal Taxation* (1937), pp. 193-4. The sales were all made at a prearranged price to Heekin employees and family friends. The artificiality of the price is indicated by its being the same in 1951, 1952, 1953 and 1954, despite the varying fortunes of the Company during these years and with the price failing to reflect, as would normally be expected, such differences in any way.

Secondly, in using the Company's full 1954 financial data, and then working back from December 31, 1954, to the respective gift dates, data were being used which would not have been available to a prospective purchaser as of the gift dates. "The valuation of the stock must be made as of the relevant dates without regard to events occurring subsequent to the crucial dates." *Bader v. United States, supra,* at p. 840. Furthermore, in the working-back procedure, general market data were used although it is evident that the stocks of a particular industry may at times run counter to the general trend. This was actually the situation here. Although the market generally advanced after August 3, 1954, container industry stocks did not.

Thirdly, the converse situation applies with respect to the data used by the third expert. His financial data only went to December 31, 1953, since the Company's last annual report prior to the gift dates was issued for the year 1953. But the Company also issued quarterly interim financial statements, and by the second gift date, the results of three-quarters of 1954 operations were available. In evaluating a stock, it is essential to obtain as recent data as is possible, as section 4 of the Revenue Ruling makes plain. Naturally, an investor would be more interested in how a corporation is currently performing then what it did last year or in even more remote periods. Although the use of interim reports reflecting only a part of a year's performance may not be satisfactory in a seasonal operation such

as canning, it is possible here to obtain a full year's operation ending on either June 30 or September 30, 1954, which would bring the financial data up closer to the valuation dates.

Fourth, it is accepted valuation practice, in ascertaining a company's past earnings, to attempt to detect abnormal or nonrecurring items and to make appropriate eliminations or adjustments. As shown, only the plaintiffs' expert who came out with the highest August 3 valuation attempted to do this by adjusting the excessive Korean war earnings and by eliminating the unusual losses suffered in 1950, 1951 and 1952 arising from the operations of a financing subsidiary (Canners Exchange, Inc.) that had been liquidated in 1952. The reason this is important is that past earnings are significant only insofar as they reasonably forecast future earnings. The only sound basis upon which to ground such a forecast is the company's normal operation, which requires the elimination or adjustment of abnormal items which will not recur. *Plaut v. Smith,* [49-1 USTC ¶ 9145] 82 F. Supp. 42 (D. C. Conn.), *aff'd, sub nom. Plaut v. Munford,* [51-1 USTC ¶ 9254] 188 F. 2d 543 (Ct. App. 2d Cir.). In *American Steel Foundries v. United States, supra,* the court similarly viewed the "earning prospects" of the company whose stock was being evaluated in light of its past earnings "as constructed by the accountants, eliminating or adjusting losses due to strikes or other nonrecurring events." And the court in *White & Wells Co. v. Commissioner,* 50 F. 2d 120 (C. C. A. 2d), also held that: "* * * past earnings * * * should be such as fairly reflect the probable future earnings" and that to this end "abnormal years" may even be entirely disregarded. The Revenue Ruling (sec. 4.02(d)) specifically points out the necessity of separating "recurrent from nonrecurrent items of income and expense."

Fifth, in deriving a past earnings figure which could be used as a reasonable basis of forecasting future earnings, none of plaintiffs' experts gave any consideration to the trend of such past earnings. They simply used the earnings of prior years and averaged them. But such averages may be deceiving. Two corporations with 5-year earnings going from the past to the present represented by the figures in one case of 5, 4, 3, 2, and 1, and in the other by the same figures of 1, 2, 3, 4, and 5, will have the same 5-year averages, but investors will quite naturally prefer the stock of the latter whose earnings are consistently moving upward. The Revenue Ruling specifically recognizes this in providing (sec. 4.02(d)) that: "Prior earnings records usually are the most reliable guide as to the future expectancy, but resort to arbitrary five-or-ten-year averages without regard to current trends or future prospects will not produce a realistic valuation. If, for instance, a record of progressively increasing or decreasing net income is found, then greater weight may be accorded the most recent years' profits in estimating earning power."

And further, since the most recent years' earnings are to be accorded the greatest weight, care must be taken to make certain that the earnings figures for such years are realistically set forth. For instance, in Heekin's case, profits for 1952-54 were understated because a noncontributory retirement plan for hourly employees was established in 1951 for which the costs attributable to 1950 and 1951 were borne in the later years of 1952-54. Similarly, 1954 profits were further understated because they reflected (1) a renegotiation refund arising out of excess profits made in 1951, and (2) they were subjected to a charge of $174,203.54 ($83,617.70 after taxes) as a result of a deduction from 1954 profits only of certain expenses attributable to both 1954 and 1955. This abnormal doubling up of 2 years' expenses in one year was permitted by a change in the tax laws which became effective in 1954 (and which was later revoked retroactively) which allowed taxpayers such as Heekin to change their methods of accounting so as to effect the accrual in 1954 of these 1955 expenses. If proper adjustments are made in Heekin's 1954 statements for these items, the earnings for the 1954 period prior to the gift dates would be realistically increased and given due weight insofar as earning trends are concerned.

None of plaintiffs' experts made any of these adjustments in connection with a trend study or otherwise.

Sixth, it is generally conceded that, as stated by the Revenue Ruling, in evaluating stocks of manufacturing corporations such as Heekin, earnings are the most important factor to be considered. *Badar v. United States, supra.* Yet only one of plaintiffs' experts, who assigned double value to this factor, gave it such weight. As shown, the other two assigned the dividend factor equal weight. Some investors may indeed depend upon dividends. In their own investment programs, they may therefore stress yield and even compare common stocks with bonds or other forms of investment to obtain the greatest yields. However others, for various reasons, may care little about dividends and may invest in common stocks for the primary purpose of seeking capital appreciation. All investors, however, are primarily concerned with earnings, which are normally a prerequisite to dividends. In addition, the declaration of dividends is sometimes simply a matter of the policy of a particular company. It may bear no relationship to dividend-paying capacity. Many investors actually prefer companies paying little or no dividends and which reinvest their earnings, for that may be the key to future growth and capital appreciation.

And further, in capitalizing the dividend at 6 and 7 percent, as did two of the experts, rates of return were used which well exceeded those being paid at the time by comparable container company stocks. And still further, one of the experts used a 35-cent dividend rate as the basis for his capitalization because that was the average paid for the 5 years ended December 31, 1954. However, it seems clear that an annual dividend rate of 50 cents a share would be the proper rate to capitalize since that was the dividend paid by Heekin every year since 1945 except for the year 1950 and the first half of 1951 when, as shown, dividends were temporarily suspended. By the end of 1951 the Company had recovered from the situation causing the suspension and the normal dividend (quarterly payments of 12½ cents per share) was then resumed. By August and October 1954, Heekin's demonstrated earning capability and financial position were such that there was little doubt it would at least continue its 50-cent annual dividend, which represented only about 25 percent of its current earnings per share. To dip back into this 1950-51 atypical period to compute an "average" of dividends paid for the past 5 years is unrealistic.

Finally, the record indicates that all three experts took too great a discount for lack of marketability. Defendant disputes the propriety of taking this factor into consideration at all. It seems clear, however, that an unlisted closely held stock of a corporation such as Heekin, in which trading is infrequent and which therefore lacks marketability, is less attractive than a similar stock which is listed on an exchange and has ready access to the investing public. This factor would naturally affect the market value of the stock. This is not to say that the market value of any unlisted stock in which trading is infrequent would automatically be reduced by a lack of marketability factor. The stock of a well-known leader in its field with a preeminent reputation might not be at all affected by such a consideration, as was the situation with Ford Motor Company stock before it was listed. *Couzens v. Commissioner,* [CCH Dec. 3931] 11 B. T. A. 1040. But the stock of a less well-known company like Heekin which is a comparatively small factor in its industry is obviously in a different position. In such a situation, a consideration of this factor is appropriate, especially where, as here, only a minority interest is involved. *Bader v. United States, supra; Baltimore National Bank v. United States,* [56-1 USTC ¶ 11,576] 136 F. Supp. 642 (D. C. Md.); *Schnorbach v. Kavanagh, supra; Cochran v. Commissioner, supra; First Trust Co. v. United States, supra.* But see *Couzens v. Commissioner, supra; Estate of Katharine H. Daily v. Commissioner,* 6 CCH Tax Ct. Mem. 114.

Defendant concedes that if such a factor is appropriate in these cases, a reasonable method of determining the diminution in value attributable to lack of marketability is to determine how much it would cost to create marketability for the block of stock in question. This was the method used by the court in *First Trust Co. v. United States, supra.* The record shows that for a company of Heekin's size, and for blocks of 30,000 and 40,000 shares, which would appear to be the appropriate considerations, flotation costs would amount to about 12.17 percent of the gross sales prices. However, as shown, the discounts taken by plaintiffs' experts for this factor ranged from 15 to 25 percent.

For all the above reasons, the opinions of plaintiffs' experts are not wholly acceptable.

[Decedent's Expert Witness]

Defendant produced one expert, an employee of a recognized appraisal company. His primary work over may years was the valuation of intangibles, including closely held stock. His opinion was that the value of the Heekin stock in question on August 3 and October 25, 1954, was $16 and $15.25 per share, respectively. This witness also used the comparative appraisal method, considering a group of stock in the can and glass container industries. As part of a very comprehensive study, he selected eight container companies, six engaged in can production and two in glass container production, glass container enterprises being similar to those engaged in can production. He considered net assets as a key factor in the determination of a stock price, and one which keeps a stock price from declining to zero when earnings become zero or even when losses are suffered and when a price-to-earnings ratio would therefore become meaningless. He therefore developed for the comparative companies percentage ratios of profits and dividends to net worth as well as market value to net worth. In developing figures for the profits and dividends of the comparative companies for the past 5 years, he gave weight to the trends thereof. He then developed Heekin's profits over the period 1950 through September 1954, making adjustments for the retirement plan costs, the losses from subsidiaries, the renegotiation refund, and the abnormal 1951 profits, in order to reflect the more nearly normal operations over the period. Adjusted profits were developed for the 12-month periods ending June 30 and September 30, 1954. Before correlating the percentages developed for the comparative companies to Heekin, however, he concluded that only two of such companies, United Can and Glass Company and Crown Cork & Seal Company, Inc., could be considered conformable to Heekin. The others, including the giants of their industries, such as American Can, Continental Can, and Owens Illinois Glass Company which, because of acquisitions, diversification, premium investment quality position, and mere size, were not considered fairly comparable, were eliminated. Correlating the data developed with respect to such two companies, he concluded that, as of August 3, Heekin would be worth 59.5 percent of net worth, or $19.72 per share, a stock exchange equivalent of 19¾ per share. The similar method produced $18.78 per share as the value as of October 25, 1954, or a trading equivalent of 18¾.

This witness too felt that the correlation process resulted in comparing Heekin with seasoned listed stocks enjoying marketability, and that an adjustment should be made for the closely held nature of the Heekin stock with its resultant lack of marketability, especially where only a minority interest was involved. Similarly equating this adjustment to deductions a seller would experience through floating the shares through an underwriter, which he calculated to be almost 20 percent, resulted in net valuations of 16 and 15¼ as of August 3 and October 25, 1954, respectively. Since these values approximate Heekin's current assets (including inventories) less all of its liabilities, without giving any value at all to any of its plants, equipment, or other noncurrent assets, he concluded they were extremely conservative. Employing the common tests of price-to-earnings ratio and yield on the basis of the current 50-cent dividend, these values would result in a price-to-earnings ratio of 7.24:1 as of August 3, based on $2.21 adjusted net profit per share for the 12 months ending June 30, as well as a 3.13 percent dividend yield, and a ratio of 8.29:1 as of October 25, based on $1.84 adjusted net profit per share for the 12 months ending September 30, as well as a 3.28 percent dividend yield.

This witness' study has certain meritorious features. It is based on justifiable adjustments in Heekin's earnings records to eliminate abnormal and nonrecurring items (although he made no adjustment for the 1954 doubling up of certain expenses). It considers earnings trend. It disregards the prior $7.50 sales prices as a major factor. And in employing the Company's financial data going up to June 30 and September 30, 1954, it is based on its most recent performance. However, it has certain weaknesses

too, the principal one being the limitation of the comparative companies to two, one of which, Crown Cork & Seal, leaves much to be desired as a comparative because its principal business is the manufacture of bottle caps and bottling machinery, an entirely different business. Only 40 percent of its business is in can production. On the basis of size too there are great differences. At that time, Crown, including its foreign subsidiaries, was doing about $115,000,000 worth of business as against Heekin's $17,000,000. And the other comparative, United Can and Glass, presents the complication that it declared periodic stock dividends to which the witness gave no consideration, although it seems that some element of value should fairly be attributed to them.[*] Although no two companies are ever exactly alike, it being rare to have such almost ideal comparatives as were present in *Cochran v. Commissioner, supra,* so that absolute comparative perfection can seldom be achieved, nevertheless the comparative appraisal method is a sound and well-accepted technique. In employing it, however, every effort should be made to select as broad a base of comparative companies as is reasonably possible, as well as to give full consideration to every possible factor in order to make the comparison more meaningful.

Further, in compiling Heekin's financial data for correlation purposes, this witness used Heekin's average dividends for the 4½ years preceding the valuation dates, thus including the atypical period when no dividends were paid.

Defendant, considering its own expert's valuations to be unduly conservative, and disagreeing as a matter of law with any deduction for lack of marketability (and in any event with the amount deducted by its expert for such factor), now offers valuations on what it claims to be a more realistic basis. It also adjusts and redistributes Heekin's profits, including the "doubling up" expenses in 1954, the renegotiation refund, and the retirement plan. As com-

---

[*] "In theory, of course, the additional stock certificate gives him [the stockholder] nothing that he would not own without it * * *. But in actuality the payment of periodic stock dividends produces important advantages. Among them are the following: * * * 4. Issues paying periodic stock dividends enjoy a higher market value than similar common stocks not paying such dividends." Graham & Dodd, *Security Analysis, Principles and Technique* (3d ed. 1951) pp. 444-5.

paratives, it uses for the purpose of developing a price-earnings ratio 11 can and glass container manufacturing companies, including American Can and Continental Can (although it concedes that with respect to the stock of such companies in this field, the investing public affords "some extra value coincident with size"), as well as Crown Cork & Seal and United Can. The dividend yield of seven comparative companies, based on their 1954 dividend payments, was 3.77 percent. Defendant too gives no cognizance to United Can's stock dividends, although it concedes that "stock dividends have some effect on market value." On Heekin's 50-cent dividend, the market price of Heekin stock would be $13.33, based solely on a 3.75 (the figure used by defendant) percent dividend yield.

Defendant then computes representative earnings for Heekin as $1.89 per share, based on 1953 and 1954 adjusted earnings. The average price to current earnings ratio of the 11 comparative companies in 1954 was 13 to 1. On this formula, Heekin's stock would sell for $24.57 per share if earnings were the sole factor. However, defendant reduces this figure to $22.50 for the purpose in question.

On the basis of the book value of Heekin stock being $33.15 as of June 30, 1954, and comparing the market prices of various alleged comparable companies to their book value (i. e., the stocks of 11 unidentified comparatives used by the Commissioner of Internal Revenue in making his valuation sold for 1.4 times book value), defendant concludes that Heekin stock would not sell for less than $33 per share.

The three factors of earnings, dividend yield, and book value are then weighted, earnings, considering their recognized im-

portance for valuation purposes and the upward trend thereof, being assigned 50 percent weight, and dividend yield and book value receiving 30 percent and 20 percent respectively. On this basis, defendant arrives at a fair market value figure of $21.85 as of August 3, 1954.[7]

Since there was a slight drop in the market price of can manufacturing stocks between August 3 and October 25, 1954, defendant concludes the fair market value on the latter date would be about 50 cents less per share, or $21.35.

Thus, defendant now seeks a fair market value determination as of the gift dates of $21.85 and $21.35 respectively, in lieu of the $24 value fixed by the Commissioner of Internal Revenue.[8]

In its selection of the three basic factors to be considered in determining fair market value, the weights to be assigned to these factors, the earnings adjustments, and the use of 50 cents per annum as the proper dividend basis, this estimate has merit. However, the selection of such companies as American Can and Continental Can as comparatives—companies held in esteem in the investment world—will obviously give an unduly high result. It simply is not fair to compare Heekin with such companies and to adopt their market ratios for application to Heekin's stock. Furthermore, defendant's use of the comparatives is confusing. The employment of different comparatives for different purposes is unorthodox. When the comparative appraisal method is employed the comparatives should be clearly identified and consistently used for all purposes. And the refusal to make any allowance for lack of marketability contributes further to the unrealistic nature of defendant's fair market value estimate.

---

[7] Earnings .... $22.50 × .5 = $11.25
   Dividend yield .... 13.33 × .3 = 4.00
   Book value .... 33.00 × .2 = 6.60

                                   $21.85

[8] This $24 value resulted from a study by the Commissioner of 11 comparatives. Their price to book value ratio was 1.4; price to average earnings, 14.3; price to current earnings, 13; and price to current dividends, 31.1.

Applying these ratios to Heekin, 1.4 times book value of $33.23 as of December 31, 1954, equals $46.52 per share. Average earnings for a 5-year period of $1.68 per share times 14.3 equals $24.02 per share. Current earnings times

13 equals $17.16 a share. Price to current dividend equals $15.55 per share.

In addition, in 1954 National Can purchased Pacific Can and the Commissioner analyzed the sale price for comparative purposes. The sales price came to 12.5 times Pacific's earnings. Application of that ratio to Heekin's 1953 earnings would price Heekin's stock at $24.38 per share. Pacific's price also represented 17 times its average 1949-1953 earnings. Application of such ratio to Heekin would price its stock at $28.39 per share. Further, Pacific's price bore a ratio of 1.6 to book value. Application of such ratio to Heekin's stock would price it at $53.17 per share.

To summarize, Heekin's stock has been valued as of August 3 and October 25, 1954, in blocks of 30,000 and 40,002 shares respectively, as follows: $10, originally, by two donors and the executor of the third; $7.50, in amended returns; $7.88 by one expert of plaintiffs (upon which valuation plaintiffs now stand); $9.50 and $9.65 respectively by plaintiffs' second expert; $11.76 and $9.47 respectively by plaintiffs' third expert; $16 and $15.25 respectively by defendant's expert; $21.85 and $21.35 respectively by defendant in these proceedings; and $24 by the Commissioner of Internal Revenue.

[*Three Valuation Factors*]

The proper use of the comparative appraisal method, applying the principles already indicated, should provide a reasonably satisfactory valuation guide in these cases.[*] In its application, it would under all the circumstances herein involved appear appropriate to select the three factors of (1) earnings, (2) dividends and dividend-paying capacity, and (3) book value, as being the important and significant ones to apply. *First Trust Co. v. United States, supra; Cochran v. Commissioner, supra; Bader v. United States, supra.*

As to earnings, an examination of them for the periods from 1950 to June 30 and September 30, 1954, which are the most recent periods in relation to the gift dates, would be most representative. For this purpose, the annual profit and loss statements, plus the Company's interim balance sheets, from which can be derived with reasonable accuracy the Company's earnings for the 12-month periods ending June 30 and September 30, 1954 (thus eliminating distortions due to seasonal factors), are the starting points. As stated, it would then be proper to make such adjustments therein as would be necessary to eliminate abnormal and nonrecurring items and to redistribute items of expense to their proper periods. In these cases, this normalizing process

would require (a) the elimination from the years 1950 to 1952 of the abnormal, non-recurring losses incident to its financing subsidiary, which had been completely liquidated by 1952; (b) the elimination of the abnormally large 1951 profits due to the Korean war; (c) the redistribution of the expenses attributable to the establishment subsequent to 1951 of a retirement plan, which expenses, although borne in later years, were also applicable to 1950 and 1951, thereby overstating 1950 and 1951 profits and similarly depressing 1953 and 1954 profits; (d) the shift from 1954 to 1951 of a renegotiation refund paid with respect to excessive 1951 profits; (e) the elimination from 1954 of the abnormally large charge relating to the accrual in 1954 of certain expenses actually attributable to 1955, as hereinabove explained, and which resulted in the doubling up of 2 years of such expenses in 1954, as permitted by a then recent change in the tax laws. The method adopted in making these adjustments, and the adjusted profit figures resulting therefrom, are set forth in detail in finding 47.

As indicated, it would then be appropriate to give due consideration and weight to the trend of such earnings. Greater weight should fairly be given to the most recent years and periods. The method adopted in finding 48 of assigning greater weight to the later periods is a reasonably accurate one, and indicates that as of June 30 and September 30, 1954, Heekin's reasonably expected annual earnings per share would be $1.93 and $1.79, based on average annual earnings of $491,460.86 and $454,492.82, respectively.

As to dividends and dividend-paying capacity, it has already been indicated that as of the gift dates, it could reasonably be expected that Heekin would continue to pay in the foreseeable future its usual 50-cent annual dividend. Indeed, on its aforesaid earnings basis, this would appear to be a conservative distribution. However,

---

[*] In the related estate tax area, § 2031(b) of the Internal Revenue Code of 1954 specifically provides that: "In the case of stock and securities of a corporation the value of which, by reason of their not being listed on an exchange and by reason of the absence of sales thereof, cannot be determined with reference to bid and asked prices or with reference to sales prices, the value thereof shall be determined by taking into consideration, in addition to all other factors, the value of stock or securities of corporations engaged in the same or a similar line of business which are listed on an exchange." 26 U. S. C. (1958 Ed.) § 2031(b).

while the declaration by the board of directors of a small increase might have been considered a possibility—a 10-cent increase would, for instance, result in a corporate outlay of only $25,412 on the 254,125 shares outstanding—it seems clear, nevertheless, that no substantially larger payment, at least for some time to come, could reasonably have been anticipated. Heekin's equipment was, as shown, not modern and the Company was in need of relatively large sums for equipment and plant modernization if it hoped to continue to be a competitive factor in the industry. For such a program, the Company would have to depend almost entirely on retained earnings. A further limitation on the Company's dividend-paying capacity was its repayment obligations on its long-term debt. Annual installments on principal of $150,000 had to be made through 1965, plus 20 percent of the net income (less $150,000) for the preceding year.

As to book value, the Company's balance sheets showed the book value per share to be, conservatively, $33.15 and $33.54 as of June 30 and September 30, 1954, respectively (findings 51-53). These statements also showed the Company to be in a current sound financial condition. As of June 30, 1954, current assets alone, amounting to almost $8,700,000, far exceeded its total liabilities of approximately $4,700,000, including its long-term debt. Its ratio of current assets to current liabilities was 3.17 to 1.

With the above basic data applicable to Heekin, it is then appropriate to select as closely comparable companies as is possible whose stocks are actively traded on an exchange, and to ascertain what ratios their market prices bear to their earnings, dividends, and book values. The application of such ratios to Heekin would then give a reasonable approximation of what Heekin's stock would sell for if it too were actively traded on an exchange.

[Proper Comparatives]

A study of all the numerous companies considered by the experts as proper comparatives indicates that five of them, i.e., Pacific Can Company, United Can and Glass Company, National Can Corporation, Brockway Glass Co., Inc., and Thatcher Glass Manufacturing Co., Inc., are, while by no means perfect comparables, certainly at least reasonably satisfactory for the purpose in question. The detailed reasons for their selection are set forth in finding 57. In size they all fall generally into Heekin's class, and the nature of their operations is also comparable. In addition, five companies give a sufficiently broad base. Such companies as American Can, Continental Can, and Crown Cork & Seal, for the reasons already indicated, are eliminated (finding 56).

After similarly computing the earnings, as adjusted, of the comparatives for the same periods as for Heekin (finding 58), and similarly weighting them to give effect to the trend factor (finding 59), the average ratio of their market prices to their adjusted earnings as of August 3 and October 25, 1954 (the "price-earnings" ratio), was 9.45 and 9.84 to 1, respectively (finding 62). Thus, on the basis only of earnings, Heekin's stock would similarly sell for $18.24 and $17.61 per share on such dates.

Similarly, the comparatives' dividend payments for the 12 months ending June 30 and September 30, 1954, after making some allowance for United's stock dividend, show an average percent yield of 3.50 and 3.56 respectively (finding 64). Thus, on the basis only of dividend yield, Heekin's stock would similarly sell for $14.29 and $14.05 per share on August 3 and October 25, 1954, respectively (finding 65).

As to book value, the average market prices of the comparatives were 83.96 and 86.39 percent, respectively, of the book values of their common stocks on said dates (finding 66). Thus, on the sole basis of the average relationship between such book values and market prices, Heekin's comparable market prices on said dates would be $27.83 and $28.98 (finding 67).

[Weight Accorded Factors]

However, since the three factors of earnings, dividends, and book value are not entitled to equal weight, it becomes necessary to consider their relative importance in the case of a company such as Heekin. In this connection, plaintiffs' contention that in these cases no factor is to be considered of greater importance than dividend yield and that no investor would reasonably be expected to buy Heekin stock at a price which would afford a yield of less than 7 percent, cannot be accepted, not only for the reasons set forth above concerning the general relative importance of this factor but also because it is not supported by the specific data relating to the container industry as shown by the comparatives' yields. Investors were purchasing the stocks of comparable container companies which were yielding much less return than 7 percent. As shown, the average dividend yield of the five comparative companies was only around 3½ percent. Investors were purchasing Pacific Can at a price which afforded a yield of less than 3 percent. Indeed, they were purchasing National Can at more than $13 a share although it was paying no dividend at all.

Considering all the circumstances, it would appear appropriate to accept defendant's proposals in this respect and to consider earnings as entitled to 50 percent of the contribution to total value, and to give dividend yield (which in this case would appear to be substantially equivalent to dividend-paying capacity) 30 percent, and book value 20 percent, thereof. Cf. *Bader v. United States, supra,* in which the court gave 50 percent weight to earnings, and divided the remaining 50 percent equally between the dividend yield and book value factors. Book value indicates how much of a company's net assets valued as a going concern stands behind each share of its stock and is therefore an important factor in valuing the shares. As defendant's expert pointed out, this is the factor that plays such a large part in giving a stock value during periods when earnings may vanish and dividends may be suspended. However, principally because book value is based upon valuing the assets as a going concern, which would not be realistic in the event of a liquidation of the corporation, a situation which a minority stockholder would be powerless to bring about in any event, and for the additional reasons set forth in finding 50, this factor is, in the case of a manufacturing company with a consistent earnings and dividend record, normally not given greater weight than the other two factors.

On the above percentage bases, the fair market value of Heekin's stock on August 3 and October 25, 1954, would be $18.98 and $18.83 respectively (finding 69).

[Lack of Marketability]

These prices, however, assume active trading for Heekin's stock on an exchange, as was the situation with the comparatives. As shown, the closely held nature of, and the infrequent trading in, Heekin's stock resulted in a lack of marketability which would affect its market value. Equating the proper discount to be taken for this factor with the costs that would be involved in creating a market for the stock, a method which defendant concedes is reasonable, results in a deduction of approximately 12.17 percent for a company of Heekin's size and for blocks of 30,000 and 40,000 shares. On this basis, the fair market values of the Heekin stock as of August 3 and October 25, 1954, would be $16.67 and $16.54 respectively.

These are the values resulting largely from strictly formula and statistical applications. While such use of figures and formulas produces, of course, results which are of important significance, and may in certain instances be given conclusive weight, it is nevertheless recognized that determinations of fair market value can not be reduced to formula alone, but depend "upon all the relevant facts," including "the elements of common sense, informed judgment and reasonableness." Revenue Ruling, sec. 3.01. The question of fair market value of a stock "is ever one of fact and not of formula" and evidence which gives "life to [the] figures" is essential. *Estate of James Smith v. Commissioner,* 46 B. T. A. 337, 341-2. The selection of comparatives has been a particularly troublesome problem in these cases. National Can's erratic earnings record, even though adjustments are attempted to normalize its situation (findings 57-58), and its nonpayment of dividends (finding 64), certainly weaken its position as a comparative, and suggest the desirability of an adjustment in the final market value figures set forth above. Pacific Can's sharp rise in price after August 3, 1954, justifies a similar adjustment for the October 25, 1954, valuation. While the inclusion of the glass container manufacturers with their higher dividend yields tends to neutralize somewhat the National Can situation, an adjustment downward would, in fairness to plaintiffs, nevertheless guard against their being prejudiced by the aforementioned selections of comparatives.

Furthermore, while the sales of Heekin stock at $7.50 warrant, as hereinabove pointed out, only minimal consideration, the figures derived from the above formula give them no cognizance whatsoever.

[*Adjustment for Comparison*]

Giving important weight to the figure of $16.67 produced by the application of the comparative appraisal method as applied herein, but viewing it in light of all the facts and circumstances involved in these cases, it is concluded that the fair market value of the 30,000 shares given on August 3, 1954, was $15.50 per share.

The market for stocks of the can and glass container manufacturing companies fell somewhat between August 3 and October 25, 1954, so that ordinarily on that basis as well as on the basis of Heekin's own financial and operating positions on October 25 as compared with August 3, a slightly lower value would be justified as of October 25 (although one of plaintiffs' experts felt that, insofar as Heekin stock is concerned, the same value should be applied to both dates, and another came out with a higher value for the second date). It seems clear, however, that the brightened prospects for increased business and profits resulting from the Company's decision in August 1954 to embark upon the beer can business and to satisfy further the demands of its largest customer for new products would, in Heekin's instance, tend to neutralize the market decline and to make its stock at least as valuable on October 25 as it had been on August 3. Accordingly, it is concluded that the fair market value of the 40,002 shares given on October 25, 1954, was also $15.50 per share.

A $15.50 valuation represents a price to adjusted earnings ratio on the gift dates of between 8 and 9 percent (somewhat less than the 9-10 percent average of the comparatives (finding 62)), a dividend yield of 3.23 percent (slightly less than the 3.5 percent average of the comparatives (finding 64)), and only 46 percent of book value (considerably less than the approximately 85 percent of the comparatives (finding 66)). On these bases, it is a figure that is fair to both sides.

Plaintiffs should consider that such a valuation prices the stock only at an amount representing the difference between current assets and total liabilities, including its long-term debt, as shown by its June 30, 1954, balance sheet. Thus, at such price, the value of the stock would be represented in whole by current assets, with no consideration whatsoever given to plant, equipment, or any other assets. As such, it would appear to be a conservative price indeed. Despite the difficulties under which it is laboring in a highly competitive industry, Heekin was, as of the valuation dates, a profitable, dividend-paying company, in sound financial condition, in an industry in which demand was at record levels, and in which it was forging ahead with relatively large investments in new fields holding bright prospects. Only a disregard of these favorable factors would warrant any lower valuation.

On the other hand, defendant should consider that such a valuation would give an investor a dividend yield of less than 3.5 percent on his investment, with little prospect of any significant increase in the foreseeable future. The fact that the Company was, on the gift dates, a relatively small one competing, with a comparatively old plant, against the giants of the industry operating at high efficiency with the most modern equipment, makes unwarranted a valuation of this closely held stock representing only a minority interest on any significantly higher basis. For these reasons also the $15.50 valuation is considered to be fair and just to both plaintiffs and defendant.

On this valuation basis, plaintiffs are entitled to recover, the amount of the recovery to be determined in accordance with Rule 38(c).

Estate of Woodbury G. Andrews, Deceased, Woodbury H. Andrews, Executor, Petitioner v. Commissioner of Internal Revenue, Respondent

Docket No. 12465-79. Filed November 29, 1982.

Franz P. Jevne III, *Michael S. Frost*, and *George R. A. Johnson*, for the petitioner.

Jeffrey D. Lerner, for the respondent.

OPINION

WHITAKER, *Judge*: Respondent determined a deficiency of $160,981.67 in the Federal estate tax of petitioner. The sole issue for decision is the date-of-death fair market value of shares of stock held by decedent in four closely held corporations. Since this case is largely factual, we have combined our findings of fact with our opinion.

Some of the facts have been stipulated and are so found. The parties have stipulated that Woodbury G. Andrews (hereinafter referred to as the decedent) was a resident of Excelsior, Minn., when he died testate on May 16, 1975. It has been further stipulated that Woodbury H. Andrews, a son of decedent, was appointed executor of the estate of decedent and resided in Minneapolis, Minn., when the petition in this case was filed.

Among the assets listed in the estate tax return of decedent were his interests in the following four closely held corporations: (1) 54 shares of W.F. & H.H. Andrews Co. (W.F. & H.H.), (2) 100 shares of St. Anthony Holding Co. (St. Anthony), (3) 50 shares of Green Mountain Investment Co. (Green Mountain), and (4) 63 shares of Andrews, Inc. Decedent owned approximately 20 percent of the total outstanding shares of each of the four corporations at the time of his death,[1] with the remainder being owned by his four siblings in approximately

---

[1] The exact percentages held by decedent were 20.4 percent of Andrews, Inc., 21.6 percent of W.F. & H.H., and 20 percent of the other two corporations.

equal proportions. The stock had been held by these five individuals since their father died in 1945. Decedent worked with these corporations from approximately 1927 until his death in 1975. His two brothers have been involved with the corporations since the early 1930's. Together, decedent and his two brothers constituted the entire management of all four corporations; the two sisters did not actively participate in management. There is no evidence of any significant internal management disputes or family discord.

As of the date of death, W.F. & H.H. had been in business 73 years; St. Anthony, 71 years; Green Mountain, 66 years; and Andrews, Inc., 53 years. All four corporations have been involved primarily in the ownership, operation, and management of commercial real estate properties, although they also held some liquid assets such as stocks, bonds, and cash.[2] The real estate holdings included warehouses, apartment buildings, factories, offices, and retail stores in the Minneapolis - St. Paul metropolitan area. Many of the properties were in rundown urban areas, and most of the buildings were quite old, having been acquired during the early years of the corporations' operations. Most of the properties were leased to small tenants under leases for periods of less than 5 years.

To handle their management and maintenance responsibilities, the corporations together employed approximately 22 persons in addition to the three Andrews brothers. Fourteen persons were listed as employed and paid by Andrews, Inc.; two by Green Mountain; and three, each, by St. Anthony and W.F. & H.H. However, the record discloses that many of the employees assigned to Andrews, Inc., performed services for all the corporations, which were billed on a monthly basis for

---

[2]Based on respondent's expert's appraisal of the assets of each corporation, W.F. & H.H. had 76.6 percent of its assets invested in real estate; Green Mountain had 80.9 percent; St. Anthony had 55.8 percent; and Andrews, Inc., had 66.4 percent as of the date of decedent's death. Additionally, most of the cash held by Andrews, Inc., was attributable to a condemnation award and fire insurance proceeds, which were to be invested in real property to avoid recognition under sec. 1033. These amounts, earmarked for the purchase of real estate, should be considered as invested in real estate for our purposes, and, after making this adjustment, Andrews, Inc., should be seen as having had 89.9 percent of its assets invested in real estate.

their allocable shares of employee payroll and related charges.
The types of employees included janitors, parking lot atten-
dants, night watchmen, office personnel, and maintenance
workers, who handled plumbing, carpentry, painting, heating,
and other maintenance and repair work.

On its estate tax return, petitioner valued decedent's stock
interest in Andrews, Inc., at $56,700; St. Anthony at $45,000;
W.F. & H.H. at $12,690; and Green Mountain at $13,000. In his
notice of deficiency, respondent determined that petitioner
had significantly undervalued these stocks, and valued Andrews, Inc., at $517,608; St. Anthony at $287,400; W.F. & H.H.
at $114,264; and Green Mountain at $93,650.

Fair market value has long been defined as the price at
which property would change hands between a willing buyer
and a willing seller, neither being under any compulsion to
buy or to sell and both having reasonable knowledge of
relevant facts. Sec. 20.2031–1(b), Estate Tax Regs.; *United
States v. Cartwright*, 411 U.S. 546, 551 (1973). This is a
question of fact, with the trier of fact having the duty to weigh
all relevant evidence of value and to draw appropriate
inferences. *Hamm v. Commissioner*, 325 F.2d 934, 938 (8th Cir.
1963), affg. a Memorandum Opinion of this Court.

In determining the value of unlisted stocks, actual arm's-
length sales of such stock in the normal course of business
within a reasonable time before or after the valuation date are
the best criteria of market value. *Duncan Industries, Inc. v.
Commissioner*, 73 T.C. 266, 276 (1979). However, the stock of
these four corporations has never been publicly traded, and
there is no evidence of any sales of stock in these corporations
at any time near the date of decedent's death. In the absence of

---

³Sec. 20.2031–2(f), Estate Tax Regs., provides:

(f) *Where selling prices or bid and asked prices are unavailable.* If the provisions of
paragraphs (b), (c), and (d) of this section are inapplicable because actual sale prices and
bona fide bid and asked prices are lacking, then the fair market value is to be determined by
taking the following factors into consideration:

(1) In the case of corporate or other bonds, the soundness of the security, the interest
yield, the date of maturity, and other relevant factors; and

(2) In the case of shares of stock, the company's net worth, prospective earning power and
dividend-paying capacity, and other relevant factors.

arm's-length sales, the value of closely held stock must be determined indirectly by weighing the corporation's net worth, prospective earning power, dividend-paying capacity, and other relevant factors. *Estate of Leyman v. Commissioner*, 40 T.C. 100, 119 (1963), remanded on other grounds 344 F.2d 763 (6th Cir. 1965); sec. 20.2031–2(f), Estate Tax Regs.[3] These factors cannot be applied with mathematical precision. Rather, the weight to be given to each factor must be tailored to account for the particular facts of each case. See *Messing v. Commissioner*, 48 T.C. 502, 512 (1967).

Both parties relied upon experts' valuations derived from analyses of intrinsic factors. However, because of fundamental differences in approach between respondent's and petitioner's experts, particularly with respect to the weight to be placed upon net asset value as opposed to earnings or dividend-paying capacity, the amounts arrived at in the valuations were extremely far apart. The following chart, which was used on the estate tax return, lists the different values arrived at by petitioner's primary expert, Sigurd Wendin; petitioner's second expert, Orville Lefko; and respondent's expert, Edward Bard:

	Andrews, Inc.	St. Anthony	W.F. & H.H.	Green Mountain
Mr. Wendin	$56,700	$45,000	$12,690	$13,000
Mr. Lefko	55,755	46,500	12,204	12,250
Mr. Bard	570,843	260,000	113,832	97,800

Respondent's Valuations

Respondent's first witness, James M. McKenzie, performed an appraisal of the assets held by the corporations. He valued

---

Some of the "other relevant factors" referred to in subparagraphs (1) and (2) of this paragraph are: the good will of the business; the economic outlook in the particular industry; the company's position in the industry and its management; the degree of control of the business represented by the block of stock to be valued; and the values of securities of corporations engaged in the same or similar lines of business which are listed on a stock exchange. However, the weight to be accorded such comparisons or any other evidentiary factors considered in the determination of a value depends upon the facts of each case. In addition to the relevant factors described above, consideration shall also be given to nonoperating assets, * * * each real property using three commonly accepted approaches to valuation—comparable sales, replacement costs, and income-producing capacity. After correlating the values found under each of these approaches, he arrived at the following total values for the assets held by the corporations:

	Andrews, Inc.	St. Anthony	W.F. & H.H.	Green Mountain
Real estate	$2,780,700	$1,239,800	$677,500	$645,500
Cash, stocks, and bonds	1,405,024	808,230	56,700	151,682
Miscellaneous assets	121,313	174,105	149,388	---
Total	4,307,037	2,222,135	883,588	797,182
Liabilities	116,493	2,667	696	515
Net asset value	4,190,544	2,219,468	882,892	796,667

Petitioner has not attacked Mr. McKenzie's valuations of the underlying assets. However, the executor has argued that in arriving at overall net asset value, adjustments should have been made to reflect costs that would have been incurred if the corporations had liquidated all their real estate properties and placed them on the market at one time. The adjustments sought by petitioner are for blockage, capital gains tax to the seller, real estate commissions, and real estate taxes and special assessments constituting a lien against the real estate. We disagree with this argument. Both parties have agreed here that there was no reasonable prospect of liquidation, and the evidence clearly supports this finding. When liquidation is only speculative, the valuation of assets should not take these costs into account because it is unlikely they will ever be incurred. See *Estate of Piper v. Commissioner*, 72 T.C. 1062, 1087 (1979); *Estate of Cruikshank v. Commissioner*, 9 T.C. 162, 165 (1947); *Estate of Huntington v. Commissioner*, 36 B.T.A. 698 (1937).[4]

---

[4]See also *Estate of Thalheimer v. Commissioner*, T.C. Memo. 1974–203, affd. on this issue and remanded without published opinion 532 F.2d 751 (4th Cir. 1976); *Gallun v. Commissioner*, T.C. Memo. 1974–284.

Respondent's second expert, Edward Bard, a financial analyst employed by respondent, initially used three approaches to value the stock of each corporation: Earnings and dividend-paying capacity, linear regression analysis, and net asset valuation. The former two methods produced values far lower than valuation based on net asset values. For instance, the values he computed for Andrews, Inc., based upon capitalization of earnings and dividends ranged from $1.1 million to $1.5 million,[5] the value based on linear regression analysis was $1.6 million but the value based on net asset value was $4.1 million.[6] He concluded that the former two values should be disregarded because they were unrealistically low, even though his computations did show that the corporations' yields on investment had consistently been exceptionally low.[7] Thus, his starting point for valuing each of these corporations was the net asset values derived from Mr. McKenzie's appraisals. Because he saw the corporations involved here as holding passive items, he believed they were comparable to closed end mutual funds, which are also corporate entities holding investment properties. He found that shares of mutual funds generally traded at a 25-percent discount from the value of the assets held by such funds, and accordingly, applied a 25-percent discount to the net asset values of the corporations. To this amount, he then applied a lack of marketability discount, varying from 11.9 percent to 20.74 percent to reflect each corporation's costs of flotation if the stock were to be publicly offered.[8]

[5]To arrive at these figures, Mr. Bard computed the price-earnings ratios of publicly owned real estate enterprises, primarily real estate investment trusts, that he considered comparable to the corporations involved here. The corporations selected as comparables had price-earnings ratios on a 3-year average of approximately 11 percent, price cash flow earnings of approximately 6.4 percent, and dividend income that averaged 9.6 percent. He applied these percentages to the earnings of Andrews, Inc., to arrive at an income valuation of $1,393,990 based on the latest 3-year average earnings; $1,134,214 based on the latest 3-year average cash flow earnings; and $1,452,073 based on dividend-paying capacity.

[6]All these values were prior to any discount for lack of control or marketability.

[7]Dividing net assets by net income for each corporation showed yields on investment of 3.1 percent for St. Anthony, 3.6 percent for Andrews, Inc., 3.5 percent for W.F. & H.H., and 4.1 percent for Green Mountain.

[8]At trial and on brief, respondent, in light of Rev. Rul. 81-253, 1981-2 C.B. 187, has taken the position, which we discuss later in this opinion, that neither of these discounts should be allowed.

Respondent argues that Mr. Bard was correct in ignoring earnings and dividend-paying capacity because all four corporations should be classified as investment companies not involved in the active operation of a business. He believes that a willing buyer would recognize that the value of his investment would be in his right to share in the value of the corporations' underlying net assets, regardless of their low earnings and dividend-paying capacity. Petitioner attacks respondent's characterization of these corporations as investment companies, stressing that the corporations employed 25 employees and actively performed real estate management and maintenance functions.[9] Characterizing these corporations as operating companies, petitioner believes greater weight should be placed on earnings and dividend-paying capacity than on net asset values.

We believe, however, the corporations here cannot be characterized for valuation purposes as solely investment companies or solely operating companies. The cases cited by respondent,[10] which involved corporations holding only cash, commercial paper, or marketable securities, are readily distinguishable on the ground that the corporations involved here were actively engaged in the real estate management business. But cases dealing with corporations owning factories and other industrial or commercial operations are also not directly on point.[11] Unlike many industrial companies, where the value of

---

[9]As we found earlier, although employees other than the three Andrews brothers were assigned to only one corporation for bookkeeping purposes, many of them actively performed services for all the corporations.

[10]The following cases were cited by respondent: *Estate of Cruikshank v. Commissioner*, 9 T.C. 162 (1947); *Gallun v. Commissioner*, *supra*; *Estate of Thalheimer v. Commissioner*, *supra*; *Estate of Cotchett v. Commissioner*, T.C. Memo. 1974–31; and *Richardson v. Commissioner*, a Memorandum Opinion of this Court dated Nov. 30, 1943, affd. 151 F.2d 102 (2d Cir. 1945). *Estate of Lee v. Commissioner*, 69 T.C. 860 (1978), in which we used net asset values in arriving at the value of a close corporation that held primarily real estate is likewise distinguishable because the real estate was not rental property but rather undeveloped property that offered no immediate prospects for taxable income to the corporation.

[11]See *Waterman v. Commissioner*, T.C. Memo. 1961–225, in which we rejected both respondent's valuation based solely on net asset values and petitioner's valuation based solely on earning capacity as inappropriate for a corporation holding improved rental property; and *Estate of Tompkins v. Commissioner*, T.C. Memo. 1961–338, in which we rejected similar contentions with respect to a corporation holding unimproved real estate.

the manufacturing equipment and plant is tied to the nature of the manufacturing operation, here, the value of the underlying real estate will retain most of its inherent value even if the corporation is not efficient in securing a stream of rental income. It seems reasonable to assume, as we did in *Estate of Heckscher v. Commissioner*, 63 T.C. 485, 493 (1975), that a—

potential buyer would have to forego some current return on his investment in exchange for an interest in a net worth much more valuable than the price he pays for the stock, and the seller would have to be willing to part with an equity interest in the company for much less than its indicated value in return for something that would produce a greater yield on his investment. * * *

Furthermore, regardless of whether the corporation is seen as primarily an operating company, as opposed to an investment company, courts should not restrict consideration to only one approach to valuation, such as capitalization of earnings or net asset values. See *Hamm v. Commissioner*, 325 F.2d 934 (8th Cir. 1963), affg. a Memorandum Opinion of this Court; *Portland Manufacturing Co. v. Commissioner*, 56 T.C. 58, 80 (1971); *Estate of Schroeder v. Commissioner*, 13 T.C. 259 (1949); *Hooper v. Commissioner*, 41 B.T.A. 114 (1940).[12] Certainly, the degree to which the corporation is actively engaged in producing income rather than merely holding property for investment should influence the weight to be given to the values arrived at under the different approaches but it should not dictate the use of one approach to the exclusion of all others.

The regulations[13] call for all relevant factors to be examined and, in a case such as this, we believe values arrived at under all the accepted valuation methods should be considered. We therefore believe respondent's expert was incorrect to simply

---

[12] See also *Estate of Dooly v. Commissioner*, T.C. Memo. 1972–164; *Lippman v. Commissioner*, T.C. Memo. 1965–73; and *Wallace v. United States*, an unpublished opinion (D. Mass. 1981, 49 AFTR 2d 82–1482, 82–1 USTC par. 13,442), in which the court stated:

"The 'willing buyer' and 'willing seller' * * * test the experts' advice, and the formulas the experts advance to bolster their advice, against common sense. The willing buyer and willing seller are not limited to choosing one formula or another among competing formulas advanced by experts. [49 AFTR 2d 82–1482.]"

[13] See sec. 20.2031–2(f), Estate Tax Regs.

reject earnings and dividend-paying capacity valuations because they produced too low a result. Certainly, a prospective
buyer would not so reject one particular type of valuation. A
buyer of stock in these corporations would necessarily look to
the earning capacity for part of his return on his investment.
Nevertheless, this would not be the only factor that he would
consider. Undoubtedly, he would also give substantial weight
to each corporation's underlying net asset value even though
he would have no ability to directly realize this value by
forcing liquidation.

Respondent argues that there is a particular reason why
only net asset values should be used in this case. Mr.
McKenzie's determination of the values of the real estate
properties held by the corporations was arrived at through a
computational method that considered, among other factors,
the projected earning capacity of the properties. Respondent
contends that in valuing each corporation it is therefore
appropriate to use only the underlying net asset value, which
is the sum of the appraised real estate values plus the values of
other assets held by the corporation, such as stocks and bonds,
minus all the corporation's liabilities.[14] However, to do so
would ignore the corporate entities. If the properties had been
held directly by decedent, respondent would undoubtedly be
correct, but here we are not faced with the question of finding
a value for the properties themselves; rather, we must find the
value of shares of the corporations that held the properties.
The corporations are businesses, engaged in the maintenance
and management of these real estate properties. Thus, some of
the value attached to the corporations must be based upon the
operating nature of the businesses, with attention paid to their
earnings and dividend history, management, and prospects for
growth.

Petitioner's Valuations

We turn now to analyze petitioner's experts' valuations,

[14]Because the corporations followed a very conservative policy of avoiding substantial
debt, St. Anthony, W.F. & H.H., and Green Mountain had virtually no liabilities, and the
liabilities of Andrews, Inc., equaled only 2 percent of the value of its assets.

which we also find to be markedly deficient, largely because of their adopting approaches that minimize the importance of the value of the underlying assets.

Petitioner's first expert, Sigurd Wendin, selected as comparables four large publicly traded real estate management corporations, although he recognized that there were differences in size, financing, number of employees, and types of activities carried on. Based on his analysis of these publicly traded corporations, he assigned price earnings multiples to the corporations involved here of five for future earnings, four for current earnings, five for the average of the last 3 years' earnings, and seven for the average earnings for the period 1970 through 1973. These multiples were somewhat lower than those obtained from the comparable companies because of the difficulty in marketing nonpublicly traded shares. He then applied these multiples to net operating income during the applicable periods, and applied a minority discount for lack of marketability of 40 percent based on his overall experience with the amount of such discounts commonly allowed.

For dividend capitalization purposes, Mr. Wendin assumed a 10-percent rate, based upon the fact that corporate bond yields were around 9 percent to 11 percent. He believed bond yields were better comparables than the yield rate on stocks because the assets involved here were frozen and stock yields had been quite variable during this time period. He applied this 10-percent rate to the last year dividend and to his estimate of the future dividend that could be expected. Again, he discounted these amounts by 40 percent for lack of marketability.

Mr. Wendin also looked at the corporate balance sheets showing net assets and liabilities of the corporations. He did not have Mr. McKenzie's or any other appraisal of underlying assets so he looked at book values instead of net asset values. He reduced the book values to 80 percent based on the market-to-book-value ratio here found in analyzing his four "comparables."[15] To this he applied a 40-percent discount for lack of marketability.

In combining all of these factors to arrive at an overall

valuation of each corporation, Mr. Wendin minimized the impact of the adjusted book value per share. He believed this approach was necessary because there were no plans to liquidate and because a minority stockholder would have had no ability to force liquidation. Listed below as an example are the weights given to each factor, the values per share, and the overall average value arrived at for Andrews, Inc., stock:

	Per share	*Weight*	*Amount*
Future dividend capitalization	900.00	5	$4,500.00
Last year dividend capitalization	770.76	4	3,083.04
Future earnings capitalization	1,167.00	3	3,501.00
Last year earnings capitalization	940.34	2	1,880.68
	Per share	*Weight*	*Amount*
Three-year average earnings capitalization	963.57	1.5	$1,445.36
1970–73 year average earnings capitalization	998.07	1.5	1,497.11
Book value	2,345.11	1	2,345.11
		18	18,252.30

Average 1,014.02

To this $1,014.02 value per share he applied an additional discount to reflect specific negative factors such as deterioration of areas, strategic location, rising inflation, taxes, future maintenance costs, and the ability to quickly adjust rentals. He ended up with an estimated value for Andrews, Inc., of $900 per share. The values for the other three companies were determined in equivalent manners. In no case was book value given more than a one-ninth weight in determining the current value.

———

[15]Exactly how he arrived at this 80-percent figure is not clear since the ratios for three of the selected "comparables" were 51 percent, 79 percent, and 92 percent, and for the fourth "comparable" an astounding 3,007 percent.

[16]Mr. Wendin apparently recognized that unadjusted book values are often unreliable for valuation purposes because they may have little relation to the assets' fair market values at the date of valuation. With an asset that appreciates in value (and thus has investment value), such as real estate, book value may be far below current fair market value. See *Estate of Poley v. Commissioner*, a Memorandum Opinion of this Court dated Mar. 7, 1947, affd. per curiam 166 F.2d 434 (3d Cir. 1948).

We find Mr. Wendin's valuations to be seriously flawed because they did not take into account each corporation's net asset value, i.e., the total value of its assets less liabilities. Although he attempted to approximate net asset values by using adjusted book values,[16] which were arrived at by reducing book values by a market-to-book ratio, the figures so computed bore no reasonable relation to actual net asset values. Mr. Wendin used a market-to-book ratio of 80 percent, but a comparison of book values to the appraised values determined by Mr. McKenzie shows the ratio was actually near 300 percent. Moreover, even if the adjusted book values had been close to actual net asset values, Mr. Wendin assured they would be of little importance in his overall computations by assigning insubstantial weights, varying from one-ninth to one-eighteenth, to them. As discussed earlier, a prospective buyer of stock in these corporations would undoubtedly give substantial weight to net asset values.

Another problem with the Wendin valuations was that he applied to his adjusted book values a 40-percent discount for lack of marketability and control. We believe this was improper because lack of control was also reflected (excessively) in the weighting of factors considered in computing an overall valuation.

Petitioner's second expert, Mr. Orville G. Lefko, was retained to prepare an analysis after the McKenzie appraisals had been made available to petitioner. Mr. Lefko employed an approach somewhat different than Mr. Wendin but still minimized the importance of net asset values and arrived at figures quite close to those computed by Mr. Wendin.

Mr. Lefko felt that both net asset value and earnings capability were not very important in comparison to dividend projections for purposes of valuing corporations such as the ones at issue here. Although the dividend history of each of the corporations had been irregular, Mr. Lefko came to the conclusion that each corporation had the ability to pay a regular dividend. To arrive at a rate of dividend capitalization, he looked at seven equity real estate investment trusts, which he selected as comparables. These "comparables" yielded a 12-

percent dividend capitalization rate, which he increased to between 15 and 17 percent because he believed that real estate investment trusts involved lower risks due to factors such as professional management, geographical diversity, and size. After applying the dividend capitalization rate to projected dividends, he applied a 45-percent discount for lack of marketability.

Mr. Lefko did not entirely dismiss the net asset value of the corporations but attempted to factor into his overall value a liquidation probability value, to reflect the buyer's prospect of realizing on liquidation a share of the underlying asset values. First, he adjusted the appraised value of the corporation's assets. He decreased the values of real properties by anticipated liquidation costs of stocks and bonds by handling charges, and receivables by a bad debt allowance. This gave him a net realized value per share of each corporation. Next, he projected when a purchaser of shares that had been held by decedent might reasonably expect to obtain his share of the underlying assets through liquidation. Because of the corporation's long history of continuing operations and no prospect of imminent liquidation, Mr. Lefko believed there was no chance of liquidation within 5 years, a 5-percent chance in 10 years, a 10-percent chance in 15 years, a 35-percent chance in 20 years, and a 50-percent chance in 25 years. He multiplied the net realized value per share by each of these percentages and then discounted the resulting amounts because of the lost time value of money prior to the assumed future liquidation. He thereafter added together all the discounted amounts and applied a 45-percent illiquidity discount. In this manner, he computed a liquidation probability value for each corporation, equal to approximately 3 percent to 5 percent of the fair market value of the underlying assets. This liquidation probability value was added to the previously determined dividend capitalization value of each of the corporations.[17]

[17]We note that it is highly unusual in a valuation to add together the values derived through two independent estimates of valuation, here the liquidation probability approach and the dividend capitalization approach. Theoretically, each approach should result in computation of the entire value of the property and although averaging of the different computations might be necessary, it would not be appropriate to add together separate valuations.

We find the liquidation probability approach to be highly speculative at best. Moreover, we believe the computation improperly reduced asset values on account of lost use of money. This discounting for lost use of money is unrealistic because it fails to recognize that the underlying assets will themselves appreciate, most probably, at a rate similar to that applied as a discount. Another problem with Mr. Lefko's valuation was his use of real estate investment trusts (REITs) as comparables. These entities are not truly comparable to the corporations involved here because of the requirement that REITs must pass through 90 percent of earnings as dividends and because REITs are generally highly leveraged while the corporations here were virtually debt free.

Petitioner's third expert, Thomas C. O'Connell, based his valuation solely upon an approximation of cumulative future dividends of all the corporations. He started with the total average dividend for all the corporations over the 3-year period from 1972 through 1974. To this amount he applied a dividend capitalization rate of between 18.75 percent and 25 percent. He explained that this capitalization rate was arrived at based upon his belief that an investor would require a return of 150 to 200 percent of the prime rate because the companies had certain negative factors such as a low return on invested capital, a low rate of cash flow, very conservative management, fragmented management control, and a lack of consistent policy in prior years. He also stressed that there was no public market for the shares, a low return on net worth and a lack of any long-term plan or growth strategy. Applying the dividend capitalization rate to the prior 3-year total average dividend, he computed a value for the four corporations of between $605,000 and $807,000. For the 20 percent of the shares involved here, he estimated the value of $121,000 to $161,000 total.

We have accorded little weight to Mr. O'Connell's valuation for several reasons. Most importantly, he did not consider earnings and took no account whatsoever of the net asset values of the corporations. Furthermore, in selecting a dividend capitalization rate, he did not examine comparable companies but simply expressed his relatively unsubstantiated opinion that an 18.75- to 25-percent rate of dividend capitalization would be desired by a willing purchaser. In the absence of more facts showing why this specific rate was chosen, it is difficult for the Court to determine whether the rate was simply an educated guess or whether he really had a substantial basis for concluding that it was appropriate. Another problem with Mr. O'Connell's approach was that in applying the dividend capitalization rate to the average dividends received for the prior 3-year period, he did not differentiate among the corporations but considered them as if they were only one single entity. Thus, there is no way in which his valuation can be used directly to arrive at the value of any particular corporation involved here.

Lack of Control and Marketability Discounts

In Mr. Bard's valuation report and in computing the amount of deficiency, the net asset values of the four corporations were each reduced first by a 25-percent discount based on a comparison with publicly traded closed end mutual fund shares, and then by discounts ranging from 11.9 percent to 20.74 percent based on Securities Exchange Commission flotation rates. These discounts were designed to reflect the shares' restricted marketability and lack of control.

Rev. Rul. 81–253, 1981–2 C.B. 187, was published by respondent after the statutory notice was issued, and it sets forth respondent's current position concerning the allowance of minority discounts in valuing stock of closely held family corporations. Based on Rev. Rul. 81–253, respondent now argues that no discounts for lack of control or restricted marketability should be applied, although he has not asserted a deficiency greater than that asserted in the statutory notice. Thus, respondent argues that discounts should not be applied to the extent they would result in reducing the values below those asserted in the notice of deficiency.

Petitioner has questioned whether it is proper for respondent to now argue against allowing a minority discount even though he allowed a discount in computing the deficiency in the statutory notice. However, this is not a case where petitioner was surprised at trial by respondent's introduction of a new issue. It is clear that petitioner was prepared for the minority discount question being raised at trial, and has devoted large portions of its briefs to rebutting respondent's position that no minority discount should be allowed. Therefore, we find no merit to petitioner's claim that the minority discount issue has been improperly raised by respondent. See *Llorente v. Commissioner*, 74 T.C. 260, 269 (1980), modified on other grounds 649 F.2d 152 (2d Cir. 1981).

Respondent argues that no discounts should be allowed because all the shareholders in the four corporations, including decedent, shared in control. According to respondent's argument, the hypothetical "willing seller" used in arriving at valuation of the stock must be presumed to be one of the five family members, including decedent, who held stock in the corporations and shared an element of control. Respondent reasons further that such a willing seller would not have sold his shares except as part of the controlling family interest, unless to another family member or the corporations, themselves. If the shares were sold in this way, respondent contends they would retain their control value, and no minority discount would be justified.

In their arguments, neither petitioner nor respondent clearly focuses on the fact that two conceptually distinct discounts are involved here, one for lack of marketability and the other for lack of control.[18] The minority shareholder discount is designed to reflect the decreased value of shares that do not convey control of a closely held corporation. The lack of marketability discount, on the other hand, is designed to reflect the fact that there is no ready market for shares in a closely held corporation. Although there may be some overlap between these two discounts in that lack of control may reduce marketability, it should be borne in mind that even controlling shares in a nonpublic corporation suffer from lack of marketability because of the absence of a ready private placement market and the fact that flotation costs would have to be incurred if the corporation were to publicly offer its stock. However, the distinction between the two discounts is not crucial for purposes of this case. Because respondent's basis for opposing both discounts is the same—that the hypothetical willing buyer must be seen as a family member—our subsequent discussion, like the parties' briefs, will consider the two discounts together.

The leading case dealing with this question is *Estate of Bright v. United States*, 658 F.2d 999 (5th Cir. 1981) (en banc), in which the court recognized that a minority interest in a corporation should not be seen as having any control value, even though the family unit had control of the corporation. The case involved whether a minority discount should be allowed in valuing a decedent's undivided one-half interest in the control block of 55 percent of the stock of a corporation, where the other one-half interest in the control block was owned by the husband of the decedent (who was also executor of the estate and subsequently trustee of the testamentary trust that received the stock in issue). Two major bases for its decision were explained by the court. First, it found that established case law did not support any type of "family attribution" in which the control of the corporation was attributed among family members. The Fifth Circuit noted that the Tax Court, since at least 1940, has uniformly valued a decedent's stock for estate tax purposes as a minority interest when the decedent, himself, owned less than 50 percent of the stock regardless of whether control of the corporation was in the decedent's family.[19] The court also cited two District Court opinions that took the same position,[20] and it stated that it had found no estate tax cases supporting respondent's position. The court found further that case authority in the analogous gift tax area also supported the taxpayer's position, although not unanimously.[21]

The second major reason cited in the *Estate of Bright* opinion for applying a minority discount was based upon the concept of the hypothetical willing-buyer, willing-seller rule. Section 20.2031–1(b), Estate Tax Regs., sets forth the following

---

[18]See Fellows & Painter, "Valuing Close Corporations for Federal Wealth Transfer Taxes: A Statutory Solution to the Disappearing Wealth Syndrome," 30 Stan. L. Rev. 895, 920 (1978).

rule, which has been universally applied by the courts and respondent:

The fair market value is the price at which the property would change hands between a willing buyer and a willing seller, neither being under any compulsion to buy or to sell and both having reasonable knowledge of relevant facts. * * *

The Fifth Circuit saw this language from the regulation as indicating that the "willing seller" is a hypothetical seller rather than the particular estate. Thus, the willing seller should not be identified with the decedent, and the decedent's stock should not be included as part of a family unit for valuation purposes. Nor was it proper, according to the Fifth Circuit, to place any weight upon the identity of the parties that actually received the stock after distribution from the estate. For purposes of valuation, one should construct a hypothetical sale from a hypothetical willing seller to a similarly hypothetical willing buyer.

In *Propstra v. United States*, 680 F.2d 1248 (9th Cir. 1982), the Ninth Circuit followed *Estate of Bright* and discounted the value of an undivided one-half interest in real estate held by the decedent and his wife as community property at the time of death. The Ninth Circuit noted that Congress has explicitly

---

[19]The following Tax Court cases were cited by the Fifth Circuit for this proposition: *Estate of Zaiger v. Commissioner*, 64 T.C. 927 (1975); *Estate of Leyman v. Commissioner*, 40 T.C. 100, 119 (1963); *Estate of DeGuebriant v. Commissioner*, 14 T.C. 611 (1950), revd. on other grounds 186 F.2d 307 (2d Cir. 1951); *Hooper v. Commissioner*, 41 B.T.A. 114 (1940); *Estate of Kirkpatrick v. Commissioner*, T.C. Memo. 1975–344; *Estate of Stoddard v. Commissioner*, T.C. Memo. 1975–207; *Estate of Thalheimer v. Commissioner, supra; Estate of Maxcy v. Commissioner*, T.C. Memo. 1969–158, revd. on other grounds 441 F.2d 192 (5th Cir. 1971); *Estate of Katz v. Commissioner*, T.C. Memo. 1968–171. We agree with the Fifth Circuit that these cases show our established view that a decedent's stock in a family controlled corporation should be seen as a minority interest whenever the decedent individually did not have control.

[20]The two District Court opinions cited by the court were *Obermer v. United States*, 238 F. Supp. 29 (D. Hawaii 1964); and *Sundquist v. United States*, an unpublished opinion (E.D. Wash. 1974, 34 AFTR 2d 74–6337, 74–2 USTC par. 13,035).

[21]Cases cited by the court for the proposition that minority discounts were allowed for gifts of stock in family controlled corporations included *Meijer v. Commissioner*, T.C. Memo. 1979–344; *Koffler v. Commissioner*, T.C. Memo. 1978–159; *Estate of Heppenstal v. Commissioner*, a Memorandum Opinion of this Court dated Jan. 31, 1949; *Whittemore v. Fitzpatrick*, 127 F. Supp. 710 (D. Conn. 1954); *Clark v. United States*, an unpublished opinion (E.D. N.C. 1975, 36 AFTR 2d 75–6417, 75–1 USTC par. 13,076).

directed that family attribution or unity of ownership principles be applied in other areas of Federal taxation, and felt that in the absence of any legislative directive, it should not judicially require such principles to be applied in the estate tax area. Furthermore, the court emphasized the advantage of using an objective hypothetical willing-buyer, willing-seller standard, instead of a subjective inquiry into the feelings, attitudes, and anticipated behavior of heirs and legatees, which might well be boundless.

Respondent argues that the Fifth Circuit misinterpreted the concept of the hypothetical willing seller and willing buyer. In his briefs, he relies primarily upon three cases to support his proposition that a minority discount should not be applied if family members control a corporation. *Richardson v. Commissioner*, a Memorandum Opinion of this Court dated November 30, 1943, affd. 151 F.2d 102 (2d Cir. 1945), involved a family holding company whose assets were readily marketable securities. On appeal, the Second Circuit upheld the value established by us but questioned whether we had used the correct standard of valuation. Our *Richardson* opinion must be read narrowly in view of the long series of subsequent cases in which we have allowed discounts in valuing shares of family corporations that held operating as well as investment assets. *Blanchard v. United States*, 291 F. Supp. 348 (S.D. Iowa 1968), contains language supportive of respondent's position. But the court stressed that it was dealing with a unique situation involving a planned sale of all the family's shares of stock in the corporation. At first blush, *Rothgery v. United States*, 201 Ct. Cl. 183, 475 F.2d 591 (1973), seems to support respondent. But even though its valuation was phrased in terms of seeing the willing buyer as a particular person (the family member who already held almost 50 percent of the shares of the corporation), the court also explicitly found that there would have been other potential buyers for the decedent's shares of the stock at the same price if the stock had been offered for sale to persons outside the Rothgery family. Thus, despite analyzing the hypothetical sale in terms of the sale to a particular person, the court evidently attributed no premium to the fact that the family member would assure himself of control by obtaining these shares.

Three cases provide at best weak support for respondent's position that no discounts should be applied here. Opposed to this meager case law in favor of respondent is the large number of cases allowing such discounts, which were discussed in the *Estate of Bright* opinion. We see no reason to depart from such established precedent but follow the Fifth Circuit's well-reasoned and thoroughly researched opinion. Respondent's approach would have us tailor "hypothetical" so that the willing seller and willing buyer were seen as the particular persons who would most likely undertake the transaction. However, the case law and regulations require a truly hypothetical willing seller and willing buyer. We must assume these hypothetical parties exist even though the reality of the situation may be that the stock will most probably be sold to a particular party or type of person. Certainly, the hypothetical sale should not be constructed in a vacuum isolated from the actual facts that affect the value of the stock in the hands of decedent, but we do not see any actual facts in this case that require the stock to be valued as anything other than minority interests in each corporation.

Overall Valuation

We have pointed out above the defects of the approaches used by both parties' experts. Having taken diametrically opposed views as to the factors to be weighed in valuing the stock involved in this case, the parties "failed successfully to conclude settlement negotiations—a process clearly more conducive to the proper disposition of disputes such as this." *Messing v. Commissioner*, 48 T.C. 502, 512 (1967). Because we have concluded that none of the experts gave appropriate weight to net assets as well as earning and dividend-paying capacity, we must necessarily make our own best judgments of value. While we have considered the valuation reports of Messrs. Wendin, Lefko, and Bard, we have also weighed all other relevant factors such as the extremely conservative business attitudes and practices of the management, the nature of the real estate holdings, the amount of cash and other liquid assets held by the corporations, and the business climate on the valuation date, both overall and for these corporations in particular. We have discounted the values because of the restricted marketability of the shares and the lack of control a hypothetical willing buyer of these minority shares would be able to exercise. Based on all these factors and on the entire record, we conclude and find as a fact the following date-of-death fair market values for the stock held by decedent:

Andrews, Inc	$302,400
St. Anthony	158,000
Green Mountain	56,000
W.F. & H.H	64,800

Decision will be entered under Rule 155.

Harriet T. Righter, Executrix of the Estate of Jessie H. Righter v. The United States

U.S. Court of Claims, No. 37-67, 3/19/71.

William J. Cosgrove, Scott P. Crampton, Stanley Worth, Suite 700, Brawner Bldg., 888 Seventeenth St., N. W., Washington, D. C., for plaintiff. E. Alan Moorhouse, Johnnie M. Walters, Assistant Attorney General, Philip R. Miller, Joseph Kovner, Department of Justice, Washington, D. C. 20530, for defendant.

SKELTON, Judge, delivered the opinion of the court:

We are indebted to Trial Commissioner Saul R. Gamer in this case for his findings of fact and conclusion of law and also for his opinion in which he held that the plaintiff was entitled to recover. We have adopted his findings of fact with minor changes and have used much of his opinion. The opinion of the court follows:

[Facts]

Miss Jessie H. Righter, a resident of Brooklyn, New York, died on April 24, 1961. The federal estate tax return filed on July 24, 1962, by her executors, which valued the assets of the decedent as of the date of death, reported a tax liability of $42,467.55, but the Commissioner of Internal Revenue, on June 25, 1965, assessed a deficiency in estate tax due of $74,833.91, together with interest thereon in the amount of $14,912.45, totaling $89,746.36. After payment of the asserted deficiency, the filing of a claim for refund, and the passage of more than six months during which the Commissioner took no action with respect thereto, the executors[1] filed the petition herein seeking a refund of said amount of $89,746.36.[2]

Included in the assets of the estate were stocks and bonds upon which the return placed a total value at date of death of $593,024.80. There were 24 items of such securities listed. The Commissioner's notice

of deficiency changed the values set forth in the return of ten of such items. The valuation changes in nine of the items were small and no issue arises in connection therewith. The change in one of the items was substantial, however, and accounts for a large part of the asserted deficiency. That item consists of 337 shares of Selchow & Righter Company, a New York corporation. The return valued this stock at $424.90 per share for a total valuation of $143,191.60, but the Commissioner concluded that the stock had a fair market value of $1,000 a share, making a total valuation of $337,000.

Another adjustment made by the Commissioner in the return related to a charitable deduction. The decedent's will creates a trust of her residuary estate, the income from which is to go to her two sisters for their lives. Upon the death of the survivor, certain general legacies are to be paid from the residuary estate, and the balance of such estate is then to go to certain named charities. To ascertain the charitable deduction to which the estate is entitled by reason of these provisions of the will, it is necessary to calculate the amount of the remainder interest of the residuary trust which will go to charity. In making such calculation, the executors used the same value of $424.90 per share of Selchow & Righter (hereinafter "S & R") stock. The charitable deduction claimed by the estate in the return was $385,821.20,[3] but in his notice of deficiency the Commissioner re-

---

[1] The executors were Miss Harriet T. Righter and Miss Katharine A. Righter, the decedent's sisters. Subsequently Katharine died and Harriet, the surviving executrix, became the plaintiff herein.

[2] Plus such other amounts as may be allowable as a result of a deduction for the fees and expenses incurred in this proceeding, and interest and costs as provided by law.

[3] There is no dispute concerning the formula used to determine the amount of the remainder interest of the residuary estate, the factor used to compute such interest being taken from the actuarial tables contained in the Commissioner's regulations.

duced such deduction by $68,270.72. This reduction apparently reflects the reduced amount which will be available for charity because of the greater tax liability resulting largely from the aforementioned increase in the S & R stock valuation. For the purpose of calculating the amount of the charitable deduction, the Commissioner did not change the $424.90 per share value of the S & R stock used by the executors.

The executrix here argues that the Commissioner, in calculating the values of the stocks and bonds as of the date of death, erred in increasing the value of the S & R stock to $1,000 per share. She says the value of $424.90 set forth in the return was proper. She further contends, alternatively, that if a higher value is to be used for such purpose, then the same higher value should be used in calculating the remainder interest of the residuary estate and the resulting charitable deduction. Such a higher value would, she continues, result in a calculation of a greater amount available for charity under the terms of the will and, therefore, would entitle the estate to a larger charitable deduction than would result from the use of the $424.90 figure.

The Issue of the Fair Market Value of the S & R Stock

S & R is a comparatively small corporation engaged in the business of manufacturing and selling games. Its plant and principal place of business are located at Bay Shore, Long Island, New York. During 1960, the last full year prior to the date of decedent's death on April 24, 1961, the company's net sales totaled approximately $3,200,000. As of such date of death, when the 337 shares of the company's stock in the estate are to be valued, there were only 2,000 shares of S & R stock outstanding.

S & R was established over 100 years ago by its cofounders, Mr. Selchow and Mr. Righter. Just prior to the death of the decedent, 1,018 of the 2,000 outstanding shares, or slightly more than one-half, were owned by the three Righter sisters, who were the daughters of one of the cofounders. As stated, the decedent, Miss Jessie H. Righter, owned 337 shares. Miss Katharine A. Righter, one of the executors (since deceased), also owned 337 shares, and Miss Harriet T. Righter, the surviving executrix

(the plaintiff herein in her representative capacity), owned 344 shares. The balance of 982 shares was owned by 21 individuals and estates. A substantial number of the other shareholders were descendants of the other cofounder.

This closely held stock was not listed on any stock exchange, nor was it available on any over-the-counter market. It has never been publicly traded.

As of the date of the decedent's death, S & R's principal products were two games which were sold under the trademarks of "Scrabble," a crossword puzzle game, and "Parcheesi," a backgammon game. Scrabble was by far the company's main item of support. In 1960, it alone furnished over 60 percent of the company's business.

Miss Harriet Righter, the executrix and plaintiff herein, has long been closely associated with and actively engaged in the running of the business. For over thirty years, *i.e.*, from 1923 to 1955, she was its President and devoted full time to the company. Since then, she has continued to serve actively as Chairman of the Board of Directors. In 1955, Mr. C. Ellsworth Tobias became its President. Mr. Tobias, a lawyer, was a partner in a firm which had been the personal attorneys of the Righter sisters. He had served as a director of the company since 1947.

Ascertaining the fair market value of infrequently sold, unlisted, closely held stock is recognized as a difficult legal problem. See *Central Trust Company v. United States* [62-2 USTC ¶ 12,092], 158 Ct. Cl. 504, 514, 305 F. 2d 393, 399 (1962). A common and accepted technique used by financial analysts and experts in such situations is to obtain, as a basic starting point, the prices of the stocks of corporations in the same or a similar business which are traded on an exchange; to develop some relationship between such prices and the per share earnings, dividends, and book values of the stocks; and then, after some indication, as a result of comparison, of what the closely held stock would sell for on the same basis of relationship to its earnings, dividends, and book value were it also actively traded, to make the necessary refinements and adjustments in such hypothetical comparative selling price as are justified by differences between the unlisted company and those listed which informed investors would reasonably take into account.

This comparative appraisal method is so logical and so highly regarded that it has found its way into the 1954 Internal Revenue Code provisions concerning estate and gift taxes. Section 2031, "Definition of gross estate," subsection (b), "Valuation of unlisted stock and securities," provides that:

In the case of stock and securities of a corporation the value of which, by reason of their not being listed on an exchange and by reason of the absence of sales thereof, cannot be determined with reference to bid and asked prices or with reference to sales prices, the value thereof shall be determined by taking into consideration, in addition to all other factors, the value of stock or securities of corporations engaged in the same or a similar line of business which are listed on an exchange.

The comparative appraisal method produces, nevertheless, no magic formula which rigidly gives the exact valuation answer. Companies are rarely identical in size, operation, or product, and allowances must be made, as the statute says, for "all other factors." This would necessarily include the very fact of unmarketability of the stock of the closely held corporation. In the last analysis, much necessarily depends on the informed judgment of the knowledgeable investor concerning the refinements and adjustments to be made in arriving at the ultimate valuation figure. Thus it is not surprising that in this field the opinions of experts are considered to be peculiarly appropriate. *Central Trust Company v. United States, supra,* 158 Ct. Cl. at 514, 305 F. 2d at 399; *Bader v. United States* [59-1 USTC ¶ 9431, 11,865], 172 F. Supp. 833, 836 (S. D. Ill. 1959). The pertinent regulations specifically so recognize. Section 20.2031-2 of the Treasury Regulations on Estate Tax (1954 Code) provides that where

(f) * * * actual sale prices and bona fide bid and asked prices are lacking, then the fair market value is to be determined by taking the following factors into consideration:

* * *

(2) In the case of shares of stock, the company's net worth, prospective earning power and dividend-paying capacity, and other relevant factors.

Some of the "other relevant factors" referred to in subparagraphs (1) and (2) of this paragraph are: the good will of the business; the economic outlook in the particular industry; the company's position in the industry and its management; the degree of control of the business represented by the block of stock to be valued; and the values of securities of corporations engaged in the same or similar lines of business which are listed on a stock exchange. However, the weight to be accorded such comparisons or any other evidentiary factors considered in the determination of a value depends upon the facts of each case. Complete financial and other data upon which the valuation is based should be submitted with the return, including copies of reports of any examinations of the company made by accountants, engineers, or any technical experts as of or near the applicable valuation date. [26 C. F. R. § 20.2031-2 (1969).]

[Sale of Stock]

In this case, however, plaintiff did not attempt to sustain the $424.90 per share valuation of the S & R stock contained in the return by anything resembling the comparative appraisal method or by any expert testimony. Instead, she relies principally on a sale of the very stock here involved which she and her coexecutor themselves made to Mr. Tobias, the company's President, his mother, and his wife. The sale was made on July 12, 1961. On that date the sale of 200 shares was completed at $424.94 per share, 100 shares being sold to Mr. Tobias and 100 shares to his mother. Such price was 50 percent of the stock's book value as of the close of the preceding year (the company's books, pursuant to an annual audit, being closed once a year at the termination of the calendar year), less the amount of the dividend paid during the early part of the year from the earnings of the prior year. This "ex dividend" price, coming so closely after the date of death, produced a figure which was 50 percent of book value both as of the date of death and as of the date of sale. On July 12, 1961, the executors and Mr. Tobias also agreed that Mr. Tobias would, on April 5, 1962, purchase the balance of the 137 shares at a price which would be calculated on the basis of 50 percent of the book value of the shares on such date, again "ex dividend," such "ex dividend" price, consisting of the book value as of the previous December 31, less the dividend, being considered as producing a figure representing book value as of the date of sale. On April 5, 1962, such sale of the balance of the shares in the estate was effected on such basis (at a price of $473.40), 100 shares being purchased by Mr. Tobias and 37 shares by his wife. It was subsequent to the completion of the sale transaction on April 5, 1962, that the executors, on July 24, 1962, filed the estate tax return with the S & R shares valued at $424.90 as of the date of the decedent's death on April 24, 1961, such valuation being calculated on the same formula basis as the sale of the 200 shares to Mr. Tobias and his mother.

The sale of the stock to the Tobiases at 50 percent of book value shortly after the death of the decedent was, plaintiff argues, an arm's-length transaction made in good faith by parties who believed that the 50 percent book value price represented fair market value. The best measure of fair market value, it is contended, is such a sale price arrived at by parties dealing independently in their own interests. The guiding principle is, plaintiff points out, as stated by the court in *Fitts' Estate v. Commissioner* [56-2 USTC ¶ 11,648], 237 F. 2d 729, 731 (8th Cir. 1956):

> * * * In determining the value of unlisted stocks, actual sales made in reasonable amounts at arm's length, in the normal course of business, within a reasonable time before or after the basic date, are the best criterion of market value.

Since there is such valid evidence of fair market value based on an arm's-length transaction, it is wholly unnecessary, and would be improper, plaintiff argues, to resort to hypothetical prices derived from such techniques as the comparative appraisal method, the use of which is justified only as a last resort when, as both the statute and the regulations make plain, actual bona fide sales prices are lacking.

The fair market value of the stock based on this one sale transaction alone is not controlling. "* * * [I]solated sales [of the stock] of closely held corporations in a restricted market offer little guide to true value." *Central Trust*

Company v. United States, supra, 158 Ct. Cl. at 519, 305 F. 2d at 402, and cases there cited. Further, certain circumstances pertaining to this particular sale transaction serve to prevent it from falling into the prerequisite "arm's-length" category. The price at which the sale was effected was not one that resulted from the usual type of bargaining or negotiation based on factors normally applicable to stock valuation. Instead, it was a price that was set by the plaintiff herein without any negotiation. And plaintiff, in turn, took the 50 percent book value price formula from a directive in her sister's will. Under the will, the decedent "authorize[d] and direct[ed]" that at the termination of the aforementioned trust of the residuary estate, the trustees

> * * * shall at such time give to the then officers of Selchow & Righter Co. the preferential opportunity to purchase the shares of said company * * * at a price equal to fifty per cent (50%) of the book value per share as of the time of my death, which, in my judgment, will be a fair and reasonable price therefor.

Under the will, the decedent appointed her sister Harriet, the plaintiff herein, and Mr. Tobias to be the trustees. However, the decedent plainly did not wish to prevent Mr. Tobias, as an officer of the company, from purchasing the stock simply because he was a trustee, for the will went on to provide that:

> * * * Authority is hereby conferred, in such circumstances, at such time or times, upon the Trustees and Executors to make sales upon such terms to such an officer at the time of sale even though such officer be at such time a Trustee or Executor hereunder.

Furthermore, the will, by the following provision, authorized such a sale of the stock at any time during the existence of the trust provided the sister-beneficiaries consented:

> * * * During the period of the trust, a like authority with respect to sale and purchase by and to a Trustee or Executor of some or all such shares of Selchow & Righter Co. * * * as shall be held at the time in the trust, is hereby given if such of my sisters as shall be living at the time thereof shall consent thereto.

It was under this provision that the sale herein was effected.

[*Sale Not Controlling*]

Thus, the sale was here made by the executors, one of whom was a trustee, to the cotrustee the selling executor-trustee also being Chairman of the Board of S & R, and the cotrustee qualifying as a purchaser by virtue of his falling into the "preferential" category of an S & R officer (its President), with the sale price on such sale (*i. e.,* of the 200 shares) being fixed by the formula contained in the will, namely, "a price equal to fifty percent (50%) of the book value per share as of the time of my death."

Of the three factors usually given consideration in attempting to arrive at the fair market value of an unlisted, closely held stock—earnings, dividends, and book value —book value is fairly considered to be the least important in the case of a manufacturing company with consistent earnings and dividend records, as was S & R. *Central Trust Company v. United States, supra,* 158 Ct. Cl. at 533-34, 305 F. 2d at 410-11.

Under the peculiar circumstances here involved, the sale upon which reliance is placed cannot be considered as the type of private transaction that would qualify as establishing fair market value. Mr. Tobias had a special relationship with both the decedent and the executrix, having been, before becoming S & R's President, a partner in the law firm that acted as their personal attorneys. He had long been a director of the company. Since 1955, he has worked actively with the executrix, who is Chairman of the Board and who preceded him as President. Mr. Tobias was the only one to whom this stock was offered, and the decedent not only made him a trustee of her residuary estate, but in another part of the will provided that, if her sisters predeceased her, her personal property should go "to my friend, C. Ellsworth Tobias, if living at the time of my death." In cases such as this, "the burden is upon the taxpayer to demonstrate that the sales relied upon are arm's length sales in the normal course of business." *Fitts' Estate v. Commissioner, supra,* 237 F. 2d at 731.

The court has considered this sale along with all the other evidence on the question of fair market value, but has given but little weight to it.

The same is true with reference to the evidence of Miss Harriet Righter and Mr. Tobias. Both testified that in their opinion the fair market value of the stock was 50 percent of its book value. Neither qualified as an expert in this particular field. However, both had long been associated with the company. Miss Harriet Righter was a stockholder of the company and had been its president for over thirty years (1923 to 1955) and during this period devoted full time to actively running the business. Since 1955, she has served actively as Chairman of the Board of Directors. Under these circumstances she no doubt knew more about the company than anyone who testified in this case. She was entitled to give her opinion as to the value of the stock. Next to Miss Harriet Righter, the person who was the most knowledgeable as to the affairs of the company was Mr. Tobias. He has been the attorney for the Righters for many years and had been a director of the company since 1947. He became its president in 1955 and was serving in that capacity at the time of the sale of the stock in 1961. This shows that he was an official of the company for over 14 years and was actively engaged in running the company, to say nothing of his prior knowledge of its affairs. We think he was entitled to give his opinion as to the value of the stock. His opinion and that of Miss Harriet Righter have been considered by the court along with all the other evidence, but, notwithstanding their intimate knowledge of the company and their honesty in giving their opinions, under the rules followed by the courts in establishing fair market value of stock, we have been unable to give much weight to their opinions.

Other evidence which plaintiff offers in support of the estate's 50 percent of book value formula is the administrative treatment of several other estates which similarly had, among their assets, various amounts of S & R stock. Plaintiff shows that in the cases of six other estates, in which the dates of the decedents' deaths ranged from July 16, 1956, to October 1, 1962, and the number of S & R shares varied from 29 to 108, the values of the shares that were accepted by the Internal Revenue Service ranged from $235 to $450 per share, and that for the five estates for which the record shows the pertinent data, such values were approximately 50 percent of book value (at the end of the year preceding the date of death) or even less. [*]

[*Other Estates*]

The valuations accepted by the Internal Revenue Service in the cases of other estates, involving the same stock and other death and valuation dates, are of probative value in the solution of the problem involved in this case and must be considered. Stocks necessarily have different values on different dates. Numerous considerations enter into the determination of value on any particular date or the acceptance of certain values set forth in any particular estate tax return. Each case necessarily stands on its own facts.

In the first two estates in point of dates of death, *i.e.*, July 16, 1956, and November 20, 1958, approximately five and two and one-half years, respectively, prior to the date herein involved, the estate tax returns valuing the shares at $235 and $275 per share, respectively (which were 36.2 percent and 39.4 percent of book value, respectively, at the end of the years preceding the dates of death), were simply accepted as filed. There is no evidence to indicate that any investigation was made by the Internal Revenue Service into the value of the blocks of 99 and 108 shares of S & R stock included in the assets of the estates.

On the third estate, in which the date of death was June 13, 1959—almost two years prior to the date herein involved—the 38 shares included in the estate were valued in the return at $275 per share. The evidence shows, however, that, in connection with its examination, the examining Internal Revenue Service office in Brooklyn, New York, obtained financial statements covering S & R's operations for prior years, and subsequently determined a deficiency based in part on increasing the fair market value of the stock to $450 per share, a deficiency which the estate apparently did not contest. The increased value constituted 58.7 percent of book value as of December 31, 1958, *i.e.*, the end of the year preceding the date of death.

On the fourth estate, in which the date of death was December 30, 1959—only six months after the date of death involved in the third estate—the 99 shares included in the estate were valued in the return at $325. In this instance too, the examining Revenue Service office (in Connecticut) obtained financial statements covering S & R's prior years' operations. The examiner originally concluded that the value per share ranged from $1,200 to $1,250, but his report shows that the estate objected to such proposed valuation and pointed out that in the recent above-mentioned third estate in the Brooklyn District, a value of $450 had been arrived at. The Connecticut examiner then concluded that acceptance of a $450 valuation would be justified in his case too in view of a provision in the Internal Revenue Service Manual stating that: "Where a valuation has been made in a prior estate, it may not be necessary to make another detailed analysis of the stock in the current investigation, provided the valuation date on the prior estate is within reasonable proximity to the current date and the pertinent facts have not changed substantially." The Connecticut examiner stated that the Brooklyn office examiner had the pertinent financial statements, and "[s]ince the determination of fair market value is a question of fact, no doubt the [Brooklyn] examiner took into account all the circumstances to arrive at the value of $450.00." He was "reluctant to press for a higher figure" because he felt that to do so "would appear to defeat the purpose of the paragraph in

[*] As shown by the following table:

Date of death	Number of shares	Value per share reported	Value per share accepted by IRS	Ratio of value to book value (at end of preceding date of death) (Percent)
July 16, 1956	99	$235	$235	36.2
November 20, 1958......	108	275	275	39.4
June 13, 1959..........	38	275	450	58.7
December 30, 1959.....	99	325	450	58.7
December 16, 1960.....	29	450	450	53.8

the Manual, which is to provide a means of obtaining uniformity in current valuations of a particular stock regardless of the district involved." Upon review of the examiner's recommendation, the reviewer suggested an $800 a share valuation, but the ultimate determination by the Connecticut District was the $450 recommended by the examiner, which the estate apparently accepted. (As was the situation on the third estate, this figure was 58.7 percent of the book value as of December 31, 1958.)

In the fifth estate, in which the date of death was December 16, 1960—about four months prior to the decedent's death herein —the estate tax return valued the 29 shares of S & R stock included in the estate's assets at $450 per share. (This was 53.8 percent of book value as of December 31, 1959.) The return was accepted as filed. There is nothing to indicate that any investigation was made of the fair market value of the 29 shares as of the date of death.

Similarly, the sixth estate, in which the date of death was October 1, 1962—almost a year and a half subsequent to the date of death here involved—the estate tax return also valued the 104 shares of S & R stock included in the estate's assets at $450 per share. The record does not indicate what the book value of the S & R stock was as of December 31, 1961, a date subsequent to the decedent's death. Accordingly, the relationship of this figure to book value is not shown. However, even if it be assumed that the figure was approximately 50 percent of book value,[5] there is nothing to indicate that the Internal Revenue Service made any investigation into the valuation of the stock set forth in the return, which was simply accepted as filed.

The plaintiff contends that the valuations accepted by the IRS for the stock of this company in these other estates are controlling and binding on the IRS regarding the fair market value of the stock in our case. On the other hand, the defendant argues that the valuations in such other estates should not even be considered by the court on the question of value here. We do not agree with either party, but follow a somewhat middle course between their widely divergent views. It is our opinion and we hold that while the values placed on this stock by the IRS in the other estates is not determinative of the question of value, in a case such as this where there is no sure way of arriving at the true market value, the value so placed by the IRS in the other estates is some evidence which may be considered.

Accordingly, it is our view that the action taken by the IRS in the six other estates in approving the value of the identical stock at about the date of the death of our decedent at from 36.2 to 58.7 percent of book value ($235 to $450 per share) is evidence we may consider in solving the problem before us. This is especially true with reference to the third and fourth estates where investigations were made as detailed above, and the valuations of $450 per share (58.7 percent of book value) were fixed in both estates after the investigations were made. It should be noted that in the fourth estate, the examiner originally fixed the value at from $1,200 to $1,250 per share, but finally recommended $450 after his investigation was concluded. However, the reviewer suggested $800 per share. The "Connecticut District" determined that the value should be $450.

Other evidence and factors favorable to the position of the plaintiff on the fair market value of the stock, besides the statement of the testatrix in her will, the opinions of Miss Harriet Righter and Mr. Tobias, and the valuations of identical stock fixed by the IRS in the six other estates, are the following:

1. The 337 shares represented a minority interest of only 17 percent of the company's stock and lacked marketability.

2. The company only produced two products (games called Scrabble and Parcheesi).

3. The company was engaged in a luxury type business that was subject to fluctuation.

---

[5] This would appear to be a valid assumption in view of the $473.40 price which Mr. Tobias and his wife paid for the 137 shares on April 5, 1962, which represented 50 percent of book value as of December 31, 1961, less the dividend paid, in an amount not shown by the record, the early part of 1962. Thus, such $473.40 price was less than 50 percent of book value as of December 31, 1961, necessarily making the $450 valuation in the sixth estate similarly less than 50 percent of such book value as of such date.

4. The business of the company was subject to lively competition from larger companies.

5. The principal product of the company was a game called Scrabble which it did not own and which it produced under a license from the owner.

6. Sixty percent of its business was from sales of Scrabble.

7. Through the years, the company had been unable to develop new products.

8. The company was relatively small compared to other companies in the entertainment field.

9. The company had recently lost the services of key sales personnel in the persons of Mr. Anderson and Miss Stringer.

10. The owner of Scrabble had the right to compete with S & R in the manufacture and sale of the game and did so as to luxury types thereof.

11. The owner of Scrabble had the right to terminate S & R's license if its sales fell below 50,000 units in any calendar year.

12. The business of the company was highly seasonal.

13. There was always the possibility and even likelihood that Scrabble and Parcheesi would become unpopular and not be saleable.

Defendant's proof offered to sustain the Commissioner's valuation of $1,000 per share is discussed below. It produced two experts who utilized the comparative appraisal method in the process of arriving at their ultimate opinions.

[Experts' Valuations]

The first expert[*] is a financial analyst in the Internal Revenue Service. Educated both in business administration and the law, he worked, prior to becoming employed by the Internal Revenue Service, as a security analyst for stockbrokers (Bache & Co. and Hayden, Stone & Co.), as a branch office assistant manager for a company in the investment business (Hess & Co.), and as an investment counselor for Standard & Poor. In these capacities, he had made many evaluations of minority blocks of stocks of small, closely held corporations. He selected, as comparatives,

four companies in the game and toy business whose stocks were publicly traded,[†] and arrived at ratios between their market prices as of April 24, 1961 and their earnings and book values. He found that, on the basis of their earnings for the most recent five full calendar years prior to the date of death (1956-1960), their market prices were 41 times earnings. On the basis of 1960 earnings alone, the ratio was 29.55 times earnings. S & R's average earnings for the five-year 1956-1960 period were $89 per share. On the 41 times earnings basis of the four comparatives, S & R's per share price would be $3,649. S & R's 1960 per share earnings were $123.32. On the 29.55 times 1960 earnings basis of the four comparatives, S & R's per share price would be $3,644.11.

As to book values, the ratio of price to such values for the four comparatives averaged 5.76 to 1 as of December 31, 1960. S & R's book value as of such date was $899.81. On the sole basis of the average relationship that the book values of the common stocks of the comparatives bore to their market prices, S & R's market price would be $5,182.91 a share.

The witness felt that these high ratios, producing in turn such high valuations when applied to S & R, might conceivably reflect unusual popularity of certain products of the comparatives at that particular time. To guard against such possibility, he took the lowest of the comparatives' ratios, instead of their averages. Of the four, the lowest price-earnings ratio was 21.70 to 1 on the five-year average basis. Multiplying this figure by S & R's $89 per share five-year average earnings gave a value, on such basis, of $1,931 per share. On a book value basis, again taking the lowest price-to-book value ratio (as of December 31, 1960) of 2.84, S & R's price per share would be $2,555.[§]

As a further check, the witness examined the general market prices as reflected in The Standard & Poor's Index of Industrial Stocks. This Index showed that publicly traded stocks were, as of April 24, 1961, selling at a price-earnings ratio of 23 to 1. Similarly, such stock prices were, as of De-

---

[*] Mr. Leo Goulston.

[†] Aurora Plastics, Mattel, Inc., Milton Bradley Company, and Remco Industries.

cember 31, 1960, approximately twice their book value. On such price-earnings ratio basis, the S & R stock would (on the basis of 1960 earnings of $123.32 per share) sell for $2,900 per share, and on such price-book value ratio basis, would sell for approximately $1,800 per share.

As a result of all these comparisons, the witness concluded that, were S & R stock similarly publicly traded as of April 24, 1961, it would have sold within a range of not less than $1,800-$2,000 a share.

The witness further concluded, however, that certain special considerations would warrant a substantial discount in such a price. Since the S & R stock was not publicly traded, it lacked marketability. Furthermore, the 337-share block being evaluated represented only a minority interest. Although the company had, during the five-year period, showed a favorable trend of steadily rising earnings,[9] it was somewhat vulnerable because it had only two principal products, indicating a lack of vitality and creativity in new product development; it was in a type of luxury business, and it was subject to lively competition from larger companies. Because of these factors, he felt a rather large discount of approximately 45-50 percent in the hypothetical $1,800-$2,000 selling price would in this case be warranted. On this basis, it was his opinion that $1,000 per share (as the Commissioner had determined) was the fair market value of the stock as of April 24, 1961. He felt this was a conservative price for the stock of such a successful, established company with increasing earnings and book values,[10] and with a principal product (Scrabble) which had attained such sustained popularity (in the industry it was considered that it had attained the status of a "staple" game).

The second expert,[11] a graduate of the Harvard Business School, worked as a security analyst and cost account manager for the Fidelity-Philadelphia Trust Company in Philadelphia, Pennsylvania. He is now president of an investment counseling firm in Washington, D. C.,[12] which furnishes advice on securities, including valuations of closely held corporations.

As comparatives, he selected three companies.[13] His studies indicated that, based on their average earnings per share for the five-year period 1956-1960, their stocks were selling, as of December 31, 1960, based on their average prices during such week, at an average of 19.3 times earnings. He further found that there was an exceedingly favorable investment climate for toy and game manufacturing companies during the early part of 1961, for between December 31, 1960 and April 24, 1961, the prices of the stocks of these three companies more than doubled. On the same five-year average price basis, the stocks of these same companies were selling, as of April 24, 1961 (based on their average prices during such week), at an average of 45.7 times earnings.

On these bases, S & R stock would have sold as of December 31, 1960, based on S & R's average earnings per share from 1956-1960 of $89 per share, at $1,718. On April 24, 1961, the stock would have sold at $4,067 per share.

On the same bases (average earnings per share during 1956-1960, and the average prices during the weeks of December 31, 1960 and April 24, 1961), Standard & Poor's Industrial Index showed a price-earnings ratio for the stocks included therein of 18.3 and 20.2 as of December 31, 1960, and April 24, 1961, respectively, indicating a much smaller rise during the early part of 1961 for stocks in general than for toy and game company stocks. On these bases, S & R stock would have sold as of December 31, 1960, and April 24, 1961, at $1,629 and $1,798, respectively.

---

[8] As to dividends, the average price to 1960 dividend ratio of the four comparatives was 109.5. The expert considered such a ratio as out of line and in this case eliminated such factor from his consideration.

[9] As shown by the following table:

Year	Per share Earnings
1956	$ 44.15
1957	64.17
1958	103.51

Year	Per share Earnings
1959	$110.00
1960	123.32

[10] The book value per share had increased every year for the prior ten years, going from $136.77 in 1950 to $899.81 in 1960.

[11] John W. Davidge.

[12] Davidge, Van Cleef, Jordan & Wood, Inc.

[13] Milton Bradley Company, Mattel, Inc., and Remco Industries.

The witness then used the same technique but with the average prices during the weeks of December 31, 1960 and April 24, 1961 applied only to the 1960 earnings per share of the three comparatives (instead of five-year averages), resulting in price-earnings ratios of 10.9 and 25.9, respectively (again reflecting the sharp rise in the stocks of the toy-game manufacturers during such four-month period). On this basis (S & R's 1960 earnings per share being, as hereinabove set forth, $123.32), S & R's stock would have sold for $1,344 as of December 31, 1960, and $3,194 as of April 24, 1961.

Applying the Standard & Poor Industrial Index test, also on the 1960 earnings basis, the witness found that the price-earnings ratio, calculated on the average prices for the week of December 31, 1960, was 18.2 (higher than the toy-game companies), and that the ratio calculated on the average prices for the week of April 24, 1961 was 20.2 (lower than the toy-game companies). On this basis, S & R's stock would have sold for $2,244 as of December 31, 1960, and $2,491 as of April 24, 1961.

The witness then gave special consideration to certain other facts relating to S & R and its operations. He found that, for the five full calendar years preceding the valuation date, sales had increased every year, going from over $1,800,000 in 1956 to over $3,200,000 in 1960, an increase of 78 percent; that earnings per share had risen from over $44 in 1956 to over $123 in 1960, an increase of 280 percent; and that the average dividend payout rate per share during such period was approximately 50 percent, a rate which he considered to be conservative and which an investor would reasonably feel would continue.[14] Although he took it into account, he did not consider the $899.81 per share book value as of December 31, 1960, to be a major factor in determining its fair market value. He gave primary weight to earning power. He also considered significant the fact that the company had good control over its costs, since costs had risen during the five-year period more slowly than sales and profits. He noted the strong liquid current asset

position of the company, as shown by its balance sheet as of December 31, 1960, as well as the lack of any substantial indebtedness. He felt these were signs of good company management. He considered too that the block of stock being valued represented only a 17 percent minority interest. He also felt that recognition should be given to the fact that the comparatives left much to be desired since they manufactured toys (and some other products) as well as games, whereas S & R manufactured only games. He did feel, however, that an investor would consider that the companies fell within the same general category, although it would, of course, be more desirable if comparatives could be found which, like S & R, produced only games.[15] However, there were no such other companies whose stocks were publicly traded. Finally, he also considered the fact that S & R was simply a licensee with respect to the particular editions of Scrabble which it was manufacturing and the owner of the copyright had reserved to itself the right to manufacture and sell the same editions for which it had licensed S & R, so that legally it could become a competitor of its licensee (the licensor also reserved the right to manufacture and sell certain higher-priced editions of the game, and did in fact do so).

Upon the basis of all the facts and figures he considered, the witness concluded that the fair market value of the S & R stock as of April 24, 1961, was $950. He recognized, however, that the valuation of any closely held security lacking a public market or a record of any significant private transactions or placements is difficult at best, and not a precise undertaking. He therefore felt that a certain flexibility was permissible, and that any valuation within the range of $900-$1,000 would not be unreasonable. He did not feel that any figure less than the lowest level of such range could be justified by rational analysis.[16]

[*Companies Not Comparable*]

Plaintiff attacks the valuation of such experts on various grounds. She says the companies they selected as comparatives are not truly comparable since they manu-

---

[14] Milton Bradley's average dividend payout rate per share during 1956-1960 was 24 percent.

[15] In this respect, Milton Bradley Company was the closest comparative, with approximately 70 percent of its sales in games.

facture such items as toys and dolls, which appeal to a younger class of consumer than does Scrabble. She further argues that not enough consideration was given to certain unfavorable factors, such as (1) the company's being, as of the valuation date, in effect only a two-product business (Scrabble and Parcheesi), with over 60 percent of its sales in one product; (2) the company's relatively small size as compared with its closest competitor (the Milton Bradley Company); (3) the loss, during the six-month period preceding the valuation date, of its two top sales executives who had long been associated with the company; (4) the nonownership by the company of the Scrabble trademarks and copyrights and its position as only a licensee; (5) the legal ability of the licensor to enter into the business of manufacturing the same type of Scrabble games as S & R was licensed to manufacture; (6) the highly seasonal nature of its business, with a substantial part of its annual volume of sales being accounted for around the Christmas season, thus making it most vulnerable to strikes both within its unionized factory, and by such outside unions as those in the trucking and shipping industries, including the longshoremen;[17] and (7) considering the type of business it is in, its peculiar vulnerability to the public's fancy.[18]

We agree with the plaintiff that the companies used by the expert witnesses of defendant as comparables were not in fact truly comparable to S & R. Our trial judge found that there are no other publicly traded companies that are comparable to S & R in terms of game manufacture and that for this reason S & R was compared by such witnesses with other companies "which are essentially in the business of manufacturing toys." We do not think a company that manufactures toys or toys and games can be accurately compared to a company like S & R that manufactures only games. Their products appeal to and are used by different age groups. They are different in many other respects as shown herein. Therefore, since the basis for the opinions of defendant's expert witnesses was grounded on the comparison of companies that were not truly comparable, their analyses based on the comparative appraisal method have but little, if any, weight in establishing the fair market value of the S & R stock. This court dealt with the principle of comparables in *Jones Bros. Bakery v. United States* [69-2 USTC ¶ 9474], 188 Ct. Cl. 226, 411 F. 2d 1282 (1969). There the problem was whether or not the company had paid its officers more than reasonable salaries and deducted the same as an expense on their income tax returns. The government offered evidence of salaries of executives of another company that it contended was comparable to the plaintiff company to show plaintiff's salaries were too high. The court held that while the two companies were similar in many respects, they were also quite different in other ways, and were not truly comparables. The court proceeded by a jury verdict on the whole record to fix proper salaries for plaintiff's officers that were lower than the amounts deducted by the plaintiff but higher than those contended for by the government.

In the case before us, the government relied on the testimony of its expert witnesses to establish the fair market value of the stock by the comparative appraisal method. Since the companies used by such witnesses

---

[16] Plaintiff contends that the second expert testified "he would not recommend that a willing buyer purchase the stock at $950.00," and that "such an admission emasculates his testimony." (Pltf. Brief at 41.) Plaintiff errs. The expert did not so testify. His testimony was only that he would not recommend such a stock to a "fiduciary" type of client, such as a church or college. He further testified, however, that he would recommend the stock at such figure to the appropriate type of investor, and that, as a matter of fact, he did have a client who he felt would be interested in purchasing such a block of S & R stock as was here involved.

[17] Most of the titles, one of the components of the Scrabble game, are imported. S & R ships its products primarily by truck.

[18] Plaintiff points to the upsurge in its 1954 and 1955 sales and profits after S & R first began marketing Scrabble, followed by the drastic drops therein in 1956, when Scrabble's initial flurry of popularity receded. From approximately $1,900,000 in 1953, sales jumped to over $5,000,000 and $4,000,000 in 1954 and 1955, respectively. They then dropped to $1,800,000 in 1956. Similarly, gross profits went from $733,000 in 1953 to $2,300,000 and $1,700,000 in 1954 and 1955, respectively, falling back to $710,000 in 1956. Plaintiff says the experts' going back only five years resulted in their failing to consider this particular period in S & R's life.

for comparison were not true comparables, it becomes necessary for the court to review the whole record and consider all the evidence to arrive at the correct value of the stock.

We held in *Penn Yan Agway Cooperative v. United States* [69-2 USTC ¶ 9719], 189 Ct. Cl. 434, 417 F. 2d 1372 (1969):

> It is a well established rule of law, carefully analyzed and stated in *Drybrough v. United States* [62-2 USTC ¶ 12,098], 208 F. Supp. 279 (W. D. Ky. 1962), that *the market value of common stock* in a closely held corporation, there being no market sales of such stock, *must be determined upon consideration of all relevant factors,* such as earning capacity, anticipated profits, book value, and dividend yield. * * * [Emphasis supplied.] [*Id.* at 446, 417 F. 2d at 1378.]

We find a similar statement in *Arc Realty Co. v. C. I. R.* [61-2 USTC ¶ 9689], 295 F. 2d 98 (8th Cir. 1961) as follows:

> The question of "fair market value," defined to be "the price at which property would change hands in a transaction between a willing buyer and a willing seller, neither being under compulsion to buy nor to sell and both being informed," *O'Malley v. Ames* [52-1 USTC ¶ 9361], 8 Cir., 197 F. 2d 256, at page 257; *Fitts' Estate v. Commissioner of Internal Revenue* [56-2 USTC ¶ 11,648], 8 Cir., 237 F. 2d 729, 731, is one of fact and cannot be established on the basis of fixed rules or formulae. Among the factors properly to be considered in making the determination are corporate assets, earnings, dividend policy, earning power of the corporation, prospects of the corporation, book value, character of the management, competition and other factors which an informed purchaser and informed seller would take into account. *O'Malley v. Ames, supra; Fitts' Estate v. Commissioner of Internal Revenue, supra.* [*Id.* at 103.]

The defendant contends that we should accept the evidence of its expert witnesses because they were experts in the field of market value analysis and were the only experts who testified. We are not required to do so. This was made clear by our decision in *United States v. Northern Paiute Nation,* 183 Ct. Cl. 321, 346, 393 F. 2d 786, 800 (1968) where we said:

> The Indians' other complaint about the findings is that the Commission rejected

its expert appraisers' views, and did not spell out why in detailed findings. In legal appraisement, however, widely divergent opinion testimony is the rule rather than the exception. The trier of fact must decide first, of course, if such testimony is competent and and admissible. Before us, no party claims that this case was decided with respect to any issue on inadmissible testimony. The Indians wanted the Commission to take up the reasoning of its appraisers step by step, and either accept each step or show reasons for rejecting it. Having competent testimony before it, the Commission was not restricted to swallowing it whole or rejecting it utterly. It did not have to refute what it did not accept as controlling. It could, and apparently did, synthesize in its mind the immense record before it, determine to what extent opinion evidence rested on facts, consider and weigh it all, and come up with figures supported by all the evidence, perhaps, though not identified with any of it. * * *

In addition to the other circumstances favorable to the plaintiff's view in this case, as set forth above, there is the significant fact that the stock involved here was a minority interest of only 17 percent in a closely held corporation. It is logical to assume that this would adversely affect its value if it were offered for sale on the open market, as few people would be interested in buying it under these circumstances. The decided cases support this view. In *Drybrough v. United States* [62-2 USTC ¶ 12,098], 208 F. Supp. 279 (W. D. Ky. 1962), the court discounted by 35 percent the value of minority interests in a corporation. In that case the court cited with approval the decision in *Whittemore v. Fitzpatrick* [54-2 USTC ¶ 10,976], 127 F. Supp. 710 (D. C. Conn., 1954), where the court allowed a 50 percent discount for a minority interest in stock of a corporation, and stated further:

> Other cases holding that minority stock interests in closed corporations are usually worth much less than the proportionate share of the assets to which they attach are *Andrew B. C. Dohrmann* [CCH Dec. 5942], (1930) 19 B. T. A. 507; *Cravens v. Welch* [35-1 USTC ¶ 9181], (D. C. Cal., 1935) 10 F. Supp. 94; *Estate of Irene DeGuebriant* [CCH Dec. 17,600], (1950) 14 T. C. 611, reversed on other grounds *Claflin v. Commissioner of Internal Revenue* [51-1 USTC ¶ 10,791], 2 Cir., 186 F. 2d 307;

Mathilde B. Hooper [CCH Dec. 10,965], (1940) 41 B. T. A. 114, 129; *Bartram v. Graham* [57-2 USTC ¶ 11,721], (D. C. Conn., 1957) 157 F. Supp. 757; *Bader v. United States* [59-1 USTC ¶ 11,865], (D. C. Ill., 1959) 172 F. Supp. 833, and *Snyder's Estate v. United States* [61-1 USTC ¶ 11,987], (4 Cir., 1961) 285 F. 2d 857. [208 F. Supp. at 287.]

The problem before us is always a difficult one. It is never possible to fix the value of corporate stock in a closely held corporation which is not sold on the open market with mathematical exactness, and we are not required to do so. This was aptly stated by the court in *Arc Realty Co. v. C. I. R., supra,* when it said:

> * * * The matter of fixing the fair market value of corporate stock for capital gains treatment, with numerous factors entering the picture, obviously cannot be accomplished with exactness or complete accuracy. * * * [295 F. 2d at 103.]

Many times courts solve problems like the one before us by considering all the evidence and the whole record and then deciding what is right and just under all the facts and circumstances. We did this as to officers' salaries in *Jones Bros. Bakery v. United States, supra,* and again in *Meredith Broadcasting Co. v. United States* [69-1 USTC ¶ 9126], 186 Ct. Cl. 1, 405 F. 2d 1214 (1968) in arriving at the value of certain intangibles. We think we are justified in following this procedure in the instant case. It ap-

pears to be fair and right and in accordance with justice to both parties that we do so.

Based on all the evidence and the whole record, we conclude that the fair market value of the 337 shares of S & R stock as of April 24, 1961, was $700 per share.

The Charitable Deduction Issue

For the purpose of computing such deduction, it is first necessary to arrive at a figure representing the amount that will go to charity at the termination of the trust. That was the way the executors computed it in the return.[19] In view of the power given in the will to the trustees to sell the stock at 50 percent of book value as of the date of the decedent's death, the executors properly used such figures in computing the amount that would go to charity, and the Commissioner was correct in accepting such figure.

Indeed, in view of the controlling regulations governing charitable bequests, it is necessary to give effect, as the executors did, to the power vested in the trustees by the will. Section 20.2055-2(b) of the Treasury Regulations on Estate Tax (1954 Code) specifically provides, with respect to charitable bequests, that if a "trustee is empowered to divert the property * * *, in whole or in part, to a use or purpose which would have rendered it, to the extent that it is subject to such power, not deductible had it been directly so bequeathed, devised, or given by the dece-

---

[19] The schedule in the return (Schedule N) in which the charitable deduction was computed contained the following statement and explanation:

"Decedent created a Trust of her residuary estate, to pay the income therefrom to her sisters—Harriet Righter, born 2/24/78, and Katharine Righter, born 9/23/79—for their lives and upon the death of the survivor directed that certain general legacies be paid from the remainder, and the balance remaining after the payments aforesaid to certain named charities. Said residuary trust is contained in Paragraph Sixteenth of decedent's Will, a copy of which is attached to this return.

"Factor used in determining the remainder interest of said residuary trust was taken from the Actuarial Tables contained in the Commissioner's Regulations. Table III, Value of $1.00 due at death of Survivor of two persons."

[20] "§ 20.2055-2 *Transfers not exclusively for charitable purposes.*
     * * *

"(b) *Transfers subject to a condition or a power.* If, as of the date of decedent's death,

a transfer for charitable purposes is dependent upon the performance of some act or the happening of a precedent event in order that it might become effective, no deduction is allowable unless the possibility that the charitable transfer will not become effective is so remote as to be negligible. If an estate or interest has passed to or is vested in charity at the time of a decedent's death and the estate or interest would be defeated by the performance of some act or the happening of some event, the occurrence of which appeared to have been highly improbable at the time of the decedent's death, the deduction is allowable. If the legatee, devisee, donee, or trustee is empowered to divert the property or fund, in whole or in part, to a use or purpose which would have rendered it, to the extent that it is subject to such power, not deductible had it been directly so bequeathed, devised, or given by the decedent, the deduction will be limited to that portion, if any, of the property or fund which is exempt from an exercise of the power. * * *" [26 C. F. R. § 20.2055-2 (1969).]

dent, *the deduction will be limited to that portion * * * of the property * * * which is exempt from an exercise of the power.*" (Italics supplied.)[21] This provision directly controls the situation here involved, where the trustees were not only empowered, but were required, at the termination of the trust, to offer the S & R stock to its then officers at a price of 50 percent of book value as of the date of the decedent's death. Thus, no matter what the fair market value of the stock was as of such date, the charities would receiye, in accordance with the exercise of the power vested in the trustees by the will, only 50 percent of book value as of the date of the decedent's death. In the words of the regulation, therefore, to the extent that the fair market value of the stock exceeded 50 percent of the book value as of the date of death, the will empowered the diversion of such excess to persons other than to charities. Only that portion of the value of the property exempt from such power to divert, *i. e.,* $424.90 per share, is accordingly deductible as a charitable bequest.

Plaintiff says that if the test is the "amount that would in fact go to charity" then defendant should at least "allow a charitable deduction of $473.40 with respect to the stock purchased [by Mr. Tobias and his wife in 1962] * * *"[21] Plaintiff herself supplies the answer to this contention, however, by also pointing out that it is "the situation at the instant of death" that controls.[22] Plaintiff elected to have the assets valued as of the date of the decedent's death, and for the purposes here involved, it is as of such date that the return, including the amount of the charitable deduction, speaks, and the tax

computed. The deduction is based on the present (as of the date of death) value, actuarially computed, of the remainder interest, and that was the way the executors computed it in the return. Accordingly, for the purpose here in question, the subsequent sales to the Tobiases, to which both parties refer, are irrelevant. Merely looking to the will, the conclusion would have to be made that the trustees were empowered to sell the stock at the termination of the trust at 50 percent of book value as of the date of the decedent's death, and such sale proceeds would therfore, fix the amount that would go to charity. Consequently, in accordance with the regulation, the charitable deduction is limited to such amount.[23] *Cf. Commissioner v. Sternberger's Estate* [55-1 USTC ¶ 11,504], 348 U. S. 187 (1954) (no part of a conditional bequest to charity allowed as a deduction from the gross estate where there was no assurance that charity would receive the bequest or a determinable part of it).

Summary

Since the deficiency which plaintiff paid was based upon a valuation of the S & R stock as of the date of death of $1,000 per share for gross estate tax purposes, and the determination herein is that such value was $700 per share, plaintiff is entitled to recover on such issue to such extent. Plaintiff is not entitled to recover on the issue of the charitable deduction.

Section 2053 of the Internal Revenue Code of 1954 allows a deduction from the value of the gross estate for "administrative expenses." Section 20.2053-3(c)(2) of the Treasury Regulations provides that such expenses include "A deduction for attorneys' fees incurred in contesting an

---

[21] Pltf. Reply Brief at 22.

[22] *Id.* at 21.

[23] The will spoke of a sale of the stock to the officers only in terms of 50 percent of book value at the date of decedent's death. The July 12, 1961 sale of 200 shares at $424.90 per share conformed to this formula. Plaintiff testified that, with respect to the July 12, 1961 transaction "• • • we [the executors] had the instructions of my sister Jessie's will"; that the executors concluded that "• • • that's all right with us, it is as near as we can guess to the probable value of it"; (Tr. at 15) and that the sale was made in accordance with the decedent's "directions" and "instructions." (Tr. at 20.) However, the April 5, 1962 sale of 137 shares

did not so conform. This sale, at $473.40 per share, was made at 50 percent of book value as of the date of the sale instead of the date of death. (It is true that the July 12, 1961 sale would conform to both standards.) Apparently the executors felt they could make the sale upon such terms and thus deviate from the terms of the will at least to such extent. At the trial, plaintiff's counsel referred to the sales as having been made "substantially" in accordance with the terms of the will. (Tr. at 6.)

asserted deficiency * * *" and that "A deduction for reasonable attorney's fees actually paid in contesting an asserted deficiency * * * will be allowed even though the deduction, as such, was not claimed in the estate tax return or in the claim for refund." The regulation goes on to provide that "A deduction for these fees shall not be denied, and the sufficiency of a claim for refund shall not be questioned, solely by reason of the fact that the amount of the fees to be paid was not established at the time that the right to the deduction was claimed." 26 C. F. R. § 20.2053-3(c)(2) (1969).

Pursuant to these provisions, plaintiff also claims such amount as may be allowable as a result of a deduction for reasonable fees and expenses incurred in connection with the prosecution of this case. Defendant concedes plaintiff's entitlement to such a deduction. No reason is apparent for not giving effect to the parties' agreement in this respect. Accordingly, the amount of the recovery should also reflect such a deduction.

Dissenting Opinion

DAVIS, Judge, dissenting in part:

Although the court's opinion adopts much of Commissioner Gamer's underlying reasoning, it balks at his most significant intermediate conclusions and also at his ultimate determination that the stock was worth no less than $900 per share. I consider his opinion and conclusion correct, and I would follow him entirely.[1]

One of the two principal differences between the court and the trial commissioner concerns the evaluation of the stock by the Internal Revenue Service for the other estates. Commissioner Gamer thought, and I agree, that the valuations accepted for these other estates "contribute little of probative value in the solution of the problem involved in this case." He cited *Fitts' Estate v. Commissioner* [56-2 USTC ¶ 11,648], 237 F. 2d 729, 733-34 (C. A. 8, 1956), in which

the court ruled that the Tax Court did not abuse its discretion in excluding testimony concerning the valuation of unlisted, closely held stock in another estate where "[t]here is no indication as to how the values [of the stocks in the other estates] were arrived at * * *."[2] After detailing the six instances of valuation of the instant stocks in other estates, the trial commissioner pointed out that:

"Thus, an analysis of the situation in each of the six estates upon which plaintiff relies so heavily fails to reveal in any of them what the considerations were that led to the acceptance by the Internal Revenue Service of the valuations indicated. In four of the six, there is no evidence that any investigation was initiated by the Service, the taxpayer's valuation merely being accepted as filed. And as to the first of the other two, in which, after a consideration of the company's financial statements for prior years, the valuation was raised from $275, as set forth in the return, to $450, there is nothing to indicate the basis for such $450 figure or why it was selected. The second simply used the figure of the first. The evidence concerning these other estates has little probative value in the solution of the factual problem here involved of determining the fair market value of the 337 shares of S & R stocks as of April 24, 1961.

The 'equality of treatment' principle applied to the excise tax problem involved in *International Business Machines Corp. v. United States* [65-1 USTC ¶ 15,629], 170 Ct. Cl. 357, 367, 343 F. 2d 914, 920 (1965),[1] *cert. denied*, 382 U. S. 1028 (1966), which plaintiff emphasizes, has no applicability to the estate tax problem here involved. The court's concern in that case was the adverse competitive effects of the inconsistent positions of the Internal Revenue Service upon the operations of two similarly situated business competitors. The Commissioner there exercised a statutorily conferred discretion by denying an application for an excise tax exemption in one situation and granting it to a competitor identically situated. The

---

[1] There is now no dispute as to the charitable deduction issue, since plaintiff does not seek review of the trial commissioner's adverse holding on that point.

[2] The Eighth Circuit also said: "* * * the valuation of the stock in the case of one taxpayer would be no binding adjudication of its value in the case of another taxpayer, and such

evidence would be of little probative value in the absence of a showing that the valuation was arrived at after a thorough investigation."

[1] "Equality of treatment is so dominant in our understanding of justice that discretion, where it is allowed a role, must pay the strictest heed."

court refused to sanction such discrimination between the two business concerns operating in the field. It construed the statute as directing the Commissioner to apply equality of excise tax treatment to competitors similarly situated. Obviously, such a situation is hardly applicable to the type of estate tax issue here involved which concerns only the factual problem of fair market value of a certain block of stock on a certain date. The Internal Revenue Manual merely provides that 'it may not be necessary to make another detailed analysis of the stock' in the situation where 'a valuation has been made in prior estate * * * provided the valuation date on the prior estate is within reasonable proximity to the current date and the pertinent facts have not changed substantially.' Surely, such a discretionary authorization in limited situations neither constitutes a directive to the agents to accept at all times in the future a stock valuation made in a prior estate, nor does it give a taxpayer anything in the nature of a vested right to have the prior valuation applied to his return. As the court stated concerning the gift tax involved in *Wagner v. United States* [68-1 USTC ¶ 12,498], 181 Ct. Cl. 807, 817-18, 387 F. 2d 966, 972 (1967), with respect to a charge of alleged discrimination against the taxpayer:

"Nor did discrimination result from the circumstances that other persons * * * may have never paid a gift tax * * *. * * * The fact that all taxpayers or all areas of the tax law cannot be dealt with by the Internal Revenue Service with equal vigor and that there thus may be some taxpayers who avoid paying the tax cannot serve to release all other taxpayers from their obligation. As this court said in *Kehaya v. United States* [66-1 USTC ¶ 9189], 174 Ct. Cl. 74, 78, 355 F. 2d 639, 641 (1966): 'The Commissioner's failure to assess deficiencies against some taxpayers who owe additional tax does not preclude him from assessing deficiencies against other taxpayers who admittedly owe additional taxes on the same type of income. The Commissioner might reasonably conclude that a reaudit of * * * returns * * * would not produce sufficient additional revenue to justify the undertaking. Such a decision would certainly not be arbitrary.' "

The other major disagreement between court and trial commissioner hinges on the treatment of the evidence given by the Government's experts. Plaintiff presented no expert evidence at all, and in the commissioner's eyes (as in mine) the material on which plaintiff does rely (the sale to Mr. Tobias, the other valuations by IRS, the testimony of Miss Righter and Mr. Tobias, the statement in the will) is all "unacceptable" as proving value. On the other hand, as the commissioner says, the "evidence of fair market value presented by defendant [through its expert witnesses] is based upon a sound approach and is, from a financial analysis viewpoint, entirely reasonable." As a result, he properly considered that he was justified in placing his ultimate conclusion as to the fair market value of the S & R stock (as of April 24, 1961) "within the confines of the opinions of defendant's experts."

The trial commissioner did not neglect the "unfavorable" factors which both the plaintiff and the court stress. He said:

"Some of these factors were, however, given ample consideration in the very large discounts from the market values indicated by the application of the comparative appraisal method which the experts took in arriving at their final conclusions. Others, such as the vulnerability to strikes, were not considered to be any more serious than generally applicable to manufacturing businesses. The loss of experienced sales personnel affected in no way the continually increasing sales under a new Sales Manager (appointed in 1959) who had substantial and successful experience with the company, first as a salesman and then as Assistant Sales Manager. And the long, apparently satisfactory association S & R had with its licensor, the manufacturing capacity and experience which S & R had and which the licensor did not, and the substantial royalties the licensor was receiving, would hardly lead an investor to believe that the licensor would soon decide to invest in greatly increased manufacturing facilities and go into direct competition with its licensee.

In view of the steadily increasing trend of the company's earnings during the five-year 1956-1960 period preceding the valuation date, the company's ability to establish Scrabble as a staple game in the industry, its steady growth in assets, its plant enlargement program initiated in 1960 and still in process as of the valuation date, indicating confidence by the management in the company's future, its efficient management, as demonstrated by its ability to produce good profit margins and effect good cost controls, and the particularly favorable investment climate at the date of valuation, both for stocks in general and for stocks in the game and toy industry in particular, it is concluded that the fair market value of the 337 shares of S & R stock as of April 24, 1961, was $900 per share. This is at the lowest end of the range testified to by defendant's experts. Such a valuation reflects an extremely conservative price-earnings ratio of 7.3 to 1, and a generous (as of such date) dividend yield, based on 1960 dividends, of 5.5 percent.[21] Such value would simply be approximately equal to the December 31, 1960 book value of $899.81. Based on this record, no lower valuation would appear to be warranted."[22]

In rendering a "jury verdict" of $700 per share, the court seems to me to have no sound basis at all for its finding since there is no evidence whatever pointing to any figure in that range, and the amount of $700 is not, as in some cases, within the span of conflicting expert testimony. I do not know how the court arrived at it, and the opinion does not explain. *Cf. United States v. Nez Perce Tribe of Indians*, Appeal No. 2-70, decided this day. For myself, rejecting as I do plaintiff's evidence as wholly unpersuasive, I must agree with Commissioner Gamer that our choice has to be within the range of values testified to by the Government's experts.[3] There is no adequate reason, in my view, to reject the views of these two qualified witnesses, one of whom was not connected with the Government and had had great experience in valuations of this type, especially since the trial commissioner heard and credited them.

    Laramore, Judge, and Durfee, Judge, join in the foregoing opinion dissenting in part.

[Findings of Fact omitted.] * * *

---

[21] As against the then 3.4 percent yield on the stocks composing the Dow-Jones industrial average.

[22] Plaintiff's proposed valuation of $424.90 would, based on the 1960 earnings of $123.32 per share, result in a price-earnings ratio of only 3.5 to 1 (at a time when such ratio of the four comparatives used by Mr. Goulston averaged 29.55 times earnings and the stocks in Standard & Poor's Industrial Index averaged 23 times earnings); a dividend return, based on 1960 dividends of $50 per share, of 11.3 percent (at a time when the Dow-Jones industrial stock average was 3.4 percent); and in a book value of one-half (as against the comparatives, whose prices averaged 5.76 times book value, and the stocks in Standard & Poor's Industrial Index, whose prices, as of the end of 1960, averaged around twice book value).

---

[3] Defendant errs in saying that one must accept the $1,000 figure (which the IRS used) once one concludes that plaintiff has failed to prove any lower figure. By putting in its own affirmative evidence of value, the defendant opens the way for the trier to take account of that evidence in coming to a final conclusion. Here, defendant's own evidence leads one to infer that $900 (rather than $1,000) is the better figure.

Albert L. Luce, Jr., Frances C. Luce, George E. Luce, Willouise B. Luce, Joseph P. Luce and Marilyn S. Luce, Plaintiffs v. The United States, Defendant

U.S. Claims Court, No. 519-81T, 12/13/83.

Theodore M. Forbes, Jr., Robert D. Strauss, Gambrell & Russell, for plaintiffs. Glenn L. Archer, Jr., Assistant Attorney General, Israel D. Shetreat, Theodore D. Peyser, Robert S. Watkins, Department of Justice, Washington, D. C. 20530, for defendant.

Opinion *

MILLER, Judge: This is a suit for refund of gift taxes paid with respect to gifts of stock of the Blue Bird Body Company, made in 1976 by the three Luce brothers, Albert L., Jr., George E. and Joseph P., who are the controlling stockholders of that company. On September 30, 1976, Albert gave 19,000 shares to a trust for his daughter. Thereafter, on October 29, 1976, Albert gave 2,000 additional shares directly to his daughter, and George and Joseph each gave 38,000 shares both directly to members of their families and to trusts for their benefit. There were a total of 16 gifts, consisting of 97,000 shares, 83,000 of which were in nine trusts with a common trustee, the Citizens and Southern National Bank of Macon, Georgia. The 97,000 shares represented 17 percent of the total of 582,000 shares which were outstanding.

Each donor filed a gift tax return valuing the shares at $39.31, which is equal to their book value as of September 30, 1975, the end of the prior fiscal year.

After filing appropriate claims for refund, plaintiffs [1] brought timely suit and now claim that the fair value of the gifts should more properly have been computed at $26 per share.

The Blue Bird Body Company was founded in 1927 by A. L. Luce, Sr., plaintiffs' father. By 1947 its shares were owned one-fourth by A. L. Luce, Sr., and his wife, and one-fourth by each of the three plaintiffs. Plaintiffs' father died in 1962, and by 1966 the three plaintiffs had acquired 100 percent

of the shares.

Starting in 1969 Blue Bird initiated a policy of selling some of its stock to executive employees and officers other than members of the Luce family. In March 1969 it sold 10 shares to Corbin J. Davis, an officer. Preliminary to such sale it amended its by-laws to provide that no stockholder or his heirs, personal representatives or assigns may sell, pledge or otherwise dispose of any shares until he first offers to sell them to the corporation at their book value as of the end of the next preceding fiscal year. If the corporation fails to repurchase the shares within 45 days, he is to offer them to the other stockholders pro rata at the same price. If any of the other stockholders fails to exercise his purchase rights, he is to assign them to the remaining stockholders. Only if the other stockholders fail to make the purchase, may the stock be sold to outsiders.

Thereafter, from 1969 through the corporation's fiscal year ending October 30, 1976, sixteen managerial and executive employees acquired a total of 33,429 shares of Blue Bird at book values as of the end of the fiscal years preceding their acquisitions. Some shares were sold to such employees for cash; others were issued as additional compensation. Blue Bird has bought back shares from the estate of one such employee and from two others who left its employment—always at book value as of the end of the preceding fiscal year.

In 1972 the three plaintiffs gave 139,320 shares of Blue Bird stock to eight trusts

---

* Since all of the pertinent findings of fact are contained in this opinion, pursuant to Rule 52(a) no separate findings will be filed.

[1] Although the wives are necessary parties to the suit by virtue of their election to treat the gifts as made by both husbands and wives, the term plaintiffs will be used hereinafter to refer exclusively to the husbands because they paid the taxes.

for their children and grandchildren, naming themselves as co-trustees with the Citizens and Southern National Bank of the trusts of which they were grantors.

Following the 1976 gifts, Blue Bird's stock was owned:

Owner	Shares	Percentage
Plaintiffs	312,251	53.6
Plaintiffs' children ...	14,000	2.4
Citizens and Southern National Bank as trustee or as co-trustee with plaintiffs..	222,320	38.2
Non-family executives	33,429	5.8
	582,000	100.0

Section 2512(a) of the Internal Revenue Code of 1954 provides that for gift tax purposes, "If the gift is made in property, the value thereof at the date of the gift shall be considered the amount of the gift." Treasury Regulations on Gift Tax (1954 Code) § 25.2512-1, (26 C. F. R.)), states that such value is "the price at which such property would change hands between a willing buyer and a willing seller, neither being under any compulsion to buy or sell, and both having reasonable knowledge of relevant facts."

One of the more difficult property valuation problems is the appropriate method and measure of valuation of the shares of the stock of a closely held corporation, which are not ordinarily traded on an open market. See *Righter v. United States* [71-1 USTC ¶ 12,758], 194 Ct. Cl. 400, 407, 439 F. 2d 1204, 1207 (1971). Section 2031 of the Code, relating to the estate tax, provides:

(b) Valuation of unlisted stock and securities.—In the case of stock and securities of a corporation the value of which, by reason of their not being listed on an exchange and by reason of the absence of sales thereof, cannot be determined with reference to bid and asked prices or with reference to sales prices, the value thereof shall be determined by taking into consideration, in addition to all other factors, the value of stock or securities of corporations engaged in the same or a similar line of business which are listed on an exchange.

While no similar provision appears in the gift tax sections of the Code, gift tax Regulations § 25.2512-2(f) provides that where selling prices or bid and asked prices are unavailable, the valuation of shares of stock is to be determined by taking into consideration the company's net worth, prospective earning power, dividend-paying capacity, goodwill, economic outlook in the industry, the company's position in the industry, its management, the degree of control of the business represented by the block of stock, the value of securities of corporations engaged in similar lines of business which are listed in a stock exchange, and other relevant factors. See also *Penn Yan Agway Cooperative, Inc. v. United States* [69-2 USTC ¶ 9719], 189 Ct. Cl. 434, 446, 417 F. 2d 1372, 1378 (1969); *Arc Realty Co. v. Commissioner* [61-2 USTC ¶ 9689], 295 F. 2d 98, 103 (8th Cir. 1961).

In 1976 Blue Bird was primarily a manufacturer and seller of school bus type vehicles, plus a limited number of small urban transit buses and luxury motor homes. As previously noted, the enterprise had been founded in 1927 by Mr. A. L. Luce, Sr. After their return from military service in World War II, his three sons, the plaintiffs, entered the business with him and have been in control of the business since their father's death in 1962. The business has grown steadily. In 1945 Blue Bird manufactured 750 bus bodies, in 1946, 1,000. By 1976 Blue Bird was producing 10,000 buses per year.

Approximately 56 percent of Blue Bird's 1976 sales revenue were derived from the sale of buses for which the chassis and engines were provided by the truck manufacturers, such as Ford, GM or International Harvester. The manufacturers inventoried their trucks on Blue Bird property, and Blue Bird's only obligation was to maintain insurance on them. Blue Bird built the bodies, including seats, electrical wiring and all other appurtenances, installed chassis and engines and shipped the finished buses to the customers. An additional 30 percent of Blue Bird's revenues came from the sale of buses for which Blue Bird manufactured the chassis as well as the bodies, installing, however, engines manufactured by such engine manufacturers as Ford, GM, Cummins or Caterpillar. The remaining 14 percent of sales volume was about evenly divided between urban transit buses and the motor homes.

Blue Bird's domestic sales are generated primarily through corporate or distributor competitive bidding for state, county, and local government sales. Approximately 20 to 30 percent of Blue Bird's revenues result from state purchases by competitive bid. The other source of domestic sales for Blue Bird comes from its distributor network. In 1976, this network was comprised of 54 distributors and five direct factory representatives. A distributor may sell on the basis of competitive bids or through negotiations with school boards or with contractors to school boards at the county level. In 1975 and 1976, Blue Bird was also very active in the export market, and, during that time, the export market was very strong. Large orders from Middle Eastern countries contributed to the 1975-76 growth in export sales.

Many of Blue Bird's distributors have been with the Company from 20 to 30 years. Many distribute solely Blue Bird products; however, some sell, in addition, trucks, autos, or other school equipment.

Although the school bus industry is highly competitive and school bus manufacturers generally have had the capacity to produce twice as many buses as the market demand, in 1976 Blue Bird was one of the top two or three companies in unit sales in the industry. It supplied 22.4 percent of the school buses sold in the United States, 45 percent of the school buses sold in Canada and approximately 25 percent of the school buses used for such purpose in all the other countries. It was a half-century old well-established company with a good, solid, basic market. Its facilities and machinery and equipment were in good condition and well maintained. Its principal executives had been with the company for substantial periods of time, its employees were well paid, and its labor relations were good. It had no significant long term debt

and it had a good line of credit. It had a network of franchises and qualified salesmen selling its products in the United States, Canada, and in the international markets. Its sales, production, and profits were on the rise, and its competitors had a difficult time competing with it. It had generally and consistently been a successful and profitable business; and its management had plans and expectations for boosting its profits by increasing its unit sales to 25 percent of the domestic maket by 1980, which would give it the number one spot. In fact, it achieved this goal by 1978 or 1979.

Plaintiff produced, as an expert witness to testify with respect to the fair market value of the gifts of stock at issue, Mr. Charles B. Shelton, III, First Vice President in the corporate finance department of The Robinson-Humphrey Company, Inc., a member of the New York, American and Midwest Stock Exchanges and a full-service investment banking and brokerage house.

He determined that, based on information provided by management and a review of market conditions in the fall of 1976, the difference in the values of Blue Bird's common stock on September 30 and October 29, 1976, when the two sets of gifts were made, was negligible, and accordingly valued them both as of the latter date.

He accepted as correct and without further investigation the financial information concerning the company provided by Blue Bird's management. Included were audited financial statements of Blue Bird for the fiscal years ended in October 1971 through 1975, but not for 1976. Because the financial statement for October 30, 1976, was not yet available on October 29, 1976, he substituted the company's earnings projection for the fiscal year ending October 30, 1976, made by the company in the summer of 1976. And he added a forecast for fiscal 1977, also made in the summer of 1976. He summarized the earnings record for 1971-75 as follows:

(000's omitted)	1971	1972	1973	1974	1975
Net Sales	$32,008	$36,888	$40,649	$55,123	$78,886
Earnings	2,125	2,520	2,507	2,071	6,381
Earnings Per Share	3.75	4.45	4.38	3.56	10.98
Net Profit Margin	7%	7%	6%	4%	8%

He set forth the 1976 and 1977 estimates comparatively with the actual results for 1974 and 1975 as follows:

	1974	1975	1976 Est.	1977 Est.
Units Sold	7,701	9,566	8,995	10,221
% Increase (Decease) in Units Sold...		24.2%	(6.0)%	13.6%
Earnings (000's omitted)	$2,071	$6,381	$5,932	$3,670
% Increase (Decrease) in Earnings....		208%	(7.0)%	(38.1)%

He also noted that the company's net worth as of November 1, 1975, was $22,839,000 (or $39.24 per share), and, after subtracting goodwill, that tangible net worth was $22,503,000 (or $38.73 per share).

In order to determine the value of the 97,000 shares which were the subject of the gift, he first found it necessary to value 100 percent of the equity in the company, which was represented by 582,000 shares of stock.

Mr. Shelton's report and testimony discussed various measure[s] of value for the stock of the entire company but he ultimately relied on only one.

He rejected the market comparison approach, which arrives at the value of a closely held company by applying to it the ratios which the market price of the stock of a publicly owned company in the same industry bears to its earnings, dividends and net book value, on the ground that he was unaware of any publicly traded company whose business was similar to that of Blue Bird in product, size and scope.

He rejected an asset appraisal approach to value on the ground that Blue Bird was a going concern and its management had no intention of liquidating the assets.

He found the book value of Blue Bird's net assets, or net worth, was $22,838,818 or $39.24 per share on November 1, 1975, and an estimated $28,189,000, or $48.43 per share on October 29, 1976 (after giving effect to a $1.00 per share dividend declared October 25, 1976), but rejected that too.

The only method he discussed to arrive at value on the basis of objective comparative data with respect to other companies was the capitalized excess earnings method of valuation. Under this method the average return of a company on its tangible net worth (the book value of tangible assets less liabilities) over a number of years is compared to that of its industry. To the extent that the company's average return on its tangible net worth is at a rate in excess of that prevailing in the industry generally, it is assumed that such excess earnings indicate it has intangible value (or goodwill) in excess of the value of its tangible net worth. To ascertain what that value is, that portion of the earnings is capitalized at a suitable rate commensurate with the investment risk. The product is then added to the value of the tangibles to determine total value.

In making this comparison, Mr. Shelton used the average net book value of Blue Bird's tangible assets for the years 1972-76 and the average earnings for the same years. For the industry comparisons for return on net worth, he used Annual Statement Studies for 1977, by Robert Morris Associates, covering eleven companies of similar asset size as Blue Bird, primarily engaged in manufacturing automobile bodies, or assembling complete passenger cars, trucks, commercial cars, buses and special purpose vehicles, with fiscal years ending in 1976; Standard & Poor's Automobile Index; Standard & Poor's Automobile Index excluding General Motors; Standard & Poor's Automobiles-Trucks & Parts Index and Standard & Poor's 400 Industrial Index. The comparison was as follows:

BLUE BIRD BODY COMPANY
COMPARISON OF RETURNS ON
NET WORTH RATIOS
(Using Tangible Net Worth,
Net of Goodwill)

Blue Bird Body Company
Return on Net Worth

1976	20.9% Est.
1975	28.4%
1974	12.2%
1973	16.1%
1972	18.4%
Average 1972-1976	19.2%

Robert Morris Associates
Industry Median Return
On Net Worth

1976	15.40%
1975	9.13%
1974	7.98%
1973	11.72%
1972	N.A.
Average 1973-1976	11.06%

Standard & Poor's
Automobile Index

1976	17.33%
1975	5.74%
1974	6.05%
1973	16.94%
1972	16.61%
Average 1972-1976	12.53%

Standard & Poor's Automobile
Index Excluding GM

1976	12.78%
1975	Def.
1974	3.82%
1973	12.89%
1972	12.86%
Average 1972-1976	8.47%

Standard & Poor's Automobiles-
Trucks & Parts Index

1976	14.28%
1975	Def.
1974	8.60%
1973	11.07%
1972	6.57%
Average 1972-1976	8.10%

Standard & Poor's 400
Industrial Index

1976	14.02%
1975	12.11%
1974	14.17%
1973	14.15%
1972	11.71%
Average 1972-1976	13.23%

Although over the preceding 5 years Blue Bird had earned a rate of return on tangible net worth substantially in excess of that earned by each group of comparables, nevertheless he applied a relatively low multiple, five times earnings, to the excess yield. Despite the low multiple, however, this method resulted in a total value of $32,373,000 for the whole company, equivalent to $55.62 per share.

All of the foregoing, however, appears to have been mere padding. Mr. Shelton disregarded the $39.24 and $48.43 book values, for the stated reason that the shares of some publicly held companies in the automotive industry in some years sold at prices below their book values and because he was of the opinion that earnings are generally the most important factor bearing on the value of a going concern. Also, after having gone to the trouble of making all of the foregoing calculations and comparisons, Shelton then repudiated the $55.62 value he determined by the capitalized excess earnings method of valuation because the industries whose rates of return were used were broader than Blue Bird and not largely confined to school buses, because Blue Bird's average rate of return was inflated by its 1975 high earnings level, and because the method did not consider all relevant factors.

Mr. Shelton arrived at his valuation of the company by a modified capitalization of earnings method. He averaged Blue Bird's reported earnings for 1972-75 together with the estimate for 1976 and the projection for 1977, and obtained an average earnings base of $3,847,000. Dividing this earnings base by the 20 percent capitalization rate (or applying a multiple of five times earnings) resulted in a total value for the company under this approach of $19,235,000. He then added to that figure a sum sufficient to increase the $19,235,000 to $21,500,000, without explanation other than that it was a matter of judgment. Dividing this figure by the 582,000 outstanding shares arrives at a per share value of $37 for the whole company.

Shelton then reduced the $37 per share by 30 percent to $26, for the 97,000 shares which were the subject of the gifts, because they represented in the aggregate only a 17 percent minority interest, which lacked an established market for sale to the public, and absent such a sale they were subject to the will of the controlling stockholders, who could use the corporation to benefit themselves at the expense of other stockholders.

Mr. Shelton's method of valuation is subject to criticism in several respects. First, the earnings he used are not necessarily representative of the earning capacity of the business. As the court stated in *Central Trust Co. v. United States* [62-2 USTC ¶ 12,092], 158 Ct. Cl. 504, 530, 305 F. 2d 393, 409 (1962), in using reported earnings as a basis for stock valuation, it is "proper to make such adjustments therein as would be necessary to eliminate abnormal and non-recurring items and to redistribute items of expense to their proper periods."

Blue Bird's 1974 earnings had been reduced by approximately $787,000 as a result of a one time change in the company's method of accounting. By converting from first-in first-out to last-in first-out inventory accounting in that year, Blue Bird decreased its closing inventory and pre-tax income by $1,430,800. Restoration of this sum less the offsetting tax savings attributable thereto (at the 45 percent rate used by Shelton) results in additional representative after-tax earnings of $787,000 for the year. Applying this increase to Shelton's capitalized average earnings computation results in a $1.13 per share increase in his valuation of the company.

The 1976 earnings estimate used in Mr. Shelton's earning's base, $5,932,000, was short of the earnings reported for that year, $6,381,000, by $449,000. The estimate relied on was made during the summer of 1976. However, monthly financial statements were available, and Mr. Pennington, Blue Bird's independent auditor, testified that by the end of September 1976 they would have enabled determination of the annual income with 80-90 percent accuracy. Plaintiffs have not shown that as the valuation date at issue, October 29, 1976, only one day prior to the close of the fiscal year, Blue Bird's auditors could not have furnished Mr. Shelton a closer approximation of actual earnings for the year than that made during the summer. Adjustment of the earnings base for this increase results in an additional increase of $0.64 per share in Mr. Shelton's valuation for the whole company.

The reported earnings were after reduction each year by approximately 10 percent for contributions to a private charitable trust (The Rainbow Fund) of which the three Luce brothers were the trustees. In 1976 the contribution was $575,000. It is difficult to understand why the earnings base for valuation of a company should be reduced by such a voluntary diversion of earnings which was not shown to benefit the corporation. Mr. Shelton argued that since the siphoning off of earnings by con-

trolling stockholders was adverse to a minority interest, an adjustment for this annual sum should not increase the value of the gift shares. However, it is a proper item for adjustment of the earnings base in determining the value of the entire corporation prior to computing the value of a minority interest; otherwise the witness' discount for a minority interest is duplicated. More important, once there is a significant unrelated minority interest, a serious question arises as to the right of the controlling stockholders to continue to divert a substantial share of the corporate earnings to their private charitable foundation without the consent of all of the stockholders. See *A. P. Smith Manufacturing Co. v. Barlow*, 13 N. J. 145, 98 A. 2d 581 (1953); Annot. 39 A. L. R. 2d 1192 (1955); 19 Am. Jur., Corporations § 1015; and H. Ballantine on Corporations (Rev. Ed.) § 85 at 228.

Mr. Shelton included in his earnings base a forecast of earnings for 1977, which had been prepared by the company in the summer of 1976. Although the forecast was for $3,670,100 in earnings and the actual 1977 earnings turned out to be $3,883,600, the propinquity of the forecast to the actual results (6 percent below) does not necessarily show the soundness of the forecast. It actually appears to be happenstance. The forecast was made in the summer of 1976, up to 5 months before the beginning of the 1977 fiscal year. The projection was for substantially increased sales, both in units and dollars, over prior years. The forecast of reduced earnings was based on projections of increased inflation rates and correspondingly higher material and labor costs generally, and was thought by Albert Luce to be a single year's break in the trend of increased earnings. The June 1980 report of a company official responsible for the forecast explains that the 1977 results were close to the forecast because "cost increases were not quite as great as anticipated", but "On the other hand price increases were not as great as anticipated."

The use of an earnings forecast made months prior to the start of the year, and which is based on predictions of the general inflation rate with respect to raw material and labor costs generally, as a base for capitalization of earnings is subject to great error. The unreliability of such an initial estimate may be inferred from the fact that the corresponding initial forecast for 1976 was for $2,985,800 in earnings, while actual earnings turned out to be $6,189,000, more than 100 percent higher. The risks associated with such forecasts of future earnings are more properly a function of the capitalization rate than the earnings base. To reflect a forecast of a possible earnings decrease for a single future year in both the base and the rate results in an exaggeration of the effect of such a forecast.

On November 5, 1981, Mr. Shelton prepared another valuation report for the plaintiff on the entire Blue Bird stock as of August 10, 1981, for purposes of a proposed recapitalization of the company. This did not involve a tax problem. In it he followed the same general method of valuation.

However, for the average earnings base he used the results of the 1976 through 1980 years and the estimate for 1981. The latter he derived from the results for the 7 months ending in May 1981. He did not include any forecast for 1982.

In addition, in constructing the earnings base in the 1981 valuation report, Mr. Shelton used a method of averaging which emphasizes the importance of the most recent experience. He used the sum of the digits method, which places greatest weight on the most recent years, to arrive at average earnings for 1976 to 1980, and then weighed that at 40 percent and the estimated whole year 1981 earnings at 60 percent to arrive at the average for 1976-81. Had he applied that method to his 1972-76 earnings the earnings base would have been much higher, to wit:

Year	Earnings	Weight Factor	Weighted Earnings
1972	2,519,845	× 1/10	251,984
1973	2,507,003	× 2/10	501,401
1974	2,071,386	× 3/10	621,416
1975	6,381,385	× 4/10	2,552,554
		10/10	3,927,355
		× weight factor of	40%
			1,570,942
1976	5,931,800 × weight factor of 60% =		3,559,140
Weighted Earnings Base			$5,130,082

This compares to the average earnings base of $3,847,000 he actually used to value the entire company as of October 29, 1976.

In *Central Trust Co. v. United States* [62-2 USTC ¶ 12,092], 158 Ct. Cl. at 522, 305 F. 2d at 404, the court pointed out that mere averages may be deceiving since they equate both increasing and decreasing earnings without regard to their trend, and that "the most recent years' earnings are to be accorded the greatest weight."

For the foregoing reasons, Mr. Shelton's average earnings were not a wholly reliable base for the capitalization of earnings method of valuation.

Second, Mr. Shelton's valuation of Blue Bird at $37 per share as of October 29, 1976, is unacceptable because it is almost a fourth less than the book value of its net assets less liabilities, $48.98, as of October 30, 1976, even though all but one percent of that book value was represented by tangible assets, cash and receivables. Indeed, an appraisal of the tangible assets at Blue Bird's main plants, made for insurance purposes as of December 12, 1975, established that the replacement cost of such assets less sustained depreciation was far in excess of their book value and that had it been substituted for the book figures the book value per share would have been increased to $61.65.

If a company's net worth consists of substantial write-ups of intangible value acquired in mergers or corporate acquisitions, if it has paid inflated prices for its assets, or if its machinery and equipment are obsolete, and it has consistently been unable to obtain a fair return on its investment, then the fair market value of the company may understandably be less than its book value. But the undisputed evidence here is that as of the valuation date Blue Bird's ownership had been in the same family since it was organized, its net worth was not inflated by any substantial intangible value, and its plant and equipment were in good condition and enabled it to be a dominant company in its industry. Moreover, Mr. Shelton's own computations showed that the company's returns on its tangible net worth ranged between 16.1 and 28.4 percent, with an average of 19.2 percent, over the preceding 5 years, returns far in excess of those earned in the closest comparable industries Mr. Shelton could find. A seller could hardly have been expected to be willing to accept 25 percent less for the company than the cost of duplicating the net depreciated tangible assets alone, without regard to its value as a going concern with goodwill, qaüfied personnel, an established national distributors' organization and high earning capacity; and a hypothetical buyer could also hardly have expected that he could obtain it for that price.[2] In such circumstances, it is reasonable to conclude that book value is at the least a floor under fair market value, which an appraiser may not properly ignore. *Cf. Schwartz v. C. I. R.* [77-2 USTC ¶ 13,201], 560 F. 2d 311, 316-17 (8th Cir. 1977); *Hamm v. C. I. R.* [64-1 USTC ¶ 12,206], 325 F. 2d 934, 937, 941 (8th Cir. 1963), *cert. denied*, 377 U. S. 993 (1964); *City Bank Farmers Trust Co. v. Commissioner* [CCH Dec. 7024], 23 B. T. A. 663, 669 (1931).

Third, the most serious weakness in Mr. Shelton's valuation of the company lies is in his failure to supply a rational objective basis for the key element thereof, the capi-

talization rate he applied to Blue Bird's average earnings. He testified that in his judgment "a buyer of such securities of the risks inherent in Blue Bird would look for a 20 percent return." However, he was unable to furnish any objective data with respect to any comparable situations underlying that judgment, so as to enable the court to determine whether it was soundly based. Nor could he supply any objective data which would tend to to support a judgment that a knowledgeable seller would be willing to dispose of the Blue Bird stock at a price so low as to be no more than he would have received in just 5 years of its average earnings or 3 years of its most recent earnings. When pressed, Mr. Shelton fell back on his "experience"; but he conceded he was not an expert on the market for school buses and had never sold stock of any company which manufactured or sold buses, and could not identify a single contemporaneous purchase or sale of the stock of any company in his experience which was the basis of his judgment. Nor, even omitting the names of the participants, could he described the circumstances of any comparative purchase or sale. Assuming (without necessarily deciding) the good faith of Mr. Shelton's testimony, it must be concluded that his judgment in this regard was merely intuitive and the basis therefor was not susceptible of rational or objective examination or evaluation by the court.[4]

Nor is Mr. Shelton's judgment that $2,265,000 should be added to the capitalized earnings base any more rationally founded. It is self-evident that it was added to raise the $19,235,000 to $21,500,000 in order to reach a predetermined round figure. It may also be inferred that it is in recognition that the other methods of valuation reached considerably higher figures. But why $21,500,000 rather than some other figure? It must be concluded that the wit-

---

[2] This is also supported by the fact that the controlling stockholders contemporaneously sold shares of stock and gave bonuses to executive employees at book value as of the end of the prior year and deemed the price to be at least fair to the employees.

[3] In support of the 20 percent capitalization rate, plaintiff argues that the government's expert witness used a 5.3 multiple of earnings which is not very far from Shelton's. The fact is, however, that the government's witness used a multiple of 7.7 times the 5 year average for

1972-76 and 5.3 times 1976 earnings, to arrive at a value of $54 per share. As noted hereinafter, the court finds it unnecessary to rely on the government's expert testimony.

[4] Also quoted with approval in *Continental Water Co. v. United States*, 49 A.F.T.R. 2d 82-1070, 1080 (1982), (Trial Judge, Court of Claims), adopted *per curiam* 231 Ct. Cl. —, 50 A.F.T.R. 82-5128 (1982).

ness' judgment in this regard is equally in-tuitive and not based on objective facts or reasoning susceptible of objective examina-tion or evaluation.

Plaintiffs argue in their brief that "The value of expert opinion testimony lies in the qualifications of the witness" and that it is not the court's role to reason why. But however difficult, the law has never deemed the valuation of the stock of a closely held company to be an arcane or accult craft beyond the ken of courts, which must be content to evaluate only the credibility of the expert witness. "[L]ike any other judg-ments, those of an expert can be no better than the soundness of the reasons that stand in support of them." (*Fehrs v. United States* [80-1 USTC ¶ 13,348], 223 Ct. Cl. 488, 508, 620 F. 2d, 255, 265 (1980).) The opinion of an expert witness is "no better than the convincing nature of the reasons offered in support of his testimony." (*Potts, Davis & Company v. C. I. R.* [70-2 USTC ¶ 9635], 431 F. 2d 1222, 1226 (9th Cir. 1970).) "Opinion evidence, to be of any value, should be based either upon admitted facts or upon facts, within the knowledge of the witness, disclosed in the record. Opinion evidence that does not appear to be based upon disclosed facts is of little or no value." (*Baliban & Katz Corp. v. Commis-sioner*, 30 F. 2d 807, 808 (7th Cir. 1929).)" "[I]n order for the opinion to have any value it must be based on assumptions which the trier of facts can find to have been proved." (*Rewis v. United States*, 369 F. 2d 595, 602 (5th Cir. 1966).) A court "is not required to surrender its judgment to the judgment of experts." (*Hamm v. Com-missioner* [64-1 USTC ¶ 12,206], 325 F. 2d 934, 941 (8th Cir. 1963).) And see also *The Con-queror*, 166 U. S. 110, 131-33 (1897); *Pumice Supply Co. v. C. I. R.*, 308 F. 2d 766, 769 (9th Cir. 1962); and *Gloyd v. Commissioner* [58-1 USTC ¶ 9251], 63 F. 2d 649, 650 (8th Cir.), *cert. denied*, 290 U. S. 633 (1933).

Finally, plaintiff's reliance upon Shelton's determination that the fair market value of the 97,000 shares which were the subject of the gifts should be reduced by 30 per-cent, to $26 per share, because as a minority interest without an established mar-ket they could not be sold to the public except at a substantial discount, is based

on a misconception of both the law and the facts. First, under the law, the appli-cable market in which the hypothetical willing buyer may be found need not be one which includes the general public. It is sufficient if there are potential buyers among those closely connected with the corpora-tion.

In *Rothgery v. United States* [73-1 USTC ¶ 12,911], 201 Ct. Cl. 183, 189, 475 F. 2d 591, 594 (1973), there was at issue the valuation for estate tax purposes of 50 per-cent of the stock of an automobile dealer-ship, the remaining 50 percent being owned by the decedent's son. Since there was no public market for the shares, the court found the value of the entire stock from the book value and appraisals of the un-derlying assets less the liabilities, and then allocated that value on a per share basis. The court responded to the estate's argu-ment that the pro rata allocation was ex-cessive because there was no public market for the decedent's shares and because the 50 percent interest of the estate was not a controlling interest, by finding that the decedent's son would have been a willing buyer of the shares from any hypothetical seller; that the son intended to continue the corporate business after his father's death; that he wished to have control of the corporation, so that his own son might have a place in the business; that this ob-jective required the acquisition of the dece-dent's stock interest in the corporation; and that the evidence warranted the inference that the son would have been willing to pay —and from a business standpoint would have been justified in paying—for the de-cedent's half-interest in the corporation an amount equal to half the value of the corporation's assets. This was a market sufficient to negate any need for a dis-count to sell the shares.

In *Couzens v. Commissioner* [CCH Dec. 3931], 11 B. T. A. 1040 (1928), the Board of Tax Appeals was required to find the value of the Ford Motor Company stock on March 1, 1913, in order to determine the late Senator Couzen's gain on the sale of his stock in 1920. Prior to the 1920 sale only ten individuals were the sole stockholders, there was no public market for the stock, and there was a restriction on the certificates giving existing shareholders the prior right to purchase the stock at the price at which it was offered to an outsider. The Commissioner argued that the limited market for the shares under such circumstances depressed the value of a minority interest below the fair market value of the shares as a whole and would have necessitated a substantial discount to make them saleable to a willing buyer. In rejecting this contention, the court stated (11 B. T. A. at 1164):

> We do not construe a fair market as meaning that the whole world must be a potential buyer, but only that there are sufficient persons available to buy to assure a fair and reasonable price in the light of the circumstances affecting value.[8]

On cross-examination, Mr. Shelton likewise concurred that if the company or its controlling stockholders pursued a policy of buying back shares from persons who were not family members or executive employees, that fact could put a greater value on the shares by providing a potential market for them.

The record in this case establishes that there was indeed an available market for the shares at issue within the company or among persons associated with the company. Plaintiff Albert L. Luce testified that it was company and Luce policy that all shares of Blue Bird's stock remain in the ownership of members of the Luce family, of trusts for their benefit, and of executive employee. This purpose motivated the adoption of the by-law in 1969, when shares were first offered to executive employee Corbin Davis, requiring any stockholder desiring to dispose of his shares to offer them first to the corporation and then to the remaining stockholders at book value. Thereafter, whenever shares were offered to an employee, Albert Luce personally told him that the company would repurchase the shares at book value if he left the company, died or desired to dispose of the shares for any other reason, and the company has in fact followed this practice.

The company's purpose for the by-law and commitment was explained by Albert as follows:

> As we offered the stock to other members, other than the Luce family, and to some of our top executives, we did not want them to dispose of their stock to our competitors or someone we would not want to know more details about our operation or our business.

He elaborated on this theme that they wanted control of the company to remain in the family and that it was their intent that no shares be held by strangers generally. Accordingly, no shares have ever been sold to outsiders.

The same intent prevailed with respect to the shares given to the trustee for the benefit of other members of their family. Luce testified that had the trustee desired to sell any of the shares on the open market he would not have allowed it, but would have bought it back, because, as a major stockholder, he wanted to retain control of the block of stock, he wanted it to remain in the family, and he had no intention of allowing it to go to outsiders. Furthermore, he conceded he would even have paid "a premium over whatever the fair market value might be not to let any Blue Bird shares get outside the Luce family and the executives or corporate management."

Even without regard to the personal funds of the Luce brothers and their families, it is clear that as of October 29, 1976, Blue Bird had the financial resources to pay for the 97,000 shares at the $39.31 1975 book value at which they were reported on the gift tax returns if they were offered to it by the trustee or by a willing buyer from the trustee. The cost of such a purchase would have been $3,813,070. The company's financial report as of October 30, 1976, shows it had net current assets (less current liabilities) of $13,375,405, of which cash and receivables were $4,697,151, and, in addition, it owned $3,480,597 in cash

---

[8] Accord: *Estate of Goldstein v. Commissioner* [CCH Dec. 24,086], 33 T. C. 1032, 1037 (1960), affirmed on another issue, 340 F. 2d 24 (2d Cir. 1965); *Smith v. Commissioner*, 46 B. T. A. 340-41 (1942), mod., *sub nom., Worcester County Trust Co. v. Commissioner* [43-1 USTC ¶ 10,029], 134 F. 2d 578 (1st Cir. 1943).

[9] Neither of the other plaintiffs testified. Joseph Luce was hospitalized at the time of trial, but no explanation was given for George's absence, nor was any effort made to obtain Joseph's testimony at another time. It is assumed therefore that there was no divergence as to the facts and Albert spoke for all three.

value of life insurance on the lives of its officers, against which it could borrow at will. It also had a good line of credit and substantial borrowing capacity, its long term liabilities being no more than $1.7 million, which was less than 6 percent of equity.

In addition to the corporation itself and its controlling stockholders there was a further market for the shares among the other managerial employees of Blue Bird. Corbin Davis, the company's vice-president for marketing, testified without contradiction that since 1976 fifteen to twenty other managerial employees who were offered stock in the corporation at book value took the opportunity to purchase it and that there were 200 other employees in the management team, every one of whom would have been eager to purchase shares at the same price if it had been offered to him.

Thus, there was no occasion for a 30 percent discount in order for the hypothetical seller to find a willing buyer.

In a suit for refund of federal income taxes, the taxpayer bears the burden of proving that he has overpaid his taxes.

This means that not only must he establish that the assessment was erroneous, but also the amount which is correct. *United States v. Janis* [76-2 USTC ¶ 16,229], 428 U. S. 433, 440 (1976), *Helvering v. Taylor*, 293 U. S. 507, 514 (1935); *Lewis v. Reynolds* [3 USTC ¶ 856], 284 U. S. 281 (1932); *E. I. DuPont De Nemours & Co. v. United States* [79-2 USTC ¶ 9633], 221 Ct. Cl. 333, 349-50, 608 F. 2d 445, 454 (1979), cert. denied, 445 U. S. 962 (1980); *Dysart v. United States* [65-1 USTC ¶ 9188], 169 Ct. Cl. 276, 340 F. 2d 624 (1965). Since plaintiffs paid gift taxes on their gifts of 97,000 shares on the basis of a $39.31 per share value, plaintiffs are only entitled to a refund if they can demonstrate the extent to which such value was excessive. Plaintiffs have failed to prove by their evidence that any portion of the $39.31 per share was excessive.[1] Accordingly, it is unnecessary to review the testimony of defendant's valuation witnesses and defendant's other arguments, such as the argument that the prices the employees paid for their stock and the deductions the corporation took on its tax return for the stock bonuses are actual transactions more persuasive than opinions on hypothetical facts.

---

[1] Indeed, to the contrary, a fair inference may be drawn that on October 29, 1976, no hypothetical informed seller with knowledge of the results shown in the monthly audit reports would have been willing to sell his shares at the $39.31 book value as of the end of the prior year, when, by waiting only one or two additional days, in all probability he could have commanded a $48.98 price, the book value as of October 30, 1976.

Estate of Mark S. Gallo, R.J. Gallo, Administrator v. Commissioner. Docket No. 24465-82. T.C. Memo. 1985-363. Filed July 22, 1985.

M. Bernard Aidinoff, Philip L. Graham, Jr., Henry Christensen III, Florence A. Davis and Dean C. Berry, Sullivan & Cromwell, 125 Broad St., N. Y., N. Y. and William D. McKee and Paul J. Sax, Orrick, Herrington & Sutcliffe, 600 Montgomery St., San Francisco, Calif., for the petitioner. Alan S. Beinhorn, for the respondent.

Memorandum Findings of Fact and Opinion

COHEN, Judge: Respondent determined a deficiency of $347,871 in petitioner's Federal estate tax. The issue for decision is the date-of-death value of a certain minority interest in the common stock of a closely held corporation.

Findings of Fact

Some of the facts have been stipulated and are so found. The stipulation of facts and exhibits attached thereto are incorporated herein.

Mark S. Gallo (decedent) died on November 1, 1978 (the valuation date), at the age of 16 years. R. J. Gallo (petitioner), father of decedent and administrator of his estate, timely filed the Federal estate tax returns with the Internal Revenue Service Center in Fresno, California. Decedent's gross estate included 1,178 shares of Class J common stock of Dry Creek Corporation (Dry Creek) held by three separate minority trusts, the assets of which were subject to decedent's powers of appointment.

Petitioner reported the stock on decedent's estate tax return at a value of $290 per share or $341,620 in the aggregate and timely paid a tax of $77,583. In the notice of deficiency, respondent valued the stock at $1,043 per share or $1,228,654 in the aggregate. At the end of trial, the Court granted petitioner's oral motion to amend the petition to conform to the evidence and to claim an overpayment.

Overview of Dry Creek

Dry Creek was a Delaware corporation organized on December 19, 1973. On the valuation date, Dry Creek had outstanding both voting common stock and cumulative preferred stock.

The common stock consisted of two classes, Class E and Class J, with an equal of number of shares of each class outstanding. Except for a small number of shares held by charity, descendants of Ernest Gallo (Ernest) owned all of the outstanding Class E common stock, with one-half being owned by the family of his son Joseph E. Gallo and one-half being owned by the family of his son David E. Gallo. Descendants of Julio Gallo (Julio) owned all of the outstanding Class J common stock, with one-half being owned by the family of his son, petitioner, and one-half being owned by the family of his daughter, Susann G. Coleman. No holder of Class J stock held Class E stock; no holder of Class E stock held Class J stock. The shares of Class J common stock includible in decedent's gross estate constituted less than 2 percent of the outstanding Class J common stock.

The Board of Directors of Dry Creek consisted of six members, three elected by majority vote of the outstanding Class E common stock and three elected by majority vote of the oustanding Class J common stock. The directors served for 3-year staggered terms, with the Class E shareholders and the Class J shareholders each electing one director each year. A majority vote of each class of directors was required for any action requiring a vote of directors.

Other than the election of directors, any corporate action requiring a vote of the common shareholders required approval of a majority of both the Class E and Class J stockholders, voting separately.

Common stock of Dry Creek had never been listed on an exchange or traded in any market. The only sales of Dry Creek common stock that have ever occurred were aggregate sales after the valuation date of 305 Class J shares held by two of the minority trusts for decedent to the third trust. As of the valuation date, no dividends had ever been declared or paid with respect to the common stock of Dry Creek.

Dry Creek issued the preferred stock in connection with a recapitalization in 1976. Ernest and Julio owned substantially all of the preferred shares outstanding on the valuation date. The preferred stock was entitled to a cumulative annual dividend of a fixed amount per share, which had been paid in full through the valuation date with respect to all outstanding preferred shares. Dry Creek generally could, at its option, redeem any portion of the preferred stock after January 1, 1982, at a predetermined price per share that varied slightly, depending upon the year of redemption. Under a sinking fund provision, Dry Creek was required to redeem for a fixed price per share any preferred shares held on or after January 1, 1984, by any owner other than a member of the Gallo family. Although the preferred stock generally did not possess voting rights, the holders of the preferred stock were entitled to elect two additional directors of Dry Creek, if either dividends on the preferred stock were in default in the amount of six quarterly dividends or Dry Creek failed to redeem shares as required in the sinking fund provision.

Dry Creek maintained a policy against public disclosure of financial information. As of the valuation date, Dry Creek had never made available to the public financial information concerning Dry Creek or its subsidiaries.

As of the valuation date, it had always been and continued to be Dry Creek's policy to remain closely held by the Gallo family. No holders of the common stock intended to sell any of his or her shares to outsiders.

Dry Creek was primarily a holding company and its principal asset was all of the stock of its wholly owned subsidiary, E. & J. Gallo Winery (Gallo), a California corporation. Any other assets or operations of Dry Creek did not materially affect the value of Dry Creek.

Founded as a partnership in 1933 by Ernest and Julio, Gallo was the largest producer of wine in the United States as of the valuation date. Ernest and Julio made all policy decisions and actively man-

aged Gallo. Ernest was chairman of the board of directors of both Dry Creek and Gallo and was responsible for sales, marketing, and distributor relations. Julio was president and a director of both Dry Creek and Gallo and was responsible for grower relations, winemaking, production, bottling, and shipping. The second generation of Gallo family members established careers with Dry Creek and Gallo and were active in management. Ernest's sons participated in his area of the business, and Julio's son and son-in-law participated in his area.

Gallo had three principal winemaking facilities in California—one in Fresno, one in Livingston, and one adjacent to the corporate headquarters in Modesto. Gallo also owned all of the shares of Gallo Glass Company (Gallo Glass), a bottle manufacturer in Modesto. Gallo Glass sold all of its output to Gallo and satisfied all of Gallo's bottle needs.

Gallo sold its products through independent distributors, with the exception of three distributorships in which Gallo had an interest, to retail outlets primarily in the United States and Canada.

The U. S. Wine Industry

As part of the alcoholic beverage industry, the wine industry was a licensed industry subject to excise taxes. The Federal Government and each of the states regulated sales, methods of operation and production, recordkeeping, labeling, packaging, advertising, interstate shipments, and trade practices.

The U. S. wine industry classified wine products in four principal categories: table wines, sparkling wines, dessert wines, and special natural wines. Table wines were unflavored wines containing not more than 14 percent alcohol by volume. Sparkling wines possessed natural carbonation and contained not more than 14 percent alcohol. Dessert wines were unflavored wines containing more than 14 percent alcohol and included sherry and port. Special natural wines were flavored and included wines made from fruit other than grapes.

The industry further classified table wines as either varietal or generic. Varietal table wines were identified by a specific grape variety (e. g., Cabernet Sauvignon). As of the valuation date, Federal regulations required that at least 51 percent of the wine sold under a varietal label be produced from the indicated grape variety. Generic table wines contained less than 51 percent of any single variety. Varietal wines generally were considered to be of higher quality and commanded higher prices than generic wines of the same producer.

The U. S. wine market possessed three major price segments: low, popular, and premium.

Total wine sales in the United States increased from 163 million gallons in 1960 to 434.7 million gallons in 1978. For the period 1970 to 1978, the greatest increase occurred from 1970 through 1972, when sales grew at a 12 percent compound annual rate. Growth slowed to a 4.3 percent compound annual rate from 1972 through 1978. In 1978 certain industry analysts predicted that wine sales would reach 1 billion gallons per year by 1990.

The various categories and price segments within the wine industry did not share equally in this growth. In general, wines perceived by consumers as possessing relatively high quality and selling for relatively high prices enjoyed greatest sales growth. From 1972 through 1978, a representative sample of wine producers in the low, popular, and premium price segments experienced compound annual growth rates in gallon sales of 1.43 percent, 13.00 percent, and 20.41 percent, respectively.

From 1970 to 1978, annual table wine sales increased by 129 percent, from 133 million gallons to 304.3 million gallons, while annual sales of all other wines decreased by 3 percent. Although annual sales of special natural wines grew steadily through 1972, sales peaked at 72.8 million gallons in that year and declined to 50.5 million gallons in 1978. Sales of dessert wines decreased from 71.9 million gallons in 1972 to 54.2 million gallons in 1978, and annual sales of sparkling wines increased only modestly. Thus the share of the wine market represented by table wines increased from 50 percent in 1972 to 70 percent in 1978. The growth in table wines and decline in dessert and special natural wines were largely attributable to the emerging consumer preference for popular and premium price wines.

During the 1970's domestic wine producers encountered strong and increasingly successful competition from foreign producers. From 1970 through 1978, the sales of imported wines in the United States grew at a much higher rate than sales of domestic wines. Imports increased their U. S. market share from 11 percent in 1970 to 22 percent in 1978. Among the factors contributing to the growth in imports were consumer perception that imports possessed higher quality and European export subsidies provided in response to vast surpluses in Europe. In contrast to the U. S. import market, the potential for successfully exporting U. S. wine was minimal.

Gallo's Position in the Wine Industry

From 1952 through 1972, Gallo was the generally acknowledged leader of the wine industry in every respect. Throughout that period, Gallo grew in size each year, possessed the largest and best distributor organization and sales force in the industry, constituted the only marketing-oriented firm in the industry, and successfully introduced a number of new wine products. After developing the special natural wines Thunderbird, Ripple, and Boone's Farm, Gallo's annual sales of wines in that category grew substantially during 1960 through 1972, before peaking in the latter year at 47.5 million gallons. Gallo's total sales of over 109 million gallons in 1972 represented 32 percent of the U. S. market.

Gallo did not fully share, however, in the growth of the U. S. wine market from 1972 through 1978. Whereas total sales in the industry grew steadily from 337 million gallons in 1972 to 434.7 million gallons in 1978, Gallo's volume declined to 107.5 million gallons in 1978, or 25 percent of the market. Moreover, from 1973 through 1976, Gallo averaged sales of only approximately 100 million gallons annually. Although Gallo's sales of table wines increased from 42 million gallons in 1972 to 60.5 million gallons in 1978, sales of special natural wines fell from their peak in 1972 to 25.4 million gallons in 1978.

A number of factors prevented Gallo's sales from keeping pace with the industry.

By 1972 Gallo had become a mature company with its vast national distribution system in place. Gallo thus could achieve further growth only by increasing sales in established markets, and merely maintaining sales at current levels became a tremendous burden.

The 1970's marked the entry of several diversified and well-financed companies with strong marketing experience into the wine industry, often through purchasing wine producers previously owned by families or agricultural cooperatives. In 1978 four of the five largest domestic suppliers of wine after Gallo were Heublein, Inc., National Distillers and Chemical Company, The Cola Cola Company, and Joseph E. Seagram and Sons—all of which were much larger than Gallo in terms of total assets, revenues, and profits. Thus, for the first time in its history, Gallo confronted effective marketing competition. Although Gallo increased its advertising substantially each year and continued to lead the industry in advertising expenditures as of 1978, Gallo's share of total industry advertising and its share of display space in wine retail establishments were steadily declining.

In August of 1976, Gallo consented to an order by the Federal Trade Commission, which prevented Gallo from engaging in certain relationships with its independent distributors. As a result of the order, distributors that had previously sold only Gallo wines began to sell wines of competitors as well.

As of the valuation date, 21 states maintained affirmation laws or warranty regulations requiring that alcoholic beverage sales within that state be at the producer's lowest U. S. price. Such provisions presented a dilemma to a wine producer, like Gallo, with national distribution: it risked losing market share in any local market if it did not meet the local market price, but must lower prices in the affirmation or warranty states if it did. This dilemma permitted certain importers who emphasized east coast markets to capture sales volume from Gallo.

Changing consumer tastes, however, represented the most significant reason for the changing role of Gallo in the industry. Virtually all of Gallo's products, including its table wines, were positioned in the low price market segment. Indeed, its most successful products prior to 1972 were special natural wines. With the shift in consumer preferences to popular and premium price wines, Gallo suffered, unfairly in the opinion of its management, from a reputation as a producer of inexpensive and lower quality wines. This image problem impeded attempts by Gallo to compete with the popular price producers in the table wine market and to introduce successful new products after 1972.

Almaden, Paul Masson, Inglenook, Taylor, and Sebastiani—often referred to collectively as the "AMITS" brands—were the primary producers in the popular price segment. Most of the AMITS producers historically produced varietal wines, but in the late 1960's they began to produce lower price generic table wines in competition with Gallo. Possessing reputations for high quality, the AMITS producers were able to attract considerable sales volume, to charge higher prices than Gallo, and to relegate Gallo to the role of "price follower" in this market segment. The entry of imported wines into the segment exacerbated Gallo's competitive problems. Thus, although Gallo's annual table wine sales increased by almost 50 percent from 1972 to 1978, its market share of table wines fell from 25 percent in 1972 to 20 percent in 1978.

In contrast to Gallo's experience prior to 1972, virtually all of its new wine products introduced between 1972 and 1978 were failures. These unsuccessful products included a special natural wine similar to Boone's Farm, various products designed to compete with imports, and a line of varietal wines to compete with the AMITS brands. The varietal wines never comprised more than 2 percent of Gallo's total annual sales, even though Gallo initially priced them equal to the lowest price AMITS generic wines and subsequently lowered prices almost to the level of Gallo generics.

As of the valuation date, Gallo planned to reintroduce its line of varietal table wines and had made a substantial investment in plant and equipment to produce the new varietals. Gallo's director of marketing research was pessimistic concerning the success of the line, however, in light of studies he conducted of consumer preferences and Gallo's image.

Gallo's ability to produce all of its bottle needs (through Gallo Glass) historically provided a unique efficiency advantage. By the valuation date, however, a major competitor in the wine industry began producing bottles. Moreover, independent bottle producers, who supplied most other wine producers, held bottle prices fixed for several years immediately prior to the valuation date, a time during which Gallo Glass' production costs increased substantially. Gallo had a large investment in Gallo Glass which was subject to the risk that plastic and "bag-in-the-box" containers would become widely utilized [in] the U. S. wine market.

As of the valuation date, Ernest and Julio were 69 and 68 years old, respectively. Although the second generation of Gallo family members possessed substantial management ability, the talents that Ernest and Julio possessed as top management would be difficult to duplicate.

In sum, although Gallo remained the largest wine producer in the United States, with a market share almost double that of the second largest producer, its performance in the years immediately preceding the valuation date and its prospects for the future were not as bright as its record prior to 1972. Gallo experienced a substantial decline in its total market share and weakness in traditional areas of strength. In light of its image as a quantity producer of inexpensive wines, Gallo appeared ill-equipped to take advantage of emerging trends in the industry.

Financial Condition of Gallo [1]

Gallo's earnings generally declined during 1972 through 1978.[2] Although nominal revenues increased steadily each year and were approximately 50 percent higher in 1978 than in 1972, after adjustment for inflation, revenues in 1978 were virtually equivalent to revenues in 1972. Cost of sales increased by 70 percent over the period. These figures reflected the shift in Gallo's product mix to

a higher percentage of table wines, which were more expensive to produce than special natural and dessert wines. Moreover, most of the growth in Gallo's table wine sales occurred in its Carlo Rossi label, the less profitable of its two primary table wine labels.

Although earnings in 1977 and 1978 were each only approximately one-half of 1972 earnings, this downward trend was by no means steady; earnings were very erratic over the 7-year period. Earnings in 1978 approximately equaled average earnings over the 5-year period immediately preceding the valuation date.

The volatile price of grapes, the most significant cost variable for Gallo, was primarily responsible for the fluctuations in earnings. Gallo grew in its own vineyards only 5 percent of its grape requirements. It purchased approximately 83 percent of its requirements from independent growers under multi-year contracts in which Gallo guaranteed the grower the higher of market price or a fixed minimum price for his entire crop.

Reflecting the increased marketing competition in the wine industry, selling and advertising expenses in 1978 were approximately 60 percent higher than in 1972. General and administrative expenses nearly doubled over this period.

The annual dividend requirements on Dry Creek preferred stock outstanding as of the valuation date equaled approximately 40 percent of Gallo's average annual earnings for the 5-year period immediately preceding the valuation date. Gallo's earnings in 1978 were not sufficient to support any dividends to common shareholders of Dry Creek.

Gallo's balance sheet as of August 31, 1978, indicated that Gallo possessed a sound financial position and carried relatively little debt. Gallo's fiscal year, however, ended immediately prior to the processing of the annual grape crop, which Gallo typically financed with substantial short-

---

[1] By order of the Court, numerous portions of the record were sealed at petitioner's request. Because most of such confidential evidence consists of sensitive financial information relating to Gallo, we have, to the extent possible, minimized specific findings concerning Gallo's financial condition. We have nevertheless considered the entire record, and our general findings are consistent therewith.

[2] Gallo maintained its financial records on the fiscal year ending August 31.

term borrowings. The average month-end balance of such debt for fiscal year 1978 was almost three times greater than the balance on August 31.

Economic Conditions as of the Valuation Date

In 1976, 1977, and 1978, the U. S. gross national product grew at rates of 5.4 percent, 5.5 percent, and 5.0 percent, respectively, and the rate of inflation (measured by the consumer price index) was 5.7 percent, 6.5 percent, and 7.6 percent, respectively. Interest rates increased over this period, most sharply in the year preceding the valuation date. The prime rate charged by Bank of America was 7.25 percent, 6.25 percent, 7.75 percent, and 10.5 percent on January 1, 1976, January 1, 1977, January 1, 1978, and November 1, 1978, respectively. The average price-earnings ratio for Standard and Poor's 400 Industrial Stocks was 10.4, 9.6, and 8.2 for the years 1976, 1977, and 1978, respectively, and the ratio for the Dow Jones Industrials was 10.4, 9.3, and 7.1 for those years, respectively. As of the valuation date, several respected economists predicted a recession in 1979.

Expert Valuations

Petitioner's primary expert witnesses, Ross J. Cadenasso (Cadenasso) and William A. Shutzer (Shutzer), and respondent's expert witness, Glenn M. Desmond (Desmond), utilized similar approaches in valuing the stock in issue. Each expert concluded that the value of Dry Creek was essentially equal to the value of Gallo. Determining the value of Dry Creek stock thus, entailed determining the value of Gallo, taking into account Dry Creek's capital structure. The experts first estimated the amount for which Dry Creek common stock would sell, if traded in an active public market, based primarily upon comparisons of various financial and operating data of Gallo with data of publicly traded companies. The experts all concluded that, as of the valuation date, there existed only two publicly traded wine companies and only one, Canandaigua Wine Company (Canandaigua), was even remotely comparable to Gallo. The experts therefore selected additional comparable companies from other industries, including the beer,

distilled spirits, food, and soft drink industries. From the estimate based on comparables, the experts deducted a percentage discount because shares in Dry Creek were not publicly traded. Despite the similarity in methodology, the ultimate value of the 1,178 Class J common shares determined by respondent's expert far exceeded the values determined by petitioner's experts.

Cadenasso

Cadenasso was a self-employed corporate financial consultant and appraiser of corporations and corporate securities. He was previously employed for a number of years by a large, national investment banking firm and served for eight years as vice president in the corporate finance department of that firm.

Petitioner reported the 1,178 Class J shares on decedent's estate tax return at $290 per share, the value for which Cadenasso appraised the shares in a report dated March 1, 1979. Cadenasso prepared an additional report dated April 4, 1984, in which he described in greater detail the valuation process that he used in 1979.

Cadenasso first analyzed the U. S. wine industry and Gallo's position therein. He noted that the industry experienced considerable growth during the years preceding the valuation date and that Gallo remained the largest producer and marketer of wines as of the valuation date. Cadenasso nevertheless concluded that Gallo would probably continue to have difficulty sustaining market share in the years after the valuation date for the following reasons: Gallo's failure to exploit the higher price segments of the table wine market, the fastest growing portion of that market; the entry of large, marketing-oriented companies into the wine industry, which diminished the competitive advantage traditionally enjoyed by Gallo in that area; the vigorous growth of imported wines; the expected continuing decline of dessert and special natural wines, which remained a significant portion of Gallo's sales as of the valuation date; and the 1976 consent order with the Federal Trade Commission.

Cadenasso next examined Gallo's financial statements for the 5 years immediately preceding the valuation date and computed various financial relationships therefrom. Although Cadenasso considered Gallo's balance sheet and compiled data therefrom, he concluded that such data were not as useful in valuing Gallo as were profitability, sales and earnings growth, and consistency in earnings. Cadenasso believed that a stock's price-earnings ratio (market price per share divided by earnings per share), computed using earnings that are representative of the company's earnings power, was a reliable indicator of market value and the ratio most widely used by investors.

Cadenasso selected 10 companies for comparison with Gallo. In addition to Canandaigua, Cadenasso chose five distilling companies and four brewing companies. Cadenasso believed that distillers and brewers provided useful comparisons because they operated in the same regulated environment as Gallo and their products competed with wine to some extent. Moreover, Cadenasso noted that three of the distillers selected as comparables owned significant California wineries. All of the comparables chosen by Cadenasso were successful companies with substantial trading volume in their stocks. Cadenasso concluded that the stock of four of the comparables possessed above-average investment attractiveness and quality and that six of the companies were average or below average.

Cadenasso ranked Gallo and the 10 comparables in terms of return on common equity, both for the immediately preceding year and for the average of the preceding 5 years; growth in sales and earnings over the preceding ·5 years; and earnings consistency, measured by the number of years earnings declined over the preceding 5 years and the total percentage decline in those years. Gallo ranked last among the 11 companies and at or near the bottom in all six measures of investment merit.

Cadenasso concluded that the fair market value of Dry Creek common stock would have been $450, per share on the valuation date, if the stock were publicly traded. At this price, the stock's price-earnings ratio would be among the highest of the six comparables considered average or below average and its price-book value ratio (market price per share divided by

book value per share) would be among the lowest of those companies. Cadenasso believed that this latter figure reflected that Gallo's profitability was the lowest among the group.

Because Dry Creek stock was not publicly traded, Cadenasso believed the value of the Class J shares to be at least 35 percent below the $450 per share figure. He therefore computed a final value of $290 per share.

Shutzer

In February 1984, Gallo retained Shearson Lehman/American Express Inc. (Lehman Brothers), an investment banking firm, to value the 1,178 shares of Class J stock as of the valuation date. Shutzer was a managing director of Lehman Brothers and participated in the appraisal of the Dry Creek stock. In early March 1984, Lehman Brothers determined a value of $237 per share. Shutzer then communicated this value to Gallo prior to Lehman Brothers' receiving any notice of the value reported on decedent's estate tax return or the conclusions reached by Cadenasso or Desmond. Lehman Brothers prepared a detailed report dated November 9, 1984, supporting its opinion as to value, and Shutzer was petitioner's principal expert witness at trial.

The valuation process used and conclusions reached by Lehman Brothers were quite similar to those of Cadenasso. After a detailed analysis of Gallo, the wine industry, and economic conditions as of the valuation date, Lehman Brothers compared Gallo with Canandaigua and representative companies in the brewing, distilling, soft drink, and single discretionary food product industries. Lehman Brothers selected the three additional beverage industries because they all competed somewhat and because the brewing and distilling companies operated in the same regulated environment as wine companies. It believed that producers of single product discretionary foods were, like Gallo, subject to fluctuations in agricultural raw material prices and to competitive market conditions. Lehman Brothers concluded that the brewing industry was most comparable to the wine industry because the two industries exhibited similar growth patterns (although growth was higher in the wine industry and was declining in the beer industry), competition among marketing-oriented companies, and product market segmentation.

Lehman Brothers believed that an investor might use one or more of the following ratio-based methods in valuing closely held stock: price-earnings, price-book value, dividend capitalization (annual dividends per share divided by market price per share), adjusted operating profit capitalization (income from operations plus interest and depreciation divided by market value of total outstanding shares plus long-term debt and other long-term liabilities), and price-revenues (market price per share divided by net revenues per share). Because stock price or value is an element of each ratio, an investor can appraise a stock by determining all elements of the ratio other than stock value and estimating the aggregate ratio by comparisons with publicly traded companies, whose ratios are readily computable.

Lehman Brothers believed that, whatever method used, the valuation of an operating business implicitly entailed an estimate of the future earnings potential of the business and that the price-earnings ratio most directly and unambiguously reflected the financial markets' assessment of such future earnings potential. According to Lehman Brothers, price-earnings was the ratio it and other investment banking firms primarily used in stock and business valuations and was most often considered by investors. Lehman Brothers believed that dividend capitalization was not useful for valuing Dry Creek common stock in part because Dry Creek's ability to pay dividends on common shares was "questionable at best" in light of preferred stock dividend requirements. Lehman Brothers considered price-revenues useful where, unlike Gallo, the subject company had little earnings history, but misleading for comparing firms in different industries and with different operating characteristics and cost structures. Lehman Brothers concluded that price-book value was an unreliable indicator of value because historic asset cost often did not reflect future earnings potential. It believed that adjusted operating profit capi-

talization was misleading for a company like Gallo that must reinvest cash flow and whose debt reported at year end was not representative of debt carried during the year. Lehman Brothers therefore used primarily the price-earnings ratio in valuing Gallo based upon comparative analysis.

Lehman Brothers did not, however, rely exclusively upon historical earnings or earnings-based financial data in valuing Dry Creek stock under the price-earnings method. In estimating the price-earnings ratio for which Dry Creek common would trade in a public market, Lehman Brothers carefully compared Gallo with each of the comparable companies and considered all factors that Lehman Brothers believed might affect the ratio. In addition to relative earnings data, these factors included relative size, market share, financial security, brand loyalty, diversification, and dividend-paying capacity. For example, Lehman Brothers concluded that Dry Creek stock would sell for a higher multiple of earnings than would Canandaigua, even though Canandaigua realized substantially greater earnings growth and return on equity than Gallo. Lehman Brothers ultimately assigned Dry Creek stock a price-earnings ratio near the average for the comparable companies in the brewing and discretionary food industries, although most of those companies experienced operating results far superior to Gallo's.

After assigning a preliminary price-earnings ratio to Dry Creek stock based upon comparisons of Gallo with each of the comparable companies, Lehman Brothers undertook similar comparative analyses using the price-book value and adjusted operating profit capitalization ratios. Although Lehman Brothers compared Gallo only with Canandaigua and the brewing companies under these methods, the results confirmed the reasonableness of the preliminary price-earnings ratio.

Lehman Brothers next examined Gallo's balance sheet and considered whether the value of Gallo's assets might justify a higher valuation for Dry Creek stock than an appraisal under the price-earnings method. Because Gallo's assets consisted primarily of operating wineries and bottle plants that could not productively be put to any other use, Lehman Brothers concluded that any liquidation value of Gallo's assets would not exceed the preliminary price-earnings valuation. Lehman Brothers specifically considered whether Gallo possessed any goodwill or other intangible asset value.

Lehman Brothers concluded that Dry Creek common shares would trade in a public market for $370 per share, computed by multiplying the estimated price-earnings ratio times Gallo's 1978 earnings (plus an immaterial amount of Dry Creek earnings) per share of Dry Creek common stock. Lehman Brothers then discounted the $370 figure by 36 percent to reflect that Dry Creek stock was not actively traded, yielding a final value of $237 per share.

Desmond

Desmond owned a firm specializing in the valuation of businesses and business assets. Respondent engaged Desmond in 1983 to value the 1,178 Dry Creek Class J shares as of the valuation date.

In performing a comparative analysis similar to the approaches of Cadenasso and Lehman Brothers, Desmond selected Canandaigua and 15 companies engaged in the brewing, distilling, and food processing industries. The 15 companies included two brewers and four distillers also selected by both Cadenasso and Lehman Brothers.

Desmond's report included a schedule listing 16 asset, leverage, turnover, and earnings relationships realized in 1976, 1977, and 1978 by Gallo and each of the 16 comparables. In 1978, Gallo ranked average (i. e., ninth) among the 17 companies with respect to two relationships, above average with respect to five relationships, and below average with respect to nine relationships. Gallo ranked below average in 1978 with respect to each of the earnings relationships and last in both pre-tax and after-tax return on equity.

Desmond computed values for Dry Creek

using each of the five ratios considered by Lehman Brothers.[2] He first determined, with respect to each ratio, the range exhibited by the 16 comparables, after eliminating the companies with the two highest and two lowest ratios. Based on these ranges, Desmond then assigned to Gallo ratios that, under each of the five valuation methods, would yield the highest value for Dry Creek. As he stated in his report: "Because of Gallo's overall superiority in terms of operating results, market domination and industry potential as compared with the 16 comparable publicly traded companies the ratios and rates Gallo [sic] fall at the most favorable end of each respective range established by the comparatives."

To value Dry Creek using the adjusted operating profit capitalization ratio, Desmond used (as an addition in the denominator of the ratio) the amount of Gallo's interest-bearing debt as of August 31, 1978, without adjustment. He utilized (as an addition in the numerator of the ratio) Gallo's total interest expense for the year ended August 31, 1978.

In applying the dividend capitalization method, Desmond first concluded that Dry Creek could pay common stock dividends totaling 40 percent of Gallo's annual net income. He therefore computed a value for Dry Creek under this method by dividing 40 percent of Gallo's total earnings for 1978 by the dividend capitalization ratio that he determined based on comparables.

In using the price-revenues method, Desmond increased Gallo's reported net revenues by Gallo Glass' net revenues. Desmond made this adjustment because Gallo and Gallo Glass did not report on a consolidated basis.

In addition to the five values for Dry Creek computed using comparative analysis, Desmond computed an unadjusted book value and an adjusted book value. The former was simply Gallo's total stockholders' equity as of August 31, 1978. In computing the latter, Desmond estimated land values

---

[2] Desmond's approach differed from Lehman Brothers' in mechanical application. Instead of using the various ratios to value directly the common stock of Dry Creek (based upon per share financial data adjusted for the effects of Dry Creek preferred stock), Desmond used the ratios to value the total equity of Dry Creek (based upon aggregate unadjusted financial data). He then determined a single value for Dry Creek through a weighting process, described *infra*. From this value he deducted the amount at which he valued the outstanding preferred stock.

based upon certain acquisitions by Gallo and upon comparable sales and property assessment data. He did not, however, appraise the other items of property, plant, and equipment. Instead, "the estimated contributory values of improvements and equipment was based upon historical cost data * * * to which certain adjustments have been made." Desmond computed the adjusted values for the various assets by multiplying the costs of the assets by various percentages (ranging from 60 percent to 100 percent) but did not explain how he determined the percentages. The adjusted values substantially exceeded the book values of these assets.

Desmond thus computed seven values for Dry Creek. These values varied over a substantial range; the highest value, computed under the price-revenues method, exceeded the lowest value, computed under the price-earnings method, by over 2½ times. Desmond stated in his report:

> In analyzing each valuation approach for its degree of applicability in estimating the minority equity value of Dry Creek Corporation stock, this appraiser accords primary consideration to the earnings and cash flow valuation methods—price earnings, adjusted operating profit capitalization, and dividend capitalization. Secondary weight is given the two formula methods: market price to book and aggregate market price to net revenues. The unadjusted book equity value is not indicative of economic value of Gallo as an operating enterprise and, therefore, is accorded little weight.

Desmond's ultimate value for Dry Creek (assuming its stock were publicly traded) was approximately equal to the unadjusted book value, the dividend capitalization value, and the average of the price-earnings, adjusted operating profit capitalization, and dividend capitalization values. This value implied a price-earnings ratio for the common stock that exceeded by more than 50 percent the price-earnings ratio determined by Desmond based on comparables. The publicly traded value for Dry Creek computed by Desmond under the price-earnings method would have yielded a per share value for the common stock virtually equal to the prediscount value computed by Lehman Brothers.[4]

Desmond concluded that, after a 10 percent discount to reflect that Dry Creek stock was not publicly traded, the value of the common stock was $689 per share.

Pratt

In August 1984, petitioner retained Shannon P. Pratt (Pratt) to determine the appropriate discount for lack of marketability for the 1,178 Class J shares, as of the valuation date. Pratt was a senior member of the American Society of Appraisers and was president of a firm specializing in the valuation of businesses and business interests. Based upon his own empirical comparisons of the initial public offering prices of selected common stocks with prices from sales occurring before the offerings, Pratt concluded that 50 percent was an appropriate discount.

Ultimate Finding Of Fact

The fair market value of the Dry Creek Class J common shares includible in decedent's gross estate was $237 per share on the valuation date.

Opinion

Property includible in the gross estate is generally included at its fair market value on the date of the decedent's death. Sec. 2031(a);[5] sec. 20.2031-1(b), Estate Tax Regs. Fair market value is the price at which the property would change hands between a willing buyer and a willing seller, neither being under any compulsion to buy or to sell and both having reasonable knowledge of all relevant facts. *United States v. Cartwright* [73-1 USTC ¶ 12,926], 411 U. S. 546, 551 (1973); sec. 20.2031-1(b),

---

[4] The price-earnings ratio assigned to Gallo by Desmond exceeded the ratio determined by Lehman Brothers by approximately 29 percent. The equivalence in ultimate common stock values reflects that Desmond valued the preferred stock at greater than liquidating value. See *supra* note 3.

[5] Unless otherwise indicated, all statutory references are to the Internal Revenue Code of 1954, as amended and in effect on the valuation date.

Estate Tax Regs. Determining fair market value is a question of fact, and the trier of fact must weigh all relevant evidence and draw appropriate inferences. *Hamm v. Commissioner* [64-1 USTC ¶ 12,206], 325 F. 2d 934, 938 (8th Cir. 1963), affg. a Memorandum Opinion of this Court; *Estate of Andrews v. Commissioner* [Dec. 39,523], 79 T. C. 938, 940 (1982).

Where the value of unlisted stock cannot be determined by reference to bid and ask or sales prices,* the value thereof should be based upon, in addition to all other factors, the value of listed stock of corporations engaged in the same or a similar line of business. Sec. 2031(b). Section 20.2031-2(f), Estate Tax Regs., provides that the company's net worth, prospective earnings power, and dividend-paying capacity should be considered, along with "other relevant factors." These other relevant factors include the goodwill of the business, the economic outlook in the particular industry, the company's position in the industry and its management, and the degree of control represented by the block of stock to be valued. Sec. 20.2031-2(f), Estate Tax Regs.

The relative weight accorded to the various factors depends upon the facts of each case. *Messing v. Commissioner* [Dec. 28,532], 48 T. C. 502, 512 (1967); sec. 20.2031-2(f), Estate Tax Regs. Earnings are relatively more important for valuing the stock of operating companies, whereas asset value is relatively more important for investment companies. *Levenson's Estate v. Commissioner* [60-2 USTC ¶ 11,969], 282 F. 2d 581, 586 (3d Cir. 1960); *Central Trust Co. v. United States* [62-2 USTC ¶ 12,092], 305 F. 2d 393, 404 (Ct. Cl. 1962). See also *Estate of Andrews v. Commissioner, supra.* "Financial data is important only to the extent it furnishes a basis for an informed judgment of the future performance of the particular company." *Snyder's Estate v. United States* [61-1 USTC ¶ 11,987], 285 F. 2d 857, 861 (4th Cir. 1961). Thus, for operating companies, the proper focus is typically upon earnings trends, if such trends are representative of future expectations. *Snyder's Estate v. United States, supra; Central Trust Co. v. United States, supra.*

* Neither petitioner nor respondent attributes any significance to the sales between the trusts for decedent.

Reliance on Expert Opinions

Opinion testimony of an expert is admissible if and because it will assist the trier of fact to understand evidence that will determine a fact in issue. See Fed. R. Evid. 702. Such evidence must be weighed in light of the demonstrated qualifications of the expert and all other evidence of value. *Estate of Christ v. Commissioner* [73-1 USTC ¶ 9454], 480 F. 2d 171, 174 (9th Cir. 1973), affg. [Dec. 30,011] 54 T. C. 493 (1970); *Anderson v. Commissioner* [58-1 USTC ¶ 9117], 250 F. 2d 242, 249 (5th Cir. 1957), affg. a Memorandum Opinion of this Court [Dec. 21,874(M)]. We are not bound by the opinion of any expert witness when that opinion is contrary to our judgment. *Kreis' Estate v. Commissioner* [56-1 USTC ¶ 9137], 227 F. 2d 753, 755 (6th Cir. 1955); *Tripp v. Commissioner* [64-2 USTC ¶ 9804], 337 F. 2d 432 (7th Cir. 1964), affg. a Memorandum Opinion of this Court [Dec. 26,298(M.)]. We may embrace or reject expert testimony, whichever, in our best judgment, is appropriate. *Helvering v. Nat. Grocery Co.* [38-2 USTC ¶ 9312], 304 U. S. 282 (1938); *Silverman v. Commissioner* [76-2 USTC ¶ 13,148], 538 F. 2d 927, 933 (2d Cir. 1976), aff'g a Memorandum Opinion of this Court [Dec. 32,831(M)]; *In Re Williams' Estate* [58-1 USTC ¶ 9252], 256 F. 2d 217, 219 (9th Cir. 1958), affg. a Memorandum Opinion of this Court [Dec. 21,990(M)]. Thus we have rejected expert testimony where the witness' opinion of value was so exaggerated that his testimony was incredible. See *Chiu v. Commissioner* [Dec. 42,027], 84 T. C. 722 (1985); *Dean v. Commissioner* [Dec. 41,348], 83 T. C. 56, 75 (1984); *Fuchs v. Commissioner* [Dec. 41,349], 83 T. C. 79, 99 (1984).

Both petitioner and respondent rely primarily upon the valuations prepared by their respective experts. Petitioner asks us to implement "the policy adopted in *Buffalo Tool & Die Manufacturing Co. v. Commissioner* [Dec. 36,977], 74 T. C. 441, 452 (1980), * * * that in proper cases the Court should adopt the value put forward by the most credible party." In that case we stated:

We are convinced that the valuation issue is capable of resolution by the parties themselves through an agreement which will reflect a compromise Solomon-like adjustment, thereby saving the expenditure of time, effort, and money by the parties and the Court—a process not likely to produce a better result. Indeed, each of the parties should keep in mind that, in the final analysis, the Court may find the evidence of valuation by one of the parties sufficiently more convincing than that of the other party, so that the final result will produce a significant financial defeat for one or the other, rather than a middle-of-the-road compromise which we suspect each of the parties expects the Court to reach. If the parties insist on our valuing any or all of the assets, we will. We do not intend to avoid our responsibilities but instead seek to administer to them more efficiently—a factor which has become increasingly important in light of the constantly expanding workload of the Court. [74 T. C. at 452.]

That language should not be misinterpreted, as some litigants apparently have, as expressing an intention of the Court to sanction a party who takes an unreasonable position. See, e. g., the argument of the taxpayer in *Estate of Kaplin v. Commissioner* [85-1 USTC ¶ 9127], 748 F. 2d 110ʃ, 1111-1112 (6th Cir. 1984), revg. on another ground a Memorandum Opinion of this Court [Dec. 39,235(M)].

Nothing in *Buffalo Tool & Die* requires us to accept any opinion that does not withstand careful analysis. If expert testimony is to serve its intended purpose, however, we should not and will not reject it without objective reasons for doing so. *Buffalo Tool & Die* simply indicates that an objective reason for doing so is that another expert's opinion is more persuasive. In addition *Buffalo Tool & Die* does not require that we find that an expert's report is more persuasive in its entirety. We can find one such report more persuasive on one ultimate element of valuation and another more persuasive on another ultimate element.

Respondent's Valuation Evidence

In the present case, we find the opinion of respondent's expert, Desmond, to be unreliable and, therefore, do not accept his opinion as a basis for our decision.

In valuing Gallo under each of the five methods based on comparables that he used, Desmond assigned to Gallo ratios that would result in the highest possible valuations. Desmond's method was pervasive and absolute: he made no real attempt to compare Gallo with any of the individual comparables. Even if Gallo were an above-average company, which it was not when ranked among the comparables, it would be unreasonable to expect Gallo to be most attractive with respect to each and every ratio. None of the 16 comparables was so positioned.

The emerging consumer preference for higher price wines with perceived higher quality was apparent as of the valuation date, as was Gallo's actual past and expected future inability to exploit this trend. Gallo also felt the effects of the entry of competitive marketing organizations and imports into the U. S. wine market, the consent order with the Federal Trade Commission, and the state affirmation laws or warranty regulations. Because of these and other factors mentioned in our findings, Gallo's earnings exhibited a sharp downward trend after 1972. By virtually any measure of investment merit, Gallo was significantly less attractive on the valuation date than in 1972.

Gallo's earnings were particularly poor relative to the comparable companies, and Desmond's testimony at trial indicated that he realized the importance of earnings in valuing an operating manufacturer like Gallo. Desmond explained the apparent inconsistency of choosing relatively favorable ratios for Gallo as reflecting his belief that earnings of closely held and publicly traded companies are not comparable. Respondent argues this point extensively in his brief and asserts that Gallo incurred expenses not typically incurred by public companies and that Gallo used accounting methods that understated its earnings relative to earnings of public companies.

With respect to expenses, respondent points to the testimony of Joseph Gallo that, unlike management of many public companies preoccupied with short-term earnings, Gallo's management made financial and operating decisions with a view toward long-term success. Respondent further focuses upon the parties' oral stipulation that the annual salaries of the four second generation members of the Gallo family were in the aggregate $200,000 more than the salaries of other Gallo employees of similar service and rank.

There is no evidence, however, that the salaries paid to the Gallo family members were excessive. Members of the second generation spent their entire business careers with Gallo and ultimately would assume top management from Ernest and Julio. More importantly, the hypothetical purchaser of 1,178 shares of Dry Creek Class J stock would have little hope to alter the compensation or other expense policies of Gallo. Earnings reflecting actual expenditures of funds, not expenditures that Gallo might incur if it were a public company, are most relevant for valuing Gallo.

With respect to accounting methods, respondent notes that Gallo utilized the sum-of-the-years'-digits method of depreciation. While a rational investor presumably would adjust the earnings of the subject company to reflect accounting methods consistent with those used by comparables, nothing indicates that such an adjustment was necessary here. The record does not indicate what Gallo's earnings would have been under different accounting methods or even which of the comparable companies used different depreciation or other accounting methods. Had Desmond or respondent possessed genuine doubts concerning the consistency of Gallo's accounting methods with those of comparables, they should have at least attempted to answer these questions.

In light of his distrust of Gallo's reported earnings, Desmond testified that he relied primarily upon Gallo's relatively strong rankings with respect to four balance sheet relationships—current ratio (fifth), quick ratio (twelfth), debt to total assets (fourth) and debt to equity (fourth)—in placing Gallo among the most attractive of the comparables. Even if, like Desmond, we disregard Gallo's poor relative earnings and earnings-based relationships (which we do not), we find serious problems with Desmond's conclusions. Gallo's current ratio (current assets divided by current liabilities) was misleadingly high at the end of its fiscal year due to its seasonal financing needs and practices. Had Desmond ad-

justed Gallo's current ratio to reflect average short-term borrowings outstanding during 1978 (with an equal increase in current assets), Gallo would have ranked below average with respect to this relationship.

The two leverage relationships (debt to total assets and debt to equity) computed for Gallo by Desmond were also misleading. In computing these relationships, Desmond made no adjustment to reflect the outstanding Dry Creek preferred stock. The parties argue on brief whether preferred stock should technically be treated as equity or debt in the computations. Either way a rational investor in Dry Creek common stock would consider the leverage relationships computed by Desmond in light of the outstanding preferred. The holders of the preferred stock possessed a substantial prior claim on assets, and preferred dividend requirements exhausted dividend-paying capacity in 1978.

Attempting to justify Desmond's overly favorable appraisal of Gallo, both Desmond and respondent noted Gallo's large size and the expected future growth in the wine industry. Although size may indeed be a source of security, we find little evidence that Gallo's being the well-established giant of the industry in terms of market share (which in fact fell significantly from 32 percent to 25 percent) implied any special promise of improved financial performance. With its national distribution system in place, Gallo could look forward to little opportunity of expanding geographic markets. As in *Snyder's Estate v. United States* [61-1 USTC ¶ 11,987], 285 F. 2d 857, 859 (4th Cir. 1961), the company's "relatively greater success in the past meant that * * * there were fewer new potential consumers to be won by vigorous advertising and promotional campaigns." More importantly, Gallo's size in fact contributed to its poor image and inability to succeed in the changing consumer market. Gallo's director of marketing research testified:

A. Well, the—Gallo was in a terrible position—perceptually in a terrible position to meet the needs of the consumer groups that were going to be the biggest and most aggressively growing groups in the table wine market. We were really not providing the kinds of imagery values that they wanted, and we were really a long way away from taking care of those things.

Q. What could be done about it?

A. Well, the only way to do it is to change the image of the brand which is a hellishly difficult task. And it was particularly complicated in this situation because some of the reasons why Gallo was struck way over on the other side of the map was that it was perceived to be this hugh monolithic mass production, you know, factory with hiᵣh speed blinds, and chemicals, all the wines made with chemicals. I mean, people didn't perceive it as a small boutique, an interesting part, you know, crafted product.

No rational investor would assume without doubt that the growth prospects of the wine industry justified ignoring the very real and substantial obstacles facing Gallo in that industry.

Respondent argues in his brief that Gallo expected to reap large profits from the reintroduction of its varietal wines and that Gallo eliminate any image problems by marketing the new varietals under a non-Gallo label. We first note that Desmond virtually ignored the prospects for the new varietals, both in his report and at trial. In light of Gallo's past experience with varietals, we believe such treatment was proper. Respondent's forecast is pure speculation unsupported by the record, and Gallo's marketing research director was pessimistic concerning varietals. As to use of another label, Gallo's executive vice president for marketing testified that the company did not expect significant sales of varietals but planned to reintroduce them to improve the image of Gallo's primary label. Using another label would defeat this purpose. In any event, respondent cannot substitute his own business judgment for that of Gallo, which had not planned to use a different label. Cf. *Snyder's Estate v. United States*, 285 F. 2d at 859.

In addition to the fatal flaws in the overall approach of Desmond's valuation, we find serious problems with his application of the specific valuation methods. We note below the more egregious of those problems.

Desmond assumed that Dry Creek could pay annual dividends to common share-holders equal to 40 percent of Gallo's earnings, in valuing Dry Creek under the dividend capitalization method. He admitted at trial, however, that preferred dividend requirements, which equaled 40 percent of Gallo's earnings for 1978, precluded payment of a dividend to common shareholders in that year. Gallo's 1978 earnings approximated average earnings for the 5 years immediately preceding the valuation date. Respondent argues that Dry Creek could redeem preferred shares beginning in 1982 and could thereafter pay common dividends. Notwithstanding respondent's speculation, no evidence suggests that Dry Creek was likely to redeem any portion of the preferred stock after it acquired the power to do so. Moreover, absent dramatic earnings increases, Gallo (or Dry Creek) presumably could finance the substantial redemption payments only through the issuance of debt, which would reduce Dry Creek's dividend-paying capacity. No evidence suggested such increases in earnings after the valuation date.

Desmond added Gallo Glass' net revenues to Gallo's reported net revenues in valuing Dry Creek under the price-revenues method. At trial he stated that the purpose of this adjustment was to consolidate the companies' revenues. He later admitted, however, that because all of Gallo Glass' sales were to Gallo, if the companies had reported on a consolidated basis, Gallo Glass' sales would properly be eliminated as intracompany transactions.

In applying the adjusted operating profit capitalization method, Desmond used Gallo's actual interest expense for 1978. He did not, however, adjust the amount of debt outstanding as of the fiscal year end to reflect the significantly higher average debt outstanding during the year.

Desmond testified at trial that the adjusted operating profit ratio entailed a "purifying" of earnings, primarily through the addition of depreciation to operating profit. We repeat that, had Desmond seriously questioned the comparability of Gallo's reported earnings with earnings of the comparable companies, he should have attempted a reasoned investigation before making arbitrary adjustments. Nothing indicates that Gallo's reported depreciation did not reflect economic reality (at least to the same extent as depreciation reported by the comparables), particularly in light of Gallo's substantial reinvestment requirements. Desmond admitted at trial that Gallo's reinvestment of earnings in plant and equipment exceeded depreciation charges during the years that he examined.

Desmond's treatment of his valuation using adjusted operating profit capitalization illustrates the difficulty confronting us in understanding exactly how Desmond weighted his various valuations. Desmond stated in his report that he gave primary consideration to price-earnings, dividend capitalization, and adjusted operating profit capitalization. At trial he testified: "Maybe it was equal weight to all three in my mind." He later stated, however: "Because of the nature of the [adjusted operating profit capitalization] method I gave it—of the three that I gave most weight to, I gave it, in my mind, the lesser weight than the other two methods." Desmond described the "nature of the method" as follows:

> That's an academic way of appraising a company. It means something to appraisers. It doesn't always mean something to other people. It's not readily understood. It's complicated to explain. A lot of assumptions go into it. Sometimes it's used because there just isn't any other way to purify the operating profit.
>
> With those caveats in mind and yet some weight, I thought, needed to be given to it, it was another run at the earnings and how the earnings looked in terms of value. I gave it some weight.

Similarly, with respect to price-book value and price-revenues, to which Desmond gave "secondary weight" according to his report, he testified: "I felt that weight given to those should be very modest at best." Respondent asserts in his brief that the valuations under these methods had "no bearing" upon Desmond's ultimate valuation.

Concerning adjusted book value, the only noncomparative method given any weight, Desmond testified: "I took a shot at the —at adjusting the balance sheets, tangible assets. I felt that that was the least im-

portant to satisfy myself as to where those values might be on a value [in] * * * place basis." Indeed, from the record before us, we cannot determine whether the adjusted values that Desmond computed for the land improvement and equipment items bore any relationship to their fair market values. His report stated that the adjusted values were "based upon historical cost data trended from the date of acquisition," but we have no way of knowing how Desmond determined the various percentages by which he multiplied the costs of the various assets. Cf. *Estate of Andrews v. Commissioner* [Dec. 39,523], 79 T. C. 938, 948 (1982).

Petitioner's Valuation Evidence

In contrast to Desmond, petitioner's experts acted reasonably in selecting comparable companies, in drawing conclusions based upon careful comparisons of Gallo with individual comparables, in focusing primarily upon earnings, and in relying primarily upon the price-earnings method of valuation.

Respondent initially asserts several subjective reasons for rejecting the testimony of petitioner's experts. He suggests that the witnesses were biased because they had long-term relationships with petitioner and were paid well for their reports. Respondent refers to valuations prepared by Cadenasso or Lehman Brothers several years before the valuation date. The Court permitted respondent to cross-examine Cadenasso and Shutzer with respect to the earlier reports to uncover any inconsistencies in methodology with their later reports. The record discloses no such inconsistencies. In any event, a close relationship with a party is obviously not, standing alone, sufficient to discredit the testimony of a witness. The result of any such rule would be to disqualify those most knowledgeable about any problem.

The Court's task is to determine the credibility of any lay or expert witness based upon objective facts, the reasonableness of the testimony, the consistency of the statements made by the witness, and, in some cases, the demeanor of the witness. In the present case, as in the ordinary case, any doubts about the reliability of an expert's testimony are based on the failure of the facts to support his assumptions and his ultimate opinion rather than any doubt as to whether the expert is expressing a truthful opinion.[1]

Based on the entire record, we conclude that Lehman Brothers was well qualified to express an opinion as to the value of the stock in issue and that Lehman Brothers' opinion has not been impeached by any objective evidence. We therefore agree with its opinion that the pre-discount value of the stock as of the valuation date was $370 per share. Cadenasso's valuation was consistent in approach and similar, if somewhat higher, in result. We nevertheless hold that the more rigorous and detailed analysis in Lehman Brothers' report justifies a lower value than that underlying the value reported in decedent's estate tax return.

Many of respondent's objections to Lehman Brothers' valuation are the same arguments made by him in support of Desmond's. We shall not repeat those arguments and our reasons for rejecting them but instead address below only respondent's arguments not previously considered.

Respondent disputes Lehman Brothers' conclusion that brewing companies were most comparable to Gallo, in light of the superior growth forecast for the wine industry. Gallo had not, however, fully participated in the past growth in the wine industry and faced substantial competitive problems in the future. Moreover, Lehman Brothers compared Gallo with each of the comparables in using the price-earnings method, its primary valuation method. Only with respect to the two secondary or "check" methods did Lehman Brothers compare Gallo exclusively with Canandaigua and beer companies. Respondent presumably believes that comparisons with the distilling and soft drink companies, which generally realized financial results superior to brewers, would yield higher valuations for Gallo. But Desmond himself rejected soft drink companies as comparables, a conclusion with which respondent agrees in his brief. More importantly, unlike Desmond, Lehman Brothers made careful and reasoned comparisons with each compara-

ble instead of arbitrarily relying upon the outer limit of a range. Nothing suggests that, under the approach taken by Lehman Brothers, considering the other companies under the other methods would yield a higher value for Gallo than that computed under the price-earnings method.

Respondent similarly asserts that Lehman Brothers relied too heavily upon the price-earnings method and should have given greater weight to the other methods used by Desmond. Lehman Brothers did not ignore the other methods but considered and rejected those methods as inappropriate. We believe Lehman Brothers' conclusions were reasonable, particularly in light of the problems Desmond had in attempting to apply the other methods. Certainly Lehman Brothers' approach was preferable to that of Desmond, who arbitrarily computed a maximum value using each method and then unsystematically derived an ultimate valuation.

Respondent's primary argument is that Lehman Brothers focused excessively upon earnings in its valuation. Respondent does not dispute that earnings were more important than assets in valuing Gallo, but he argues that Lehman Brothers incorrectly ignored asset value. See *Estate of Andrews v. Commissioner* [Dec. 39,523], 79 T. C. 938, 945 (1982).

Lehman Brothers did not ignore asset value but concluded, after considering Gallo's assets, that Gallo did not possess sufficient asset value to sustain a value for Dry Creek stock exceeding the price-earnings valuation. Lehman Brothers admittedly did not appraise Gallo's assets, but, with the exception of land, nor did Desmond. Unlike *Estate of Andrews,* the current case does not present a situation where net asset value per share demonstrably exceeded an earnings-based valuation. See also *Hamm v. Commissioner* [64-1 USTC ¶ 12,206], 325 F. 2d 934 (8th Cir. 1963), affg. a Memorandum Opinion of this Court; *Portland Manufacturing Co. v. Commissioner* [Dec. 30,729], 56 T. C. 58 (1971), affd. by unpublished opinion on another issue 35 AFTR 2d 75-1439, 75-1 USTC ¶ 9449 (9th Cir. 1975). Des-

[1] A different problem may arise where the expert is called upon to vindicate an opinion that was the original basis for the transaction in dispute. See *Chiu v. Commissioner* [Dec. 42,027], 84 T. C. 722 (1985).

mond's report contains the only evidence of the value of Gallo's assets. As previously indicated, we are quite skeptical of the asset values determined by Desmond. Indeed, even Desmond apparently gave little weight to his adjusted book value computation. As he stated at trial:

> But, the value could not be placed heavily, in light of the higher tangible net worth, merely because it was—they were valuable assets. Those assets are worth what they'll earn. And, if they're not producing wine, those assets aren't worth anything at all.

We need only consider asset value; we need not attribute any weight to it, if to do so would be unreasonable. As the Ninth Circuit Court of Appeals, to which this case is appealable (barring stipulation to the contrary), stated:

> [T]he statutory standard for evaluating closely held stock incorporates a number of alternative methods of valuation, and merely directs the trial court to consider all relevant methods. The applicable case law directs the trial court to consider all relevant information, but grants it broad discretion in determining what method of valuation most fairly represents the fair market value of the stock in issue in light of the facts presented at trial. In light of * * * the wide discretion given the trial court to weigh the credibility of witnesses at trial and to determine the appropriate weight to give various methods of valuation, we do not believe the Tax Court erred in its choice of a method other than net asset value. [Citations omitted.] [*Estate of O'Connell v. Commissioner* [81-1 USTC ¶ 13,395], 640 F. 2d 249, 251-252 (9th Cir. 1981), affg. a Memorandum Opinion of this Court [Dec. 35,173(M)].]

Considering the entire record, we do not believe that the value of Gallo's assets justified a higher valuation for the Dry Creek stock than that determined by Lehman Brothers.

In sum, respondent's objections are unsupported by any evidence from which we could conclude that the methods and calculations used by Lehman Brothers were incorrect. Respondent is, in effect, merely asking us to substitute numbers that would achieve a higher valuation and to reject Lehman Brothers' approach because it produced a relatively low valuation. If we were to do so, we would be merely substituting our guess for the expert opinion, when the original purpose of the expert opinion is to provide us with the assistance of persons specially qualified in the areas in issue.

Discount for Lack of Marketability

Both parties agree that the fair market value of 1,178 shares of Dry Creek Class J common was less than the publicly traded value of the stock. The only issue is the proper amount of the discount to reflect the absence of a public market for the stock.

Desmond concluded in his report that a relatively low discount of 10 percent was appropriate, primarily for the following reasons:

1. The popularity and opportunity associated with the wine industry during this period (as reflected by the multitude of acquisitions that took place).

2. Gallo's dominant position within the industry.

3. Ernest and Julio Gallo's unique value to the company's operations, which could enhance the possibility of a merger, acquisition or public offering, due to their respective ages.

Desmond testified at trial that, because of the above factors, a sophisticated and well-financed investor might consider the purchase of the 1,178 Class J shares an opportunity to establish a position from which he could later acquire a larger, perhaps controlling, interest in Dry Creek. Desmond believed that the hypothetical investor could not reasonably foresee a public market for the stock but would instead make the purchase "[j]ust to get on the inside to see what * * * [he] could see."

We have found as facts that Dry Creek intended to remain closely held by the Gallo family and that none of the common shareholders intended to sell any shares to outsiders, as of the valuation date. These findings were supported by substantial evidence, including the extensive and uncontradicted testimony by two members of the second generation of Gallos. A rational investor would not assume that the purchase of the 1,178 Class J shares would lead to the acquisition of a larger interest in Dry Creek.

The hypothetical purchaser would acquire only a very small interest in a family-dominated corporation, for which there existed no ready market and little reasonable expectation for significant dividend income.[*] Dry Creek's capital structure and voting provisions, which required a majority vote of both classes of common shares for shareholder action, exacerbated the problems facing an outside investor in Dry Creek.

Citing *Luce v. United States* [84-1 USTC ¶ 13,549], 4 Cl. Ct. 212 (1983), respondent implies in his brief that we should presume the purchaser of the 1,178 Class J shares to be a member of the Gallo family.[10] Respondent is desperately reaching for some support for the unsupportable. As respondent admits, such a presumption would be inconsistent with the holding of *Estate of Bright v. United States* [81-2 USTC ¶ 13,436], 658 F. 2d 999 (5th Cir. 1981) (en banc), expressly adopted by both the Ninth Circuit Court of Appeals and this Court. See *Propstra v. United States* [82-2 USTC ¶ 13,475], 680 F. 2d 1248, 1251-1253 (9th Cir. 1982); *Estate of Andrews v. Commissioner* [Dec. 39,523], 79 T. C. 938, 953-956 (1982). See also *Estate of Lee v. Commissioner* [Dec. 35,017], 69 T. C. 860 (1978). For our purposes, the assumed purchaser of the shares in issue must be hypothetical, not a Gallo family member.

Respondent further argues that a pub-

lished empirical study, considered by both Desmond and petitioner's experts, supports the 10 percent discount determined by Desmond. The study relied upon by respondent concerned discounts applicable to restricted stock of publicly traded companies. Although such shares were typically issued in private placements and were not immediately tradeable, a purchaser of the shares could reasonably expect them to be publicly traded in the future. The purchaser of Dry Creek shares, by contrast, could foresee no reasonable prospect of his shares becoming freely traded.

We thus reject Desmond's 10 percent discount figure as too low. Considering the entire record, we believe that the 36 percent figure determined by Lehman Brothers, which was substantially equal to that used by Cadenasso, was a reasonable discount to reflect the illiquidity of the 1,178 Class J shares. Although Pratt concluded that 50 percent was an appropriate discount, we believe that the conclusions of Cadenasso and Lehman Brothers, as integral portions of comprehensive analyses, were more reliable in the present case.

Conclusion

As permitted under section 6512(b), we find that petitioner made an overpayment in decedent's estate tax. Because the amount of the overpayment depends upon the credit for state death taxes paid,

Decision will be entered under Rule 155

---

[*] Desmond stated at trial:
I know that Gallo management itself made it very clear to me, and they reiterated it here on the stand here yesterday, that there was no discussion, other than in 1972 no interest in selling stock. Well, the assignment here * * * is the assumption — it may be hypothetical, but that's what I'm saddled with — that there is a willing seller, not just a willing buyer.
Our task is to value the 1,178 Class J shares. It is only for these shares that we must visualize a willing buyer and a willing seller. No prospective purchaser of the 1,178 shares would, like Desmond, ignore the stated intention of the Gallo family members.

[9] Cf. *Estate of Katz v. Commissioner* [Dec. 29,081(M)], T. C. Memo. 1968-171. None of the experts concluded that the size of the block of shares in issue, standing alone, justified a discount from the publicly traded value of the shares. Like the experts, we have considered the relatively small interest represented by the block only as it affected the discount for illiquidity.

[10] Desmond's report contained a similar implication, but he stated at trial that he did not consider, in his valuation, the possibility that Gallo family members might purchase the stock.

APPENDIX D
Key Ratios Used in Valuation

TYPES OF KEY RATIOS

A number of key ratios are considered primary valuation tools and are often used in valuing a privately held business. An example of the raw data used in compiling these ratios and complete ratios is provided in this appendix.

Key ratios can be divided into three groups:

1. *Liquidity ratios* measure (a) the ability of the business to meet its current obligations or (b) the efficiency and productivity of the business in utilizing its available resources and expenditures (ratios that fall into category (b) are also referred to as "activity ratios").
2. *Leverage ratios* indicate the amount of the business' operations that are debt rather than equity financed.
3. *Profitability ratios* measure the nitty gritty of the business—does it make money (rate of return) on its sales, equity, and investments?

LIQUIDITY RATIOS

Liquidity ratios measure a company's ability to meet all of its current financial obligations. If necessary, how much cash could the company come up with at short notice? Could the company sell enough of its assets to meet its current liabilities without endangering its ongoing operations? A high liquidity ratio indicates that the company not only has a cushion against capricious creditors, but is also able to take advantage of windfall business opportunities.

$$\text{Current ratio} = \frac{\text{Current assets}}{\text{Current liabilities}}$$

This measures the extent to which short-term debt can be distinguished by current assets—cash, net trade receivables, inventories, prepaid expenses, and other current assets.

$$\text{Quick ratio} = \frac{\text{Quick assets}}{\text{Current liabilities}}$$

This measures the extent to which short-term debt can be extinguished by quick assets—cash, net trade receivables, and other current assets easily convertible to cash.

$$\text{Collection period} = \frac{\text{Accounts receivable}}{\text{Average daily sales}}$$

This measures the average period of time (days) between a sale and payment. The shorter the period, the larger the company's cash flow. Average daily sales are net yearly sales divided by 360.

$$\text{Inventory turnover} = \frac{\text{Cost of goods sold}}{\text{Year-end inventory}}$$

This measures the number of times inventory is replenished during the year. A good inventory turnover is a high one. For example, if cost of goods sold is $1 million, the lower the year-end inventory, the higher the inventory turnover. What this means is that the investment needed to carry inventory is lower, freeing more working capital for other needs.

$$\text{Fixed assets to net worth} = \frac{\text{Depreciable assets}}{\text{Net worth}}$$

This measures the amount of working capital tied up in depreciable assets. A high percentage, common for capital-intensive industries, indicates that a substantial amount of working capital will have to be expended each year in renewing fixed assets, and hence, represent a significant drain on working capital.

$$\text{Sale to net working capital} = \frac{\text{Sale (receipts)}}{\text{Current assets} - \text{Current liabilities}}$$

This measures the turnover of working capital in a given period. The higher the turnover, the more efficient the use of working capital, allowing more of it to be used for other current needs.

LEVERAGE RATIOS

Leverage ratios show the degree to which a business' operations and capital expenditures are funded by borrowed funds or the owner's equity. The higher the degree of debt involved, the higher the risk an investment in such a business entails. Debt is a fixed charge that must be met yearly regardless of profitability of a business. If the business can earn a higher return on investment on borrowed funds than the cost of borrowing those funds, the difference increases shareholder equity. For example, if the cost of borrowing funds used to finance operations is 12 percent and the operations are returning 25 percent, the 13 percent difference represents an incremental increase in equity. This is called trading on equity.

Lenders use leverage ratios to determine the ability of a business to not only pay back borrowed funds but make a respectable profit at the same time. The owners of the business have little incentive to continue operations if all the profits will be eaten up by debt service. On the other hand, these ratios arc the birthing tools for the current craze of leveraged buyouts.

$$\text{Long-term debt to net worth} = \frac{\text{Long-term liabilities}}{\text{Owner's equity}}$$

Who really owns the company? The shareholders or the business' long-term lenders? Creditors have priority upon liquidation. What is the liquidation value to a shareholder of a highly-leveraged business? Not much. If this ratio is more than 1 (i.e., the lenders have more long-term capital than the shareholders), the degree of risk in investing in such a business can become prohibitively high.

$$\text{Total debt to worth} = \frac{\text{Total liabilities}}{\text{Owner's equity}}$$

Similar to the immediately preceding ratio, this measures the overall position of the shareholders versus the business' creditors. The larger the percentage of all creditors in the assets of the business, the smaller the cushion the business has against adverse operating periods. A trend that shows an increase in this percentage could indicate that shareholder's equity in the business' assets eventually may be reduced to zero.

$$\text{Total debt to total assets} = \frac{\text{Total liabilities}}{\text{Total assets}}$$

This represents the percentage of assets supplied by the creditors. The same principals discussed in the previous two leverage ratios apply.

$$\text{Times interest earned} = \frac{\text{Earnings before interest and taxes}}{\text{Interest expense}}$$

How capable is a business of paying its interest obligations? Put another way, can it shoulder the burden of its debt service and make a reasonable profit? That question is answered by this ratio, which measures the number of extra times that fixed interest has been earned in a year. The more times earned, the larger the cushion the business has and the smaller the effect of debt service on the ability of the business to turn a profit.

A decision must be made when calculating this ratio about whether to use pre-tax or after-tax earnings. It is wise to make both calculations because the difference between the two reveals the extent to which taxes affect the cash earnings of the business.

PROFITABILITY RATIOS

These are the most important ratios. Does the business make money? Can it generate the profits for continued growth or survival? These ratios also reflect directly on management's abilities and decisions and how well it has used the business' resources to benefit the shareholders.

$$\text{Pre-tax return on investment} = \frac{\text{Pre-tax profit}}{\text{Owner's equity}} \times 100$$

$$\text{After-tax return on investment} = \frac{\text{After-tax profit}}{\text{Owner's equity}} \times 100$$

These two ratios are literally the bottom line. How much of the owner's or shareholder's money was returned in profit? Again it is wise to compare the results to determine if taxes in the particular geographical area or industry make investing in the company unwise, or whether a discount is necessary to compensate.

$$\text{Turnover of owner's equity} = \frac{\text{Sales (receipts)}}{\text{Owner's equity}}$$

This ratio measures the amount of sales generated by the capital employed. It is another type of ratio indicating the efficiency of management in utilizing shareholder's equity. Caution should be used with this ratio: a very high ratio could indicate inadequate capitalization as well as efficient use of capital.

$$\text{Sales to fixed assets} = \frac{\text{Sales (receipts)}}{\text{Fixed assets}}$$

This ratio measures the amount of sales generated by the depreciable assets of the business. It also indicates the ability of management to use available operating resources. A decision to invest more in plant and equipment as a way of boosting sales can often hinge on this ratio.

$$\text{Sales to total assets} = \frac{\text{Sales (receipts)}}{\text{Total assets}}$$

This ratio indicates how much in sales one dollar of assets generates. It is also an overall measure of management capability. When compared to the immediately preceding ratio, it reveals the relative importance of plant and equipment to revenue generation.

Example

Key Ratios of Astro Electronics. The following example is taken from the software package put out by Aardvark/McGraw-Hill entitled *Business Valuation.* It uses the same 15 key ratios explained in the preceding pages. The ratios cover a five-year period and are based on historical and adjusted balance sheet and income statement date.

Also included with the financial statements and key ratios is an Income Statement Percentages. This statement takes items from the income statement, and lists all debits as a percentage of sales/receipts. It covers a five-year period and is based on historical and adjusted income statement data. The income statement percentages give a good idea of what expense items are the greatest depressers of the business' bottom-line profit margin.

Astro Electronics
Valuation Date: January 15, 1986
Key Ratios

Estate of John Smith.
Minority shareholder.

	1985		*1984*		*1983*		*1982*		*1981*	
	Hist	*Adj*	*Hist*	*Adj*	*Hist*	*Adj*	*Hist*	*Adj*	*Hist*	*Adj*
Liquidity ratios										
Current	2.15	2.67	2.11	2.43	1.99	2.30	1.94	2.24	1.89	2.19
Quick	1.26	1.53	1.25	1.39	1.15	1.26	1.10	1.24	1.07	1.20
Collection per	81	77	81	79	84	79	84	81	90	86
Inventory turn	3.26	3.21	3.37	3.11	3.28	2.93	3.24	3.17	3.11	2.96
Fixed assets to worth	0.35	0.43	0.34	0.42	0.38	0.44	0.44	0.49	0.47	0.51
Sales to net working capital	3.84	3.34	3.87	3.40	4.00	3.48	4.06	3.59	3.86	3.38
Debt ratios										
Long-term debt to worth	0.06	0.05	0.06	0.05	0.05	0.04	0.05	0.04	0.05	0.04
Total debt to worth	0.43	0.28	0.42	0.31	0.42	0.30	0.39	0.28	0.39	0.28
Total debt to total assets	0.29	0.22	0.28	0.24	0.28	0.23	0.27	0.22	0.27	0.22
Times interest earned	12.22	12.62	9.39	10.00	7.04	7.99	5.10	5.49	3.50	4.00
Profitability ratios										
Pretax profit to worth (%)	34.77	29.10	28.75	25.21	21.94	20.53	15.52	13.88	9.84	9.55
After-tax profit to worth (%)	18.78	15.71	15.53	13.61	11.85	11.08	8.38	7.49	5.31	5.16
Worth turnover	1.63	1.31	1.56	1.28	1.44	1.17	1.31	1.07	1.18	0.95
Sales to fixed assets	4.70	3.07	4.67	3.06	3.82	2.62	2.96	2.19	2.53	1.87
Sales to total assets	1.10	1.03	1.05	0.98	0.97	0.90	0.90	0.83	0.80	0.75

Astro Electronics   **Estate of John Smith.**
Valuation Date: January 15, 1986   **Minority shareholder.**
Key Ratios

| | Income Statement Percentages | | | | | | | | | |
| | 1985 | | 1984 | | 1983 | | 1982 | | 1981 | |
	Hist	Adj	Hist	Adj	Hist	Adj	Hist	Adj	Hist	Adj
Sales/receipts	100.0	100.0	100.0	100.0	100.0	100.0	100.0	100.0	100.0	100.0
Cost goods sold	63.0	62.7	64.7	63.9	66.4	64.6	68.2	67.8	70.0	69.2
Gross profit	37.0	37.3	35.3	36.1	33.6	35.4	31.8	32.2	30.0	30.8
Operating exp	13.7	13.3	14.8	14.2	15.9	15.2	17.1	16.3	18.3	17.5
Operating prof	23.3	24.0	20.5	21.9	17.7	20.2	14.7	15.9	11.7	13.3
Interest exp	1.9	1.9	2.2	2.2	2.5	2.5	2.9	2.9	3.3	3.3
Pretax profit	21.4	22.1	18.3	19.7	15.2	17.7	11.8	13.0	8.4	10.0
Income taxes	9.8	10.2	8.5	9.1	7.0	8.1	5.5	6.0	3.8	4.6
After-tax prof	11.6	11.9	9.8	10.6	8.2	9.6	6.3	7.0	4.6	5.4

Astro Electronics
Valuation Date: January 15, 1986
Key Ratios

Estate of John Smith.
Minority shareholder.

	Adjusted Balance Sheet				
	1985	*1984*	*1983*	*1982*	*1981*
Cash	50,540	55,750	55,000	50,245	51,550
Net trade receiv	450,000	400,000	350,000	310,500	285,000
Inventories	410,500	375,000	350,000	295,000	280,000
Prepaid expenses	16,596	15,660	15,481	15,075	14,950
Other current	75,000	65,000	35,000	24,000	24,000
TOT CURR ASSETS	1,002,636	911,410	805,481	694,820	655,500
Land	265,000	255,000	245,000	235,000	225,000
Fixed assets	682,875	595,900	605,490	629,310	641,250
Econ intangibles	40,000	50,000	60,000	70,000	60,000
Other intang	0	0	0	0	0
Other long-term	56,259	56,259	56,259	25,000	25,000
TOTAL ASSETS	2,046,770	1,868,569	1,772,230	1,654,130	1,606,750
Current liab	375,000	375,000	350,000	310,000	300,000
Long-term liab	75,000	65,000	60,000	50,000	50,000
Deferred taxes	0	0	0	0	0
TOT LIABILITIES	450,000	440,000	410,000	360,000	350,000
TOTAL CAPITAL	1,596,770	1,428,569	1,362,230	1,294,130	1,256,750
TOTAL LIABILITIES AND CAPITAL	2,046,770	1,868,569	1,772,230	1,654,130	1,606,750

Astro Electronics   **Estate of John Smith.**
Valuation Date: January 15, 1986   **Minority shareholder.**
Key Ratios

| | Historical Balance Sheet | | | | |
	1985	1984	1983	1982	1981
Cash	50,540	55,750	55,000	50,245	51,550
Net trade receiv	475,000	410,000	370,000	320,560	300,150
Inventories	405,100	350,000	321,500	290,100	270,000
Prepaid expenses	16,596	15,660	15,481	15,075	14,950
Other current	75,000	65,000	35,000	24,000	24,000
TOT CURR ASSETS	1,022,236	896,410	796,981	699,980	660,650
Land	195,600	195,600	195,600	195,600	195,600
Fixed assets	446,300	390,888	415,208	466,156	475,000
Econ intangibles	120,000	117,266	96,506	78,396	60,000
Other intang	76,000	76,000	76,000	76,000	76,000
Other long-term	56,259	56,259	56,259	25,000	25,000
TOTAL ASSETS	1,916,395	1,732,423	1,636,554	1,541,132	1,492,250
Current liab	475,000	425,000	400,000	360,000	350,000
Long-term liab	75,000	65,000	60,000	50,000	50,000
Deferred taxes	0	0	0	0	0
TOT LIABILITIES	550,000	490,000	460,000	410,000	400,000
TOTAL CAPITAL	1,366,395	1,242,423	1,176,554	1,131,132	1,092,250
TOTAL LIABILITIES AND CAPITAL	1,916,395	1,732,423	1,636,554	1,541,132	1,492,250

Astro Electronics   **Estate of John Smith.**
Valuation Date: January 15, 1986   **Minority shareholder.**
Key Ratios

	Historical Income Statement				
	1985	1984	1983	1982	1981
Sales/receipts	2,098,808	1,825,050	1,587,000	1,380,000	1,200,000
Cost goods sold	1,321,756	1,180,140	1,053,696	940,800	840,000
GROSS PROFIT	777,052	644,910	533,304	439,200	360,000
Operating exp	288,375	269,509	251,878	235,400	220,000
OPERATING PROF	488,677	375,401	281,426	203,800	140,000
Interest exp	40,000	40,000	40,000	40,000	40,000
PRETAX PROFIT	448,677	335,401	241,426	163,800	100,000
Income taxes	206,391	154,284	111,056	75,348	46,000
NET PROFIT AFTER TAXES	242,286	181,117	130,370	88,452	54,000

	Adjusted Income Statement				
	1985	1984	1983	1982	1981
Sales/receipts	2,098,808	1,825,050	1,587,000	1,380,000	1,200,000
Cost goods sold	1,315,750	1,165,430	1,025,500	935,000	830,000
GROSS PROFIT	783,058	659,620	561,500	445,000	370,000
Operating exp	278,375	259,509	241,878	225,400	210,000
OPERATING PROF	504,683	400,111	319,622	219,600	160,000
Interest exp	40,000	40,000	40,000	40,000	40,000
PRETAX PROFIT	464,683	360,111	279,622	179,600	120,000
Income taxes	213,754	165,651	128,626	82,616	55,200
NET PROFIT AFTER TAXES	250,929	194,460	150,996	96,984	64,800

Astro Electronics   **Estate of John Smith.**
Valuation Date: January 15, 1986   **Minority shareholder.**
Key Ratios

	Balance Sheet Percentages									
	1985		1984		1983		1982		1981	
	Hist	Adj	Hist	Adj	Hist	Adj	Hist	Adj	Hist	Adj
Cash	2.6	2.5	3.2	3.0	3.4	3.1	3.3	3.0	3.5	3.2
Net trade rec	24.8	22.0	23.7	21.4	22.6	19.7	20.8	18.8	20.1	17.8
Inventories	21.1	20.1	20.2	20.1	19.6	19.7	18.8	17.8	18.1	17.4
Prepaid exp	0.9	0.8	0.9	0.8	1.0	0.9	1.0	0.9	1.0	0.9
Other current	3.9	3.7	3.7	3.5	2.1	2.0	1.6	1.5	1.6	1.5
Tot curr assets	53.3	49.1	51.7	48.8	48.7	45.4	45.5	42.0	44.3	40.8
Land	10.2	12.9	11.3	13.6	12.0	13.8	12.7	14.2	13.1	14.0
Fixed assets	23.3	33.4	22.6	31.9	25.4	34.2	30.2	38.1	31.8	39.9
Econ intang	6.3	1.9	6.8	2.7	5.9	3.4	5.1	4.2	4.0	3.7
Other intang	4.0	0.0	4.4	0.0	4.6	0.0	4.9	0.0	5.1	0.0
Other long-term	2.9	2.7	3.2	3.0	3.4	3.2	1.6	1.5	1.7	1.6
TOTAL ASSETS	100.0	100.0	100.0	100.0	100.0	100.0	100.0	100.0	100.0	100.0
Current liab	24.8	18.3	24.5	20.1	24.4	19.7	23.4	18.7	23.5	18.7
Long-term liab	3.9	3.7	3.8	3.5	3.7	3.4	3.2	3.0	3.4	3.1
Deferred taxes	0.0	0.0	0.0	0.0	0.0	0.0	0.0	0.0	0.0	0.0
Tot liabilities	28.7	22.0	28.3	23.6	28.1	23.1	26.6	21.7	26.9	21.8
Total capital	71.3	78.0	71.7	76.4	71.9	76.9	73.4	78.3	73.1	78.2
TOTAL LIABILITIES AND CAPITAL	100.0	100.0	100.0	100.0	100.0	100.0	100.0	100.0	100.0	100.0

APPENDIX E
Unified Gift and Estate Tax
For 1988 and After

APPENDIX E

Unified Gift and Estate Tax for 1988 and After

Taxable amount ($)	Tax ($)	Percentage on excess (%)
0	0	18
10,000	1,800	20
20,000	3,800	22
40,000	8,200	24
60,000	13,000	26
80,000	18,200	28
100,000	23,800	30
150,000	38,800	32
250,000	70,800	34
500,000	155,800	37
750,000	248,300	39
1,000,000	345,800	41
1,250,000	448,300	43
1,500,000	555,800	45
2,000,000	780,800	49
2,500,000*	1,025,800*	50*

*Note: For years after 1983 and before 1988, substitute the following in the above schedule:

Taxable amount ($)	Tax ($)	Percentage on excess (%)
2,500,000	1,025,800	53
3,000,000	1,290,800	55

Index

Index

favorable rate of, 16, A-35
on redemption profits, 17
and divorce property settlements, 23
Capital loss carryforward in a distribution of appreciated property in redemption, 187
Cash flow
negative, 5
present value of, as a valuation factor, 66
Central Trust Co., Exr. v. *U.S.*
case transcript, C-1, C-3–C-19
comparables used in, 80–83
discount for lack of marketability stated in, 134, A-26
lack of marketability discount lumped with minority interest in, 136–37
weighting process used in, 42, 47–52, 69–70
Charitable contributions, 202–4
Charitable deduction of property, 207–8
Closely held business
as collateral, using a 12
definition of a, 11
destruction of a, 13
price of a, determination of the, 6
sale or purchase of a, 22
valuation of a, 5, 18, 29, 80
Closely held corporation
fair market value fluctuation for a, causes of, 12
IRS ruling on valuing a, 78
merger involving a, 22, 67, A-60
minority interest discount for a, 134–35
Rev. Rul. 65-192's ruling on, definition of the, 11, 36–37
uniqueness of the, as negation of comparables method, 82
Closely held stock
valuation of, 15, 35, 105
valuation of donation of, 203–4
Cluett, Peabody as comparable company to J.J. Bean, A-41, A-42–A-46, A-63, A-66
Combination buy-sell agreement, 144
Combinations and variations approach to valuation, 71–72
Commodity, value of a, 5
Companies, comparable. *See* Comparables
Comparables, 73–86
basics about usage of, 75–77
capitalized excess earnings approach compared with, 101–3
comparative value based on, A-52–A-53
courts and the use of, 79–80
definition of, 32
difficulty finding, 75, 78–79
drawbacks of, 83–84
fluctuating stock prices forces weighting prices for use as, 75–76
IRS and the use of, 77–78, 79, 80–83
lack of buy-sell experience in using, 77
missed significance of adjusted book value for, 76
problems of using, 75–77
proper use of, 84
in Royal Oil, Inc. sample valuation, 112–13
sample valuation using, A-37–A-67
used in valuation, 65–66

Comparative approach to valuation, 50
Competition as a weighing factor, 38, 48
Concord Control, Inc. independent appraisal case, 123–24
Continental Can, 48, 81
Contracts
as intangible assets, 122
as valuation factors, 59
Contributions, charitable, 202–4
stock as one of, 12, 25
Copyrights as intangible assets, 122
Corporation
closely held. *See* Closely held corporation
control of a, retaining, 199–201
Court(s). *See also* U.S. Appellate Courts, U.S. District Courts, and U.S. Supreme Court
allocation issues considered by the, 127–29
buy-sell agreement rulings by the, 147–50
cases, appendix of, C-1–C-90
comparables use and the, 79–80
tax. *See* Tax Court
valuation by the, 32
valuation penalties imposed by the, 209–10
Covenant not to compete, 59, 126–27
Cross-purchase agreement, 144
Crummey v. *Commissioner* and the Crummey provision for trust distributions, 199
Curtis Noll Corp. case involving going-concern value, 124–25

D

Deferred compensation, appraisal of, 211, A-60
Depreciation, 58, 188, 216
Dewing, A. S., A-58
Directory of Companies Required to File Annual Reports, 84
Discounted cash flow approach, 67
Discounts
factors in determining, 67
for controlling interest, 47
from the fair market value, 94, 133–39
for general lack of marketability, 133–34, A-11–A-12, A-25–A-35, A-53–A-54
for lack of marketability of a minority interest, 25, 39, 49, 50, 92, 212
for minority interests, 47, 134–36, 139, 212
minority interests versus lack of marketability regarding, 136–37
for net asset value, A-61
Rev. Ruling 77–287 decision on arbitrary percentages for, 134
size of, 137–39
"Discounts Involved in Purchases of Common Stock" study by SEC, A-26–A-27
Dividend-paying capacity, as valuation factor, 44, 49, 50, 69, 82, 212, A-61–A-62, A-64
Divorce
division of closely held business during a, 12
and valuation of a closely held business, 22–23

Index

Index

Index

Index

V